How to Think About Arms Control, Disarmament, and Defense

How to Think About Arms Control, Disarmament, and Defense

Christopher J. Lamb

PRENTICE HALL, Englewood Cliffs, New Jersey 07632

LIBRARY OF CONGRESS
Library of Congress Cataloging-in-Publication Data

Lamb, Christopher.
    How to think about arms control, disarmament, and defense /
Christopher J. Lamb.
        p.   cm.
    Includes bibliographies and index.
    ISBN 0-13-435462-1 :
    1. Arms control--History. 2. Disarmament--History. 3. Nuclear
arms control--History. 4. Nuclear disarmament--History. 5. United
States--Defenses--History.   I. Title.
JX1974.L26 1988
327.1'74'09--dc19   87-30190
                                                                    CIP

Editorial/production supervision and
  interior design: **Rob DeGeorge**
Cover design: **George Cornell**
Manufacturing buyer: **Margaret Rizzi**

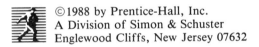 ©1988 by Prentice-Hall, Inc.
A Division of Simon & Schuster
Englewood Cliffs, New Jersey 07632

Printed in the United States of America

10   9   8   7   6   5   4   3   2   1

ISBN 0-13-435462-1

PRENTICE-HALL INTERNATIONAL (UK) LIMITED, *London*
PRENTICE-HALL OF AUSTRALIA PTY. LIMITED, *Sydney*
PRENTICE-HALL CANADA INC., *Toronto*
PRENTICE-HALL HISPANOAMERICANA, S.A., *Mexico*
PRENTICE-HALL OF INDIA PRIVATE LIMITED, *New Delhi*
PRENTICE-HALL OF JAPAN, INC., *Tokyo*
SIMON & SCHUSTER ASIA PTE. LTD., *Singapore*
EDITORA PRENTICE-HALL DO BRASIL, LTDA., *Rio de Janeiro*

This book is dedicated to our parents,
Ted, Ellie, Mirtili, and George.

Contents

PART III   THE MECHANICS OF ARMS CONTROL:
  Nine Practical Questions for Negotiating
  an Arms Control Agreement

Preface

In 1960 Henry Kissinger wrote an influential article encouraging Americans to study arms control more seriously:

> No aspect of American policy has received less systematic attention than arms control. Substantial intellectual as well as material resources have been devoted to the study of strategy. Yet arms control, which is its reverse side, has lacked a focus of attention. . . . Before there can be a successful negotiation on arms control we must get our intellectual house in order.[1]

Thousands of books and articles have been written on arms control since Kissinger made his appeal for serious thought on the subject. Despite all this attention and intellectual exertion, twenty-five years after Kissinger's original exhortation for study and reflection, he had to admit that "our intellectual house" was still not in order. In fact, the situation was worse:

> The subject has become so esoteric that it fits Lord Palmerston's description of the Schleswig-Holstein question of the 19th century: Only three people ever understood it, he said. One was dead. The second was in a lunatic asylum. He was the third and he had forgotten it. Arms control positions do not reflect an

overall concept because they emerge from bureaucratic controversies and because there is no longer any intellectual theory outside of government to sustain them. Heads of state cannot cut through this fog in a single meeting: their lack of sophistication on the subject makes matters worse.[2]

One could attribute the growing complexity of arms control issues to the influence of intellectuals, who seem to complicate even the simplest of questions. Or, it could be argued that the world has grown more complex, and political thinking must become more discriminating to keep pace. Then again, many believe that arms control and disarmament, like all issues concerning war and peace, are inherently very complex and always have been so.

Whatever the cause, Kissinger was certainly correct in observing that the debate on arms control has become more esoteric and difficult to master. Readers who want to cut through the fog of confusion surrounding controversies on arms control and disarmament need assistance—a book that simplifies alternative approaches without obscuring critical if subtle distinctions between them. This book is designed to meet this demand by providing the means to identify quickly the premises and assumptions of the principal competing schools of thought on U.S. national security.

Specifically, the reader is offered four sets of tools. First, the book identifies and discusses eighteen perennial issues in the study of arms control and disarmament which are explicit or implicit in all negotiations on all types of weapons, nuclear and nonnuclear. These eighteen questions do not constitute a catechism on arms control, but rather a conceptual chart for exploring complex subject matter. Second, the reader is introduced to the two most popular competing explanations for war and the two most influential yet antagonistic strategies for deterring war, especially nuclear war. An understanding of these competing theories allows access to the origins of national decision makers' most significant assumptions and beliefs.

Third, the book provides a taxonomy for identifying and categorizing the major schools of thought on national security and their major points of agreement and contention. Fourth, the book is designed to assist the development of a sober sense of historical perspective. A sense of historical perspective on arms control means more than an awareness of past successes and failures. It means removing oneself from the current debate, abandoning ephemeral fervency and ideological consistency, recognizing in a detached manner premises, patterns, and prescriptions of alternative schools of opinion, and evaluating these opinions by comparing current historical trends with past experience.

In summary, the purpose of this book is to help readers think about a confusing and complex subject: arms control and disarmament. The only conviction readers are asked to accept as a premise is that the subject matter deserves serious contemplation. In this regard, it is important to emphasize that one should not associate calm judgment with moderate or "middle-of-the-road" views. "Extreme" and "radical" are employed only as descriptive modifiers, not as derogatory labels. Moderate views are discussed at greater length because they are more subtle and difficult to explain than extreme opinions, but I do not wish to assert that they are somehow more respectable.

ACKNOWLEDGMENTS

I would like to thank a number of people whose support and encouragement contributed to this book. My wife, Ismini, supplied critical moral support, and my family, along with my friends, Janie Coates and Tom Glakas, helped me track down citations which I could not obtain while in Port-au-Prince, Haiti. My father responded to my spur of the moment request for immediate illustrations with his usual aplomb and talent.

Bernard Noe, a close friend and superb educator, was instrumental in the initiation of the book and a source of inspiration and determination. Much of the first draft of the manuscript was completed during my tenure as a fellow at Georgetown University's National Security Studies Program. I thank Dr. Steven Gibert, Director of the NSS Program, for giving me support and freedom to pursue my interests, and for being a valued source of ideas.

Dr. William O'Brien, who rightly and firmly directed my studies when I was inclined to stray into less important activities, supported this project when conventional wisdom would have counseled otherwise. I am also thankful to Dr. O'Brien for introducing me to James E. Dougherty's *How to Think About Arms Control and Disarmament*. As my footnotes demonstrate, I drew on much more than the title of this valuable little volume, which is regrettably out of print.

Dr. Richard Bald, the most demanding scholar I have studied under, read the entire manuscript. I am grateful to him for his rigor and vast knowledge, which made major contributions to my education and to this book in the form of numerous corrections and insights. Above all, I thank Dr. Alberto Coll. I greatly benefited from his many comments on the structure and content of the book and on how to improve its readability. I am even more appreciative of his trustworthy friendship, sound advice, and steady encouragement, which never flagged throughout the duration of this much longer than anticipated project.

NOTES

1. Henry Kissinger, "Arms Control, Inspection and Surprise Attack," *Foreign Affairs* (July 1960), p. 573. These remarks by Kissinger anticipated the rapid growth of professional research on arms control. For an argument that all this interest was misguided, and that the United States should have learned the essential lessons on arms control from its encounters with Soviet representatives in 1958, see Colin Gray, *Strategic Studies and Public Policy: The American Experience* (Lexington, KY: University of Kentucky Press, 1982), p. 74.
2. Henry Kissinger, "A Reagan-Gorbachev Summit: It Will Have to Go Beyond Arms Control," © *The Washington Post,* May 5, 1985, p. C8.

How to Think About Arms Control, Disarmament, and Defense

PART I

CONTROLLING WEAPONS—PAST AND FUTURE

Chapter One

The Relevance of History

Some of the admirers of the eighteenth-century German poet Klopstock made a journey from Gottingen to Hamburg to ask him to explain a difficult passage in his works. Klopstock received them graciously, read the passage, and said: "I cannot recollect what I meant when I wrote it, but I remember it was the finest thing I ever wrote, and you cannot do better than devote your lives to the discovery of its meaning.[1]

Like Klopstock's obscure passage of poetry, the significance of history often seems most evident when it is being made or written. Critical issues seem much less critical with each passing year, and people are naturally more interested in current events and issues than obscure historical cases. Realizing this, few savants—unlike Klopstock—would simply exhort their followers to devote themselves to studying the past with nothing more than the vague assertion that doing so could only be to their benefit. Instead, they often condense the "lessons of history" for their audience and then apply these historical "truths" to current events.

This is troublesome, for the real parallel between history and Klopstock's poetry passage is not history's irrelevance but the difficulty of its interpretation. The meaning of Klopstock's poetry originated in his mind, and it would reflect the mind of anyone else who undertook its reconstruction. The same is true of history. It is hard to reconstruct exactly what happened in the past and even more difficult to isolate its origins. The result is that the lessons of history, which are anything but self-evident, almost invariably bear the personal marks of their creators. In history, meaning is often conferred as much as discovered. Thus the first lesson of history is that the past yields its lessons reluctantly, and one must be alert for hidden biases.[2]

One of the most popular historical allegories in the contemporary literature on arms control and disarmament is the myth of Prometheus.

A HISTORICAL ALLEGORY ON MANKIND
AND WEAPONS

PROMETHEUS: I placed in them blind hopes.
     CHORUS: That was a great gift you gave to man.
PROMETHEUS: Besides this I gave them fire . . . and from it they shall learn many
              crafts.

PROMETHEUS: Time in its aging course teaches all things.
    HERMES: But you have not yet learned a wise discretion.

—Aeschylus, *Prometheus Bound*

It is common when discussing the control of modern weapons to use the myth of Prometheus as a characterization of humanity's nuclear dilemma. In Greek mythology Prometheus was the hero who dared to rise to the sun and steal the gods' fire. Then, returning to earth, he gave the knowledge of fire to mortals in order that they should learn many crafts and have superiority over other animals. Zeus, King of the gods, sent his servants, Force and Violence, to punish Prometheus for his audacity. They chained Prometheus to a mountainside and doomed him to eternal captivity and torture.

The development of nuclear weapons is often seen as analogous. Humans discovered one of nature's most awesome and powerful secrets—atomic energy—and force and violence soon followed as atomic power was immediately put to work as an agent of death and destruction. Since then our nuclear knowledge has tortured us with the omnipresent threat of nuclear war and doomed the entire human race to coexist with weapons powerful enough to destroy whole cities in a matter of minutes.

This interpretation of the Promethean myth contains a subtle bias. Comparing nuclear power with Promethean fire draws a parallel with the inexorable advance of technology through the ages and implies technology is the key historical issue in understanding humanity's poor record in controlling the use of weapons. With technology as its central focus, the myth becomes a lesson on mankind's entrapment by technological momentum, a historical allegory on how mankind abdicated control of its future to the inexorable march of science. It is then argued that weapons "have taken on a life of their own, and man has become, to some degree, their dependent."[3] There certainly is truth in this understanding of the Promethean myth, but there is also truth in the myth's broader meaning, which emerges when the focus is on Prometheus himself.

The myth of Prometheus, as recorded in Aeschylus' profound tragedy *Prometheus Bound,* deals with one of the great, recurring themes in man's continuing struggle to understand his nature and his relationship to eternal powers. When Force and Violence seized Prometheus, they told him:

> Forever shall the intolerable present grind you down.
> And he who will release you is not yet born.
> Such fruit you shall reap for your man-loving ways.
> A god yourself, you did not dread God's anger,
> But gave mortals honor not their due.
> And therefore you must guard this joyless rock—
> No rest, no sleep, no moment's respite.

Hermes, the messenger of Zeus, advised Prometheus to "bring his proud heart to know a true discretion," but Prometheus was unrepentant; his will remained unbroken despite his tortured circumstances.

Defying the powers that be and assuming the burdens and benefits of knowledge are the essence of the epic theme found in many great works of Western literature and religion.[4] Captain Ahab, King Lear, and the Grand Inquisitor are just a few of the many vivid Promethean characters brought to life by poets and writers. Promethean characters are alternatively championed, villified, or lamented, depending largely on whether one believes that man or God "is the measure of all things." However Prometheus is portrayed, the consequences of his nature are evident in the historical record: Mankind's daring has brought greater knowledge of and control over nature, but a desire to test the bounds of power in an arena which resolutely defies our complete comprehension and control has also led to great tragedy and suffering.

When Prometheus is the central focus of the allegory, the issue is not so much the uncontrollable power of technology as the inevitability of *choice* and *responsibility* that accompanies power. The human race has not abdicated responsibility for its future by seizing knowledge, but rather has forced upon itself the necessity of choice. No longer interested in guidance from God, and armed with the double-edged sword of knowledge, we are free to choose barbarism or civilization, war or peace, life or death. This is the broader interpretation of the Promethean myth; having seized power, mortals "will have no moment's respite" from the endless vigil which must be kept against the abuse of power.

The distinction between these two interpretations of the Promethean allegory is not trivial. When thinking about **arms control** and **disarmament** (and implicitly about the future of civilization), it is critical whether one concentrates on technology or human nature. Does conflict emanate from a profu-

Fig. 1.1   Mankind's willful pursuit of knowledge and power has led to triumphs and tragedies. Source: New York Public Library (Adam and Eve) NASA (Space Shuttle))

sion of weapons, or from innate human characteristics? Should nations seek "moral" or "material" disarmament first? Do distinctions between offensive and defensive weapons matter, and is it possible to distinguish wars of aggression from wars of liberation? Is arms control or disarmament a more effective peace strategy? As will become apparent in later chapters, answers to these questions often reflect the difference in focusing on Prometheus (humanity) or fire (weapons).

The discussion of the Promethean allegory raises two issues that are addressed in the remainder of this chapter. First, although the role of advancing technology is a fundamental issue in arms control and disarmament, history reveals it always has been within mankind's power to apply knowledge on behalf of peace or violence. It is at least as important to consider why people choose one or the other as it is to think about the means or technology with which either end is accomplished. What did people hope to achieve with violence in the past, and have they ever been successful? Second, human knowledge has now advanced to the point where we can command practically instantaneous annihilation of entire cities. Cities have been destroyed before, but many believe nuclear weapons threaten the survival of the entire human race. Faced with the unprecedented peril of thermonuclear weapons, it is fair to ask whether there are any helpful lessons to be learned from the study of history other than that mankind cannot afford to repeat previous mistakes. If not, the only value of familiarity with the past is that it can serve as a backdrop against which the "intolerable present" may be highlighted and better understood.

THE QUIXOTIC QUEST FOR ABSOLUTE SECURITY

> Again I saw that under the sun the race is not to the swift, nor the battle to the strong, nor bread to the wise, nor riches to the intelligent, nor favor to the men of skill; but time and chance happen to them all. For man does not know his time. Like fish taken in an evil net, and like birds caught in a snare, so the sons of men are snared at an evil time, when it suddenly falls upon them.
>
> —Ecclesiastes, 9:11–12

Jenghiz Khan is one of history's most notorious villains; wherever he went death reaped a gruesome bonus. In China alone it is estimated that he killed some eighteen million people. In Central and Southeast Asia he left a prosperous and highly developed Moslem civilization in ashes and weeds:

> The [Khan's] sack of Bokhara served as a first object lesson. The few who survived that horror bore tales of infamies which made death seem a reward. As a climax of terrorism the great city was burned to the ground, with the loss of a priceless heritage of Islamic art and manuscripts. Even the outlying gardens of apricots, cherries, melons, roses and poppies were laid waste, leaving the site a wilderness.
> The physical effects [of Jenghiz Khan's campaigns] left permanent scars. Today only an arid region and a few dull provincial towns survive from a Moslem civilization which once supported several cities claiming a million people each.[5]

The Khan calmly reasoned that his own safety demanded such wholesale slaughter: "The vanquished can never be the friends of the victors; the death of the former is necessary therefore for the safety of the latter."[6]

Jenghiz Khan waged total war because he believed that limited war was too dangerous, but he did not argue that his victims forced him to initiate war. He is an exception since most victors have rationalized total war as defensive and therefore justified. Timur the Lame followed Jenghiz Khan by about one hundred years and equaled the Khan's reputation for rapacity and barbarity. He is remembered for piling the skulls of his victims in columns and pyramids in order to shock his next victims into minimal resistance. On December 12, 1398, Timur sat before the gates of Delhi watching this process begin with the massacre of one hundred thousand prisoners. Speaking to whomever, he absolved himself of blame: "I am not a man of blood; and God is my witness that in all my wars I have never been the aggressor and my enemies have always been the authors of their own calamity."[7]

It would be a mistake to explain away such behavior because the perpetrators were barbarians. The Christian Crusaders viciously sacked Constantinople and Jerusalem, and the ancient Israelites received this standing rule from their great leader Moses:

> When you draw near a city to fight against it, offer terms of peace to it. And if its answer to you is peace and it opens to you, then all the people who are found in it shall do forced labor for you and shall serve you. But if it makes war against you, then you shall besiege it; and when the Lord your God gives it into your hand you shall put all its males to the sword, but the women and the little ones, the cattle and everything else in the city, all its spoil, you shall take as booty for yourselves . . . [8]

Numerous other "highly civilized" societies as diverse as Periclean Athens (400 B.C.) and modern Germany (both considered the most refined cultural centers of their times) have deemed the extermination of whole cities, even whole nations, both justifiable and necessary for their security. It would also be a mistake to think that the quest for absolute security is necessarily a relic from our unenlightened past, or to assume that a preference for peace is deeply entrenched in contemporary society. Previous generations have made the mistake of an overly sanguine assessment of mankind's prospects for peace.

Writing well before the outbreak of the first World War, the Swiss historian Jacob Burckhardt lamented the European ethnocentric egoism of his time, which presumed for itself a moral superiority over other cultures, past and present.[9] He noted it was a false sense of security which prompted this delusion and once security was suspended every conceivable horror would rear its head. Sadly, history proved Burckhardt correct. During the first World War 15 million civilians died, and in World War II 51 million civilians perished. Since 1945, some 67 conventional wars have been fought, and over the past decade the world has been marred by over forty different regional conflicts of varying scope and intensity. Living in a period of relative tranquility, many Americans do not appreciate how difficult it is to achieve peace.

PARTIAL LIST OF COUNTRIES MARRED BY CONFLICT IN THE 1980s

Afghanistan (Insurgency)
Angola (Insurgency)
Cambodia (Insurgency)
Chad (Insurgency/Border War)
Chile (Urban Insurgency)
China (Border War)
Columbia (Insurgency)
Cuba (Intervention)
El Salvador (Insurgency)
Ethiopia (Separatist Insurgency)
France (Intervention)
Grenada (Invasion)
Guatemala (Insurgency)
Honduras (Insurgency/Border Conflict)
India (Separatist Insurgency)
Indonesia (Separatist Insurgency)
Iran (Border War)
Iraq (Border War)
Israel (Border Conflicts/Intervention)
Lebanon (Urban Insurgencies & Foreign Occupation)
Laos (Insurgency)
Libya (Border Conflicts)
Morocco (Separatist Insurgency)
Mozambique (Insurgency)
Nambia (Insurgency)
Nicaragua (Insurgency)
Northern Ireland (Urban Insurgency)
North & South Yemen (Border Conflict)
North & South Korea (Border Conflict)
Somalia (Insurgency)
Pakistan (Border Conflict)
Peru (Insurgency)
Philippines (Insurgency)
South Africa (Insurgency)
Spain (Separatist Insurgency)
Sri Lanka (Separatist Insurgency)
Sudan (Border Conflict/Insurgency)
Syria (Border Conflict/Intervention)
Thailand (Border Conflict)
Uganda (Insurgency)
United States (Intervention)
Vietnam (Border Conflict/Insurgency)
Zaire (Intervention)

Not all of these conflicts were the result of absolute security strategies. There is always the possibility, though, that a state will move from a limited struggle for freedom or security to a desire for absolute security. For example, ancient Rome began by defending itself against and eventually conquering its immediate neighbors on the Italian peninsula. Rome then found itself in an epic struggle with Carthage, another Mediterranean power. In the course of three terrifying wars with Carthage, during which the very existence of Rome was repeatedly threatened, Rome became convinced it would have absolute security or none at all. Finally Rome devastated Carthage at the conclusion of the **Third Punic War** (146 B.C.). Rome razed Carthage to the ground, slaughtered or sold its citizens into slavery, and sowed its fields with salt. Yet Rome still did not have absolute security. Centuries later it was still expanding, running up against and eliminating one security threat after another.

Originally concerned with security, the Romans came to believe their poet Virgil who said that Jupiter had destined Rome for greatness, promising them "no end to empire" and "authority without limit." The Roman "art" was "to impose the custom of peace, to spare the humbled and wear down the proud," and in the words of the Roman historian Livy, all Rome's wars were "just and pious."[10] Rome's success with local security concerns burgeoned into a supposed mandate to civilize the world.

The Roman Empire may be the most noteworthy case, but history is dotted with both "civilized" and barbaric attempts to achieve absolute security, and never has this chimera been obtainable. Even the Roman Empire was plagued at the zenith of its power by wars on the periphery of its domain with the Parthians, the Germans, the Vandals, and others. Even should some future power come to dominate the entire planet, it would no doubt find itself subject to the same malady of civil war which periodically wracked the Roman Empire. And, as many historians have noted, civil wars frequently prove to be the bloodiest and most desperate of all struggles for power.

ARMS CONTROL AND DISARMAMENT: THE SEARCH FOR SECURITY IN AN UNTRUSTING WORLD

I have also seen this example of wisdom under the sun, and it seemed great to me. There was a little city with few men in it; and a great king came against it and besieged it, building great siegeworks against it. But there was found in it a poor wise man, and he by his wisdom delivered the city. Yet no one remembered that poor man. But I say that wisdom is better than might, though the poor man's wisdom is despised, and his words are not heeded. The words of the wise heard in quiet are better than the shouting of a ruler among fools. Wisdom is better than weapons of war, but one sinner destroys much good.

Ecclesiastes, 9:13–18

One student of arms control has categorized the quest for absolute security as "disarmament by extermination."[11] Militant absolute security strategies need not require the extermination of an adversary, but they do deny the possibility of peaceful coexistence. Leaving no room for compromise, such strategies are pursued with the highest stakes riding in the balance. In 1071 the brash young Byzantine emperor Romanus Diogenes ignored the peace overtures of a formidable enemy in hopes of securing a total victory on the battlefield. At first the emperor's confidence proved well-founded as he swept the enemy forces before him, but then the tide of battle turned. As darkness and the enemy both fell on his overextended forces a total rout ensued. The result of the battle of Manzikert was a decade of anarchy in Asia Minor which enervated the Byzantine empire and set in motion its slow decline.[12]

Militant absolute security strategies eschew cooperation or compromise with other states. Pacific absolute security strategies share the assumption with militant absolute security strategies that trust between states is unnecessary, or they assume perfect trust is necessary. Non-violent resistance does not call for trust or cooperation with other states; i.e. for negotiating arms limitation agreements or allocating defence resources based on estimates of which states may be trusted and to what extent. Instead a general policy of resisting force without resort to violence is adopted. In short, since no armed resistance to foreign occupation is contemplated, there is no concern about the ultimate intentions of other powers and thus trust is irrelevant.

Pacifism assumes that the danger of coercion from or even occupation by other powers is less to be feared than the dangers of resistance and war. Some forms of pacifism, like nonviolent resistance strategies, assume no trust is necessary because surrender is preferable to resistance. Other types of pacifism, rooted in the belief that war is always the result of mutual fear, assume the opposite: that absolute trust is necessary for peace. Only when states categorically trust one another and are willing to prove it by disarming unilaterally will the fear which causes war disappear.

There has been a lot of debate over the historical record of pacifism and nonviolent resistance. The Indian resistance to British colonial rule led by Mahatma Ghandi is often cited as an example of successful nonviolent resistance to foreign occupation. Others argue that while Ghandi was successful, it was only due to the fact that the British had a code of morality which restrained their response to Ghandi's tactics. Other more ruthless powers would have executed Ghandi early on, taken away other leaders in the middle of the night, and used selective and mass murder to terrorize the population.

Most people believe the success of nonviolent tactics depends greatly on historical circumstances: the nature of the occupying power, its strategic ambitions, the nature of the indigenous population, and so forth. The historical record on the efficacy of nonviolent resistance is confused by the fact that in every case where forces committed to nonviolence succeeded, there were also forces working toward the same goals that threatened or actually used violence. For example, Thomas Merton has cited the effectiveness of the Danish passive resistance to the Nazis in World War II, nonviolent resistance which contrasted favorably with the bloody Italian resistance movement which led to five Italian civilians being shot to death for every German killed by the resistance.[13] The problem with this comparison is that there is no way of knowing how harshly Hitler would have responded to the Danes and their heroic resistance to Nazi anti-Jewish measures if he had not been preoccupied with eliminating other armed opponents.

Most would accept the general historical observation that nonviolent resistance has had some qualified success, but it is also true that there has never been a case of nonviolent resistance which forced the withdrawal of invading forces. Some proponents of nonviolent resistance argue that the absence of clear-cut historical success for nonviolent resistance can be attributed to the fact that governments have never really trained their populations in nonviolent techniques, establishing the communication networks and political organizations that would be necessary to carry on a nonviolent defense. If such precautions were taken prior to invasion, it is argued, a successful nonviolent resistance would be possible. Those skeptical of nonviolent defense tactics, believe that regardless of preparations, a ruthless occupation power would crush nonviolent defenders with brutal terror, forcing resistance leaders to choose between armed resistance and mass sacrifice.

The debate over pacifism and nonviolent resistance cannot be resolved here. What is clear from the historical record is that both the quest for universal empire and universal peace have long motivated various elements of mankind. Nations always have pursued empires earnestly, and it is to be assumed that this temptation has not disappeared, despite the fact that history suggests the quest for empire entails great costs and brings only short-term security at best. Efforts for world peace through pacifism and nonviolent resistance have been pursued mostly in the writings of intellectuals, the efforts of relatively small subnational and international groups, and in some cases, through popular national movements. Still, the quest for universal peace remains a popular ideal, even if history offers few unambiguous examples for encouragement.

The alternative to absolute security strategies like militarism and pacifism are limited security strategies. Unlike absolute security strategies, which either assume that no trust or absolute trust is necessary, limited security strategies assume that some less-than-absolute level of trust is required for peace between nations. The level of trust assumed by limited security strategies ranges from the minimum trust assumed in supposing the enemy is rational enough to be deterred by sufficient defense preparations, to the greater amounts of trust required by various types of negotiated arms control and disarmament agreements.

There are two practical difficulties with negotiated or tacit security agreements. First, leaders must decide which countries are possibly trustworthy and to what extent. With regard to the first point it must be remembered that some trust is unavoidable inasmuch as no country has unlimited resources for defense. Every state must decide which adversaries it has most reason to distrust and deploy its defenses accordingly. For example, the United States trusts that neither Mexico nor Canada will attempt to invade U.S. territory and consequently makes little effort to defend its borders with these nations. In Europe, on the other hand, the United States has some three hundred thousand troops facing forces led by the Soviet Union, a nation it believes it has less reason to trust.

Second, with those countries deemed untrustworthy, statesmen must decide how to encourage some means of accommodation. Ameliorating antagonisms between rival hostile powers still requires risking an element of trust. Some trust must exist between nations before they will even move to the negotiating table. They must believe that their negotiating partners are entering negotiations in good faith and not in order to gain some unilateral advantage, as occasionally happens.

For example, in the fifth century B.C., the Greek city-state Sparta entered into negotiations with its archrival, Athens, in order to prevent the Athenians from building newer and better fortifications around their city.[14] The Spartans knew that the huge city walls which Athens intended to build would be impregnable, and felt they would allow Athens a security advantage which would upset the stability of the Greek world. The Athenians professed good will and feigned interest in the negotiations. They ordered their ambassadors to stall negotiations and fervently deny reports that they were continuing with the construction of the walls. Working as fast as possible, Athens completed its fortifications, at which point the Spartans had little choice but to accept the Athenian action or go to war. Later, when war did break out between Athens and Sparta, it took the Spartans twenty-seven years to breach the Athenian wall.[15] Rather than negotiate in good will, Athens opted for unilateral security measures which enhanced its power and frightened Sparta and the other Greek city-states.

It is this fear of giving a potentially rival nation an advantage that makes many countries reluctant to risk the trust which serious negotiations entail. Even if neither side uses negotiations as a cover for seizing unilateral advantages and the negotiations proceed to a conclusion, there is no foolproof method of determining whether or not parties to an agreement will adhere to all of its established terms. It is impossible, in any absolute sense, to perfectly "verify" compliance with an agreement and thus there is always an element of trust and commensurate risk in negotiated agreements.

Negotiations cannot be avoided simply because they are risky. Every security strategy entails some element of risk, and it may be more dangerous not to negotiate than to negotiate. If in the past negotiations have proved to be a mistake, they have also led on occasion to some long periods of peace. For example, after a series of fierce border clashes, and a momentous battle in

1296 B.C., the leaders of the ancient Egyptian and Hittite empires (Hittite King Muwatallis and Egyptian Pharaoh Ramses II) signed a detailed and very long treaty of peace. The treaty helped end over a century of conflict and brought seventy years of peace to what was then the better part of the known world.[16]

In summary, absolute security strategies like militarism, pacifism and nonviolent resistance, assume that either no trust or absolute trust is possible between nations. In contrast, limited security strategies assume some degree of trust is necessary and possible for peace and security. There are historical cases where both militarism and nonviolent policies have succeeded for a limited period of time in bringing about peace and security, but they also have failed and led to catastrophic loss of life. The precise historical circumstances are obviously important in estimating the likely result of an absolute security policy.

Most arms control, disarmament and defense plans are limited security strategies. Before moving on to discuss these limited security strategies, two other fundamental questions must be introduced. The first is the matter of whether nuclear weapons have radically affected calculations of risk and trust, and thereby also affected the relative dangers of absolute and limited security strategies. Second, if nuclear weapons have altered forever the risks involved in choosing an absolute or limited security strategy, we need to ask whether it is possible to use knowledge of the past as an aid or guide for future security policies.

ABSOLUTE AND LIMITED SECURITY IN A NUCLEAR WORLD

A bad peace is even worse than war.

—Tacitus, *Annals,* 110 B.C.

The most disadvantageous peace is better than the most just war.

—Erasmus, *Adages,* 1508

People have long debated whether war ever justifies its obvious costs. Today, though, many believe that nuclear weapons have brought this debate to an end. They contend that the destructive power of modern atomic warheads raises the costs of war so high that no possible cause or principle can justify armed conflict. As Barbara Tuchman writes, "The Mongols may have left pyramids of skulls and the Nazis the equivalent in their gas chambers, but capacity [for destruction] was not global."[17] Tuchman agrees that in the past nations were subject to wars that had devastating consequences. Whole cities have been destroyed by unmerciful victors and, as Michael Walzer has noted, the conventional means of siege and starvation may exceed nuclear attack in death toll:

> Siege is the oldest form of total war. . . . More civilians died in the siege of Leningrad than in the modernist infernoes of Hamburg, Dresden, Tokyo, Hiroshima, and Nagasaki taken together. They probably died more painfully too, even if in old fashioned ways.[18]

Walzer goes on to cite the ancient historian Josephus's terrifying account of the devastating Roman siege of Jerusalem in A.D. 72, a graphic reminder that a nuclear blast may be considered merciful compared to other forms of man's inhumanity to man. Others have also argued that despite the symbolic and psychological significance of the atomic bombing of Japan, the obliteration of two cities was a less costly way to end World War II. Mounting an invasion of Japan would have entailed much greater hardship and suffering for both Japan and the Allies.[19]

In the past, not only cities, but whole nations have ceased to exist, either through the extermination and scattering of the population, or by political and military fiat. The ancient Hittites, Babylonians, and Aztecs met with virtually complete destruction through war, as did many North American Indian nations. In 722 B.C. the Kingdom of Israel was conquered by the Assyrians and its inhabitants scattered throughout the region, not to be rejoined under political sovereignty for another two-and-a-half-thousand years.

Tuchman acknowledges the precarious existence of nations throughout history, but her concern is that today the destructive power of man's weapons is so great that an all-out nuclear exchange between the two superpowers could obliterate most, if not all, human life, by means of both direct casualties and by delayed damage to the environment. In contrast to Dresden and Tokyo, Hiroshima and Nagasaki were destroyed by single bombs, bombs which contained only a fraction of the destructive power contained in the warheads of contemporary nuclear arsenals. The assumed consequences of a nuclear exchange today magnify the horrors of war beyond anything previously experienced by mankind as a whole.[20]

In fact, there is currently great concern within the scientific community that the long-term ecological effects of nuclear war could mean the extinction of human life. Dr. Carl Sagan of Cornell University has postulated that an all-out superpower nuclear exchange would throw up a layer of nuclear ash and smoke that would block out the sun's rays and usher in a **"nuclear winter"** of subfreezing temperatures. Sagan claims such a phenomenon would mean a massive disruption of the earth's ecosystems and result in mass starvation of those surviving a nuclear exchange. Sagan has concluded that there must be a 90 percent reduction in the world's stock of nuclear weapons to eliminate the threat of a nuclear winter.[21] While the danger of a nuclear exchange receives the most attention, modern chemical and biological weapons also contribute to the magnitude of the contemporary threat to human life.

In short, science has raised the stakes, perhaps as high as they can possibly go, and many wonder if mankind will have to find a radically new solution to end the threat posed by weapons of mass destruction. If so, why waste time consulting the historical record? Unprecedented danger calls for unprecedented action and not for lengthy studies of past failures. Such an attitude was the prevailing opinion in the early postthermonuclear world:

> The destructive potential of thermonuclear arms made their threat cosmic and immediate . . . modern civilization—human existence itself—was felt to be in jeopardy . . . [Since] the new weapons created wholly new hazards, [it was believed] that the control of these arms could be achieved best by those who understood how they were made, how they might be deployed, what damage they were capable of, and how they could be monitored and controlled. . . . the historical record was thought to provide nothing new in the way of useful data [and] the guidance that historians and others who lived on a knowledge of the past could offer was minimal.[22]

Such stark choices between life and liberty may not be necessary. Many people believe that an appropriate choice of strategies can both prevent war and preserve liberty, or at least minimize the likelihood of nuclear war while preserving liberty and human dignity. Again those who hold nuclear weapons have radically altered all previous calculations of values and security strategies have a different view. A happy medium is not possible in the era of "hair-trigger" nuclear holocaust, they say. Either we disarm or prepare to perish altogether. Mankind must accept radically new peace strategies and the risks they entail if we are going to prevent the eventual false step that leads to war and the end of the world.[23]

CONCLUSION: THE VALUE
OF A HISTORICAL PERSPECTIVE

For those who believe the world needs new efforts, values and strategies for peace, the study of the past is tedious and irrelevant. It may seem that nuclear weapons give these sentiments new urgency, but they are not novel. In 1927 representatives of the young revolutionary Soviet government arrived in Geneva for a League of Nations Disarmament Commission meeting. They brought with them a plan for "immediate, general and complete disarmament." A league official, Salvador De Madariaga, relates how Soviet Foreign Minister Litvinoff was received:

> When M. Litvinoff, whom I had met years before in London before he became a world figure, called on me, he asked me whether the Commission would reject his scheme. "My dear Litvinoff," I answered, "they will do something much

worse than that. They will consider it very carefully." The Soviet delegation imagined that they were going to get drama out of the Commission [but] . . . the bourgeois devils grinned . . . They knew too much. The Commission enjoyed a speech by M. Paul-Boncour who, the Commission had perhaps forgotten, is a Socialist. M. Paul-Bancour fraternally upbraided Messieurs Litvinoff and Luna-charsky for their schoolboy enthusiasm and inexperience. M. Paul-Bancour . . . smiled with his eyes, scorned with his intellect, caressed while chastizing with his graceful and modulating voice and crushed the Bolsheviks with the experience which shone on his hoary head. "That is how *we* began, my friends. You bring us nothing new."[24]

It is worthwhile knowing how radical new peace proposals have fared in the past, when and why they failed or succeeded. The purpose of cultivating a historical perspective is not to follow Mr. Paul-Bancour and extinguish any "schoolboy enthusiasm," but to direct the enthusiasm in realistic directions. Even if the future does demand radically new peace strategies, it is not possible to know what is new without a knowledge of what has already been tried. Thus at the very least historical knowledge makes it possible to avoid peace strategies that in similar circumstances have failed in the past. It is also important to understand the advantages and disadvantages of alternative novel solutions, and those with a historical perspective on arms control and disarmament are better able to defend their preferred peace strategies. In short, a historical perspective gives one a sense of the possible and the necessary, even if the necessary turns out to be the unprecedented.

*   *   *

Absolute security strategies have been contrasted in this chapter with limited security strategies, and this contrast is developed throughout the remainder of the book. The next several chapters deal principally with limited security strategies, the category that includes most plans for deterrence, arms control, and disarmament. Chapters 2 and 3 categorize alternative types of arms control and disarmament and provide historical examples of each category. Chapter 4 then discusses the role of deterrence, which is an inseparable element of all limited security strategies, including those which rely primarily upon plans for arms control and disarmament.

DISCUSSION QUESTIONS

1. Martin Luther King said that "If a man hasn't discovered something that he will die for, he isn't fit to live." Do you agree or disagree?
2. Would you be willing to turn over yourself, your family and friends to foreign authorities in hopes of preventing a nuclear confrontation which might lead to global disaster?
3. If Hitler's scientists had created the atomic bomb in time to defeat England and

the Soviet Union, what would have been the best strategy for the United States at that point? What if Hitler declared war on the United States and demanded unconditional surrender?

4. It is widely believed that Israel has nuclear as well as conventional defenses. If neighboring Arab states attacked Israel today and it became apparent that Israel's conventional defenses were being overwhelmed, what ought Israel to do?

5. Is it reasonable to believe nuclear weapons can be retained and never used, or if used, abandoned before they create a global holocaust?

6. Do you know enough history to judge its usefulness in planning current and future peace and security strategies? Can you name one historical example of a successful peace and security strategy? Why was it successful?

SUGGESTED READINGS FOR CHAPTER 1: THE RELEVANCE OF HISTORY

AESCHYLUS. *Prometheus Bound.*
COLL, ALBERTO R. *The Wisdom of Statecraft.* Part II: "The Wisdom of History." Durham, NC: Duke University Press, 1985.
DURANT, WILL and ARIEL. *The Lessons of History* (New York: Simon and Schuster, 1968).
The Effects of Nuclear War. Office of Technology Assessment. Washington, DC: Government Printing Office, 1979.
GRAUBARD, STEPHEN R. "Preface to the Issue: U.S. Defense Policy in the 1980s." *Daedalus* 109 (Fall 1980).
GREGG, RICHARD B. *The Power of Nonviolence.* New York: Schocken Books, 1966.
HARVARD NUCLEAR STUDY GROUP. *Living with Nuclear Weapons.* Cambridge: Harvard University Press, 1983.
HERZ, JOHN. *Political Realism and Political Idealism.* Chicago: University of Chicago Press, 1951.
KNORR, KLAUSS. *On the Uses of Military Power in the Nuclear Age.* Princeton: Princeton University Press, 1966.
MERTON, THOMAS. *The Non-violent Alternative.* New York: Farrar, Straus and Giroux, 1980. In revised edition of Thomas Merton *On Peace* 1971.
SCHELL, JONATHAN. *The Abolition.* New York: Alfred A. Knopf, 1984.
———. *The Fate of the Earth.* New York: Alfred A. Knopf, 1982.
SCHROEDER, PAUL. "Does Murphy's Law Apply to History?" *Wilson Quarterly* 9 (1985): 84–93.
SHARP, GENE. *Exploring Non-violent Alternatives.* Boston: Porter Sargent, 1970.
———. "The Political Equivalent of War: Civilian Defense." *International Conciliation* (November 1965).
SIBLEY, MULFORD Q. *The Quiet Battle.* Boston: Beacon Press, 1968.
TUCHMAN, BARBARA. "The Alternative to Arms Control." *New York Times Magazine.* April 18, 1982. Reprinted in Roman Kolkowicz and Neil Joeck, eds. *Arms Control and International Security.* Boulder, CO: Westview Press, 1984.
VAGTS, ALFRED. *A History of Militarism.* New York: W. W. Norton, 1937.

NOTES

1. Edmund Fuller, *2500 Anecdotes for All Occasions* (Garden City: Doubleday, 1961), p. 213.

2. The gifted British historian, Herbert Butterfield, analyzed as well as anyone the problems historians have in isolating their biases from their research. He also repeatedly cautioned against a willingness to draw broad generalized lessons from history. His book, *The Whig*

Interpretation of History, is an excellent starting point for investigating these issues. The best book on Butterfield and his scholarship is Alberto Coll's *The Wisdom of Statecraft: Sir Herbert Butterfield and the Philosophy of International Politics* (Durham, NC: Duke University Press, 1985). Any student interested in the significance of historical scholarship for the study of international relations could profit handsomely by reading this book.

3. Russell Warren Howe, *Weapons: The International Game of Arms* (Garden City, New York: Doubleday, 1980), p. xxxiii. For another strong statement on how technology has "assumed command," see Solly Zuckerman, *Nuclear Illusion and Reality* (New York: Vintage Books, 1983). For a contrary view see Jonathan B. Stein *From H-Bomb to Star Wars: The Politics of Strategic Decision Making* (Lexington, Mass.: Lexington Books, 1984). Stein uses the H bomb and Ballistic Missile Defense programs to show that politics and strategy can control technological developments.

4. The parallels between the myth of Prometheus and the biblical account of Adam and Eve are particularly evident:

> But of the tree of the knowledge of good and evil you shall not eat, for in the day that you eat of it you shall die. . . . But the serpent said to the woman, "You shall not die. For God knows that when you eat of it your eyes will be opened. . . . "

Defying God by seizing forbidden knowledge is not the only parallel between the biblical and Greek stories of mankind's fall and hopes for salvation. Readers might find a closer comparison interesting.

5. Lynn Montross, *War Through the Ages* (New York: Harper and Row, 1960), p. 145.

6. Ibid.

7. Edward Gibbon, *The Decline and Fall of the Roman Empire,* cited in Hans Morganthau, *Politics Among Nations* (New York: Alfred A. Knopf, 1954), p. 249.

8. Deuteronomy 20, cited in Leon Friedman, ed., *The Law of War: A Documentary History* (New York: Random House, 1972), p. 4.

9. Jacob Burckhardt, *Reflections on History* (Indianapolis, IN: Liberty Classics, 1979), p. 102.

10. Edith Hamilton, *The Roman Way* (New York: W. W. Norton, 1972).

11. Henry Forbes, *The Strategy of Disarmament* (Washington, DC: Public Affairs Press, 1962), p. 4.

12. It was Machravelli's opinion that "Wise princes and Republics should content themselves with victory; for when they aim at more than generally lose." *The Discourses* Bk. 11, Chap. 27.

13. Thomas Merton, "Danish Nonviolent Resistance to Hitler," in Thomas Merton *The Nonviolent Alternative.* New York: Farrar, Straus and Giroux revised edition of Thomas Merton *On Peace,* 1971, 1980; pp. 165–167. For a more recent argument in favor of civilian defence, see Gene Sharp *Making Europe Unconquerable: The Potential of Civilian-Based Deterrence & Defense* Cambridge: Ballinger, 1986.

14. The former walls were destroyed by the Persians during a brief occupation of Athens. Momentarily setting aside their own hostility, the Spartans and Athenians repelled the Persian invasion in what many consider one of history's most significant military conflicts.

15. Thucydides, *The Peloponnesian War,* trans. Rex Warner (Middlesex, England: Penguin Books, 1954), pp. 86–90.

16. C. W. Ceram, *The Secret of the Hittites,* translated by Clara and Richard Winston (New York: Alfred A. Knopf, Inc., 1973), p. 190.

17. Barbara Tuchman, "The Alternative to Arms Control," *New York Times Magazine,* April 18, 1982, p. 95. Reprinted by permission of Russell and Volkering, as agents for the author.

18. Michael Walzer, *Just and Unjust Wars* (New York: Basic Books, 1977), pp. 160–161.

19. This is a very controversial issue about which much has been written. Some argue that the critical factor in Truman's decision to drop the bomb was his desire to intimidate the USSR, while others maintain it was principally the desire to end the war quickly with as few casualties as possible. A short and very readable article on the subject is Roger Rosenblatt, "The Atomic Age," Special Section, *Time,* July 29, 1985, pp. 32–59.

Of course, the issue is less controversial in Japan, where most people see the bombings as unmitigated disasters, but even in Japan there are differences of opinion on the subject. See "Tokyo Physician Sees Dropping of Atomic Bomb as 'Having Saved Japan,'" *Washington Post,* August 5, 1983, p. D1.

20. Opinions differ on the exact effects of a nuclear exchange. Of course, much would depend on how well the war could be contained and stopped, if at all. For a good initial discussion of the subject, see *The Effects of Nuclear War* (Office of Technology Assessment: U.S. Government Printing Office, 1979), and K. N. Lewis, "The Prompt and Delayed Effects of Nuclear War," *Scientific American* 241 (1979).

21. Carl Sagan, "Nuclear Winter and Climatic Catastrophe," *Foreign Affairs* (Winter 1983–1984): 274. The National Academy of Sciences released a report on December 11, 1985, with conclusions that differ substantially from Sagan's findings. See also Stanley C. Thompson and Stephen H. Schneider, "Nuclear Winter Reappraised," *Foreign Affairs* (Summer 1986); especially p. 983.

22. Stephen R. Graubard, "Preface to the Issue: 'U.S. Defense Policy in the 1980s,'" *Daedalus* 109 (Fall 1980), p. vi.

23. Two popular and readable opposing points of view on this issue are Jonathan Schell's *The Fate of the Earth* (New York: Alfred A. Knopf, 1982) and the Harvard Nuclear Study Group's *Living with Nuclear Weapons* (New York: Bantam Books, 1983). The Harvard Study Group criticized Schell's book, and his rejoinder can be found in "The Abolition: II—A Deliberate Policy," *The New Yorker,* January 9, 1984, pp. 61–64, reprinted in Levine and Carlton, *The Nuclear Arms Race Debated,* pp. 75–79.

24. Salvador De Madariaga, *Disarmament* (New York: Coward McCann, 1929), pp. 247–48.

Chapter Two

A Historical Survey of Disarmament

A DISTINCTION BETWEEN ARMS CONTROL
AND DISARMAMENT

The terms **arms control** and **disarmament** are often used together, yet there are significant differences as well as similarities between them. Professor James E. Dougherty explained the distinctions well:

> The term "arms control" in contrast to "disarmament" (which has as its goal the elimination or reduction of armaments), refers to a broad range of policies which presuppose the continued existence of national military establishments and other political-military organizations (such as revolutionary guerrilla movements). Arms control policies usually aim at some kind of restraint or regulation in qualitative design, qualitative production, deployment, protection control, transfer, and planned, threatened, or actual use of arms for political-strategic purposes. Advocates of arms control assume that a general and complete disarmament (GCD) for a number of complex reasons . . . lies beyond the world's reach, at least under present conditions.[1]

Disarmament is much more ambitious in its scope than arms control, but both seek to reduce the likelihood of war. Since disarmament assumes weapons lead to war, it seeks a reduction in the number of weapons as a means of reducing the likelihood of war. Arms control seeks to reduce the chances of war primarily by "stabilizing" the military competition between countries and reducing mutual fear. Other mutual goals of arms control and disarmament are reducing the cost of defense[2] and the cost of war, should it occur.[3]

In this and the following chapter the principal historical categories of arms control and disarmament agreements are introduced. The categories and examples offered are not exhaustive. For example, international attempts to use budgetary limitations as a means of restraining the growth of armaments are not reviewed in this chapter.[4] In addition, other categories could have been used, such as the broad distinction between manpower and hardware in arms limitation agreements (see also footnote 5 below). Moreover, the categories used are not mutually exclusive. Those discussed under disarmament could apply, in certain cases, to arms control agreements, and vice versa. For example, the Philistine prohibitions (1100 B.C.) against Israelites obtaining the means to make iron weapons was both an "involuntary" disarmament agreement and a "nonproliferation agreement."[5] Involuntary agreements are discussed in this chapter as a category of disarmament, and attempts to prevent proliferation are discussed in the following chapter under arms control. In summary, the categories are not exhaustive nor mutually exclusive. They are helpful, though, for making rudimentary distinctions, introducing popular terminology and numerous examples of various types of arms limitation agreements.

SEVEN CATEGORIES OF DISARMAMENT:
A HISTORICAL SURVEY

Disarmament programs are (1) nuclear or nonnuclear, (2) voluntary or involuntary, (3) partial or complete, (4) material or moral, and may be conducted either (5) unilaterally,[6] (6) bilaterally, or (7) multilaterally.

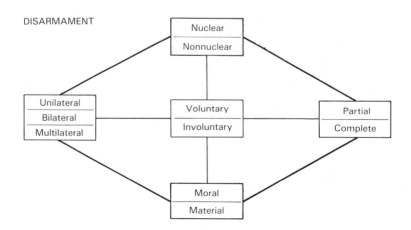

The distinction between *nuclear* and *nonnuclear* arms limitation agreements recognizes the vast qualitative difference between nuclear weapons and most other types of armaments. Negotiations normally do not cover both nuclear and nonnuclear arms since they are so dissimilar, although there are exceptions. For example, in the **MBFR** (Mutual and Balanced Force Reductions) negotiations, which seek to reduce **NATO** and **WTO** forces in central Europe, there have been numerous proposals to reduce the NATO advantage in nuclear weapons in exchange for reductions in the WTO advantage in conventional arms. Also, some treaties, such as the 1971 Seabed Treaty, prohibit all means of mass destruction, nonnuclear as well as nuclear weapons.

The nuclear/nonnuclear distinction is a critical one for many advocates of arms limitation agreements. While some people make little or no distinction between the two, others argue that nonnuclear arms control is a distant secondary concern compared to nuclear arms limitations. They may also believe that nonnuclear arms limitation is just not possible given current political conditions, while nuclear arms represent such a salient threat to all mankind that their reduction or elimination is as possible as it is necessary.

Since there is no safe way to disarm a state armed with nuclear weapons against its will, most people agree that negotiating reductions in nuclear weapons must be a voluntary process. Preemptive strikes against smaller nuclear powers have been suggested in the past, but always rejected as too risky. Thus nuclear disarmament must be *voluntary disarmament,* which occurs when nations, of their own accord, agree to negotiate a reduction in military forces. US-Soviet negotiations to eliminate medium range nuclear missiles in Europe would be an example of a voluntary nuclear disarmament agreement.

Involuntary disarmament results from nations having disarmament imposed upon them, usually after defeat in war. For example, in the Treaty of Zama (201 B.C.) a victorious Rome imposed limits on the number of ships and elephants Carthage could maintain, and destroyed its city walls. Similarly, Napoleon forced disarmament on Prussia in the Treaty of Tilsit (1806). Prussia was forced to pay France a large war indemnity and was compelled to limit the size of its army to forty-two thousand men. Also, after both World War I and World War II, the Allied governments imposed disarmament on their defeated opponents with great vigor. With the exception of World War II, in each of these cases the defeated parties found ways to rebuild their military forces and fight their old adversaries again.

History records no cases of voluntary and *complete unilateral* disarmament, and very few cases of voluntary *partial unilateral* disarmament. One popular example of a partial unilateral disarmament initiative was the 12th century effort to eliminate the crossbow. In 1139 Conrad III of Germany renounced the use of the crossbow and for thirteen years prohibited its use in his armies. However, since none of his adversaries followed his lead he revoked his prohibition of the crossbow in 1152.[7] The history of unilateral restraint in chemical weapons development in the United States may be considered a modern example of partial voluntary disarmament. As the U.S. Chemical Warfare Review Commission noted in its June 11, 1985, report:

> The United States unilaterally abandoned chemical weapons production sixteen years ago. The Soviet response was a massive chemical weapons buildup and even actual use of these weapons.[8]

Following the same reasoning as that used by Conrad III in the twelfth century, the commission did not believe the United States could afford restraint any longer, and it recommended the modernization of U.S. chemical warfare capabilities.

Bilateral negotiations are the historical norm, but both negotiating states may be in constant touch with allies, and may even make their agreements contingent upon the approval of allies. In the past there have been many bilateral treaties limiting weapons (for example, the Anglo-French Naval Pact of 1787 and the Ottoman limitation of Egyptian arms in 1841), but the first *multilateral* conventions called for the express purpose of disarmament were the **Hague conferences** of 1899 and 1907. At the first conference weapons such as expanding "dum-dum bullets" (designed by the British for colonial warfare) and asphyxiating gases were outlawed, but nothing approaching a general disarmament settlement was reached. At the second conference international conditions had degenerated to the point where the subject of disarmament came up only briefly. Given the intense competition and suspicion rampant in Europe prior to World War I, negotiators were unwilling to trust other nations enough to agree to do away with any of their own nation's weapons.

World War I consumed almost an entire generation of Europe's youth, and many concluded that the prewar arms race was responsible for this catastrophe. Support for some form of disarmament was nearly universal. President Woodrow Wilson's "fourteen points" included a call for disarmament and became the basis for the World War I peace settlement. The Allied governments imposed disarmament on defeated Germany, reducing its army to one hundred thousand men, its navy to one tenth its former size, and eliminating its air force entirely.

The European nations also organized the League of Nations as a multilateral forum for the pursuit of peace. The League's charter indicated that the quest for disarmament was to be taken up with renewed determination. Article 1 stipulated that membership in the League was contingent upon willingness to accept League regulations on military, naval, and air armaments, and Article 8 established disarmament as a League goal:

> The members of the League recognize that the maintenance of peace requires the reduction of national armaments to the lowest level consistent with national safety and the enforcement by common action of international obligations.[9]

Article 8 also condemned the production of armaments by private manufacturers, set up plans for the reduction of armaments, stated that annual reviews of weapons policies were necessary, and encouraged communication between governments on the level of armaments in each country. The League established a permanent commission to oversee the execution of Articles 1 and 8.

The apparently senseless origins of World War I and its futile trench warfare convinced European publics of the need for disarmament, but there was a difference of opinion among experts on how to pursue this goal. A great debate developed between those who believed the first step toward peace was a reduction in weapons (called *material disarmament*) and those who believed the first step was a reduction in mistrust (called *moral disarmament*). Moral disarmers believed weapons reduction was meaningless unless mutual distrust was reduced, and material disarmers argued mutual trust could only follow from weapons reduction, since it was the arms race which produced mistrust. As it turned out, the leading naval powers of the world were able to conclude a multilateral material disarmament treaty, and the leading European land powers were able to conclude a multilateral moral disarmament treaty.

In 1925 five Western European powers signed the **Locarno Pact.** France, Germany, Belgium, Great Britain, and Italy all agreed to come to the immediate aid of France and Belgium, or Germany, if either side were attacked by the other. The object of the treaty was to provide guarantees of safety to potential belligerents, thereby reducing insecurity and creating an atmosphere more conducive to material disarmament agreements, which the League of Nations was then promoting. Numerous efforts to create a similar pact, referred to as an "Eastern Locarno," between Russia, Germany, Czechoslovakia, Poland, and other Eastern European nations, failed. The European land powers of the 1920s and 1930s also failed to follow up the Locarno Pact with any significant material disarmament treaties.

Instead, it was the world's great naval powers which signed the most substantive material disarmament agreements of the era: the Washington Naval Agreement of 1922 and its practical extension, the London Naval Treaty of 1930s. The terms of the 1922 agreement limited the five signatories to a battleship ratio based on tonnage, set at 5 tons for Britain and the United States, 3 for Japan, 1.7 each for France and Italy. The treaty was extended by the 1930 agreement to include cruisers. The strict treaty limitations on tonnage required the signatories to scrap sixty-eight ships, a voluntary military sacrifice perhaps unprecedented in history. Most of the European powers scrapped older ships, but the United States scrapped fifteen new vessels worth $300 million, a huge sum in 1922.[10]

Lord Balfour, the head of the British delegation, proclaimed the 1922 treaty an "absolute unmixed benefit to mankind, which carried no seeds of future misfortune." But those who believed that moral disarmament was a necessary prerequisite for meaningful material disarmament were skeptical.

The following anecdote, circulating at the time of the treaty signing, illustrated their skepticism:

> . . . in the old days when Florence led the world both in the arts of the spirit and in those of trade there were five bankers in the city well known for their friendly rivalry. They all were solid and sound men, fearful of God, loving their good wives and enjoying their still better mistresses. Of these, Signor Jonathani and Signor Toro had so many that neither the curious town nor the fortunate bankers themselves knew the exact number thereof; Signor Nipponi, Signor Gallo and Signor Savoia had a lesser though still comfortable number. But winds cannot always blow fair, and a foul weather having set in on the seas of business, the five rivals and friends bethought themselves of the necessity of reducing costly establishments. So, Signor Jonathani . . . called a conference . . . and it was decided, not without difficulty, for the five men were healthy and loved their flesh and the ladies were fair and brought them much pleasure and prestige, it was decided, I say, that Signor Jonathani and Signor Giovanni Toro should limit the number of their fair friends to five apiece; Signor Nipponi to three, while Signori Gallo and Savoia should be reduced to one each with occasional visits to one other, which visits they would carefully keep equal in number—and, in order that their credit . . . should not suffer thereby, the five friendly rivals agreed to make it quite clear to the curious city that their sacrifices were made in deference to the sanctity of marriage.[11]

Just as the Florentine bankers were more interested in their finances than moral scruples, the five signatories to the 1922 Washington Naval Treaty were motivated by budgetary constraints more than a desire for disarmament. To enlarge upon the point, moral disarmers would say that just as the reduction in Florentine adultery did not signal an improvement in Florentine integrity, reductions in weapons do not necessarily signal a shift to peaceful intentions.

The anecdote is also a reminder that disarmament can be a by-product of other national security concerns rather than a top priority, that nations can have multiple reasons for their decisions, and that their reasons are debatable and not always readily apparent. Nevertheless, as material disarmers would note, a multilateral agreement to destroy weapons is a significant step in the right direction. Even if such an agreement does not dissolve mutual distrust instantly, it makes future cooperation and goodwill much more feasible. The 1922 naval agreement was rightly considered an unparalleled achievement, and at the time popular sentiment also believed it represented great progress in disarmament.

Unfortunately both the 1922 and 1930 naval agreements were as exceptional as they were unprecedented, for they did not succeed in stimulating any other significant disarmament agreements. The several other agreements that were reached between the two world wars were symbolic but did not require the reduction of existing weaponry. Moreover, none of the naval treaties of the period were renewed (including the Argentine-Chilean Treaty of 1902, the Washington Naval Treaty of 1922, and the London treaty of 1930). By the mid 1930s, mistrust and militarism were on the rise again.

In fact, shortly after the World Conference on the Reduction and Limitation of Armaments convened in Geneva, in February of 1932, it became clear that the political climate in Europe was no longer conducive to disarmament negotiations. By 1936 a resurgent and increasingly powerful Germany had reoccupied the Rhineland and was demanding arms parity with France, while France, fearful of the rising tide of German nationalism, would neither countenance reductions in its armaments nor willingly acquiesce in arms parity with Germany. In addition, the League of Nation's failure to stop Japanese aggression in Manchuria and Italian aggression in Ethiopia ruined its authority in international politics and with it any hopes of ending war through a collective security agreement.

World War II did not dampen enthusiasm for arms control and disarmament. However, the Charter of the United Nations did place more emphasis on the control as opposed to the reduction of arms than the League of Nations's Charter.[12] The United Nations also recognized the pivotal role of the superpowers in any scheme for arms control or disarmament. Article 11 gave the General Assembly the right to

> consider the general principles of co-operation in the maintenance of peace and security, including the principles governing disarmament and the regulation of armaments, and may make recommendations with regard to such principles to the members or to the Security Council or both.[13]

Also, Article 26 of the UN Charter gave the Security Council (Britain, China, France, USSR and US) responsibility for formulating "plans for the establishment of a system for the regulation of armaments." These provisions revealed a presumption that the success of any international arms control plan required the support of the major powers, that is, the Security Council members. However, differences rather than cooperation have marked the efforts of major powers to advance the causes of arms control and disarmament through the United Nations.

Since 1945 the United States and the USSR have competed for public attention with proposals and counterproposals for a multitude of arms control and disarmament plans.[14] What they almost all bear (or bore) in common, though, is a general pattern of debate that was set with the very first U.S. nuclear disarmament proposal on March 21, 1946. Known as the Baruch plan, this initiative (a joint U.S.-Canadian-British proposal) recommended the establishment of a United Nations **Atomic Development Authority (ADA)** which would assume control of all nuclear energy activities and all highly concentrated uranium and thorium deposits. The ADA would allow use of nuclear technology and raw materials for peaceful purposes only. If any states were found to be in violation of this rule the ADA would take it on itself to warn all other nations of possible aggressive intent on the part of the violating nation. Variations of the proposal also included provisions for punishing violators of the accord.

There were two key features of the Baruch plan. First, the ADA would not be subject to UN Security Council vetoes. Thus the power of the Soviet Union to interfere with the ADA through its Security Council veto power was negated. Second, only the United States had atomic weapons at the time, and under the terms of the Baruch plan the United States reserved the right to retain its weapons until the international agency had established control over all atomic energy activities and thorough international inspection procedures were in place.[15]

The Baruch plan was not accepted by the Soviet Union, which demanded that the United States disarm before institutions for inspection were established and put into operation. The United States and Soviet Union fought many a rhetorical battle over the Baruch plan, but the simple explanation for its failure was that the two former wartime allies profoundly distrusted each other. The Second World War had closed with high hopes for friendship between the allies, but political differences and tests of military strength soon put the United States and Soviet Union at odds.

The controversy over the Baruch plan established an enduring pattern of distrust for U.S.-Soviet disarmament proposals. The United States refused to disarm unless the Soviet Union agreed to stringent verification measures and the Soviet Union refused to consider stringent verification measures until the United States disarmed. To use a frequently employed metaphor, the nuclear genie could not be put back inside the bottle and the world had to accommodate itself to the spectre of nuclear competition.

IS DISARMAMENT POSSIBLE?
THE CONTINUING DEBATE

The failure to negotiate disarmament agreements in the nuclear age has not discouraged disarmament advocates. The United Nations, for example, has never stopped campaigning for disarmament. In 1978 a First Special Session of the General Assembly devoted to disarmament led to the creation of the UN Department of Disarmament, and in 1982 the UN General Assembly launched its World Disarmament Campaign. The UN agenda for disarmament was ambitious:

> The ultimate objective . . . is to achieve general and complete disarmament under effective international control. The immediate goals are to eliminate the danger of war, in particular, nuclear war, and to implement measures to halt and reverse the arms race and clear the path towards lasting peace.[16]

Perhaps remembering the failure of the naval conferences conducted under the auspices of the League of Nations, the United Nations chose to concentrate its efforts on moral disarmament.[17] The UN disarmament campaign is primarily an educational effort. UN publications such as the *United Nations Disarmament Yearbook,* its disarmament *Fact Sheets,* and *Disarmament Newsletter* are aimed at "elected representatives, media, nongovernmental organizations, educationai communities and research institutes."[18]

The United Nations's disarmament campaign has received much support from private citizens and organizations. Another recent and popular case for disarmament is Jonathan Schell's book, *The Fate of the Earth.*[19] Schell, like many others before him, recommended world government as the only viable solution to an armed and hostile world. With world government, disputes would be settled by law:

> Armaments have not been built up entirely out of sheer cussedness. They have been built up in part at least, to perform a legitimate function: that of trying to protect the state against wrongful infringements of its rights, including its right to security. It follows that we cannot merely get rid of armaments and leave a vacuum. Something has to be put in their place. In the human story that something has always been the law.[20]

There is a wealth of literature on the problems and prospects of world government and international law. The majority of informed observers do not consider these options a plausible alternative to the current international system.[21] In fact, Schell's call for world government generated so much criticism that upon reconsideration he agreed it was not a practical alternative.

Prospects for disarmament do not hinge on world government alone. Schell later proposed, for example, that the abolition of nuclear weapons by treaty might be possible if accompanied by strict verification procedures and antinuclear defenses. He admitted that no perfect system of verifying compliance existed. However, he argued that if one side clandestinely harbored nuclear weapons, its advantage would be negated by the other side's defensive forces. In addition, the signatories of the treaty would remain ready for nuclear rearmament so they could respond if they discovered the other side was cheating.[22]

The critical element of Schell's second disarmament plan is the creation of antinuclear defense forces. Opponents of nuclear disarmament have always argued that if one side kept even a handful of hidden nuclear weapons, it would have a tremendous advantage over more honest signatories to the treaty. But with a defense against nuclear weapons such as Schell proposed, this advantage would be substantially reduced. The few hidden nuclear weapons would be negated by active anti-nuclear **defenses**. At the moment such defenses are not in existence, but their construction is being given serious consideration under the U.S. **Strategic Defense Initiative (SDI)** initiated by President Ronald Reagan.

Official interest in disarmament, as opposed to arms control, enjoyed a comeback of sorts under the Reagan administration. Prior to Reagan, in the 1960s and 1970s, the U.S. government and most informed opinion agreed that disarmament was too ambitious, and that arms control initiatives were more practical. Reagan came to office criticizing past arms control agreements as counterproductive. He committed himself to substantial reductions in the nuclear arsenals of the superpowers and advocated their total elimination. Later in his first term Reagan promoted SDI, a plan for researching and then building defenses against nuclear-armed **ICBMs.**

SDI is part of a larger continuing debate on whether new defenses can be used to stimulate major disarmament agreements, both nuclear and nonnuclear. For example, Randall Forsberg has argued for a "defensive disarmament," which she compared with and distinguished from pacifism and arms control:

> Most arms control efforts are intended to reduce the risk of nuclear war while allowing large nuclear arsenals to be maintained indefinitely. But the risk of global nuclear holocaust cannot be substantively reduced until the capability to perpetrate such a holocaust has been virtually eliminated. . . . we must eliminate 99 percent of the current nuclear arsenals.
>
> The defense-oriented approach to disarmament resembles that of pacifists and differs from that of arms controllers in that it is aimed, ultimately, at eliminating the military system. It differs from the pacifist approach, however, in that it concentrates on institutional change and condones the maintenance of defensive armed forces until a stable peace has been achieved. It shares with arms controllers the view that progress toward disarmament cannot be made in a single step, quickly or unilaterally. It assumes that progress will require a series of steps taken over a period of decades through cooperative international action.[23]

Forsberg's approach assumes that there is a significant and identifiable distinction between offensive and defensive weapons that would allow states to eliminate "threatening" offensive weapons and retain "reassuring" defensive weapons. The offensive-defensive delineation is a contentious assumption (discussed in the following chapter) emphasized less by arms controllers and more by disarmers. It has made a comeback in U.S. policy circles since Ronald Reagan announced his plans for SDI.

It may be that one of SDI's most significant long-term effects is to stimulate renewed interest in disarmament through its emphasis on defensive systems. Reagan began negotiations with the Soviet Union in early 1985 with different sets of talks for offensive and defensive weapon systems, and although many doubt their sincerity, the leaders of the United States and the Soviet Union have been assuring the world of their interest in disarmament, above and beyond mere "control" of arms. In January 1986, Soviet leader Mikhail Gorbachev proposed plans to abolish nuclear weapons by the end of 1999. Similarly, President Reagan stated repeatedly his preference for radical reductions (50 percent) in strategic nuclear arms, and the eventual elimination of all nuclear weapons.[24]

Another approach to disarmament, besides world government, and elaborate new defenses, is unilateral disarmament. Proponents of unilateral disarmament believe unilaterally disarming will encourage other nations to do the same. It might be necessary to start slowly, and wait for the other side to reciprocate. Hopefully the adversary would respond positively, but even if the opposite occurred, and unilateral disarmament encouraged an enemy to strike, many believe surrender would be preferable to any resistance that required the use of nuclear arms.[25]

While disarmament has enjoyed a resurgence in policy circles in the 1980s, many remain unconvinced by the arguments reviewed above. With respect to the nuclear winter thesis, they point to alternative studies that challenge the validity of Dr. Sagan's conclusions.[26] More importantly, opponents of the disarmers argue that dwelling on the possibility of nuclear winter confuses the issue, which is not whether nuclear war would be horrible—for all agree it would be—but how to prevent such a war. Indeed, to the extent the nuclear winter thesis is valid, it provides a commensurate degree of deterrence to nuclear war. In other words, if the nuclear winter thesis is correct, any state that launched a nuclear strike would be automatically committing suicide. Thus the nuclear winter thesis does not require disarmament, but instead reinforces deterrence of nuclear war.

Calls for world government, as mentioned above, are simply not practical alternatives. If nations will not trust each other enough to *disarm,* they can hardly be expected to relinquish their sovereignty to a fledgling world government, a step that would require much more trust than signing a disarmament agreement. The same could be said of any radical disarmament plan. If states are unwilling to agree to more modest arms limitation agreements, it is not realistic to expect them to participate in disarmament plans that would involve greater risks.

Further, even if a plan for radical disarmament such as Jonathan Schell's were possible, it is not at all clear that it would be desirable. Some critics of nuclear disarmament believe that the elimination of nuclear weapons alone would only make a return to large-scale conventional war more likely. Perhaps the presence of nuclear weapons and their awesome destructive power inhibits the outbreak of all types of war, in which case it might be a mistake to suddenly dispose of such weapons.[27]

Only an outline of the arguments for and against disarmament was presented in the foregoing discussion. The greater depth and sophistication of the debate over disarmament will become apparent in later chapters. At this point, it is important to recognize both the continuity of the substance of the disarmament debate, especially over the past half-century, and the rise and fall of the disarmament ideal as a guide for official policy. As mentioned, disarmament recently has gained a renewed respectability. However, for the past three decades it was arms control that received most official interest and generated concrete arms limitation agreements.

DISCUSSION QUESTIONS

1. From what you know of history, do you think arms control or disarmament strategies are more realistic? (Draw on the distinctions between the two noted on page one of the chapter.)
2. Is it possible for states to separate nuclear and nonnuclear disarmament efforts? Is it advisable?
3. Can you think of historical circumstances during which material disarmament would improve the chances for peace more than moral disarmament, or vice-versa?
4. Is complete disarmament possible? Is it advisable?
5. Can a weapon be classified as either offensive or defensive? If so, would a major technological breakthrough in defensive weapons improve the chances for disarmament, as opposed to arms control?

SUGGESTED READINGS FOR CHAPTER TWO: A HISTORICAL SURVEY OF DISARMAMENT

BECHOEFER, BERNHARD. *Postwar Negotiations for Arms Control.* Washington, DC: Brookings Institution, 1961.
BURNS, RICHARD DEAN. *Arms Control and Disarmament: A Bibliography.* Santa Barbara, CA: ABC Clio, Co., 1977.
DE MADARIAGA, SALVADOR. *Disarmament.* New York: Coward McCann, 1929.
DOUGHERTY, JAMES E. *How to Think About Arms Control and Disarmament.* New York: Crane, Russak, and Co., 1973.

DUPUY, TREVOR N., and GAY M. HAMMERMAN. *A Documentary History of Arms Control and Disarmament.* New York: R. R. Bowker, 1973.

INDEPENDENT COMMISSION ON DISARMAMENT AND SECURITY ISSUES. *Common Security: A Blueprint for Survival.* New York: Simon and Schuster, 1982.

KALDER, MARY. "Disarmament: The Armament Process in Reverse." In Burns H. Weston, ed. *Toward Nuclear Disarmament and Global Security: A Search for Alternatives.* Boulder, CO: Westview Press, 1984.

NOEL-BAKER, PHILIP. *The Arms Race.* London: Atlantic Books, 1958.

TUCHMAN, BARBARA W. *The Proud Tower.* New York: Macmillan, 1966.

WHEELER-BENNET, J. W. *Disarmament and Security Since Locarno, 1925-31.* New York: Macmillan, 1932.

WOLFERS, ARNOLD, ET AL. *The United States in a Disarmed World.* Baltimore: Johns Hopkins University Press, 1966.

YEFREMOV, A. Y. *Nuclear Disarmament.* Moscow: Progress Pub., 1980.

YOUNG, WAYLAND. "Disarmament: 30 Years of Failure." *International Security* 1 (Fall 1976): 98–116.

NOTES

1. James E. Dougherty, *How to Think About Arms Control and Disarmament* (New York: Crane, Russak, and Company, 1973), pp. 29–30.

2. According to one source the first discussion of arms reductions in the modern era was prompted by budgetary concerns. In 1766 the Austrian Chancellor, Prince Kaunitz, approached Prussian representatives with a suggestion that both states reduce their standing armies by three-quarters to reduce the burden of defense spending. Austrian as well as Prussian finances had been depleted by the Seven Years' War, which ended three years prior to Kaunitz's offer. William R. Hawkins, "Arms Control: Three Centuries of Failure," *National Review,* August 9, 1985, p. 26.

3. Arms control can cost as well as save money. For example, many U.S. nuclear weapons use a system called PAL/CD (Permissive Action Link/Command Disable) to prevent their accidental or unauthorized use. The system is essentially an electronic lock inside each weapon which can only be opened by electronic code on command from the President of the United States. The system also has an electronically activated explosive system that permits the weapon to be disabled harmlessly if seized by unauthorized persons. The system is expensive. At one point, the Department of Defense decided to use an older system instead of PAL in its new B-1 bombers in order to avoid a $200 million cost overrun.

    Some argue that disarmament also can be costly. See the discussion of the "displacement effect" in Chapter 13.

4. Discussion on controlling military budgets was especially popular in the early 1900s. Nations with relatively low manpower costs and thus a comparative advantage in financing military competition were particularly enthusiastic about the prospects for such agreements. The difficulty of defining and monitoring military expenditures, or even establishing a basis for comparing the relative purchasing powers of different national currencies, helps explain why a budget limitation agreement has never been concluded.

5. Richard Dean Burns, *Arms Control and Disarmament: A Bibliography* (Santa Barbara, CA: ABC Clio, Co., 1977), p. 3.

6. As an example of another category, Richard Dean Burns distinguishes between unilateral neglect and unilateral disarmament. The former "refers to a nation's failure to provide for an adequate defense" and the latter is "a consciously decided policy of self-imposed restrictions or limitations." Burns cites British policy after World War I as a case of unilateral neglect and Japan's post–World War II constitutional limits on defense forces as a case of unilateral disarmament. This distinction is an important one, but it is also controversial when applied. British defense spending was thoroughly debated prior to World War I, and only clearly appears to be "neglect" when considered in retrospect. Japan's unilateral disar-

mament must be considered in view of the U.S. defense forces which are pledged to defend Japan. See Ibid.

7. Walter R. Fisher and Richard Dean Burns, *Armament and Disarmament: The Continuing Dispute* (Belmont, CA: Wadsworth Publishing Co., 1974), p. 214.

8. The congressionally established and presidentially appointed *Report of the Chemical Warfare Review Commission, June 1985* (Washington, DC: Government Printing Office, 1985), p. 39.

9. Josef Goldblat, *Agreements for Arms Control: A Critical Survey* (London: Taylor and Francis, 1982), p. 131.

10. This sum was slightly less than one twentieth of the entire federal budget in 1920, and just about one tenth of all federal appropriations in 1925. *The World Almanac and Book of Facts, 1986* (New York: Newspaper Enterprise Associate, 1986), p. 103.

11. Salvador De Madariaga, *Disarmament* (New York: Coward McCann, 1929), pp. 100–101.

12. See footnote 18 in Chapter 10 for the relevant passages from the UN and League Charters.

13. Keesings Special Reports, *Disarmament: Negotiations and Treaties* (New York: Charles Scribner's Sons, 1972), p. 42.

14. See James E. Dougherty, *Arms Control and Disarmament: The Critical Issues* (Washington, DC: Center for Strategic Studies, 1966), pp. 4–5; and William Epstein, *Disarmament: 25 Years of Effort* (Toronto: Canadian Institute of International Affairs, 1971).

15. See Joseph L. Lieberman, *The Scorpion and the Tarantula: The Struggle to Control Atomic Weapons, 1945–1949* (Boston: 1970); and Joseph Nogee, *Soviet Policy Towards International Control of Atomic Energy* (Notre Dame, IN: University of Notre Dame Press, 1961).

16. David Brook, "The United Nations Disarmament Campaign: A Progress Report," *International Studies Newsletter* 12 (June/July 1985): 6–7.

17. Albert Einstein believed in moral disarmament, and his sentiments reflect the strategy the UN has followed to date:

> There is no scientific antidote [to the atomic bomb], only education. You've got to change the way people think. I am not interested in disarmament talks between nations. . . . What I want to do is to disarm the mind. After that, everything else will automatically follow. The ultimate weapon for such mental disarmament is international education.

The United Nations is interested in disarmament talks, but it has concentrated its efforts on international education. Quoted in Charles W. Kegley and Eugene R. Wittkopf, *The Global Agenda: Issues and Perspectives* (New York: Random House, 1984), p. v, preface.

18. Brook, "United Nations Disarmament Campaign," pp. 6–7.

19. Jonathan Schell, *The Fate of the Earth* (New York: Knopf and Random House, 1982).

20. Arther Larson, "Arms Control Through World Law," in Donald G. Brennen, ed., *Arms Control, Disarmament and National Security* (New York: George Braziller, 1961), p. 423.

21. The best place to start an investigation of the problems and prospects of world government is still the classic work by Inis L. Claude, Jr., *Power and International Relations* (New York: Random House, 1962).

22. See Jonathan Schell, "The Abolition: II—A Deliberate Policy," *The New Yorker* (January 9, 1984), in Herbert M. Levine and David Carlton, eds., *The Nuclear Arms Race Debated* (New York: McGraw-Hill, 1986).

23. Randall Forsberg, "Confining the Military to Defense as a Route to Disarmament," *World Policy Journal* (Winter 1984): 285, 318.

24. For example, in a prepared statement of May 7, 1986, President Reagan explained the purpose of U.S.-Soviet negotiations on Nuclear and Space Arms in Geneva as "the achievement of deep, equitable, and verifiable reductions in the nuclear arsenals of the United States and USSR and [through these reductions] to work toward our ultimate goal of eliminating all nuclear weapons."

25. Writing immediately after World War II, Bertrand Russell expressed this sentiment with the expression "better red than dead." Russell thought the long-lasting consequences of a global Soviet empire less pernicious than the potential for nuclear war. In response, Soviet dissident

Alexander Solzenitsyn has argued that "to be Red means to become dead." Alexander Sol-zhenitsyn, "Those Who Would Disarm," *The Washington Post,* June 28, 1983, p. A15. For Russell's quotation, see Bertrand Russell, "The Case for British Unilateralism," in Ernest Lefever, ed., *Arms and Arms Control* (New York: Frederick Praeger, 1962), pp. 154–155.

Interestingly Bertrand Russell has advocated policies from both ends of the absolute secu-rity spectrum. In 1948 he argued for a preventive war against the Soviet Union. See Daniel Frei, *Risks of Unintentional Nuclear War* (Totowa, NJ: Rowman and Allanheld, 1983), p. 170.

26. Caspar W. Weinberger, "The Potential Effects of Nuclear War on the Climate: A Report to the U.S. Congress," *Congressional Record,* 99th Congress, 1st Session (March 6, 1985); and Starley C. Thompson and Stephen H. Schneider, "Nuclear Winter Reappraised" *For-eign Affairs* (Summer 1986).

27. For a discussion of the merits of nuclear disarmament, see essays by six experts in "A World Without Nuclear Weapons" *New York Times Magazine* 5 April 1987.

Chapter Three

A Historical Survey of Arms Control

ARMS CONTROL: LOWERING EXPECTATIONS OR MOVING TOWARD DISARMAMENT?

Consistent with its long-established interest in disarmament, the United Nations in 1969 designated the 1970s the "Decade of Disarmament." In reality, the "Era of Arms Control" would have been a more prophetic pronouncement. The most notable treaties of the 1970s were arms control efforts, and opinion in the scholarly community and decision-making circles was strongly disposed toward arms control instead of disarmament. The shift from disarmament to arms control as the preferred strategy for enhancing limited security began in the early 1960s—but not without much acrimonious debate.

Writing in 1962, Lincoln Bloomfield characterized arms control and disarmament as "two terms which seem to be at war with each other," the disarmers considering arms controllers to be amoral, and the arms controllers considering the disarmers hopelessly utopian.[1] While the differences of opinion endure, the arms controllers clearly gained the upper hand in official policy circles during the 1960s and 1970s. Hence it is worthwhile to investigate the goals and methods of arms control more closely. Arms control is considered a means to accomplish some or all of the following goals:

1. The reduction of the likelihood of war.
2. The reduction of incidents of violent conflict at all levels and, should a war begin, the reduction of the risk of uncontrollable war, especially nuclear war.
3. The diversion of finances from expensive arms to alternative social needs.
4. The end of the spread of nuclear weapons technology to non-nuclear countries.
5. The reinforcement of existing restraints on violent behavior by adding the onus of international public outrage should a treaty be broken.
6. And finally, for some, the setting of the stage for significant disarmament or even world government.

Arms control, like disarmament, has its critics (and they are often the same people). Those who object to arms control raise the following general criticisms. Arms control agreements

1. lead to a false sense of security which both encourages the neglect of necessary defenses and distracts attention from more serious and meaningful efforts to build peace; and
2. can serve as a smoke screen to disguise an aggressor's true intentions.
3. Also, fair arms control treaties cannot be negotiated by democratic nations as public impatience and pressure for progress in negotiations eventually translates into a negotiating advantage for nondemocratic countries.
4. There are those who object to arms control because they believe it interferes with the more important task of disarmament; and
5. many believe the United States and Soviet Union only feign interest in arms control in order to maintain their joint hegemony over the rest of the world (currently a third-world complaint).

As with disarmament, the pros and cons of arms control are explored more fully in later chapters, but at this point it will be helpful to continue with some rudimentary categorization.

SEVEN CATEGORIES OF ARMS CONTROL: A HISTORICAL SURVEY

The types of initiatives governments take to achieve arms control objectives are numerous and varied, and overlap in their functions, but for illustrative purposes they may be divided into seven groupings:

1. Rules of war
2. Communication and administration agreements
3. Confidence-building measures
4. Geographic agreements
5. Quantitative limitation agreements

6. Qualitative limitation agreements
7. Horizontal and vertical proliferation controls

Rules of War

Rules of war—sometimes referred to as just war theory—is a centuries-old field of study. Rules of war are often overlooked in contemporary discussions on arms control when arms control is too narrowly construed as merely the attempt to limit numbers of weapons. In fact, both traditional subdivisions of just war theory are forms of arms control. *Jus ad bellum,* or justice of war, concerns prohibitions on the initiation of hostilities, and *jus in bello,* or justice in war, concerns restraints on violence once hostilities have begun. Both reducing the likelihood of war and limiting its scope and duration are professed objectives of modern arms control advocates, and insomuch as the laws of war facilitate these objectives, they constitute arms control measures.

Laws of war are often derided as merely unenforceable conventions that lack any efficacy, but the same is often said of arms control and disarmament treaties. Just as mankind's interest in arms limitation persists, so does its enduring concern with moral and legal justification for the use of force:

> Virtually every civilization of which we have record placed some limitations on the conduct of its own warfare. As early as the Egyptian and Sumerian wars of the second millennium B.C., there were rules defining the circumstances under which war might be initiated (*jus ad bellum*). Among the Hittites of the fourteenth century B.C., a formal exchange of letters and demands generally preceded hostilities. In ancient China hostilities were circumscribed with many chivalric rules. For example, it was prohibited to wage war during the planting and harvesting seasons.[2]

Christian authorities also tried to impose periods of peace on warring Christians. The first "Peace of God," declared in A.D. 989, forbade war from Thursday through Sunday, and the "Truce of God," proclaimed in 1035 by the Archbishop of Arles, prohibited violence

> from vespers on Wednesday to sunrise on Monday, so that during these four days and five nights, all persons may have peace, and, trusting in this peace, go about their business without fear of their enemies.[3]

In addition to attempts to regulate the duration of hostilities, people have sought to define rules for justifying, and conversely proscribing, resort to force. Greek and Roman laws "specified that an enemy nation could be attacked only if it violated a treaty, injured an ambassador, desecrated holy places, or attacked an ally. Not only was just cause required but a formal demand for redress and a declaration of war was necessary."[4]

Although many ancient societies dealt explicitly with criteria for initiating a "just" conflict (Cicero and St. Augustine are notable ancient contributors to "just war" theory), it was the Christian philosopher Thomas Aquinas who outlined the requisite set of conditions for launching a just war that are still being debated today. The validity and efficacy of Aquinas's prescriptions always have been controversial, but the principles he set down in his *Summa Theologica* have defined the terms of debate on just war theory for Christians and non-Christians alike.

Traditionally, discussion on *jus ad bellum* has focused on ultimate moral principles embued with natural or supernatural significance ("natural law"), but people have also tried to establish positive legal criteria for initiating conflict; that is, law whose authority resides merely in human convention, or formal legal agreements. The best historical examples are the collective security provisions established in the League of Nations and United Nations Charters. Both of these documents contain procedures for international punishment of states that initiate acts of aggression. This led to many attempts to define aggression, but only resulted in one actual collective security action—the UN response to the North Korean invasion of South Korea in 1950. The United States bore the brunt of the fighting for UN forces in the Korean War, and the situation proved so unsatisfactory enough for all concerned that the United Nations never repeated the effort. Instead the United Nations has limited itself to the more manageable task of inserting peacekeeping forces between poten-

St. Aquinas' Principles of Just War

JUS AD BELLUM	JUS IN BELLO
1. *Competent Authority:* The conflict must be ordered and conducted by public authority for public and not private good.	1. All conflict must be justifiable as militarily necessary, i.e. as a direct and significant contribution to military victory.
2. *Just Cause:* For the cause to be just four criteria must be met: —The society is worth protecting. —Peaceful alternatives are exhausted. —There is a reasonable probability of success. —Probable good from the war exceeds significantly the likely evil it will entail.	2. Combatants must be discriminating; that is they must avoid harming non-combatants to the extent possible.
3. *Right Intentions:* The purpose of fighting must always be a just and lasting peace rather than unacceptable motives such as revenge or personal glory.	

For a much fuller explanation of just war theory, see William V. O'Brien, *The Conduct of Just and Limited War* (New York, Praeger, 1981).

tial or active belligerents who request UN assistance. Nevertheless, moral guidelines for resort to force are still a current and contentious concern of contemporary society, as the recent heated debates over tactics for fighting terrorism and statements by religious leaders on the morality of nuclear deterrence demonstrate.

Jus in bello also remains a contemporary concern despite an ancient heritage. Ancient Hindu, Chinese, Babylonian and Hebrew civilizations all left records of rules regulating the conduct of war. Indeed, rules for regulating the conduct of war (*jus in bello*) have received more attention throughout history than rules for initiating war, albeit sometimes for less ideal reasons. Sun Tsu, in his fourth century B.C. Chinese classic *The Art of War,* advises "All the soldiers taken must be cared for with magnanimity and sincerity so that they may be used by us."

It must be admitted that almost all attempts to restrain the behavior of combatants have a self-serving element. First, it is hoped that restraint will be reciprocated by the adversary. Second, the conservation of resources (the military principle of economy of force) requires restraint in the use of military forces. Finally, rules of war are necessary for the maintenance of the basic discipline so necessary to effective military organization. It may be difficult to accomplish military objectives if soldiers are allowed to rape, pillage, and plunder at will. Self-interest is a major consideration in adherence to rules of war, but there is also an element of principle involved. Military men do make voluntary sacrifices on behalf of common moral principles. Medieval knights took their chivalric code very seriously, as have many other warrior elites throughout history. Recently, for example, U.S. pilots suffered higher casualties during the Vietnam War due to their attempts to minimize unintended civilian casualties.[5]

Historically most self-imposed rules on military conduct dealt with the protection of prisoners and noncombatants, but some dealt with larger social concerns, such as prohibitions against poisoning water supplies, or the biblical injunction against the destruction of trees:

> When you besiege a city for a long time, making war against it in order to take it, you shall not destroy its trees by wielding an axe against them. . . . Only the trees which you know are not for food you may destroy and cut down that you may build siegeworks against the city that makes war with you, until it falls.[6]

Of course an attacker would not want to destroy food supplies that he could use himself. However, such restraint may also served larger social and ecological interests, as an example of unrestrained tree-chopping illustrates. When Alexander the Great lay siege to Tyre (300 B.C.), the city had already withstood thirteen years of siege by the Assyrians. Alexander took the city in a mere seven months, but he did it by enslaving the entire population of the surround-

ing area and by destroying an entire forest in the construction of his siegeworks, thereby permanently scarring the area.[7]

Modern leaders confronted with the awesome power of new technologies
have had to envision the possibility of large-scale ecological damage. Since
1977 over thirty nations have signed the Environmental Modification Convention, pledging "not to engage in military or any other hostile use of environmental modification techniques having widespread, long-lasting or severe effects as the means of destruction, damage or injury to any other State."[8] The
1972 Biological Weapons Convention, which prohibits the production, stockpiling, or acquisition of biological agents or toxins was also prompted, in part,
by environmental concerns. Yet biological and chemical weapons[9] (restricted
in the 1925 Geneva Protocol Prohibiting the Use in War of Asphyxiating,
Poisonous or other Gases, and of Bacteriological Methods of Warfare) have
also been outlawed as *mala in se,* or evil by their very nature.

There is a long history of *mala in se* prohibitions (which are a form of
qualitative arms limitation) against certain kinds of weapons. According to the
Book of Manu, the ancient Hindus outlawed the use of barbed, poisonous,
and flaming projectiles. Since then attempts have been made to outlaw cross-
bows, "that deadly and God-detested art of slingers and archers,"[10] submarines, expanding bullets, and nuclear weapons. In some cases the outlawing of
weapons has been motivated more by a desire to curb a new area of military
competition than by any sense of moral revulsion; for example, the 1909 Declaration Prohibiting the Discharge of Projectiles and Explosives from Balloons.

During conflict the punishment of individuals who commit war crimes is
left to the discretion of national authorities, who are also free to define criminal behavior in war as they see fit.[11] However, after a conflict is terminated,
the victors may choose to hold individuals responsible for crimes committed
during battle. Most often the justice of the victor is based on political expedi-
ency or a lust for revenge. Less frequently, the victor(s) will go to the trouble
to make a case for adherence to transnational principles of justice.

The outstanding example of an international war crimes tribunal is the
Allied prosecution of Germans at Nuremberg following World War II. The
issues of command and personal responsibility for German atrocities were fervently debated at Nuremberg, and in the many books and articles that followed the trials.[12] Opinions differ on the success of the trials and the extent to
which they served justice, but they remain the sole modern example of an
international effort to punish men for criminal behavior in time of war. Judg-
ing by the conduct of war since Nuremberg, the punishments handed out by
the Allied powers have not had as much deterrent effect on barbaric behavior
as most would have hoped.

It is difficult to render a general verdict on the utility of rules of war. It
would be easy to be cynical. As for *jus in bello,* the fact is that every weapon

Fig. 3.1   American troops oc-
cupied Nuremburg,
Germany in 1945.
Shortly thereafter, in-
dividual Germans
would be tried for
war crimes. (Source:
National Archives)

that has proved its utility has been used on the battlefield, regardless of treaties to the contrary. For example, the 1930 Treaty of London obliged submarines to save the crews of all ships they torpedoed, yet *every* nation with submarines violated the rule in World War II. In cases where available weapons have not been used, such as poisonous gas during World War II, fear of retaliation in kind rather than any inherent opprobrium seemed the more likely source of motivation for restraint.

Concerning *jus ad bellum,* the following opinion is a widely held one:

> The theory of just war also tends to shade over into a justification of war. It is an easy transition from "ethics permit me to fight this war" to "ethics require me to fight this war."[13]

To illustrate the point, part of the church's motivation for the Truce of God was to prevent intra-Christian fighting long enough to organize Christendom to fight in the Crusades.

Measured by mankind's hopes, the basic limitations on organized violence surveyed above seem meager, but measured against the full length of man's record of gruesome excesses they are welcome respites whenever they are observed. Rules of war also are commended to our attention by Western civilization's deep-rooted concern with justice and morality. Many cynics dismiss discussion of abstract ideals in the arena of human conflict as irrelevant, but they are at least as relevant as the public's demand for some moral justification for the use of force. In representative polities such a justification is almost a prerequisite for sustained military operations, and often a factor in the formulation of defense planning and strategies.

Communication and Administration Agreements

Administrative agreements are meant to reduce tension in the international environment by facilitating communication and procedural cooperation between nations. Ancient conventions on diplomatic immunity which protected ambassadors and negotiators from harm are an example of this type of agreement. Prior to diplomatic immunity the corpse of a messenger would be returned on occasion to indicate the proposal he carried was unacceptable. This practice had the virtue of brevity and directness, but it also tended to foreclose further options for negotiating a peaceful settlement. Thus heads of state, and especially their messengers, found diplomatic immunity a useful first step toward exploring alternatives to violence.

A modern example of an administrative agreement is the U.S.-Soviet "hotline." The 1962 Cuban missile crisis is generally agreed to be the origin of the hotline agreements. During the crisis American and Soviet leaders had to cope with delays in communications and mixed signals. Established in 1963 and modernized twice since then, the Hotline Agreement linked the United States to the Soviet Union, allowing the leaders of both states to communicate directly. The first hotline consisted of a cable running from the United States to the Soviet Union. It proved a rather tenuous connection, however:

> In 1964, a thief cut out a 20-foot section of the cable near Helsinki. In the same year, the communications link was put out of operation when a power station was damaged by a thunderstorm in southern Finland. In 1965, a fire in Rosedale, Maryland, cut the circuit, and later the same year a farmer in Finland ploughed through the cable. In 1966, a Finnish postal strike made the circuit inoperable for several hours, and several months later a Soviet freighter in Denmark severed the cable when it ran aground.[14]

The availability of new technologies prompted a second agreement that utilized communication satellites and is reportedly so secure as to be capable of operating throughout a nuclear war. This agreement has been updated again under the Reagan administration, and in November 1985 President Reagan and Soviet General Secretary Gorbachev agreed to discuss the construction of nuclear crisis centers to improve superpower communication.[15]

The United States and the Soviet Union also signed agreements in 1972 and 1973 that require each nation to inform the other of naval exercises and to limit their surveillance of each other's fleets, thereby reducing the possibility of confrontation on the high seas. This latter agreement has enjoyed a practical success, virtually eliminating the once frequent collisions between U.S. and Soviet ships monitoring each other's maneuvers.[16]

Confidence Building Measures

Communication and administration agreements can be considered **confidence-building measures** (CBMs) inasmuch as they promote the incremental growth of trust by building confidence in the peaceful intentions of an adversary. With such a broad interpretation, trade agreements (sustained over time), arms control treaties that have been adhered to, crisis management rules and structures, limitations on military options, or agreements on military doctrine could all be considered CBMs.

However, the term CBM is usually defined more narrowly, referring specifically to agreements on immediate military concerns; for example, the voluntary sharing of information on troop movements, mutual restraint on weapon transfers to politically unstable areas, cooperation on the verification of previous arms control agreements, and so forth. According to one authority on CBMs, openness, transparency, and predictability are the keys to effective CBMs.[17] By allowing inspection of military forces, their testing and deployment, and by agreeing not to maneuver them without forewarning, the adversary has access (openness) to information on enemy forces, can monitor their condition (transparency), and can judge their status according to predetermined criteria (predictability). These factors strengthen confidence in the inability of an adversary to launch a surprise attack, and over time they also may strengthen confidence in the adversary's peaceful intentions.

CBMs usually do not seriously restrict a nation's capabilities. That is, they do not affect the overall size or functioning of a country's military forces, and so they do not affect power distributions. Instead, CBMs potentially affect perceptions of intentions to use power. As a result, proponents of CBMs consider them valuable preliminary steps toward more substantive agreements. Opponents of CBMs consider them steps toward a false sense of security.

At the 1975 **Conference on Security and Cooperation in Europe (CSCE)**, Warsaw Pact forces and NATO countries were able to successfully negotiate a package of CBMs. They agreed to provide each other with a twenty-one day advance warning of maneuvers involving more than twenty-five thousand troops, and each side agreed to allow observers from the other side to witness such maneuvers. These measures were strengthened by another set of CBMs agreed to by 35 CSCE participants on September 22, 1986.

It is important that CBM agreements be worded very precisely, for ambiguity can lead to misunderstandings that undermine rather than build mutual trust. The spirit of an arms control agreement can be broken even while the letter of the agreement is (arguably) adhered to. For example, in third-century Greece, Macedonia and Athens entered into negotiations to stem their drift towards war. During the negotiations Philip of Macedon agreed not to carry out military operations in the "Chersonese," territory that straddled the Hellespont straits. Athens considered the Chersonese vital to its security since most of its food supplies were shipped through the Hellespont. Taking advantage of some uncertainty as to the precise boundaries of the Chersonese, Philip went ahead and captured the towns of Serrium and Doriscus. The great Athenian orator Demosthenes used these violations of the spirit of the agreement as evidence of Philip's fundamentally hostile intentions towards Athens.[18]

If the spirit of an agreement is clearly broken,[19] then the agreement is actually counterproductive, reinforcing rather than reducing mutual distrust. For example, some Americans charged the USSR with violating a CBM when it failed to notify the United States of the impending Egyptian invasion of Israel in 1973. Those protesting a violation cite the 1972 U.S.-Soviet understanding that each superpower was to notify the other and engage in mutual consultation in the case of a crisis with the potential for superpower conflict. The actual 1972 agreement on "Basic Principles" bound each side to "attach major importance to preventing the development of situations capable of causing a dangerous exacerbation of their relations."[20] There is no question but that the USSR knew about the pending Egyptian attack and knew, also, that another Arab-Israeli war would exacerbate the tension between it and the United States. However, it is questionable whether the USSR violated the agreement, which after all only bound each side to "attach major importance" to preventing such an occurrence. In retrospect it seems that the broad and vague provisions of this CBM encouraged an eventual disagreement over compliance.

Geographic Arms Control Limitations

Geographic arms control measures restrict arms competition in particular geographic areas of the world. For example:

YEAR	TREATY	TERMS
1959	Antarctic Treaty	Demilitarized the Antarctic region
1967	Treaty of Tlatelolco	Banned nuclear weapons in Latin America/Caribbean region
1967	Outer Space Treaty	Banned the placing of weapons of mass destruction in space
1971	Seabed Arms Control Treaty	Banned the placing of weapons of mass destruction on the ocean floor

One advantage to a geographical demarcation in arms control is that it can be relatively unambiguous and thus is not as susceptible to misunderstanding as are other agreements. Most geographical arms control agreements aim at avoiding spiraling arms races by removing an entire area from arms competition. Geographical limitations on nuclear weapons are the most notable of such agreements. In addition to the treaties cited above, there have been numerous proposals for the denuclearization of various regions. In August 1985 the leaders of eight South Pacific countries, including New Zealand and Australia, signed a nuclear-free zone treaty that banned the manufacture, acquisition, or receipt of nuclear explosives in their region. Proposals for a nuclear-free Balkans, Indian Ocean Basin, Central Europe, and Scandinavia have been discussed frequently, but have not yet materialized.

Denuclearization and general demilitarization agreements can encompass whole regions and continents, but much more limited geographic arms control agreements are the historical norm, such as the demilitarization of lakes, border areas, small seas, and other regions. For example, the Peace of Callais (448 B.C.) set limits on the movement of Athenian and Persian warships in the Aegean Sea; the Russo-Turkish Treaty of Kuchuk Kainarji (1774) prohibited the Turkish fortification of the Crimean Peninsula; the Great Lakes were demilitarized in the **Rush-Bagot Agreement** of 1817; a twenty-mile-wide strip along the Norwegian-Swedish border was demilitarized in the Karlstad Convention of 1905, as were the Turkish Straits in the Lausanne Convention of 1923, and the border between North and South Korea in 1953. On occasion an entire country will have its neutrality defined in a mutual agreement by hostile powers to abstain from deploying forces on its territory. The neutralization of Austria with the Austrian State Treaty of 1955 is an example.

Qualitative and Quantitative Limitations

Geographic arms control agreements are either *quantitative* (limiting the number of military forces in a region) or *qualitative* (limiting the type and sophistication of military forces allowed in a region). The 1890 Brussels Act was a qualitative geographic arms control treaty. The agreement was ostensibly designed to repress the African slave trade by prohibiting the "introduction into Africa between latitudes 20 degrees North and 22 degrees South firearms and ammunition other than flintlock guns and gunpowder, except under effective guarantees."[21]

The 1924 Convention on the Limitation of Armaments of Central American States was basically a quantitative geographic agreement. It limited each of five small Central American states to a small standing army of between two thousand and five thousand troops, the precise numbers having been negotiated on the basis of populations, areas, and lengths of borders. In addition, each country was limited to no more than ten warplanes, and all deep-sea warships were prohibited.

Most geographic agreements that include a quantitative provision also include a qualitative provision because the number of weapons to be limited (the quantitative dimension) must be defined precisely (a qualitative distinction). Even so, many agreements clearly emphasize one element over the other. Primarily qualitative arms control agreements prohibit the development or deployment of new types of weapons or improvements of existing weapons systems. Primarily quantitative arms control agreements seek to limit the number of certain types of existing weapons usually already deployed in some quantity by the signatories to the treaty.

Horizontal and Vertical Proliferation

Qualitative and quantitative limitations on the production and deployment of weapons by the signatories to an agreement are referred to as *vertical* controls; that is, they prevent a country from adding to or improving its own weapons. When nations enter into agreements to limit arms transfers to other countries (either qualitative or quantitative), they are referred to in arms control literature as *horizontal* arms control agreements. The most prominent horizontal arms control agreement is the **Nonproliferation Treaty (NPT),** intended to prevent states without nuclear weapons from acquiring any.

Limiting horizontal nuclear proliferation requires restrictions on two kinds of assets: materials and knowledge. The general spread of knowledge through internationally shared educational services and facilities is a vexing problem for those seeking to control nuclear proliferation. Students in U.S. universities using publicly available information have put together workable plans for a nuclear bomb, and one U.S. periodical (*The Progressive*) even tried to publish an explanation on how to build an atomic bomb. Espionage is another reason it is difficult to control the spread of technological know-how. For example, the USSR obtained sketches of the atomic bomb mechanism from secret agents two months before the United States dropped it on Japan.[22]

Another problem for countries desiring nuclear weapons is the acquisition of enough uranium 235 or plutonium 239 to make a bomb. Neither material is readily available and the technology needed to enrich uranium (necessary for use in weapons production) is more difficult to obtain. However, plutonium 239 is produced as a by-product of spent nuclear reactor fuel. With a chemical separation facility, which is needed to extract plutonium from spent uranium and other materials contained in fuel rods, any nation with a reactor has the potential to produce the plutonium necessary to manufacture a nuclear weapon. As a result, any attempt to control horizontal proliferation must involve measures to control spent fuel and the technology needed to produce plutonium 239.

By 1957 such an attempt was underway. The **International Atomic Energy Association** (IAEA) was set up in that year for the express purpose of ensuring that no nuclear fuel was diverted for use in making bombs. Today the IAEA administers safeguards for more than six hundred nuclear facilities throughout the world. A decade after the establishment of the IAEA a major effort to control horizontal proliferation culminated in the 1968 signing of the **Nuclear Nonproliferation Treaty** (NPT) by ninety-seven nations. The NPT was designed to control the export of nuclear technology from **nuclear weapons states** (NWS) to **nonnuclear weapons states** (NNWS). According to the terms of the treaty:

1. No nuclear weapons state party to the agreement would transfer nuclear explosive devices or assist any non nuclear weapons state (NNWS) in acquiring or manufacturing a nuclear explosive device. In turn no NNWS party to the treaty would seek to acquire a nuclear explosive device.
2. All NNWS party to the treaty agreed to submit to IAEA safeguards which would insure that nuclear materials located in NNWS would be used solely for peaceful purposes.
3. Nuclear weapons states agreed to share the benefits of peaceful nuclear technology with NNWS.
4. Each of the parties to the agreement undertook "to pursue negotiations in good faith on effective measures relating to the cessation of the nuclear arms race at an early date and to nuclear disarmament, and on a treaty on general and complete disarmament under strict and effective international control.[23]

A NPT Review Conference met in 1985 and several familiar complaints about the NPT were heard. In particular, many NNWS have been disenchanted with the NPT. Initially they viewed the NPT as part of a universal effort to reduce the level of nuclear weapons, as the provisions of the treaty (see point four above) gave reason to hope. But the United States-Soviet failure to negotiate lower levels of armaments at the **SALT** talks and the paucity of progress in any other arms control and disarmament negotiations was disillusioning. In addition, many NNWS charge that the superpowers are not categorically sincere about stopping nuclear proliferation since they have helped or allowed some close allies to acquire nuclear weapons. Before the NPT was signed, Britain and China obtained their nuclear capabilities with the assistance of the United States and the USSR, respectively. Since the signing of the NPT, the United States has provided Israel with billions of dollars in aid despite its apparently successful efforts to acquire an "undeclared" nuclear weapons capability. Similarly, the United States provided Pakistan with large amounts of aid following the Soviet invasion of Afghanistan despite its determined efforts to produce an atomic capability. In short, immediate strategic interests have taken precedence over the long-term need to uphold the NPT.

Despite such grumbling, supporters of the NPT insist that the treaty has proven remarkably successful.[24] They point out that the gloomy predictions of widespread proliferation in the 1960s have not come to pass, and since the advent of the NPT only India has chosen to publicly explode a nuclear weapon. Moreover, nations are still signing the NPT; between 1980 and 1984, ten new countries signed the treaty. Finally, NPT supporters argue it is imperative to continue efforts to stop nuclear proliferation for the following reasons:

1. The acquisition of nuclear weapons by one power in a region will lead to a desire by other local powers to do the same, as was the case with Pakistan after India exploded a nuclear device in 1974. Pakistan's president was adamant: "We will eat grass, even go hungry, but we will have to get one of our own. We have no alternative."
2. The more countries possessing nuclear weapons the more unstable the world will be. Even an accidental launch from a small nation could escalate into a major nuclear exchange if the origins and responsibility for the attack were unclear.
3. A war between two small nuclear powers could draw in the nuclear arsenals of the superpowers.
4. If a small country used nuclear weapons to achieve a decisive victory, the current "psychological barrier" against the use of nuclear weapons might be broken, and then their use might more readily be contemplated by the superpowers.
5. As more nuclear weapons become available there is a greater chance that one could be stolen by terrorists, or even given to terrorists by those nations that regularly cooperate with them.

Not everyone is so concerned about nuclear proliferation.[25] There is a minority that believes proliferation is inevitable and might even help to stabilize the international environment. This group points out that no power possessing nuclear weapons has ever been directly attacked and concludes that the use of nuclear weapons may be so inherently risky for all concerned that, in effect, they provide perfect territorial security. However, there are signs that the value of nuclear weapons as deterrents against conventional attack may be wearing thin. The Argentine attack on the Falkland Islands, which nuclear-armed Great Britain claimed as its territory, marked the first time in history a nonnuclear power directly attacked the forces and territory of an established nuclear power.

While opponents of nuclear proliferation definitely form the majority opinion on the subject, the debate over proliferation of conventional weapons is more balanced. Advocates of proliferation control take the position that limitations on the sale and transfer of conventional weapons, if properly regulated, can contribute to the three most frequently cited goals of arms control (and disarmament, as mentioned above):

1. To make the outbreak of war less likely
2. To decrease the probable damage if war should occur
3. To lessen the peacetime cost of preparation for war

According to this point of view, limits on proliferation of conventional weapons would make wars less likely because low levels of armaments would make surprise attack impossible, and large-scale hostilities of any kind would be more difficult to undertake due to shortages of weapons. It is also argued that preventing a sudden influx of weapons into a region would preserve political stability because states could be more confident in their assessments of the regional balance of forces.

Furthermore, if a war did start, restrictions on the import of conventional arms would reduce potential damage and risks in a war by reducing the possibility that a small conflict could drag in the superpowers and escalate into a full-scale nuclear confrontation. Without a decisive advantage in arms, it would be difficult to obtain the kind of decisive victory that might tempt outside powers to intervene in order to save an ally or take advantage of a redistribution of power.

Finally, it is argued that without the importation of ever more sophisticated weapons, the cost of peacetime defense and military competition would be lower—an especially important consideration for developing countries. Considering the impoverished conditions of most developing countries, their arms expenditures are a particularly painful burden.

Policies for preventing or restricting conventional arms proliferation frequently take one of the following forms:

1. Restrictions on sales of weapons that are considered particularly loathsome because they inflict superfluous pain and suffering
2. Restrictions on arms sales to certain regions that are considered especially unstable and politically volatile
3. Restrictions on arms sales to regimes considered especially repressive
4. Limits on the quantity of weapons sold to a certain area

Historically nations have negotiated both bilateral and multilateral constraints on conventional weapons proliferation. Bilateral agreements that prohibit the recipient of arms from transferring them to third parties are called "end-use" agreements. End-use agreements often are surreptitiously circumvented or broken outright because sellers are reluctant to enforce them. Sellers need a market just as buyers need a supplier. For example, neutral Switzerland believes that its policy of armed neutrality depends on some domestic weapons production. However, the cost per unit of modern weapons can only be kept down by mass production, and thus Switzerland must find foreign buyers for its weapons, despite public disenchantment with a national role as "arms merchant."[26]

There are financial and political costs involved in switching to a new supplier, and these costs provide the seller with some negotiating leverage should it decide to enforce an end-use agreement. Some governments are less discriminating about their arms sales than others, but private manufacturers are seldom given a free hand in marketing anymore. Since World War II almost all governments have established tight controls over their domestic arms manufacturers. Private manufacturers still account for arms sales, and there is a thriving black market in weapons, especially small arms. But today the overwhelming number of international weapons transfers are conducted on an intergovernmental basis, or with official approval.

Multilateral arms embargoes have not been much more successful than bilateral restrictions. Both the League of Nations and the United Nations organized multilateral arms embargoes. League embargoes failed to pressure Italy and Japan to desist from their acts of aggression prior to World War II, and the UN arms embargoes against Portugal, Rhodesia, and South Africa, designed to stop their colonial and racist policies, were not successful either. However, arms embargoes can and have created real inconveniences for countries by raising the political and financial costs of procuring weapons through alternative means such as espionage, the black market, and domestic arms industries.

Some observers argue that restraints on conventional arms exports are not only ineffectual but also are counterproductive. They contend that there is no evidence to indicate that reductions of worldwide sales of weapons would serve any of the three goals of arms control enumerated above. Contrary to the assertion that reductions in armaments reduce the risk of war, they argue that if the level of armaments were directly related to the causes of war, the most highly armed nations would fight most often, which has not been the case. Weapons are bought and sold because force is considered a viable option in international affairs, not because other nations have weapons. In short, these observers do not believe, as many others do, that arms races start wars.

As for stability, these critics claim that the failure to sell arms can sometimes lead to instability. Agreeing with the renowned student of war, Quincy Wright, they argue that "Neutral arms embargoes if equally applied to all belligerents actually favor the aggressor, who is usually better prepared than his victim."[27] The League response to the pre–World War II Italian-Ethiopian conflict illustrates Wright's point. The League arms embargo of these belligerents left well-armed Italy free to ravage comparatively defenseless Ethiopia.

Moreover, these critics point out that selling arms can be an effective means of restraining nations from conflict. Leaders contemplating war will need to ensure a steady supply of spare parts and replacements for weapons destroyed in combat. If their supplier nation refuses to cooperate in a critical period, when it would be difficult to find another supplier, they may be forced to postpone or even abandon plans for conflict. The United States has exercised such influence in Latin America and the Middle East through its arms sales. In fact, U.S. controls have encouraged some nations—for example, Brazil and Israel—to begin their own domestic arms industries.

As for reducing the damage resulting from war, critics of arms proliferation agreements argue that wars fought with few or relatively unsophisticated arms often are more bloody and destructive than ones fought with highly advanced weaponry. The long Iraq-Iran war is a case in point. In the early stages of the war, Iran was cut off from sources of spare parts for its U.S.-made weapons. It compensated for its inferiority in weaponry by resorting to mass conscription (including the very young) and human-wave assaults, willingly sustaining a very high casualty rate.

Hopes of economic savings are also considered unrealistic. Given disparities in size, population, and levels of industrialization, some nations will feel the necessity of maintaining high levels of armaments regardless of how neighboring states choose to build or reduce their arsenals. Although pointing to the arsenals of neighboring states is a popular justification for defense spending, it rarely is the sole or even the major determinant of arms purchases. As Prince Metternich argued in rejecting Russia's 1816 offer of arms reductions: "The size of a nation's forces must necessarily be determined by its geographic situation, its resources, its domestic situation, and other parochial factors."[28]

Finally, opponents of arms proliferation agreements insist that history demonstrates controls on conventional arms sales just do not work. In the words of one student of the subject, despite the many international efforts to limit the conventional arms trade, "the best of these attempts were innocuous failures, the worst were fiascoes." He adds that the only "principle of arms transfer limitation on which everyone could agree" is "do not give weapons to an enemy."[29] In short, notwithstanding periodic pronouncements to the contrary, nations always end up considering it more important to sell or give arms in order to further some national security objective.

An instuctive case in point is President Jimmy Carter's May 1977 pledge to severely restrain U.S. arms transfers. His presidential directive promised that arms transfers would henceforth be viewed as "an exceptional foreign policy implement," and that the burden of persuasion would "be on those who favor a particular arms sale, rather than on those who oppose it." Yet two years later this promise was all but forgotten. President Carter discovered his European allies were happy to step in where the United States left off in supplying Latin America with arms, and more importantly, that the Soviet invasion of Afghanistan created a need for new and larger U.S. arms transfers in the Middle East. In fact, arms sales actually ended up increasing under the Carter administration despite his sincere original intentions.[30] To summarize, these critics argue that arms transfers are inevitable and thus the United States should use them to promote its own security goals and whenever possible to restrain buyer nations from aggressive behavior.

Implicit in this discussion of conventional arms transfers is the issue of *qualitative* controls. Virtually any nation can produce weapons; the problem is that everyone wants the latest and most technologically sophisticated weapons. Those who believe that arms races lead to war see the history of human conflict as a series of spiraling competitions to produce the latest and greatest weapons. Thus they consider qualitative arms control—that is, the control of the type and sophistication of weapons systems—one of, if not the most important form of arms control.

Throughout history there have been attempts to control qualitative advances in weaponry. One frequently cited example is the Pope's interdict against the use of the crossbow. In 1139 he singled out the crossbow as too murderous "for Christian warfare" but approved its use against the infidels.[31] Like the longbow, the crossbow was capable of piercing armor and thus was a major advance in missile technology. Why there is an appreciable difference between a knight being killed by a bolt from a crossbow rather than an arrow shot from a longbow is not immediately apparent at this late date. Perhaps it was because the crossbow could be used by unskilled peasants, but the longbow required highly skilled archers. Thus the crossbow made the lowest peasant the military equal of the most distinguished knight.

Whatever the Pope's reasons, Christian princes used the crossbow to the extent they considered it expedient. King Richard the Lionhearted was one of many who refused to heed the Pope. Ironically, he was killed by a bolt from a crossbow. While many considered this a very just end for his chaffing at the Pope's authority, the event did little to curb the crossbow's popularity. The crossbow was not abandoned until it was rendered obsolete by firearms.

Occasionally, technological advances prove decisive on the battlefield. For example, in 1866 the Prussians used new breech-loading rifles to defeat the Austrians in the Austro-Prussian War. Four years later their use of steel breech-loading artillery aided them in crushing the French,[32] and forty-four years later submarines almost secured a victory for Germany in World War I. In World War II it was the allies' sudden invention and deployment of shortwave radar that dramatically reversed the fortunes of the naval war with German submarines.

Although it is difficult to negotiate restrictions on technology, nations have managed to do so in the past. Hugo Grotius records that the ancient Chalcidians and Eretrians agreed "not to make use of missile weapons."[33] Much more recently the United States and the USSR agreed to the opposite. The **Antiballistic Missile (ABM) Treaty,** signed by the United States and the Soviet Union in 1972, was an agreement not to make use of antimissile weapons. Neither country wanted to be involved in an expensive arms race involving new weapons systems. Moreover, the USSR had the added incentive that the United States was ahead in ABM technology, and the U.S. government was encouraged to negotiate because the ABM system was unpopular with Congress. As a result, the two nations were able to agree to limit ABM deployment to two sites in each country made up of one hundred missiles at each site and a specified number of radar installations. (In 1974, both agreed to limit the sites to one in each country.)

The ABM Treaty was a tacit recognition of the most basic qualitative distinction in weaponry: the difference between offensive and defensive weapons. The offensive-defensive issue was debated extensively under the auspices of the League of Nations, without much success, an experience paralleled by the United Nations's more recent but equally unsuccessful attempts to define aggression.[34] Although they may be difficult to define, these qualitative distinctions are still considered by many to be critical concepts for progress in arms control and disarmament.

CONCLUSION TO PART I: CONTROLLING WEAPONS— PAST AND FUTURE

In the final chapter of this book we shall return to the "lesson of history" as it applies to arms control and disarmament. It will be easier to assess the relevance of history after more detailed reviews of such important concepts and issues as deterrence, **escalation,** parity, and advancing technology. However, at this point, a few preliminary observations are possible.

From the historical record it is clear states do not voluntarily disarm completely, and partial involuntary disarmament has produced mixed results with defeated states occasionally rebounding to renew past hostilities, for example, Athens and Thebes against Macedon, Carthage against Rome, and Germany against France. Partial voluntary arms control and disarmament also has produced mixed results with the successes being of limited duration and scope. In the case of disarmament, demilitarized zones and armed neutrality have the best record for contributing to peace. For arms control, one could argue that all extended periods of peace have been in part the result of explicit agreements between states or implicit mutually understood measures that are the essential equivalent of arms control.

In short, history advises that complete disarmament is not likely, and instead of the very risky recourse to limited war with the intention of imposing involuntary limited disarmament, it is more reasonable to hope for partial voluntary arms control and disarmament measures which will contribute to limited security. This is particularly true for limited security strategies tailored to fit the sweeping hope of our times: perpetual prevention of nuclear war.

The most important precondition for successful partial arms control and disarmament measures has been identified by Richard Dean Burns in his historical overview of arms control and disarmament:

> Evidently the key to successful contracts is *mutual self-interest:* when this mutuality persists the agreements continue to function, when this mutuality disintegrates so does the effectiveness of the agreement.[35] (emphasis added)

But how do states define mutual self-interest? Kautilya, a fourth century B.C. Brahman statesman, provided a fundamental definition of mutual self-interest that remains pertinent today:

> Just as the collision of an unbaked mud-vessel with a similar vessel is destructive to both, so war with an equal king brings ruin to both.[36]

Avoiding mutual destruction is clearly in the mutual self-interest of adversaries, but how do adversaries know that war would be likely to end in mutual self-destruction? Kautilya suggested the answer to this question was the relative balance of power. "Equal" kings should not fight, and equality was a function of resources and military capabilities:

> If any two kings, hostile to each other, find the time of achieving results from their respective works to be equal, . . . [or] expect to acquire equal amounts of wealth in equal time, they shall make peace with each other.[37]

Kautilya was saying that a balance of power between adversaries should deter war.

In summary, arms limitation agreements must be based on mutual self-interest to succeed, and avoiding mutual destruction is the pre-eminent goal for mutually self-interested parties. Avoiding mutual self-destruction means avoiding war between military equals; that is, military equals should be deterred from fighting one another. Thus at the very least arms limitation should help reinforce **deterrence** between military equals. This simple chain of reasoning, which leads from arms limitation to deterrence of war, obscures some important questions about the relationship between arms limitation and deterrence.

Some arms limitation advocates believe that a balance of military forces provides a foundation for productive arms control negotiations, and may even be a prerequisite for successful negotiations.[38] Others consider arms control merely a means of enhancing a military balance which will deter war,[39] and still others believe a military balance which reinforces mutual deterrence is essentially a substitute for arms control agreements.[40] In contrast to all these opinions, disarmers reject arms control as inadequate precisely because of its relationship to deterrence, since they support disarmament as a means of "reducing the importance of the deterrence system itself."[41] These various points of view are considered at length in later chapters. First, however, we need a thorough familiarity with the concept of deterrence, which is provided in the next two chapters.

DISCUSSION QUESTIONS

1. If you were a military commander, would you order your subordinates to follow established rules of war if doing so would obviously increase their casualties?
2. What ought to be the criteria for classifying weapons *mala in se?*
3. Should revolutionaries be limited by conventional rules of war?
4. Should arms limitation agreements be negotiated with the expectation that the signatories will respect the "spirit" as well as the "letter" of the agreement? What should the response be if the spirit of the agreement is violated?

5. Is it possible to halt the proliferation of new weapons? Is it advisable? If so, under what circumstances?

SUGGESTED READINGS FOR CHAPTER THREE:
A HISTORICAL SURVEY OF ARMS CONTROL

BAILEY, SYDNEY D. *Prohibitions and Restraints in War.* New York: Oxford University Press, 1972.

BLACKER, COIT D., and GLORIA DUFFY, eds. *International Arms Control: Issues and Agreements.* Stanford, CA: Stanford University Press, 1984.

BRENNAN, DONALD G., ed. *Arms Control, Disarmament and National Security.* New York: Braziller, 1961. Based on the Fall 1960 issue of *Daedalus.*

BULL, HEDLEY. *The Control of the Arms Race: Disarmament and Arms Control in the Missile Age.* New York: Praeger, 1961.

CALDWELL, DAN. "Strategic and Conventional Arms Control: An Historical Perspective." *Stanford Journal of International Studies* 14 (Spring 1979): 7–27.

DUNN, LEWIS A. *Controlling the Bomb: Nuclear Proliferation in the 1980s.* New Haven: Yale University Press, 1982.

FRIEDMAN, LEON. *The Law of War: A Documentary History.* New York: Random House, 1972.

GOLDBLAT, JOSEF. *Arms Control Agreements: A Handbook.* London: Taylor and Francis, 1983.

——. *Agreements for Arms Control: A Critical Survey.* London: Taylor and Francis, 1982.

JASANI, BHUPENDRA. *Space Weapons: The Arms Control Dilemma.* Stockholm International Peace Research Institute. London: Taylor and Francis, 1984.

NATIONAL ACADEMY OF SCIENCES. *Nuclear Arms Control: Background and Issues.* Washington, DC: National Academy Press, 1985.

PFALTZGRAFF, ROBERT L., ed. *Contrasting Approaches to Strategic Arms Control.* Lexington, MA: Lexington Books, 1974.

PIERRE, ANDREW J. *The Global Politics of Arms Sales.* Princeton: Princeton University Press, 1982.

STARES, PAUL B. *The Militarization of Space: U.S. Policy, 1945–84.* Ithaca, NY: Cornell University Press, 1985.

STOCKHOLM INTERNATIONAL PEACE RESEARCH INSTITUTE. *World Armaments and Disarmament: SIPRI Yearbook 1985.* London: Taylor and Francis, 1985.

UNITED STATES ARMS CONTROL AND DISARMAMENT AGENCY. *Arms Control and Disarmament Agreements.* New Brunswick, NJ: Transaction Books, 1982.

U.S. CONGRESS. HOUSE. COMMITTEE ON FOREIGN AFFAIRS, SUBCOMMITTEE ON ARMS CONTROL, INTERNATIONAL SECURITY AND SCIENCE. *Fundamentals of Nuclear Arms Control: Part I.* "Nuclear Arms Control: A Brief Historical Survey." Report prepared for the Subcommittee on Arms Control, International Security and Science by the Congressional Research Service. Washington, DC: Government Printing Office, 1985.

WISEMAN, HENRY, ed. *Peacekeeping.* New York: Pergamon Press, 1983.

NOTES

1. Lincoln P. Bloomfield, "Arms Control Theory," in Walter Fisher and Richard Dean Burns, *Armament and Disarmament: The Continuing Dispute* (Belmont, CA: Wadsworth Publishing Co., 1974), p. 258.

2. Leon Friedman, *The Law of War: A Documentary History* (New York: Random House, 1972), p. 3.

3. Ibid., p. 9.
4. Ibid., p. 5.
5. Despite requests from the Secretary of the Air Force to lift restrictions on bombing tactics due to "the present scrupulous concern for collateral civilian damage and casualties," permission was denied and "many pilots were shot down because the rules of engagement required approach angles and other tactics designed to reduce civilian casualties rather than afford maximum protection to the attacking planes." Guenter Lewy, *America in Vietnam* (New York: Oxford University Press, 1978), p. 403.
6. Leon Friedman, *The Law of War: A Documentary History* (New York: Random House, 1972), p. 4. However, no *mala in se* prohibition has been uniformly observed. For example, Polyaenus told of the Amphictyones, who

   > at the siege of Cyrrha, having discovered an aqueduct, that supplied the city with water, by the advice of Eurylochus, poisoned the water with hellbore; a great quantity of which they procured from Anticyra. The Cyrrhaeans, who made constant use of it, were attacked with violent cholics, and disabled from duty. Under such circumstances the Amphictyones easily defeated them, and made themselves masters of the place.

   Polyaenus's Stratagems of War, trans. R. Shepherd (Chicago: Ares Publishers, 1914; an unchanged reprint of the 1793 London edition), p. 244.
7. Lynn Montross, *War Through the Ages* (New York: Harper and Row, 1960), p. 32.
8. United States Arms Control and Disarmament Agency, *Arms Control and Disarmament Agreements* (New Brunswick, NJ: Transaction Books, 1982), p. 193.
9. The distinction between chemical and biological weapons is that biological weapons are living organisms, while chemical weapons are not. Some substances fall between the two categories, like toxins, which are chemical byproducts of biological processes.
   Biological and chemical weapons are not modern inventions. The ancient Chinese had poisonous hand grenades. They hurled earthenware pots filled with highly poisonous snakes at the advancing enemy, whereupon the agitated snakes attacked the closest moving objects. Ian Padden, *The Fighting Elite: US Marines* (New York: Bantam Books, 1985).
10. Friedman, *The Law of War*, p. 9.
11. The most famous case in modern American history was the trial of Lieutenant William Calley by the U.S. Army for the massacre of Vietnamese civilians at My Lai.
12. See Bradley F. Smith, *Reaching Judgment at Nuremberg: The Untold Story of How the Nazi War Criminals Were Judged* (New York: 1976).
13. Coit D. Blacker and Gloria Duffy, eds., *International Arms Control: Issues and Agreements* (Stanford, CA: Stanford University Press, 1984), p. 27.
14. Dan Caldwell, Introduction, *Arms Control and Disarmament Agreements,* p. xxiii.
15. For further discussion, see U.S. Congress, Senate, Committee on Armed Services, *Hotline Upgrade: Report to Accompany Senate Joint Resolution 108,* 99th Congress, 1st Session (Washington, DC: Government Printing Office, 1985); and William L. Ury, *Beyond the Hotline: Crisis Control to Prevent Nuclear War* (Boston: Houghton Mifflin, 1985).
16. See Sean M. Lynn-Jones, "A Quiet Success for Arms Control," *International Security* 9 (Spring 1985): 154–184; and Josef Goldblat, *Agreements for Arms Control: A Critical Survey* (London: Taylor and Francis, 1982), pp. 195, 207.
17. Ibid. Jonathan Alford offered a helpful hypothetical and condensed dialogue between adversaries that illustrates the supposed spirit of CBMs:

   > if you are *genuinely* concerned about security and not about launching an aggressive war against me, then I have the right to insist that I should have adequate warning of an attack as proof of your good intentions. I accept that you may be entitled to strike first if you feel your security to be threatened, but then I am also entitled to warning. For my part, if I am assured of fair warning, I can adopt a position which is less threatening to you. As I am prepared to give you an assurance that I do not mean to attack you, I will reduce my readiness. I do not ask that you should not be *able* to attack me but only that you cannot do it before I am ready to meet such an attack. If I do not have that confidence, I am going to have to maintain my alert position, and so are you.

Jonathan Alford, "Confidence-Building Measures in Europe: The Military Aspects," from Christoph Bertram, ed., *Arms Control and Military Force* (Montclair, NJ: Allanheld, Osmun and Co., 1980), pp. 188–89.

18. See Demosthenes, "Philippic III," in *Greek Political Oratory*, trans. A. N. W. Saunders (Middlesex, England: Penguin Books, 1970), p. 252, footnote 4.

19. An example of evading the spirit if not the letter of an agreement was Prussia's circumvention of the disarmament treaty forced on it by Napoleon in 1806 (the Treaty of Tilsit). Prussia agreed to a ceiling of 42,000 men in its army, but it compensated for this restriction by shortening the period of service and rushing great numbers of men through the regular army and then into the reserves. When fully mobilized, the Prussian army far exceeded the treaty limits. Frederick H. Hartman, *The Relations of Nations* (New York: Macmillan, 1983), pp. 268–269.

20. *Arms Control and Disarmament Agreements,* p. 205.

21. Goldblat, *Agreements for Arms Control,* p. 4.

22. Hartman, *The Relations of Nations,* p. 282.

23. *Arms Control and Disarmament Agreements,* p. 91.

24. Secretary of State George Schultz, "Preventing the Proliferation of Nuclear Weapons" (Washington, DC: U.S. Department of State, Bureau of Public Affairs, Current Policy # 63, November 1, 1984), p. 1.
    To further strengthen the NPT, in April 1987 the Reagan Administration negotiated with six other major industrialized nations an agreement to restrict the export of missiles capable of carrying nuclear warheads.

25. See Kenneth Waltz, *The Spread of Nuclear Weapons: More May be Better,* Adelphi Paper # 171 (London: International Institute for Strategic Studies, 1981).

26. In response to public protest in 1973, Switzerland decided to export only defensive weapons, and not to any governments of "zones of tension," but the Swiss government's definitions of "defensive" and "tension" have proven flexible. *The Economist* 22 (March 1986): 50. See also, "Everybody's Doing It: Selling Arms to Iran, That is, Notably the Europeans." *Time* 16 March 1987, p. 31.

27. Richard Burt, *Arms Control in the 1980s* (Boulder, CO: Westview Press, 1984), p. 115.

28. Blacker and Duffy, *International Arms Control,* p. 32.

29. Some would say that the Reagan administration's decision to sell weapons to Iran in 1986 shows there are even exceptions to this rule. Cited in Burt, *Arms Control in the 1980s,* p. 110.

30. Andrew J. Pierre, *The Global Politics of Arms Sales* (Princeton, NJ: Princeton University Press, 1982), pp. 52, 58.

31. Edwin Tunis, *Weapons: A Pictorial History* (New York: World Publishing Co., 1954), p. 65.

32. Michael Howard, "Theater Nuclear Warfare: The Forgotten Dimensions of Strategy," in John Reichart and Steven Sturm, *American Defense Policy* (Baltimore: Johns Hopkins University Press, 1982), p. 352.

33. Friedman, *The Law of War,* p. 38.

34. For example, in 1974 the United Nations approved a convention that identified and firmly condemned seven general categories of aggression, but then ended up approving wars of "self-determination, freedom and independence," thereby blurring the clear distinction it had just made. Theodore A. Couloumbis and James Wolfe, *Introduction to International Relations* (Englewood Cliffs, NJ: Prentice-Hall, 1982), p. 215. See also, Benjamin B. Ferencz, *Defining International Aggression in the Search for World Peace: A Documentary History and Analysis* (Dobbs Ferry, NY: Oceana Publishing, 1975).

35. Richard Dean Burns, *Arms Control and Disarmament: A Bibliography* (Santa Barbara, CA: ABC Clio, Co., 1977), p. 3.

36. R. Shamasastry, *Kautilya's Arthasastra,* 8th ed. (Mysore, India: Mysore Printing and Publishing House, 1967), p. 301.

37. Ibid., p. 296.

38. For example, see Richard Smoke, *War: Controlling Escalation* (Cambridge: Harvard University Press, 1977), cited in Charles E. Kegley and Eugene R. Wittkopf, *The Global Agenda: Issues and Perspectives* (New York: Random House), p. 413.

39. As Burns notes, this is generally true of arms controllers. See Burns, *Arms Control and Disarmament,* p. 1.

40. Unilateral measures designed to strengthen deterrence and encourage reciprocal actions on the part of the adversary are sometimes referred to as "indirect arms control." See "Arms Control at the Crossroads," *Newsweek,* October 1, 1984, p. 30.

41. Burns, *Arms Control and Disarmament,* p. 1.

PART II

Chapter Four

Arms Control and Defense Planning

Mark Twain once observed that, "For every complex and difficult problem there is always a simple and easy solution—and it is always wrong." Simple and easy solutions can seem effective temporarily, but they usually manage to leave the real problem unsolved. A good example is the solution Alexander the Great supposedly chose when confronted with the Gordian knot, a piece of chariot thong tied in an impossibly intricate knot. The tangle of thong was presented to him with the explanation that he who could solve its riddle would rule the world. Without hesitation Alexander simply drew his sword and easily hewed the knot in two. Wouldn't it be nice if every problem could be so quickly resolved? But a moment's reflection convinces us that Alexander merely succeeded in avoiding the problem. He personally no longer had to deal with it, but the riddle of the knot was not solved. The simple and easy solution was really no solution at all.

Today many see arms limitation as the solution and *alternative* to the outmoded policies of defense and deterrence rather than as interrelated components in a larger national security strategy. Yet majority opinion holds that the above point of view is too simple. Most experts, public officials, and politicians still believe that, like the Gordian knot, arms limitation and defense policy remain intricately and inextricably intertwined. It might be convenient to neatly separate the two in one clean analytical blow, but the riddle of arms control as a solution to war cannot really be resolved without understanding its relation to defense policy, and in particular to deterrence strategy.

ARMS LIMITATION AND DEFENSE POLICY

> I am sure you will be on your guard against the capital fault of letting diplomacy get ahead of naval preparedness.
>
> —Winston Churchill: Letter to Sir Samuel Hoare, August 25, 1935[1]

> Military influence on arms control negotiation is like the influence of a heroin pusher on drug traffic.
>
> —John Kenneth Galbraith[2]

Hedley Bull has observed: "Arms control and military strategy have been regarded as opposites; the first directed towards the removal of the second, the second toward avoiding the shackles of the first."[3] But unless a state decides either to disarm unilaterally or forswear all arms control negotiations, it must necessarily pursue arms control and defense concurrently. In other words, states must maintain military forces while trying to negotiate their limitation and control. However, the relationship between arms control, disarmament and defense can be more or less salient, as the following cases suggest.

The most obvious interaction between arms control and defense planning occurs when a treaty stimulates, bans, or severely restricts the development or deployment of certain types of weapons. For example, the **antiballistic missile (ABM)** protocol in **SALT I** restricted the United States and the Soviet Union from deploying systems capable of destroying incoming nuclear missiles **(ICBMs)**. On the other hand, there are times when arms control negotiations are postponed or ignored in order to avoid their interfering with defense programs, such as when France and China refused to sign a nuclear test ban treaty which they believed would unsafely restrict their own nuclear weapons programs. Sometimes arms control and defense stimulate rather than inhibit one another. It is not uncommon to note a correlation between arms control negotiations and accelerating arms programs, a phenomenon referred to in arms control literature as the "displacement effect."[4]

Less obvious are cases in which a military program is only delayed or made contingent upon arms control negotiations, or vice versa. Two examples are the May 16, 1984, House of Representatives's decision to refuse funding for a new ICBM (the MX missile) if the Soviet Union decided to return to the negotiating table, and the May 24, 1985, Senate decision to approve the testing of a U.S. antisatellite weapon only upon confirmation by the President that tests would not disrupt negotiations aimed at banning antisatellite weapons.

Another case occurred in Great Britain between 1932 and 1935 when hopes for successful negotiations in the Geneva Disarmament Conference were a primary reason Britain repeatedly postponed rearmament of the British Air Force.[5] Arms control is also made contingent upon weapons development on occasion. For his support of the Kellogg-Briand Pact, Senator Borah required an increase in naval spending,[6] and Senator Henry Jackson reportedly made his support in 1963 for a **partial nuclear test ban** contingent upon increased underground nuclear warhead testing.[7]

Even more subtle are those cases in which an arms limitation agreement is postponed or abandoned because it will hinder weapons development, or cases in which a defense option is either ignored because it might complicate arms control efforts or perpetuated for its utility as a **"bargaining chip"** in arms control negotiations. The term bargaining chip refers to the continuation of a defense program only in order to provide an incentive for opposing nations to negotiate an arms control agreement. Bargaining chips may never receive serious attention as defense programs. When a government is not serious about the development and deployment of a weapons system, and only desires its continuation for purposes of negotiating advantages, defense officials may be reluctant to devote scarce resources to the program, in which case the program will languish. Henry Kissinger expressed this concern in 1979 during SALT II testimony:

> Whatever the tactical utility of this argument [new weapons programs as bargaining chips], it tended to reduce the energy with which such programs were pursued. The Pentagon found it difficult to muster enthusiasm—or scarce resources—for programs which were ephemeral by definition.[8]

Alternatively, it is often the case that a program that initially was justified as a "bargaining chip" absorbs so many resources and accumulates so many supporters that it eventually is deployed, regardless of its impact on arms control negotiations. The **cruise missile** has been cited as an illustration of both possible outcomes for bargaining chip programs. The Department of Defense was initially less than enthusiastic about its development when it was being justified as a bargaining chip,[9] but it was eventually deployed and seems sure to become a major addition to U.S. strategic nuclear forces.

Finally, there are those cases where the exigencies of arms control negotiations and defense planning help define the specific form each eventually takes. For example, under the Carter administration the design of the MX missile was "strongly influenced by projected requirements for verifying future negotiated limitations on strategic weapons."[10] In particular, it was deemed unacceptable to make the MX missile without providing means for the Soviet Union to monitor U.S. deployments of the missile.

The previous examples illustrate why arms limitation and defense *cannot* be studied as mutually exclusive topics. While the existence of the relationship between arms limitation and defense is not in doubt, the nature of the relationship is often disputed. Official policy statements, defense programs, and negotiations under both Republican and Democratic administrations leave little doubt that the majority view in the United States supports the view that both arms control and defense are fundamental to national security, and thus can be complementary.

However, as the Hedley Bull quotation opening this section suggested, many other observers believe arms control and defense work at cross-purposes to the detriment of national security. In part this is because arms limitation policy and defense planning often are not properly synchronized. However, there are those who believe arms control and defense are mutually exclusive. At one end of the policy spectrum are those who argue as if every defense effort would increase the security of the nation, but no arms control effort would; and at the other end of the spectrum are those who believe every arms control effort would further the cause of peace, but no defense program would. Unilateral disarmers believe modern weapons are so dangerous that global security has supplanted national security as a requisite for any viable political community and must be pursued even at the risk of domination by another power. Those who believe that conflicting political systems make war inevitable in the long term, believe in the preparation for war without any hindrance from arms control efforts.

Neither unilateralism nor militarism has yet captured the allegiance of a significant portion of U.S. decision makers. The majority opinion oscillates between these two extremes, sometimes moving toward one and sometimes toward the other, but always assuming arms control and defense can coexist and together contribute to peace and national security. This middle ground might be referred to as the orthodox approach. In theory the orthodox position on national security holds that there is no necessary contradiction between arms control and defense. In practice it proves difficult to synchronize the two objectives, and proponents of each tend to emphasize their own immediate concerns. Over the past two decades there has been a notable shift of opinion among orthodox theorists as to the origin of resistance to synchronizing arms control and defense policy.

Twenty years ago most orthodox national security strategists believed it was the U.S. military who insisted on arms control and defense as contradictory goals. In a classic work on arms control, the authors observed:

> Military collaboration with potential enemies is not a concept that comes naturally. Tradition is against it. . . . The military and diplomatic worlds have been kept unnaturally apart for so long that their separation came to seem natural. Arms control is a recognition that nearly all serious diplomacy involves sanctions, coercion and assurances involving some kind of power or force, and that a main function of military force is to influence the behavior of other countries, not simply to spend itself in their destruction. It is the conservatism of military

policy that has caused "arms control" to appear as an alternative, even antithetical, field of action.[11]

Today, however, the pendulum seems to be swinging, and more and more observers are complaining that it is the proponents of arms control who have lost sight of the potentially complementary relationship between arms control and defense. As a former State Department official asserts:

> In sum, arms control has become less a component of national strategic military planning and more of an alternative; negotiating propositions have become an escape from the dilemmas of long-term programming. Stability is thus sought in marginal bargains about changes in some Soviet systems, rather than in the creation of an equilibrium through a combination of U.S. programs and negotiated agreements.[12]

It is difficult to say whether the military establishment or arms limitation enthusiasts are now more responsible for unduly emphasizing their concerns to the exclusion of the other. What is clear and important to understand is that the tension between these competing attitudes (represented in the following chart) is a persistent characteristic of the national security debate, and that for the time being the orthodox view is held by the majority of national decision makers and the public at large. Even though at any given time an orthodox theorist may believe more emphasis is needed for one or the other approach, his short-term general goal remains the prevention of war through arms and arms control, or to use a term more specifically defined in the next section, through stable deterrence.

Three Points of View on Armaments and Defense

UNILATERAL DISARMAMENT	THE ORTHODOX VIEW: ARMS LIMITATION & DEFENSE		UNAVOIDABLE CONFLICT
	DISARMAMENT/ DETERRENCE	ARMS CONTROL/ DETERRENCE	
Occupation by an adversary is preferable to war in the nuclear age, though passive resistance may be effective	The number of weapons must be reduced	Weapons and state behavior must be controlled	War, even in the nuclear era, will occur, and constant preparation for war is necessary for security
	Meanwhile, deterrence is a necessary part of war prevention strategy, as are		
	some existing defenses	continuing defenses	
[Only Arms Limitation ─────────────────────────────────────── Only Defense]			

ARMS CONTROL AND DETERRENCE

> When there is mutual fear, men think twice before they make aggression upon one another.

> —Hermocrates, quoted in **Thucydides**
> *The Peloponnesian War*

This chapter concentrates only on those elements basic to all concepts of deterrence. While considering deterrence it is important to remember that this concept is important for arms control because *all orthodox debate on arms limitation revolves around whether or not arms limitation policies contributes to or undermines stable deterrence.* To understand the national debate on arms control strategy, it is necessary to understand different opinions on deterrence.

What Is Deterrence?

Deterrence means simply this: Making sure any adversary who thinks about attacking the United States or our allies or our vital interests concludes that the risks to him outweigh any potential gains. Once he understands that, he won't attack. (Ronald Reagan, March 23, 1983)

As a general concept, deterrence is relatively simple, yet it quickly becomes a complicated issue when applied to specific situations and strategies. Deterrence is the ability to dissuade a potential enemy from hostile actions. It involves presenting the opponent with a prospect of costs and risks that outweigh his prospective hopes for gain. This is not nearly so easy as it might sound, for calculations of power lack mathematical rigor. They depend on human perceptions, which are subject to interference from emotions like hope and fear. But to the extent a sober assessment of what contributes to successful deterrence is possible, it must focus on two critical characteristics of deterrence: credibility and stability.

Credibility

A credible deterrent is based on two fundamental criteria: capabilities and will. A nation's *capacity* to deter an enemy is determined by the means for defense at its disposal: numbers of soldiers, quality of weapons, industrial capacity, and so forth. Without sufficient defense capabilities, a state's ability to deter attack is not credible. *Will* is an abstract concept compared to capabilities and more difficult to estimate, so much so that often it is just assumed that a state's military capabilities accurately reflect its will to defend itself.[13] While it is true that capabilities are frequently used by statesmen as a barometer of national will, assuming that capabilities perfectly reflect a nation's will can be dangerous, as the following example illustrates:

During President John F. Kennedy's first year in office, his administration sponsored an invasion of Cuba which failed horribly. Some charged that the failure was due to inadequate U.S. support, and that America's enemies would interpret the failure as a reflection of weak U.S. resolve. U.S. prestige suffered badly, Kennedy's critics argued, and by extension, so had U.S. credibility. Kennedy responded to these critics by asking, "What is prestige? Is it the shadow of power or the substance of power?" Kennedy's rhetorical questions implied that he believed capabilities are the substance of a nation's power, and a nation's apparent willingness to use those capabilities is of peripheral concern for deterring aggression.

Yet only a year later, during the Cuban Missile Crisis, Kennedy took the United States to the brink of nuclear confrontation in an effort to communicate U.S. will. The USSR placed nuclear missiles in Cuba and Kennedy demanded their withdrawal. He refused to accept a compromise wherein the Soviet Union would withdraw the nuclear missiles it had tried to sneak into Cuba if the United States would withdraw a similar type of nuclear missile it had deployed some years earlier in Turkey. Kennedy argued it would *appear* as if the United States had been coerced into the compromise by the bold Soviet move to secretly install missiles in Cuba, and this he found unacceptable. The issue was not one of *capabilities,* as Kennedy had actually ordered the removal of the missiles in Turkey some time earlier. Kennedy was willing to accept the risk of nuclear confrontation simply in order to convince the Soviet Union that America was *willing* to fight and could not be coerced; in other words, that America's will to defend itself was equal to its military capabilities, something Kennedy had come to fear the Soviet Union doubted.

Will is a less tangible ingredient of credibility than military capability, but it is no less important. An imbalance in will (that is, determination) helps explain why a country far superior to another in capabilities cannot always coerce or deter the apparently weaker state. In retrospect, Dean Rusk (former Secretary of State and a major architect of America's Vietnam War policy) suggested that a disparity in will at least partially explained the failure of the United States in the Vietnam War: "Personally, I made two mistakes. I underestimated the tenacity of the North Vietnamese and overestimated the patience of the American people."[14]

Although will is probably the more difficult of the two to estimate, both capability and will are subject to misperceptions. Hence there is a third factor critical for credible deterrence, as former Secretary of State Henry Kissinger has noted:

> Deterrence requires a combination of power, the will to use it, *and* the assessment of these by the potential aggressor. Moreover, deterrence is a product of those factors and not a sum. If any one of them is zero, deterrence fails.[15]

Even if a nation has both the will and capability to punish an act of aggression, but does not successfully communicate these facts to the aggressor,

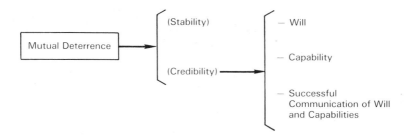

deterrence could fail. Successful communication of will and capability to a potential enemy is complicated by the fact that capabilities and will interact, each influencing perceptions of the other. For discussion purposes capability and will can be considered separately, but in their historical context they always are linked, as can be demonstrated with the following two cases of unsuccessful deterrence.

In an analysis of British diplomacy and defense policy prior to World War II, John F. Kennedy argued that France and Great Britain were incapable of deterring Hitler because they simply lacked the *means* to do so. He concluded that the decision taken at Munich by France and Britain to capitulate to Hitler's demands on Czechoslovakia was "inevitable on the ground of lack of armaments alone."[16] However, the failure to deter Hitler was not simply a function of inadequate capabilities. As Kennedy also noted, the British public was unwilling to finance armaments because it was not willing to fight a war it feared would just repeat the senseless horrors of World War I. Hence, inadequate British capabilities reflected, in large part, lack of popular will to fight.

The Soviet invasion of Finland in 1939 offers another historical example of failed deterrence and the interrelationship of will and capabilities. In 1939 Stalin wanted Finland, which lay within artillery range of Leningrad, to cede Finnish territory near Leningrad to the USSR. The two countries entered negotiations, but the Finns refused to agree to Stalin's demands. Stalin threatened war, expecting the Finns to capitulate without fighting. Nikita Khrushchev, at the time a close aide to Stalin, later recorded Soviet thinking on the situation in his memoirs:

> None of us thought there would be a war. We were sure that the Finns would accept our demands without forcing us to go to war. All we had to do was raise our voices a little bit, and the Finns would obey. If that didn't work, we could fire one shot and the Finns would put up their hands and surrender. Or so we thought.[17]

The reason for the Soviet leaders' confidence in their low assessment of Finnish will to fight was the vast disparity between Soviet and Finnish military capabilities. Khrushchev continues:

> A few days after the war began, I left for the Ukraine. Like everyone else I was confident that our advantage would prove immeasurable and that our dispute would be solved quickly, without many casualties for us. So we thought and so we hoped. But the history of that conflict turned out very differently.[18]

The examples of Hitler and Britain, and Stalin and Finland illustrate two reasons why will and capability interact, but also why they are perceived as relative to one another. In the first case, Britain seemed unwilling to keep pace with German rearmament, and this encouraged Hitler to believe Britain would make concessions rather than fight. Thus how well a nation is *prepared* to fight is often considered an indication of how *willing* it is to fight. Also, as the Soviet-Finnish example demonstrates, an aggressor may doubt the *will* of a people to fight simply because the odds against them are so hopeless. The Soviet Union assumed Soviet military superiority would undermine Finland's will to resist. In both cases perceptions of will reflected assessments of military capabilities, and in both cases will and capabilities were inseparable in their combined impact on the aggressor's perceptions.

Second, as the surprising success of the Finnish resistance demonstrates, firm resolve can in some measure compensate for relatively weaker capabilities. In short, will and capabilities interact, both in reality and in international perceptions of reality. The interrelationship of will and capability explains why national leaders so often insist that diplomacy (including arms control negotiations) is insufficient without a strong military. Even Neville Chamberlain, who is often characterized as naive for trying to appease Hitler, returned to England from Munich with these awkward but revealing words:

> Our past experience has shown us only too clearly that weakness in armed strength means weakness in diplomacy, and if we want to secure lasting peace, I realize diplomacy cannot be effective unless the consciousness exists, not here alone but elsewhere, that behind the diplomacy is the strength to give effect to it.[19]

Frederick the Great, the laconic King of Prussia, made the point more succinctly: "Diplomacy without armaments is like music without instruments."

Nuclear weapons have not suspended the belief that capabilities and will interact as essential elements of successful deterrence. Brent Scowcroft, chairman of a blue-ribbon bipartisan panel of experts established by President Reagan to investigate the need for the MX missile, justified the new missile first and foremost because of its importance as a symbol of national will. The reason the United States must have the MX, Scowcroft argued, was

> First of all, to demonstrate U.S. national will and cohesion; four Presidents have now stated that the MX is important, if not vital to our national security. To back away from that as a country and to reject requests for that system it seemed to the Commission would reflect an absence of that critical element of deterrence, and that is national will and determination.[20]

The interaction between capabilities and will complicates precise estimates of each, as does the fact that they are subject to perceptual errors and manipulation. Hence, it is difficult to know precisely the requirements for successful deterrence. Unfortunately, neither history nor more specific empirical indices provide much guidance on this matter. It is fairly obvious when deterrence fails, but historical cases of successful deterrence are necessarily highly conjectural as there are always multiple possible explanations for the unwillingness of a nation to attack a neighbor, ranging from a basic preference for peace to alternative policy priorities.

So, although it is clear that will and capability are crucial to credible deterrence, it is not at all clear "how much is enough," either for deterrence, defense or aggression. War is just too unpredictable, as Khrushchev had reason to lament in 1939:

> In our war against the Finns we had an opportunity to choose the time and the place. We outnumbered the enemy, and we had all the time in the world to prepare for our operation. Yet even in these favorable conditions it was only after great difficulty and enormous losses that we were finally able to win. A victory at such a cost was actually a moral defeat.[21]

In fact it was something far worse than a moral defeat as the poor Soviet performance against tiny Finland helped confirm the Nazi view of the USSR as a degenerate society. After following accounts of the damage the Finns were able to inflict on invading Soviet forces, Hitler boasted in 1941: "We have only to kick in the [Russian] door, and the whole rotten structure will come crashing down."[22] A year later Hitler kicked in the door and soon found he had repeated Stalin's mistake of underestimating the resolution of his opponent. Both Khrushchev's retrospective commentary and Hitler's miscalculated optimism about his pending invasion of the USSR point out how unpredictable war is and how difficult accurate assessments of capability and will can be.

Stability

A stable deterrent posture presumes a credible deterrent, but it also presumes that defense preparations will not be overly threatening and thus invite **preemptive attack.** In other words, a nation needs enough demonstrable capability and expressed will to deter an enemy, but not so much that the enemy is frightened into attacking before its security situation deteriorates further. A classic example of a nation frightened into a preemptive strike occurred in 1587 when the Englishman, Sir Francis Drake, sailed into the Spanish harbor of Cadiz and destroyed a sizable portion of the Spanish Armada, a fleet England rightly feared was being prepared for an invasion of the British Isles. England also launched a surprise naval strike in 1807, destroying the Danish fleet at Copenhagen. The danger presented by the Danish fleet is not so clear in retrospect as that of the Spanish Armada, which illustrates how subjective assessments of immediate threat can be. Two more recent examples of destabilizing deterrence postures may be cited for illustrative purposes. The first highlights destabilizing capabilities, and the second, destabilizing manifestations of national will.

On a Sunday afternoon in June 1981, Israeli jets flew 650 miles to the heart of Iraq. Suddenly dropping out of the sky and catching Iraqi defenses completely by surprise, the eight Israeli F-15 fighter-bombers took less than two minutes to destroy Iraq's Osirak nuclear reactor. The reactor had been scheduled to go into operation just two months later, and would have been producing the weapons-grade plutonium necessary for building a nuclear bomb. Israel's preventive air strike ended or at least postponed this capability. Unable to effect and unwilling to trust Iraqi intentions, Israel moved to eliminate a particularly threatening Iraqi military capability. Israel defended its action by citing intelligence reports indicating Iraq was intent on building the bomb and by calling attention to Iraqi rhetoric that seemed to substantiate the will to use such a device against Israel. Here again there is evidence that perceptions of will and capability interact, but Israel's first concern was preventing Iraq from acquiring a nuclear capability.

Years before the Osirak raid Israel coordinated another preventive military operation with allies whose goal was primarily to destroy the *will* to threaten harm before it led to a commensurate capability to do so. In 1956, after Egypt's charismatic Gamel Abdel Nasser illegally closed the economically and strategically important Suez canal, Israel, Great Britain, and France launched a surprise attack on Egypt. They did not do so because Egypt was capable of immediately threatening their vital interests, but because they believed Nasser's rhetoric and flouting of international law boded ill for their long-term security interests. The leaders of Britain and France thought Nasser's behavior was reminiscent of Hitler's bellicose posturing in the years preceding World War II.

British Prime Minister Anthony Eden openly compared Nasser to Hitler, as did French Premier, Guy Mollet, who considered Nasser's book, *Philosophy of Revolution,* a facsimile of Hitler's *Mein Kampf.* Both Eden and Mollet had overwhelming public support, and even if their comparison with Hitler seems a bit overdrawn in retrospect, it is clear they considered Nasser's intentions and ability to galvanize broad popular support in the Middle East most threatening. Prior to World War II Britain and France failed to take Hitler's rhetoric and posturing seriously until he had the capability to put his plans into action and then it was too late. They did not intend to make the same mistake with Nasser.[23]

It is possible, for any number of reasons, that a nation will believe it has to accept a significant shift in power to an adversary's advantage, but nations are most reluctant to do so. As the above examples illustrate, on occasion a nation's will (usually as it is articulated in belligerent threats) and capabilities (usually when suddenly and significantly enhanced) seem too threatening and invite **preventive attack.** The attacker postulates that it is safer to attack and try to reestablish the status quo of mutual deterrence or realign the balance of power in its favor before it is too late. In such cases the nation that was attacked can be said to have had a deterrent posture sufficient to alarm its adversaries but not sufficient to deter them from attacking. In other words its deterrent posture was destabilizing.

FIVE PROBLEMS WITH DETERRENCE[24]

This section began by noting that unless one opts for unilateral disarmament or unbridled national security competition, arms limitation and defense policy must aim at stable deterrence and thus *should* be mutually reinforcing. In contrast, unilateral disarmers and inevitable conflict theorists tend to denigrate a "preoccupation with stable deterrence." The avid disarmer often sees an emphasis on credible deterrence as a cover for rampant militarism, and the inevitable conflict theorist often sees stability as a code word for appeasing enemy hostility.

Because these two extremes are influential, and because it is important to give each position its due, it is worthwhile to review briefly five frequently cited problems with "stable deterrence."

1. Stable mutual deterrence assumes too much rationality on the part of decision makers. When translated into particular historical circumstances and deterrence strategies, it tends to assume leaders will be able to make fine distinctions coolly and rationally, even under great pressure and severe time constraints. This, critics claim, is not a safe assumption.

2. Stable mutual deterrence can be easily upset by factors that are increasingly characteristic of the modern world: (a) technological breakthroughs that would give one side a sudden, overwhelming advantage; (b) the proliferation of weapons of mass destruction to more countries, many of which are less sophisticated, less stable, and more likely to use such weapons; (c) greater reliance, to monitor and control nuclear weapons, on technical mechanisms that bypass human control and are subject to malfunction; and (d) the speed of modern weapons, which reduces time for negotiation and might make escalation to all-out war a certainty.

3. Stable mutual deterrence may be an ethnocentric concept. It is essentially Western in its reliance on rationality and its presumption that costs and benefits can be relatively accurately assessed. Many argue, for example, that the Soviet Union has never accepted the American concept of deterrence (or arms control either). If the concept of stable mutual deterrence is too ethnocentric, it means only one side is working toward a goal, the success of which is critically dependent on the best efforts of both parties.

4. Stable mutual deterrence does not explain how to defuse tensions or build peace,

only how to limit the chances of war. For some, this is a hopelessly inadequate limitation; for others, it is too optimistic an aspiration.

5.   Finally, the concept of nuclear deterrence is handicapped by one gigantic presumption of irrationality. An enemy is deterred from launching an all-out surprise nuclear strike by the fear of similar retaliation. However, most believe such a retaliatory strike could not be based on anything other than an irrational desire for revenge, since the complete destruction of the retaliating society would have been accomplished already, thus ending any rational debate about its future interests, including how to deal with enemies.

In summary, stable mutual deterrence is criticized as too optimistic, too pessimistic, too rational, too irrational, and too ethnocentric. All these criticisms can in turn be criticized, but they are not easily dismissed, and they are alarming because mutual deterrence is, for the time being, what the world must rely on for the prevention of a nuclear war.

"The knowledge that he is to be hanged in a fortnight," Samuel Johnson once observed, "wonderfully concentrates a man's mind." Hopefully the same may be said for mankind in general, living under the threat of nuclear holocaust. Either a way must be found to avoid reliance on deterrence, or we must be very careful to adopt a deterrence strategy that will not fail at some critical point. Unfortunately, at the moment there is not a consensus on the most appropriate nuclear deterrence strategy. Instead there are currently two national strategies for stable mutual deterrence, flexible response and assured destruction, and they are very much at odds with one another in theory. Living in the shadow of the grim reaper's nuclear noose provokes a healthy curiosity about which of these two strategies for stable mutual deterrence would make us more secure.

DISCUSSION QUESTIONS

1.   Are peace strategies which combine arms limitation and deterrence policies necessary, or can either of these approaches to security be pursued independently of the other?
2.   In the context of domestic politics, how should the government act to ensure that arms limitation and defense programs are synchronized?
3.   Is political will or military capability more important in deterring an adversary from attack? Which is more important for victory in a conflict? Which is easier to communicate to potential adversaries?
4.   A state's deterrence posture must be sufficient to deter an attack but not so formidable that it alarms other states and leads them to launch preemptive strikes. How can arms limitation agreements assist states in arriving at the proper balance in deterrence posture?
5.   Which of the 5 frequently cited criticisms of deterrence reviewed at the end of the chapter do you find most convincing? Can you think of any others?

SUGGESTED READINGS FOR CHAPTER FOUR: ARMS CONTROL AND DEFENSE PLANNING

BURT, RICHARD. "The Perils of Arms Control in the 1980s." *Daedalus* 110 (Winter 1981).

GEORGE, ALEXANDER L., and RICHARD SMOKE. *Deterrence in American Foreign Policy: Theory and Practice.* New York: Columbia University Press, 1974.

GREENWOOD, TED. *Making the MIRV: A Study of Defense Decision Making.* Cambridge: Ballinger, 1975.

JERVIS, ROBERT, RICHARD NED LEBOW, and JANICE GROSS STEIN. *Psychology and Deterrence.* Baltimore: Johns Hopkins University Press, 1986.

LUTTWAK, EDWARD N. *Strategic Power: Military Capabilities and Political Utility.* Beverly Hills, CA: Sage Publications, 1976.

MACLEAN, DOUGLAS, ed. *The Security Gamble: Deterrence Dilemmas in the Nuclear Age.* Maryland Studies in Public Philosophy. University of Maryland, 1984.

QUESTER, GEORGE H. *Deterrence Before Hiroshima.* New York: Wiley, 1966.

SCHELLING, THOMAS C. *Arms and Influence.* New Haven: Yale University Press, 1966.

SCHELLING, THOMAS C., and MORTON H. HALPERIN. *Strategy and Arms Control.* New York: Twentieth Century Fund, 1961.

STEGENGA, JAMES A. "Nuclear Deterrence: Bankrupt Ideology." *Policy Sciences* 16 (1983): 127–145.

STEINBRUNER, JOHN D. "Beyond Rational Deterrence." *World Politics* 28 (January 1976): 223–245.

WESTON, BURNS H., ed. *Toward Nuclear Disarmament and Global Security: A Search for Alternatives.* Boulder, CO: Westview Press, 1984. Chapter 5: "Rethinking Deterrence."

NOTES

1. Churchill quotation from *Dictionary of Military and Naval Quotations,* compiled and edited by Colonel Robert Debs Heinl, Jr., USMC (Ret.). Copyright © 1966, U.S. Naval Institute, Annapolis, Maryland, p. 264.

2. Galbraith quoted in Jeffrey S. McKitrick, "Arms Control and the Joint Chiefs of Staff," *Parameters* (Autumn 1984).

3. Hedley Bull, *The Control of the Arms Race* (New York: Frederick Praeger, 1961).

4. Displacement effect is discussed in greater detail in Chapter 11.

5. John F. Kennedy, *Why England Slept* (New York: Wilfred Funk, 1961), pp. 62–83.

6. See Salvador De Madariaga, *Disarmament* (New York: Coward McCann, 1929), pp. 345–346.

7. See G. B. Kistiakowsky, "The Good and the Bad of Nuclear Arms Control," *The Bulletin of Atomic Scientists,* May 1979, pp. 7–9.

   In addition, see the discussion of an attempt by Congress to prohibit construction of the Diego Garcia naval base in an effort to further a demilitarized Indian Ocean, in Admiral Thomas Moorer's foreword to Alvin Cottrell and Walter Hahn, *Naval Race or Arms Control in the Indian Ocean?* (New York: National Strategy Information Center Agenda Paper 8, 1978).

8. Colin S. Gray, *Strategy and the MX* (Washington, DC: Heritage Foundation, 1983), p. 7.

9. Richard Burt, ed., *Arms Control and Defense Postures in the 1980s* (Boulder, CO: Westview Press, 1982), p. 107.

10. John F. Reichart and Steven R. Sturm, eds., *American Defense Policy,* 5th ed. (Baltimore: Johns Hopkins University Press, 1982), p. 408.

11. Thomas C. Schelling and Morton H. Halperin, *Strategy and Arms Control* (New York: Twentieth Century Fund, 1961), pp. 142–143.

12. William C. Hyland, "Institutional Impediments," in Burt, *Arms Control and Defense,* p. 98.

13. When will is assumed from capabilities, credibility becomes a function of comparative military capabilities alone. Defense analysts who believe an adversary's intentions are not evident will concentrate solely on relative military power. This issue is explored in depth in Chapter 14.

14. John G. Stoessinger, *Why Nations Go to War* (New York: St. Martin's Press, 1982), p. 110.

15. James Dougherty and Robert Pfaltzgraff, *Contending Theories of International Relations* (New York: Harper & Row, 1981), p. 376.

16. Kennedy, *Why England Slept,* p. 186.

17. Nikita Khrushchev, *Khrushchev Remembers,* trans. and ed. Stobe Talbott (Boston: Little, Brown, 1970), p. 152.

18. Ibid., p. 153.

19. Kennedy, *Why England Slept,* p. 197.

20. U.S. Congress, Senate Foreign Relations Committee, Hearing on "The Arms Control and Foreign Policy Implications of the Scowcroft Commission Report," (Washington, DC: Government Printing Office, 1983), p. 3.

21. Khrushchev, *Khrushchev Remembers,* p. 156.

22. Allan Bullock, *Hitler: A Study In Tyranny* (New York: Abridged Ed., Perennial Library, Harper & Row, 1962), p. 382.

23. John G. Stoessinger, *Crusaders and Pragmatists: Movers of Modern American Foreign Policy* (New York: W. W. Norton, 1979), pp. 115, 118.

24. For more on the problems associated with deterrence, see Robert Jervis, Richard Ned Ledbow, and Janice Gross Stein, *Psychology and Deterrence* (Baltimore: Johns Hopkins University Press, 1986); Michael MacGwire, "Dilemmas and Delusions of Deterrence," *World Policy Journal* 1 (Summer 1984): 745–767; and James A. Stegenga, "Nuclear Deterrence: Bankrupt Ideology," in Herbert M. Levine and David Carlton, *The Nuclear Arms Race Debated* (New York: McGraw-Hill, 1986). For a particularly negative review of current deterrence policies, see the collected essays of one of Europe's leading disarmament advocates, E. P. Thompson *Beyond the Cold War: A New Approach to the Arms Race and Nuclear Annihilation* (New York: Pantheon, 1982).

Chapter Five

Arms Control and
Nuclear Deterrence Strategy

When the axe is blunt and has not first been sharpened, then one must use more force.

—Ecclesiastes, 10:10

The components of deterrence discussed in the previous chapter are applicable to deterrence and arms control at any level (strategic, conventional, and unconventional) and concerning any weapons. This chapter has a narrower focus: nuclear weapons and their deployment doctrine according to two opposing deterrence strategies. The two schools of thought on nuclear deterrence may be referred to as "**assured destruction**" and "**flexible response**" (sometimes called finite deterrence and graduated deterrence). A state's choice of nuclear deterrence strategy will not only determine the composition of nuclear forces and the strategy for their deployment and contingent employment, it will also strongly influence the national policy toward arms control. For these reasons it is important to understand the assured destruction/flexible response debate, which is essentially a question of whether the state's axe ought to be sharpened or not.

ASSURED DESTRUCTION STRATEGY

> It was a custom with the Tauri, a people of Scythia, always before a battle to dig ditches, throw up mounds, and render the ground impassable behind: that conscious of their retreat being thus cut off, they might know no alternative, but victory, or death.
>
> —Polyaenus
> *Stratagems of War*[1]

Assured destruction strategists begin with the premise that nuclear weapons have revolutionized strategic thinking. Bernard Brodie is quoted most frequently on this point. After the bombing of Hiroshima and Nagasaki in 1945, he observed that "everything about the atomic bomb is overshadowed by the twin facts that it exists and that its destructive power is fantastically great." As a result:

> The whole character of war as a means of settling differences has been transformed beyond all recognition.[2]

And:

> Thus far the chief purpose of a military establishment has been to win wars. From now on its chief purpose must be to avert them. It can have almost no other useful purpose.[3]

Brodie was the first to claim that nuclear weapons broke the previously necessary linkage between deterrence and defense. This assertion requires closer scrutiny since it is a fundamental premise of the assured destruction theorists.

Deterrence or Defense?

In the past the defense value of military forces was calculated by their ability to *minimize losses* to friendly territory and populace while *maximizing gains* by destroying enemy forces and occupying enemy territory. The anticipation of their being able to accomplish these twin objectives established the *deterrence value* of the military forces. The same military forces that *deterred* prior to an attack would then *defend* after an attack (that is, after deterrence failed). Assured destruction theorists claim this relationship came to an end with nuclear weapons. Nuclear weapons may deter a nuclear attack through the threat of retaliation in kind, but because their destructive power is so great they cannot defend territory or people if deterrence fails. Glenn Snyder aptly summarized this interpretation of the impact of nuclear weapons on national security strategy:

This is the most striking difference between nuclear and pre-nuclear strategy: the partial separation of the functions of pre-attack deterrence and post-attack defense, and the possibility that deterrence may now be accompanied by weapons which might have no rational use for defense should deterrence fail.[4]

The assertion that nuclear weapons have no defense value is a key tenet of assured destruction deterrence strategy. To demonstrate why it will be necessary to review the old controversy over the distinction between offensive and defensive weapons.

Offensive and Defensive Weapons

The true strength of a prince does not consist so much in his ability to conquer his neighbors, as in the difficulty they find in attacking him.

—Montesquieu
The Spirit of the Laws, 1748

Students of arms limitation have long debated whether or not weapons can be categorized as offensive or defensive. In theory, it would enormously benefit arms limitation efforts if weapons were clearly either offensive or defensive, for then nations could agree to restrict only weapons that were offensive and could be used for aggression, while allowing the construction of non-threatening defensive forces. In such an environment, all nations could defend and none could attack. Everyone would feel more secure.

However, in practice it is extremely difficult to classify a weapon as exclusively offensive or defensive because the function of most weapons is ambiguous. This point was made by a British naval officer who, when required by his superiors to determine whether a 15-inch naval gun was an offensive or defensive weapon, reportedly quipped that it depended "wholly on which end one was standing at."[5] Reviewing the history of the debate over the offensive/defensive distinction makes this eye-of-the-beholder analogy seem especially apt.

At the 1932 World Disarmament Conference the United States and Britain argued that battleships were defensive and submarines offensive, while nations without large surface navies argued the reverse, and so on, according to each state's assessment of its own strategic needs. The same pattern was repeated in the discussion on land weapons.[6] It is not just that states resolutely adhere to their own preferred interpretations of what constitutes an offensive or defensive weapon; there really is an element of ambiguity in weapons categorization. Even students of arms control and disarmament who strain for objectivity find it difficult to categorize weapons as either offensive or defensive.

For example, one commentator has argued that the Washington Naval Treaty of 1922 was defective because it prohibited fortified bases, which are *defensive* and thus help deter rather than encourage war.[7] But another prominent student of war has argued such bases were *offensive* because they gave the most feared offensive naval weapon of the day—the battleship—the fourth essential element of an offensive weapon: holding power. According to this scholar, the battleship already possessed the first three elements of offensive weapons: mobility, protection and striking power. The overseas bases that could resupply the battleship gave it greater range and endurance, and thus holding power.[8]

Part of the ambiguity surrounding the offensive and defensive nature of weapons is that often they can be used for either purpose. The United States's use of riot control gas in Vietnam is an example. Ostensibly the gas was a defensive weapon intended to quell riotous prisoners so they would not have to be harmed, but the gas was also used in an offensive mode to force insurgents from caves and tunnels so they could then be shot. Another example is offered by the merchant marine ships of World War I. Cargo vessels hardly seem like offensive weapons, but after a deck gun had been deployed and hidden on such a ship it could be lethal for any submarine that surfaced to warn the crew to abandon the ship before it was sunk. After a few submarines had been sunk by this subterfuge, submarine captains no longer bothered to provide warnings before they attacked.

Even what appear to be unambiguous defensive fortifications can be an important element of a larger strategic offensive. At the outset of World War II Germany utilized a set of defensive fortifications in western Germany—the Siegfried line—to contain French forces while it destroyed Polish resistance in the East. Afterwards Germany was able to turn its full attention on France. A modern parallel to the Siegfried line is the plan to defend the United States from ICBMs. President Reagan called it a purely defensive system, but many of those opposed to the idea claim it could be used in the same manner as the Siegfried line, that is, to allow the United States to launch a nuclear strike while itself being protected from a similar attack. Thus, when defensive forces and fortifications free offensive forces to do their job more effectively and with impunity, they may be considered to have offensive value.

Whether the distinction between offensive and defensive weapons is meaningful enough to guide arms limitation negotiations remains an unresolved issue, yet negotiators have never abandoned their efforts to single out and limit dangerous and destabilizing weapons while allowing defensive or second-strike weapons to reinforce stable mutual deterrence. For example, in 1974 eight Latin American countries signed the Ayacucho Pact, an agreement to limit the purchase of "offensive weapons" and "put an end to their acquisition for offensive warlike purposes."[9]

Also, as the parallel between the Siegfried line and SDI illustrates, nuclear weapons have not brought an end to the offensive-defensive debate. Nevertheless, from the assured destruction theorists' point of view the debate is largely a moot point since they hold that nuclear weapons have no defensive value. They are not concerned with defense, but rather with deterrence. In deterrence strategy the parallel to the distinction between offensive and defensive weapons is the distinction between first and second strike weapons.

First-or Second-Strike Weapons

The possibility of war increases in direct proportion to the effectiveness of the instruments of war.

—Norman Cousins

The offensive/defensive distinction is still a central feature of most disarmament plans,[10] (and flexible response strategies) but it is less important in arms control debate. Like assured destruction strategists, but for different reasons, arms controllers are more interested in deterrence than defense. Arms controllers generally believe that most, if not all, weapons can be employed in either an offensive or defensive mode, although they may be much more effective in one or the other. Thus arms controllers tend to focus on whether a weapon is *more* offensive or defensive. They do not seek to eliminate offensive weapons, but instead to control the composition of forces to make war less likely. In other words, they move from the question of defense to deterrence, and consider whether weapons have **first-strike** or **second-strike capabilities.** In general a first-strike weapon is any weapon that is vulnerable to a quick strike, yet is itself lethal if used quickly. Such weapons must be used before they are destroyed, and thus in a tense situation they encourage a state to strike first. In contrast, second-strike weapons are not vulnerable to quick strikes, nor can they strike quickly themselves.

For example, the same commentator who found the Washington Naval Treaty flawed because it limited "defensive" weapons such as fortified bases also concluded the treaty failed to limit the most lethal first-strike naval weapon, which in his opinion was not the battleship but the aircraft carrier:

As Pearl Harbor made clear, the aircraft carrier was a weapon that, as compared with the battleship, encouraged striking first in a crisis, and therefore somewhat increased the chances of war. The aircraft carrier was far better adapted to carry out swift attack from a distance than the lumbering battleship. . . . At Midway and other carrier battles there was a strong tendency for the side that struck first to win. If one wants to do everything that would make war less likely—the primary objective of all arms limitation agreements—one will not want to encourage the shifting of the weapons mix towards weapons, like the aircraft carrier, that may encourage a first strike. But the Washington treaty had precisely this effect.[11]

But just as there is disagreement on the possibility of clearly identifying offensive and defensive weapons, there is also disagreement over whether distinctions between first-and second-strike weapons can be made. Many would

Fig. 5.1 Were battleships first- or second-strike weapons? (Source: Library of Congress)

disagree that aircraft carriers are necessarily first-strike weapons. One could construct a scenario for their use in a defensive posture, such as NATO's intention to use aircraft carriers to defend Atlantic convoys in case of a war in Europe. Moreover, it was not the availability of aircraft carriers which led Japan to launch a first strike. Japan launched a similar surprise first strike against Russia in 1904 with battleships. In short, many would argue that what finally determines whether a weapon is a first or second strike weapon, or offensive or defensive, is the intention of its possessor.

Despite the degree of ambiguity, assured destruction theorists (like disarmers vis-a-vis the offensive-defensive distinction) still maintain that the distinction between first and second strike weapons is critical. They reason as follows: A first-strike nuclear weapon is one that is both vulnerable to an enemy first strike and accurate enough itself to be used in a first strike. In theory such weapons encourage both sides to fire their weapons first in order to eliminate the enemy's missiles before the enemy can eliminate theirs. A second-strike weapon is one that is relatively invulnerable to an enemy first strike, and thus discourages the enemy from attempting a first strike, but that is also not accurate enough to destroy enemy nuclear weapons, and thus does not constitute a first-strike threat to the enemy. Therefore, if predominantly first-strike ("offensive") nuclear weapons can be identified and eliminated or reduced, allowing only predominantly second-strike ("defensive") nuclear weapons to remain, neither side would have the means for a successful surprise first strike and hence both sides would feel much more secure. This chain of reasoning directs assured destruction theorists negotiating arms limitation agreements.

The Historical Significance of Assured Destruction Theory

The origin of the term **assured destruction** reflects the assured destruction theorists' concern that there be no delusions about the catastrophic results of any nuclear exchange:

> The term [assured destruction] was first used in 1964. The concept was originally to be known as assured retaliation, but this was felt to be too bland. The harshness of the term and the inescapable tragedy described in its definition were intentional. McNamara [then Secretary of Defense] was concerned that, through euphemistic language, the circumlocutions endemic to military briefings and ill-disciplined logic, the Air Force and its Congressional supporters were deluding themselves into believing that there was a tolerable way of fighting a nuclear war. Talking, for example, about "urban-industrial fatalities" rather than "people killed" cushioned the senses against any attempt to comprehend the extent of the human catastrophe inherent in any nuclear war.[12]

Assured-destruction theorists stressed there was no possible defense against or with nuclear weapons, and they strongly discouraged speculation that obscured this reality. It took about a decade for the assured destruction theorists to gain the upper hand in policy circles. By 1969 mutual assured destruction was official U.S. strategic policy, and it was codified with the signing of SALT I in 1972.

A summary of the internal logic of the assured destruction position juxtaposed with essential elements of the SALT I agreements better illustrates why most observers consider SALT I the codification of assured destruction strategy. The case for assured destruction can be made in three simple steps.

1. Should either the United States or the Soviet Union ever employ nuclear weapons it is most likely if not inevitable that the war would escalate to a general nuclear exchange causing catastrophic damage to both sides.

2. Since this is true, there can be no meaningful distinction made between targeting military forces and installations (counterforce targeting) and targeting population centers (countervalue targeting). Even if the war did not escalate into an all-out nuclear exchange, the distinction between civil and military targets is ridiculous because (a) most major population centers contain or are close to military targets and (b) even if no major population center was hit, damage due to fallout, high winds, fires, disease, and so on, would kill so many civilians that the distinction would be senseless.

3. This is especially true since talk of **damage limitation** leads to quixotic efforts that fuel the arms race and make nuclear war more likely. Why? Because a counterforce strategy that assumes damage limitation is possible requires (1) highly accurate weapons (a missile silo is much smaller than a city), (2) good intelligence (to locate mobile targets), and (3) elaborate C3 (C3 = command, control, and communication) facilities. An assured destruction strategy, on the other hand, requires retaining only enough weapons to threaten population centers, and so is less expensive than a counterforce strategy. Assured destruction theorists argue

that elaborate forces encourage people to believe weapons could be used to limit damage to their own country, but for the reasons stated above, this is a delusion.

The provisions of the SALT I treaty were based on the assumptions and beliefs underlying assured destruction theory.

SALT I

banned major ABM systems (in keeping with the belief that there is no defense against nuclear weapons, and thus their only utility is in deterrence)

limited ICBM forces, which need only be able to inflict "unacceptable damage"[13] on a potential enemy contemplating nuclear aggression (in keeping with the belief that only enough weapons for countervalue targeting are necessary; counterforce is unnecessary)

and made no attempt to provide for damage limitation; that is, such defensive precautions as civil defense, an ABM system, limitations on the number of warheads, and so forth.

In summary, the negotiation of SALT I was based on three policy prescriptions implicit in assured destruction doctrine:

1. The mutual vulnerability of civilian populations to nuclear weapons.
2. The mutual invulnerability of nuclear weapons employed against populations.
3. The willingness to destroy an enemy society after the enemy destroys yours. His knowing this, or even just fearing this, deters him from attacking in the first place.

Since the signing of SALT I assured destruction theorists have continued to resist all attempts to obscure or qualify these three policy prescriptions because they believe doing so undermines stable mutual deterrence. For example:

1. If precautions were taken to defend a population against nuclear attack, it might encourage the erroneous belief that a nuclear attack (retaliatory or first strike) could be endured and therefore that a crippling nuclear exchange could be won by the state that hit the "fastest and hardest."

2. If weapons were developed and deployed that could defend against nuclear attack (destroying or disarming enemy missiles) the same danger would arise. That is, a nation might conclude it could cripple or destroy an enemy while protecting itself from retaliation.

3. If a nation, for whatever reason, made it seem as though it could not or would not retaliate after the enemy had launched a nuclear strike, then the enemy might be tempted to strike first, believing the chances for doing so with impunity were good.

In summary, two premises and three policy principles constitute the essential elements of the assured destruction point of view on mutual deterrence. The premises are:

1. Escalation could not be controlled in a nuclear exchange.
2. Significant damage limitation could not be achieved in a general nuclear exchange.

The policy principles were:

1. Retain the mutual vulnerability of civilian populations by not providing for their defense.
2. Retain the mutual invulnerability of strategic offensive forces through negotiations or *some* defensive measures.
3. Retain the capability and will to respond to an enemy nuclear strike by inflicting unacceptable damage on the enemy's society.

The logic of assured destruction is relatively simple, and it is dictated by the awesome power of nuclear weapons. While not denying the power of nuclear arms, opponents of assured destruction nonetheless criticize the strategy for an insufficiently sophisticated understanding of nuclear weapons and their operational characteristics.

FLEXIBLE RESPONSE

Nobody is driven into war by ignorance, and no one who thinks that he will gain anything from it is deterred by fear.

—Hermocrates of Syracuse,
quoted by Thucydides

The flexible response theorist rejects the premises, and thus the policy prescriptions, of the assured destruction theorists. Flexible response advocates argue that the premises underlying assured destruction strategy are based on a historical myth, and that even considered in the abstract, assured destruction is not a credible strategy of deterrence. The first point, that the precepts of assured destruction strategy are a historical myth, is important because interpretations of historical precedents are used to justify or attack various policy prescriptions in the perennial debates over deterrence strategy. Assured destruction advocates have their interpretation of the historical significance of nuclear weapons, which has been reviewed. Flexible response advocates believe assured destruction theorists misrepresent the historical record on nuclear deterrence. They frequently try to set the historical record straight before arguing their case for a different nuclear deterrence strategy in the abstract.

The Historical Evolution of Nuclear Defense and Flexible Targeting

Most flexible response theorists concede that the assured destruction advocates won the war of words in the 1960s. In fact, assured destruction became so widely accepted that most people today are unaware that there ever was an intense debate between the two schools of thought. However, flexible response theorists assert there has been a major difference between official explanations of policy, which on balance were more supportive of the assured destruction viewpoint, and the implementation of policy, which actually has increasingly reflected the concerns of the flexible response theorists.[14]

Flexible response theorists acknowledge that the obliteration of Hiroshima and Nagasaki in 1945 made a powerful impact on the subsequent discussion of atomic war and deterrence strategy. Those awesome examples of the destructive power of atomic weapons immediately shifted the attention of decision makers and strategists from the vulnerability of military forces to the vulnerability of urban populations. Although the destruction of Dresden and Tokyo with thousands of conventional bombs resulted in greater numbers of civilian fatalities than the atomic attacks on Hiroshima and Nagasaki, the impact of just *one* atomic bomb was astonishing to the world. It seemed to many as if the ultimate weapon, so long feared and predicted, had finally been created and used.

However, even then, there were those who questioned whether such damage could be limited by various methods of defense or by preventive attacks on those enemy military installations that controlled or delivered nuclear weapons. As a matter of fact, the list of potential targets for U.S. nuclear forces in event of war has always included military installations as well as economic and urban centers. Over the years, both Republican and Democratic administrations have steadily developed ever more sophisticated means of controlling, directing, and targeting nuclear weapons. Although different administrations have explained and defended these adjustments under different policy labels—for example, escalation dominance, counterforce, and countervailing strategy—all have had essentially the same goal in mind: broadening the theoretical range of policy options for the use of nuclear weapons and ensuring their command and control in a hostile environment. In addition, the rationale for these objectives has always been the same: to enhance the credibility of the deterrent value of U.S. nuclear forces.

One recent and controversial manifestation of this trend was President Carter's Presidential Directive 59 (PD-59), which gave priority to (1) developing missiles accurate enough to destroy Soviet missiles still on the ground and (2) to take additional steps to ensure a C3 capability that would theoretically allow the United States to maintain control over its nuclear forces in the event of a nuclear attack on the United States. Some assured destruction advocates saw PD-59 as the official displacement of mutual assured destruction strategy.

However, the Carter administration argued it was not deviating from past policy at all. Harold Brown, then Secretary of Defense, argued:

> This doctrine, as I emphasized earlier, is *not* a new departure. The United States has never had a doctrine based simply and solely on reflexive, massive attacks on Soviet cities. Instead, we have always planned both more selectively (options limiting urban-industrial damage) and more comprehensively (a range of military targets). Previous administrations, going back well into the 1960s, recognized the inadequacy of a strategic doctrine that would give us too narrow a range of options. . . . This evolution in our doctrine enhances our deterrence, and reduces the likelihood of nuclear war.[15]

By citing the policy of previous administrations, Harold Brown was trying to deflect criticism which characterized PD-59 as somehow radical and thus destabilizing.

In summary, the flexible response theorist argues that assured destruction strategy has been promulgated by official US government sources, but that in force doctrine, posture and deployment it is a historical myth. The United States has always been prepared for discriminate use of nuclear weapons rather than a reflexive mutual and complete destruction of the United States' and an adversary's society.

How Flexible Response Differs from Assured Destruction

Flexible response requires nuclear forces with four characteristics:

1. Maximum survivability
2. Precise accuracy
3. Quick retargeting capability
4. Assured command, control, and communications

These capabilities are needed in order to facilitate (1) escalation control and (2) damage limitation, the two goals that assured destruction theorists deny are possible. It is precisely this belief in damage limitation and escalation control that the assured destruction theorist believes makes nuclear war *more* likely. The flexible response theorist argues exactly the opposite: that the capability to control escalation and limit damage will enhance the deterrent value of U.S. forces and thus make war *less* likely. How did these two schools of deterrence doctrine come to such contrary conclusions?

The flexible response theorist believes in a flexible targeting policy, and argues, as did Harold Brown, that the United States has always had one. The rationale for flexible targeting is twofold:

1. It allows the United States to reply to a limited (even very limited) nuclear attack on its allies or itself with something less than the destruction of whole cities. Since the enemy might not believe the United States would be willing to take such a drastic step as attacking cities in response to a "relatively" minor provocation, flexible targeting provides for more credible retaliatory threats.
2. If nuclear war should begin and move beyond its lowest levels, the ability to destroy enemy military forces could limit the damage to U.S. territory and populace, either by convincing the enemy to stop attacking or by destroying weapons that otherwise would be used to attack the United States.

This second point is particularly controversial. It was explained above that assured destruction theorists believe nuclear weapons have no defense value, that they can only destroy and not protect, and thus have only a preattack deterrent value. But the flexible response theorist argues there have always been both offensive and defensive elements in nuclear strategy. To date, the defensive components of nuclear forces have been (1) those means used to defend atomic weapons themselves and (2) the use of atomic weapons to defend a country by limiting the enemy's ability to destroy it. The defensive element of nuclear strategy is critical because it highlights the essential difference between assured destruction and flexible response theorists.

To elaborate, the flexible response theorist argues the following two points concerning nuclear weapons and defense:

1. To defend nuclear weapons, their delivery systems must be protected. Bombers are rotated and some kept constantly aloft to make them less vulnerable, missile silos are "hardened" to make them less vulnerable to attack, and missiles are placed on submarines that use mobility and concealment for defense.

As will be explained in more detail below, some assured destruction theorists do accept the need for limited defense of nuclear weapons to protect their deterrent value. However, *all* assured destruction theorists reject the notion that nuclear weapons have a role in defending a country. Flexible response theorists argue to the contrary:

2. To limit the ability of the enemy to destroy the United States with nuclear weapons, the enemy's strategic nuclear forces have been targeted, steps have been taken to increase the accuracy of ICBMs so that they can destroy enemy missiles before they are launched, or so that the launching pad cannot be used a second time.

Since, according to flexible response theorists, there has *always* been a *mixture* of offense and defense in nuclear deterrence strategy, the SALT I protocol that limited ABM deployment did not expunge defense from the deterrence equation as is popularly supposed. At most SALT I was an acknowledgment of the transitory offensive superiority of ICBMs. It was to be expected that this offensive superiority might pass away, which many flexible response theorists think has come to pass with the development of SDI.

Even more to the point concerning deterrence strategy, it follows that flexible response advocates also disagree with the assured destruction position that there is no meaningful distinction between counterforce and countervalue targeting. They agree that a nuclear strike on military installations would certainly entail much **"collateral"** damage to urban populations, but it would certainly be far less than a direct strike on a city, and thus they believe that the difference between counterforce and countervalue targeting is worth preserving. Notice that in making this argument the flexible response theorist is assuming escalation can be controlled (which is denied by assured destruction theorists) and that the environmental side effects (the nuclear winter thesis, for example) of a limited nuclear exchange would not be catastrophic (again denied by the assured destruction theorist).

Flexible response theorists argue that if the distinction between **counterforce** and **countervalue** attacks was not really meaningful, or if assured destruction advocates really wanted to ensure that there could be no distinction between counterforce and countervalue targeting, the logical (if not politically feasible) policy would be to place nuclear missiles in the middle of large urban concentrations. If U.S. nuclear forces were all located in or near major urban concentrations, an attack on U.S. missiles would necessarily be an attack on the U.S. population as a whole, and the United States would have no choice but to respond accordingly—the preferred deterrence posture of the assured destruction theorists. As it is, however, the vast majority of U.S. missile fields are not located near the largest population centers and could be attacked without maximum damage to major U.S. cities.

The Credibility of Defense

As discussed above, flexible response theorists see a twofold role for defense in nuclear deterrence strategy. However, they do not insist on an offensive-defensive dichotomy. Instead, they assert:

1. There are *no perfect* offensive or defensive forces. Thus a nation's deterrence policy invariably includes a combination of offensive and defensive measures.[16]
2. If there ever was a perfect offensive or defensive weapon it would be highly destabilizing. A perfect offensive weapon would encourage a nation to launch a surprise strike against its enemy, destroying the enemy's means of retaliation. A perfect defensive weapon would allow a nation to attack an enemy without fear of damage from a retaliatory strike.
3. So the question is, what *combination* of offensive and defensive measures contributes most effectively to stable mutual deterrence?

With this reasoning, flexible response theorists justify the need to defend atomic weapons themselves. To go further and justify defending the state and its population with atomic weapons requires a more complex and controversial argument.

It will be remembered that the fundamental premise of assured destruction theorists is that "nuclear weapons have separated the function of preattack deterrence and postattack defense." Flexible response theorists deny this premise. They argue that the need for "credibility" links preattack deterrence and postattack defense conceptually,[17] and dictates a defensive role for nuclear weapons in nuclear deterrence strategy.

Flexible response theorists start with the proposition that the deterrence value of any weapon is dependent on its credibility. In other words, *a potential aggressor must be convinced the weapon can and will be used if necessary,* and if the enemy does not believe this capability would be used in the manner threatened, then it does not constitute a credible deterrent threat. This is as true for nuclear weapons as for conventional forces. An incredible deterrent posture will incite probing by the enemy, probing that will go unanswered because the country making the incredible threats will not want to reveal its unwillingness to make good its threats. Henry Kissinger expressed this concern about the credibility of assured destruction doctrine before the Senate Foreign Relations Committee:

> The side that can defend its interests only by threatening to initiate the mutual mass extermination of civilians will gradually slide towards strategic, and therefore essentially geopolitical paralysis.[18]

In short, the only way to make an enemy believe nuclear weapons can and will be used is to give them a realistic strategic objective. For flexible response theorists, mutual national suicide is not a credible rationale for the use of nuclear weapons, but the defense of a society (that is, damage limitation) is a credible rationale for using nuclear forces. Thus, to deter war, the threatened use of nuclear weapons must be credible, and this means a state must articulate their intended use for the *defense* of the state. On the basis of this reasoning, the flexible response theorist denies nuclear weapons have separated deterrence from defense. On the contrary, they maintain deterrence is not credible without a plan for defense.

The flexible response point of view on the inseparable link between defense and offense may be condensed and added to the conclusions enumerated above:

1. There are no perfect offensive or defensive weapons. Thus a *combination* of offensive and defensive means are required for stable mutual deterrence.
2. Credible nuclear deterrence strategy requires a plan for defending the state, and a state's nuclear force posture must allow weapons and plans for such a defense (including a plan of attack designed to eliminate enemy military forces). Therefore, nuclear weapons have not negated the linkage between pre-attack deterrence and postattack defense.
3. In practice, then, a credible, stable mutual deterrence requires a configuration of offensive and defensive capabilities that can absorb an enemy first strike and still retaliate in kind *without fear of emerging in a highly disadvantaged position.*[19]

COMPARING THE PREMISES AND POLICY PRESCRIPTIONS OF ASSURED DESTRUCTION AND FLEXIBLE RESPONSE

The following chart summarizes all the significant differences between the flexible response and assured destruction points of view. It explains how they reach contradictory conclusions on one of the most strenuously debated questions in current arms control and deterrence literature: Do more discriminating nuclear forces increase or decrease the likelihood of war? In essence, the assured destruction advocate answers yes, because more usable weapons tend to get used, and the flexible response advocate answers no, because more usable weapons are credible and thus deter more effectively.

ASSURED DESTRUCTION (AD)

1. The advent of nuclear weapons separated the function of postattack defense from preattack deterrence. They are so destructive they cannot defend, only destroy, and hence are suitable only to deter the enemy.

2. This is true because any nuclear exchange would automatically escalate into a general nuclear conflagration with catastrophic consequences, making damage limitation impossible.

3. It follows that no meaningful distinction can be made between counterforce and countervalue targeting. Nuclear weapons and their consequences are so destructive that one can never consider their use "discriminate."

4. Since escalation is likely and damage limitation not at all likely, pretending the contrary is a delusion that might encourage the use of nuclear weapons in the erroneous belief that their use could be controlled.

5. Moreover, a policy that anticipates the controlled use of nuclear weapons and damage limitation fuels the arms race. Damage limitation efforts such as civil defense force the enemy to build greater destructive capabilities in order to preserve its

FLEXIBLE RESPONSE (FR)

1. The United States has always had a number of offensive and defensive measures in its nuclear strategy precisely because—even with nuclear weapons—preattack deterrence and postattack defense are always linked by the need for credibility.

2. Preparation for postattack defense not only lends deterrence its credibility, it is the most prudent means of trying to control and stop an escalation of nuclear exchanges, thereby limiting damage.

3. While nuclear weapons are or can be used indiscriminately, they can also be used with more rather than less discrimination, and the difference in lives saved between an attack on military targets and an attack on civilian targets is significant.

4. Escalation is not automatic and the more sophisticated one's weapons and C3 capabilities, the greater the chances a nuclear exchange could be contained and damage limited. Failure to prepare for such a contingency increases the likelihood of escalation and catastrophic damage.

5. It is not a question of whether there will be military competition, for that is a given. The issue

ASSURED DESTRUCTION (AD)

AD capability. Also, controlled use of nuclear weapons requires more sophisticated weapons and C3 facilities, which (1) encourage the enemy to reciprocate and (2) even worse, undermine stable mutual deterrence because such weapons have a first-strike capability and could lead an enemy to believe the United States was preparing to fight a nuclear war, and so should be attacked before it was fully prepared to do so.

FLEXIBLE RESPONSE (FR)

is whether it will be a competition that is stable and prevents war. A strategy that solely relies on a massive countercity retaliatory strike undermines deterrence because it is not credible. Indeed, it encourages an enemy first strike against U.S. military targets, after which the enemy could deter a U.S. response by threatening a second strike against U.S. population centers. Finally, there need not be a spiraling arms race because the United States opts for a credible deterrence posture. Both sides can agree to negotiate an arms control agreement that enhances stability by encouraging secure counterforce capabilities, that is, a FR deterrence posture.

From the foregoing premises, the assured destruction and flexible response theorists come to the following policy prescriptions for arms control and defense. Stable mutual deterrence requires states

1. To encourage measures to ensure the mutual vulnerability of civilian populations to nuclear weapons (like the ABM protocol)
2. Not to encourage measures that enhance our ability to destroy nuclear weapons (like highly accurate ICBMs with multiple warheads)
3. To insist on a readiness to retaliate against enemy population centers should the enemy launch a first strike against the United States

1. To encourage a mixture of offensive and defensive measures that could be used to limit damage in the event of an enemy attack, thus contributing to deterrence by convincing an enemy that there is no possible advantage to launching a first strike
2. Not to allow arms control agreements to foreclose options that would contribute to these measures unless, in the balance, they contribute to stability because of their restraining impact on enemy force development

In opening the chapter, the question was raised as to whether or not the state's nuclear axe ought to be sharpened. Comparing the policy prescriptions of assured destruction and flexible response theorists shows they answer the question differently. The assured destruction theorist says no, a blunt nuclear axe means more force and unacceptable damage, which means the nuclear axe will not be used. The flexible response theorist says yes, because a sharp nuclear axe is a credible weapon, and thus will deter attack.

It should be said again that the simplified points of view presented in this chapter are archetypes. Most informed opinion will tend toward one or the other, but numerous more complex variations of deterrence strategy exist. The next chapter explores some of the more subtle points of agreement and controversy on nuclear deterrence. It also applies what has been learned about strategic deterrence and arms control to the most controversial contemporary issue in arms control and strategic debate: plans for a strategic defense with space-based weapons.

DISCUSSION QUESTIONS

1. Is the threat of a massive nuclear retaliatory strike against civilian population centers a credible deterrent? If so, what range of threatening behavior is such a threat capable of deterring?

2. Once a nuclear exchange began, could its consequences be limited in any meaningful or significant way? If so, how?

3. If a partially effective defense against nuclear missiles was technologically feasible, would it be a good idea to build and deploy such a defense? Would it have any potential offensive value? How so?

4. In the previous chapter it was argued that both will and capabilities are critical components of deterrence. Do assured destruction and flexible response rely more on one or the other to deter an adversary?

5. Considering our current historical and technological circumstances, which nuclear deterrence strategy is most likely to deter a nuclear war?

SUGGESTED READINGS FOR CHAPTER FIVE: ARMS CONTROL AND NUCLEAR DETERRENCE STRATEGY

BRODIE, BERNARD. "On the Objectives of Nuclear Arms Control." *International Security* 1 (Summer 1976): 17–36.

——. *Strategy in the Missile Age.* Princeton: Princeton University Press, 1959.

——., ed. *The Absolute Weapon.* New York: Harcourt Brace, 1946.

DYSON, FREEMAN. *Weapons and Hope.* New York: Harper/Bessie, 1984.

FREEDMAN, LAWRENCE. *The Evolution of Nuclear Strategy.* New York: St. Martin's Press, 1981.

GREEN, PHILIP. *The Deadly Logic: The Theory of Nuclear Deterrence.* Columbus: Ohio State University Press, 1966.

HERKEN, GREG. *Counsels of War.* New York: Alfred A. Knopf, 1985.

IKLE, FRED C. "Can Nuclear Deterrence Last Out the Century?" *Foreign Affairs* 51 (1973): 267–285.

JERVIS, ROBERT. "Deterrence Theory Revisited." *World Politics* 31 (January 1979): 289–324.

KAHAN, JEROME H. *Security in the Nuclear Age: Developing U.S. Strategic Arms Policy.* Washington, DC: Brookings Institution, 1975.

KAPLAN, FRED. *The Wizards of Armageddon.* New York: Simon and Schuster, 1983.

KAHN, HERMAN. *On Thermonuclear War.* 2nd ed. New York: Macmillan, 1969.
KREPON, MICHAEL. *Strategic Stalemate: Nuclear Weapons and Arms Control in American Politics.* 1985.
LEVINE, HERBERT. *The Arms Debate.* Cambridge, MA: Harvard University Press, 1963.
MORGAN, PATRICK M. *Deterrence: A Conceptual Analysis.* 2nd ed. Beverly Hills, CA: Sage Publications, 1983.
NITZE, PAUL H. "Deterring Our Deterrent." *Foreign Policy* 25 (Winter 1976–77): 195–210.
PRANGER, ROBERT J., and ROBERT P. LABRIE, eds. *Nuclear Strategy and National Security: Points of View.* Washington, DC: American Enterprise Institute, 1977.
ROSENBERG, DAVID ALAN. "The Origins of Overkill: Nuclear Weapons and American Strategy, 1945–1960." *International Security* 7 (Spring 1983).
RUSSETT, BRUCE. *The Prisoners of Insecurity: Nuclear Deterrence, the Arms Race and Arms Control.* San Francisco: W. H. Freeman & Co., 1983.
SNYDER, GLENN. *Deterrence and Defense: Toward a Theory of National Security.* Princeton: Princeton University Press, 1961.

NOTES

1. *Polyaenus's Stratagems of War,* trans. R. Shepherd (Chicago: Ares Publishers, 1914; reprint of original 1793 London edition), p. 301.

2. Bernard Brodie, *The Absolute Weapon* quoted in John F. Reichart and Steven R. Sturm, *American Defense Policy,* 5th ed. (Baltimore: Johns Hopkins University Press, 1982), pp. 145, 172.

3. Bernard Brodie, (ed.) *The Absolute Weapon* (New York: Harcourt Brace, 1946), p. 76.

4. Glenn H. Snyder, *Deterrence and Defense: Toward a Theory of National Security.* Copyright © 1961 by Princeton University Press, p. 9.

5. Walter Millis, "Essential Conditions of Disarmament," *Social Sciences* (October 1958): 228. For a survey of efforts to distinguish between offensive and defensive weapons see Jack S. Levy, "The Offensive/Defensive Balance of Military Technology: A Theoretical and Historical Analysis," *International Studies Quarterly* 28 (June 1984).

6. See Frederick H. Hartman, *The Relations of Nations,* 6th ed. (New York: Macmillan Co., 1983), p. 276, and Hans Morgenthau, *Politics Among Nations,* 4th ed. (New York: Alfred A. Knopf, 1967), pp. 392–393.

7. Charles Fairbanks, Jr. "An Earlier Attempt to Limit Arms," *Wall Street Journal* 21 June 1979, p. 26, col. 5. Dr. Fairbanks is a Professor at Yale University and Research Director of Arms Races and Arms Control Project.

8. Quincy Wright, *A Study of War* (Chicago: University of Chicago Press, 1965), p. 809.

9. However, subsequent negotiations between the signatories failed to make any progress on a more detailed agreement and after two years they were abandoned. See Andrew Pierre, *The Global Politics of Arms Sales* (New Jersey: Princeton University Press, 1982), pp. 283–84.

10. Some notable efforts are still directed toward refining the theoretical distinction between offensive and defensive weapons. Dietrich Fischer, for example, began with the following:

    I propose the following definition of defensive and offensive arms: purely defensive arms increase the security of the country acquiring them but do not reduce the security of any other country. Purely offensive arms threaten the security of potential opponents, but do not strengthen the security of the country acquiring them.

    The rest of his book then elaborated on this distinction in terms of contemporary defense policy. See Dietrich Fischer, *Preventing War in the Nuclear Age* (Totowa, NJ: Rowman and Allanheld, 1984), p. 48. For a shorter version of the same thesis, see Dietrich Fischer, "Invulnerability without Threat: The Swiss Concept of General Defense," in Burns H. Weston, *Toward Nuclear Disarmament and Global Security: A Search for Alternatives* (Boulder, CO: Westview Press, 1984), pp. 504–531.

11. Fairbanks, "An Earlier Attempt to Limit Arms," p. 26.

12. Freedman, *The Evolution of Nuclear Strategy,* p. 246.

13. What constitutes unacceptable damage may lie in the eye of the destroyer (or deterrer), but while serving as Secretary of Defense, Robert McNamara offered the admittedly arbitrary definition of unacceptable damage as one fifth to one quarter of the population and one half of the industrial capacity. See Robert S. McNamara, Statement before the Senate Armed Services Committee on the FY 1969–73 Defense Program and 1969 Defense Budget (Washington, DC: Department of Defense, 1968), p. 50.

14. The apparent contradiction can be explained in part by the fact that while the United States adopted an assured destruction posture it also tried to extend its strategic nuclear deterrent to Western Europe (hence the term *extended deterrence*), where it was easier to contemplate the use of tactical nuclear weapons to stop a Soviet conventional attack. To make extended deterrence credible it seemed necessary to have more limited nuclear options than attacking cities. Further, it must be noted that there has been considerable ambiguity in the policy statements of American secretaries of defense, some asserting a flexible response point of view and others an assured destruction point of view. What is unambiguous is the steady growth of a flexible response *capability* in U.S. strategic nuclear forces.

15. Harold Brown, "Remarks for Convocation Ceremonies for the 97th Naval War College Class," August 20, 1980. See also, Desmond Ball, "Counterforce Targeting: How New? How Viable?" in Reichart and Sturm, *American Defense Policy,* pp. 227–233 and Aaron Friedberg in Samuel Huntington, *The Strategic Imperative* (Cambridge, MA: Ballinger Pub. Co., 1982).

    Brown was quite clear about the aims of the policy:

    At the President's direction, the Department of Defense has, since 1977, been working to increase the flexibility of our plans to make use of the inherent capabilities of our forces. We are also acting to improve our ability to maintain effective communications, command and control of our forces, even in the highly uncertain and chaotic conditions that would prevail in a nuclear war. These actions greatly strengthen our deterrent.

    While citing Harold Brown as a spokesman for flexible response, it is only fair to point out that he has, like other secretaries of Defense, also articulated the assured destruction point of view:

    The Soviets might—and should—fear that, in response (to a Soviet first strike) we would retaliate with a massive attack on Soviet cities and industry. [And] the Soviets would face great uncertainties in [planning a first strike and] they must recognize the formidable task of executing a highly complex massive attack in a cosmic throw of the dice.

    That the Secretary of Defense should articulate both the assured destruction and flexible response points of view is an indication of how complex, or less charitably, confused, the politics of arms control strategy can be. For the quote, see Wolfram F. Hanrieder, ed., *Arms Control and Security: Current Issues* (Boulder, CO.: Westview Press, 1979), p. 234.

16. On this point see Colin Gray, *Strategic Studies and Public Policy: The American Experience* (Lexington, KY: University of Kentucky Press, 1982), page 18. Gray observed that "Every area of military activity reveals a dialectic between the offense and the defense. . . . " And again, in Reichart and Sturm, *American Defense Policy,* Gray complains that:

    Unlike the Soviet Union, the United States has declined to recognize (courtesy of its still-authoritative stability theory) that an adequate strategic posture requires the striking of a balance between offensive and defensive elements.

    Gray goes on to offer several reasons for why the United States should integrate defensive forces into its strategic posture, pp. 181–182.

17. Again, Colin Gray provides an apt example of the flexible response point of view:

    In principle, as any Soviet defense analyst would maintain, no inherent tension should exist between the requirements of (pre-and early intra-war) deterrence, and the requirements of *operational* strategy.

    Colin Gray, *Strategy and the MX* (Washington, DC: Heritage Foundation), p. 4.

18. Gray, *Strategy and the MX,* p. 5.

19. In the words of Harold Brown, "We must ensure that no adversary could see himself better off after a limited [nuclear] exchange than before it. We cannot permit an enemy to believe that he could create any kind of military or psychological asymmetry that he could then exploit to his advantage." Assured destruction and flexible response theorists sharply disagree on the precise capabilities required for this critical condition, as will be explained below. The quotation is from Robert Jervis, "What Deters", in Reichart and Sturm, *American Defense Policy,* p. 166.

Chapter Six

The Current Debate on Arms Control, Nuclear Deterrence, and Strategic Defense

Some prominent decision makers subscribe exclusively to either the assured destruction or flexible response point of view, positions which may be referred to as *minimum assured destruction* and *maximum flexible response.* Between these two groups are the moderates who occupy the middle ground on the deterrence strategy spectrum and accept some blend of the assured destruction and flexible response rationales.

BETWEEN MINIMUM ASSURED DESTRUCTION
AND MAXIMUM FLEXIBLE RESPONSE

[Alternative Deterrence Strategies]

DISARMAMENT ONLY	MINIMUM MUTUAL AD	MODERATE AD & FR	MAXIMUM FR	DEFENSE ONLY

AD = Assured Destruction
FR = Flexible Response

On the left end of the above chart are the nuclear disarmament and minimum assured destruction theorists. Some disarmers accept no role for nuclear deterrence and others accept a minimum assured destruction strategy as necessary during the transition to a nuclear disarmed world. Lawrence Freedman provides a succinct description of their point of view on deterrence:

> Despite finding deterrence obnoxious, these groups [disarmament enthusiasts], to the extent that they have a strategic framework, promote mutual assured destruction. They object to anything—civil defense, counterforce weapons, and counterforce doctrines—that suggests nuclear war is in any way less than terrible, let alone winnable. They fear that a genuine strategy—i.e., one based on a plausible war plan—might prompt nuclear use whereas threats of unrestrained terror are so suicidal that they will be kept for the very last resort.[1]

Moderate assured destruction advocates generally agree with these sentiments, but they also accept a modicum of flexible response thinking. In the previous chapter Bernard Brodie was quoted on a fundamental assured destruction premise: that nuclear weapons revolutionized strategy and broke the linkage between defense and deterrence. However, Brodie refined this assured destruction position with a bit of flexible response thinking. He noted the revolutionary deterrence value of nuclear weapons held true *only* so long as the nuclear weapons themselves were invulnerable to a first strike:

> Even the frequently-encountered supposition that total war is now impossible, because its mutually annihilistic or "suicidal" consequences must henceforth be obvious to all, is based on the implicit assumption that at least the retaliatory forces of each side are automatically defended, or anyway easily defended.[2]

Brodie argued that as the accuracy of ICBMs improved to the point where they could destroy other ICBMs, provisions would have to be made for defending ICBMs in order to preserve the balance of terror that made mutual deterrence possible:

> [A] balance of terror exists between two nuclear powers when neither can strike first at the other without receiving a completely intolerable retaliatory blow in return. A balance does not exist when one power, in striking first, can eliminate all but a tolerable portion of the opponent's capacity to strike back.[3]

In other words, by defending ICBMs a state could preserve its retaliatory second-strike capability and thus deter a surprise first strike. At the time (1959) Brodie thought building shelters for ICBMs or making them mobile would be the most likely way to preserve their invulnerability.[4] Brodie was prescient, for this is exactly what transpired during the next decade.

Over the course of the 1960s, the United States developed what has come to be known as "**the triad**," which included airborne, land-based, and sea-based nuclear weapons (respectively, bombers with nuclear bombs and later cruise missiles; submarines with ICBMs, called **SLBMs**; and land-based ICBMs). The vulnerability of each of these three "legs" of the triad depended on its natural defense capabilities and the offensive capabilities of an adversary. Airborne nuclear forces are protected by their mobility, which is relative to the amount of warning time prior to an attack. SLBMs are protected by their mobility and concealment, which is relative to enemy antisubmarine warfare capabilities. Land-based ICBMs are protected by "hardening" their launching silos to a point where they can withstand close nuclear detonations, a defense that is relative to the accuracy of enemy warheads.

Brodie and others[5] did not argue that the defense of nuclear weapons had to provide perfect invulnerability, but that it was necessary to ensure that enough weapons would survive a first strike to permit an unacceptably devastating retaliatory blow. Deterring a first strike also required that the adversary not be allowed to believe it was possible to strike first so successfully that no counterstrike would be launched:

> the various factors which will bear on a "go" or "no-go" decision may very well be dominated by a developing conviction that it is possible to paralyze our response. It is necessary to do all we can to prevent such a conviction from taking hold in the enemy camp.[6]

In other words, the enemy must not be left with the belief that a surprise nuclear attack could so cripple U.S. forces that the United States would, upon reflection, consider total surrender preferable to retaliation and additional nuclear exchanges.

Some nuclear deterrence strategists are worried that a significant first strike capability might actually be used, but most consider it more likely that a first strike capability would be used for intimidation. If upon calculation it is apparent to both sides that the balance of forces is skewed enough to allow one side first-strike superiority, then the superior side will use this knowledge in a crisis to extract concessions from its inferior opponent—a sort of nuclear blackmail.

To offer a specific example, during the early 1980s the concern of some U.S. strategists was that the USSR might launch a sizable portion of its nuclear forces in an effort to destroy the most accurate and reliable elements of the United States's nuclear forces (generally considered to be land-based ICBMs). Having done so, only less reliable and less accurate U.S. forces would be left (that is, bombers, which might not be able to penetrate Soviet air defenses, and submarines, which had relatively inaccurate SLBMs and which might be impossible to communicate with in a nuclear environment). As Bruce Russett has hypothesized, the USSR might then deliver the following ultimatum to decision makers in Washington:

> Quit while you're only somewhat behind. Whatever you do, don't fire at our cities because we have enough missiles in reserve to wipe out your cities in response.[7]

After a Soviet strike which destroyed the U.S. ICBMs accurate enough to destroy Soviet ICBMs, the only available U.S. option would be to retaliate with its less accurate sea and air nuclear forces against Soviet *cities*. However, the United States would be deterred from attacking Soviet cities by the remaining Soviet nuclear weapons which could destroy U.S. cities in counterretaliation. According to this reasoning, the United States would simply have to accept the destruction of most of its nuclear forces and whatever civilian casualties this entailed in order to prevent the total destruction of U.S. population centers. Moreover, as noted above, simply knowing the potential for this train of events existed might give the Soviet Union an edge in a crisis, and allow it to coerce concessions from the United States.

The scenario could be turned around and viewed from the Soviet perspective of concern about a U.S. first-strike capability. Whether the U.S. or the USSR or both acquired a first-strike capability, moderate assured destruction and flexible response theorists propose defense and arms limitation strategies designed to prevent either side from acquiring such a destabilizing capability.

In contrast, minimum assured destruction theorists dismiss the entire first-strike scenario as unrealistic. They argue that (1) the enemy could never be sure that if it launched a surprise attack, it would succeed in destroying *all* the necessary land-based ICBMs. The timing, coordination and implementation of such an extensive first strike would present numerous technical difficulties and uncertainties. For example, the USSR would have to consider the United States' alert level at the time of attack. The U.S. alert level would determine how many U.S. bombers would still be on the ground, how many U.S. submarines in port, and how many U.S. ICBMs would still be in their silos. If the attack achieved complete surprise, many U.S. forces might be caught unprepared and easily destroyed; they could then be subtracted from those forces capable of retaliating. However, the USSR could not be sure it would accomplish complete surprise. In addition, the USSR would have to consider technical uncertainties. Would the Soviet missiles fire as planned? Would they be as accurate as supposed? Would the detonations of those missiles arriving first destroy or reduce the accuracy of warheads arriving at their targets several seconds later? Secretary of State Henry Kissinger emphasized these uncertainties in a 1976 speech:

> No nuclear weapon has ever been used in modern wartime conditions or against an opponent possessing means of retaliation. Indeed neither side has ever tested the launching of more than a few missiles at a time; neither side has ever fired them in a North-South direction as would be required in wartime.[8]

(2) Even if the USSR mistakenly assumed it had the technical capability to launch a successful first strike, it still could not be sure the United States would not respond in a spasmatic retaliatory strike against Soviet cities with

its remaining SLBMs and bombers. Furthermore, (3) the USSR could not be sure the United States would wait and absorb the first strike. The United States could retaliate while Soviet missiles were still in flight, thereby avoiding the loss of U.S. ICBMs and instead using them to launch a counterblow.

Moderate assured destruction theorists agree that the USSR *may* be deterred by these considerations, but they believe it is safer not to count on Soviet doubts. They believe a **"launch on warning"** policy (that is, the launching of U.S. missiles while enemy missiles are still on the way to targets in the United States) is unwise since the detection of incoming enemy missiles is subject to technical error. It would be a fatal error to launch a retaliatory strike when an incoming strike had been incorrectly identified. It is true that the United States would not actually have to adopt a launch on warning policy. The United States could promulgate the policy without putting it into effect and then the USSR could not be *sure* the United States would wait and absorb a Soviet first strike. However, the Soviet Union might be willing to gamble that the United States *probably* would not launch on warning. Thus moderate assured destruction theorists believe it is safer for the United States to develop an invulnerable retaliatory capability that would remove all doubt about the United States's ability to retaliate.

Bernard Brodie, a moderate assured destruction theorist, argued that it is better not to rely on an adversary's willingness to gamble on escaping a retaliatory blow. He cited the historical example of Pearl Harbor. The Japanese launched their surprise attack in 1941 against U.S. Pacific naval forces in the hopes of crippling U.S. capabilities so that the United States would have to accept Japanese imperial expansion in the Far East and sue for peace.[9] The fact that the Japanese miscalculated does not negate the fact that they *thought* a strategic first strike would be a good gamble and acted on this assumption. Minimum assured destruction theorists respond that the stakes in a nuclear first strike would be too high to take such a gamble.

Since moderate assured destruction theorists disagree with minimum assured destruction theorists and assert it is necessary to have an invulnerable and sufficient second-strike capability, how, then, do they differ from moderate flexible response theorists who make the same assertion? The answer is that the two groups of moderates disagree over precisely what kind of second-strike capability is necessary. The moderate assured destruction theorist believes it would suffice if the United States had enough accurate warheads surviving a Soviet first strike to retaliate against Soviet cities. The moderate flexible response theorist wants more: whatever is required to match the first Soviet counterforce strike with enough left over to threaten the nuclear forces and cities of the Soviet Union.

The points of agreement and disagreement just reviewed are summarized below and in the following chart. Moderate assured destruction and flexible response theorists agree on the need for a secure retaliatory capability, but they disagree on the precise measures required for such a capability: for example, whether or not it is necessary to have the MX missile, or the **B-1 bomber,** or **cruise missiles,** and so forth. Minimum assured destruction theorists believe none of these systems are necessary since more than enough nuclear weapons for assured destruction are already in existence. Maximum flexible response theorists believe that if the USSR has a capability, the United States needs an offsetting capability. The moderates on both sides look at each weapon system and try to decide if it is necessary for ensuring an invulnerable second-strike capability. The difference between the moderates is that those in the assured destruction camp only want a second-strike *countervalue* capability, while the moderate flexible response advocates argue that a second-strike *counterforce* capability is necessary.

A Tripartite Division of the Orthodox AD-FR Deterrence Spectrum

MINIMUM AD	MODERATE AD & FR		MAXIMUM FR
A retaliatory capability the USSR could not be sure it could destroy, and one that could deliver unacceptable damage to the USSR	An invulnerable retaliatory capability that ensures the U.S. would have a credible response after a Soviet first strike		An invulnerable retaliatory capability that can perfectly match the capabilities of the USSR and would convince the USSR it could never profit from a first strike
	AD: The second-strike capability need only be counter value	FR: The second-strike capability needs to be counterforce	

AD = Assured Destruction
FR = Flexible Response

Moderate assured destruction and flexible response theorists, occupying the middle of the deterrence spectrum, have areas of agreement and disagreement. The same is true of the minimum assured destruction and maximum flexible response positions on the end of the spectrum. The last chapter showed all the points about which the minimum assured destruction and maximum flexible response theorists disagree. The one point about which they are likely to agree is the current futility of superpower nuclear arms control. Unlike moderates, they do not think it is necessary to regulate specific weapons to stabilize deterrence.

Minimum assured destruction theorists (and disarmers) believe there is already so much "overkill" capability in the superpower nuclear arsenals that efforts to fine-tune the balance with arms control agreements are irrelevant. To really reduce the threat posed by nuclear weapons, massive disarmament is necessary. Maximum flexible response theorists (and defense-only advocates) also believe current superpower nuclear arms control efforts are not able to improve the stability of deterrence. They believe that maintaining deterrence requires constant updating of nuclear forces, including nuclear defenses, and arms control often inhibits this process.

Until recently, minimum assured destruction and maximum flexible response critics of superpower nuclear arms control were very much on the periphery of U.S. policy-making circles. U.S. policy making was dominated by moderate assured destruction and flexible response theorists who were content to work on stable deterrence through a combination of selective force modernization programs and modest arms limitation agreements. President Reagan's insistence on negotiations for major cuts in nuclear weapons and his decision to pursue a space-based strategic defense against nuclear weapons moved plans for radical disarmament and strategic defense to center stage, thereby drawing support from elements within two previously antagonistic policy groups: advocates of both minimum assured destruction and maximum flexible response strategy. The following section discusses how President Reagan's strategic defense initiative (SDI) completely changed the terms of debate on arms control and deterrence in the United States.

STRATEGIC DEFENSE FROM OUTER SPACE

I have approved a research program to find, if we can, a security shield that will destroy nuclear missiles before they reach their target. It wouldn't kill people, it would destroy weapons; it wouldn't militarize space, it would help demilitarize the arsenals of Earth. It would render nuclear weapons obsolete.

—Reagan Inaugural Address,
January 21, 1985

Background

On March 23, 1983, President Reagan announced his intention to have the United States pursue research on new defensive systems "to give us the means of rendering . . . nuclear weapons impotent and obsolete." Reagan had long been dissatisfied with the only options available to him in the event of a Soviet nuclear strike: surrender or retaliation in kind. It was not until 1983, though, when several close advisers suggested the technology necessary for **ballistic missile defense (BMD)** was sufficiently advanced, that he publicly threw his support behind strategic defense.

Reagan's 1983 speech and continuing ongoing support have focused attention on an old topic. In the 1960s there was a heated debate in the United States over BMD,[10] but it was finally rejected as too costly, technically deficient, and destabilizing. In the 1970s old ABM advocates and a new generation of BMD proponents emerged, arguing that the failure of the SALT process and advancing technology made BMD an attractive option. They, too, failed to gain majority support for their point of view. While strategic defense against **ballistic missiles** is not a new idea, it was only with Reagan's 1983 initiative, subsequent budgetary support, and refusal to negotiate restraints on SDI research that strategic defense became the most important strategic force and arms control issue.

Defense Against ICBMs

The merits and drawbacks to SDI, from both the U.S. and Soviet point of view, can better be discussed after a brief review of how ICBMs work and how future BMD systems might operate. From launch point to target, an ICBM passes through four stages.

First, the ICBM's silo door is opened and the ICBM is ejected from the silo with pressurized gases. The first-stage rockets ignite, and for the next five minutes or so the ICBM is in its *boost phase,* being propelled toward outer space until it has used all of its fuel and the body of the rocket falls away, leaving nothing but the "bus." The bus is a device which carries the ICBM's warheads. Each warhead is enclosed by a **reentry vehicle (RV)** that protects the warhead during its descent back through the atmosphere.

During the second stage, the *postboost phase,* the bus with its RVs travels silently through space on its preprogrammed trajectory, which takes about twenty or thirty minutes. During this time the bus computers control the trajectory of the bus by firing small rockets.

As the bus turns first this way and then that, the RVs are released one by one, each taking a different trajectory toward its target. Once the RVs are released and speeding toward their targets, they are said to be in their third, or *midcourse phase.* The reentry of the RVs through the earth's atmosphere and the final plunge to their targets is called the *terminal phase.*

Each of these four stages presents special opportunities and drawbacks for attack by BMD systems. Taking account of the advantages and disadvantages of attacking during any given phase, most SDI advocates envision a multilayed BMD using different weapons to attack the ICBMs at each stage of their flight. Those ICBMs that escaped destruction in the boost phase would be picked off in the postboost phase, and those survivors would then be attacked in midcourse, and then finally, the remaining RVs would have to be destroyed by "point" defenses as they entered the terminal phase.

Kinetic energy weapons and directed energy weapons are the two principal means of destroying ICBMs now under study. Kinetic energy is the energy inherent in motion, and weapons of this type destroy their targets by the impact of their collision. These self-guided projectiles are often referred to as "smart rocks," since no matter how sophisticated their propulsion and control systems, they destroy objects the same way a rock does when it is hurled at a target. Directed energy weapons use powerful beams of energy to melt and disrupt the electronics of an ICBM, or throw it off course. Particle beam weapons and lasers[11] are the two types of directed energy weapons considered most feasible for BMD.

Lasers may be fueled by chemical, gas, or nuclear power sources. Laser beams travel at the velocity of light and they damage a target by thermal weakening, shock-wave propagation, radiation, or a combination of the three. When a laser strikes its target, radiation and energy transfer sharply raise the temperature of the target surface, causing it to vaporize and explode, sending a shock wave through the rest of the target. The destructive value of particle beams comes from firing a stream of subatomic particles (protons or electrons) at a target so that on impact each particle transfers some of its kinetic energy to the target. As with lasers, particle beams travel near the speed of light. Unlike lasers, which must remain on the target long enough to cause thermal stress, particle beams provide almost instantaneous destruction through ionized radiation or deep particle penetration of the target.

ICBMs are most vulnerable in their boost phase. At this point the missile is moving relatively slowly and its large exhaust flames make it an easy target to locate with infrared sensors. Destroying an ICBM at this stage eliminates up to ten warheads, which is far more efficient than trying to track and destroy the warheads individually after they have left the ICBM's bus. Any ballistic missile defense that did not eliminate a large number of ICBMs in the boost

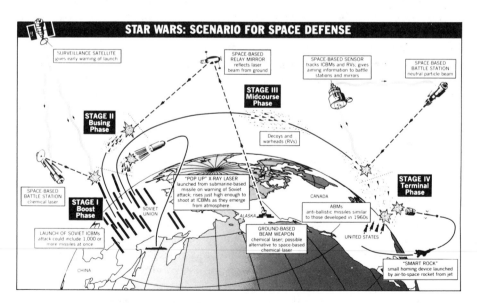

Fig. 6.1 (Source: Illustration by Larry Fogel, "Star Wars: Scenario for Space-Defense," (c) *The Washington Post* March 3, 1985, p. A 18. Reprinted with the permission of *The Washington Post.)*

phase would be in danger of being overwhelmed in later stages of the ICBM attack.

Once an ICBM reaches the bus stage and starts releasing its warheads, it could also release hundreds of decoys—flat-packed, aluminum-coated balloons that would inflate into the shape of real warheads. The missile buses could also release clouds of metallic chaff to further complicate the detection and tracking of the real warheads. When the warheads begin to reach the terminal phase and reenter the earth's atmosphere the decoys will burn up, but by then only earth-based systems remain to try to destroy the warheads before they reach their target. Warheads destroyed in the terminal stage of flight would still be a danger to human life since their destruction might cause nuclear detonations within the earth's atmosphere where radioactive fallout would present a potent hazard. As a strategic deterrent, however, the principal virtue of destroying warheads in the terminal phase would be the protection of hardened ICBM silos to ensure a retaliatory capability.

Kinetic energy weapons and directed energy weapons are potentially effective options at any of the four stages just described, but every weapon system has its own special advantages and disadvantages. For example, the great advantage of kinetic energy weapons is that they are well advanced in development. Kinetic energy weapons for terminal defense have already been produced and tested successfully, and more advanced forms for placement in outer space are feasible. The biggest drawback to kinetic energy weapons is that they are slow compared to beam weapons,[12] and thus an effective kinetic energy weapon defense would have to be deployed in much greater numbers to equal the potential effectiveness of beam weapons.

There are several different options for directed energy weapons. One possibility would be to deploy them in space. The principal problem with this scheme is figuring out how to get the bulky apparatus and huge fuel supplies into space on a cost-effective basis. Another possibility would be land-based directed energy weapons that shot their beams into outer space where they would be reflected off giant mirrors and directed onto their targets. This option would require overcoming interference from the earth's atmosphere and developing perfect mirrors for aiming the beams. Finally, some believe it would be possible to "pop up" a nuclear-powered X-ray laser weapon. The idea would be to launch a weapon system at the first sign of an ICBM attack, possibly from submarines off the coast of the USSR. Once the weapon is in space, a controlled atomic explosion would be used to generate X-ray laser beams that could be directed against enemy missiles. These weapons platforms might be difficult to communicate with and very vulnerable to attacks from enemy territory.

The effectiveness of any of the BMD systems just described is debatable. Even if the design of such systems proves feasible, many believe their value would be easily negated by countermeasures. Indeed, countermeasures are widely considered to be the critical drawback to SDI. Many observers think that after spending billions or even trillions of dollars in a Herculean effort to build a sophisticated missile defense it would be circumvented by relatively simple and inexpensive countermeasures. Thus the technical feasibility of SDI is debated on two levels: the prospects for a layered BMD in principle, and the prospects for a BMD taking into account enemy countermeasures.

Technical Feasibility

> What is centrally and fundamentally wrong with the President's objective is that it cannot be achieved.[13]

Without question the building of a space-based ballistic missile defense would be the largest and most sophisticated technological feat ever accomplished. Naturally there is a great deal of debate over whether such a project is feasible or not. Much of the debate over SDI's feasibility has been misdirected by ambiguity over the success requirements for any future BMD.[14] Limited terminal-phase ballistic missile defense, which could provide some defense for ICBM sites, was proven technically feasible twenty years ago. On the other hand, no one claims that anything close to a perfect nation-wide impenetrable shield against ICBMs will be possible during the next two decades, if ever.

When President Reagan announced his plans for SDI, he spoke of making nuclear weapons "impotent and obsolete." Many opponents of SDI have ridiculed the notion that there will ever be an "Astrodome" shield against nuclear missiles that could protect the entire U.S. population. Like the Great Wall of the ancient Chinese designed to keep out Mongel hordes, or the **Maginot Line** built by the French to defend against the Germans, SDI would be a magnificent engineering feat, but ineffectual at providing absolute security.

After demonstrating that a perfect shield is not possible in the foreseeable future, SDI critics emphasize the horrendous consequences of such a "leaky nuclear umbrella." As is often pointed out, even if the BMD were 92 percent to 97 percent effective, this would still mean that 3 to 8 percent of the ten thousand incoming Soviet warheads would hit U.S. urban targets, thereby destroying three hundred to eight hundred cities and killing the overwhelming majority of the U.S. population.[15]

Proponents of SDI, however, are not dissuaded by the short-term impossibility of a perfect population defense. Without abandoning the long-term hope for a perfect defense against nuclear weapons, they claim their current research objective is much more limited. They want a system that would provide protection against small nuclear powers and accidental launches, and some damage limitation in the event of limited nuclear war. Most importantly, they want a BMD that will ensure the survival of a U.S. retaliatory capability after a Soviet first strike.

In other words, SDI supporters admit that a defense of the civilian population would have to be nearly 100 percent effective; but they point out that a defense that protected even 50 percent of U.S. ICBMs would eliminate the incentive for a first strike since an aggressor would know that half of his opponent's ICBMs would remain to retaliate in kind. Thus the long-term objective of transcending deterrence (mutual assured survival through perfect defenses) remains, but the short-term goal is reinforcing current nuclear deterrence policy.

While the feasibility of even this more limited objective is seriously questioned by opponents of SDI, its supporters like to point out that BMD research already has produced positive results that even a decade ago were ridiculed as impossible. Lasers have destroyed small antitank and anti-aircraft missiles, and more recently, one was beamed a half mile across the New Mexico desert floor and glanced off a mirror and onto a section of a Titan missile, which it destroyed. Even more impressive was the test of a U.S. rocket interceptor against an incoming ballistic missile warhead. The warhead was caught at 100 miles above the western Pacific Ocean and destroyed in a grand collision. Tests like these are an outgrowth of the technological revolutions in precision guidance and computer science[16] that have followed the development of nuclear energy. According to SDI supporters, these new technologies make some sort of BMD technologically feasible.

Nevertheless, SDI supporters readily agree that mighty technological problems remain to be solved. Foremost among these are the following: a computer software system powerful enough to control and command a vast BMD system; smooth and efficient communication between the components of the BMD system; sensors for quickly identifying and tracking ICBMs and later their warheads; efficient power sources able to meet the enormous energy demands of a directed energy BMD; and finally, cost-effective transportation for placing the millions of pounds of SDI equipment in orbit.

It is interesting to note that critics and supporters alike agree that the toughest technological problems for SDI will not be the weapons themselves but rather the computer software programs necessary for coordinating and controlling their operation. These programs will be fantastically complex. As an example, the space shuttle's software, which was not "bug-free" even when finally used, required fifty thousand lines of information code, whereas it is estimated that a space-based BMD would require at least fifty million lines of code.[17]

Another problem separate from producing the weapons themselves would be getting all the hardware into space on a cost-effective basis. The space shuttle can carry about sixty-five thousand pounds of payload, but it is generally assumed a BMD with a space-based component would require placing many millions of pounds of weapons and sensors into orbit. Currently the cost of satellite transport is about $1,400 per pound, but SDI officials estimate this figure would have to be reduced by a factor of ten, to about $140 a pound, before space transport of a space-based BMD system would be financially feasible.[18]

In addition to the above systemic, operational, and logistical problems, the weapons systems themselves face major engineering difficulties, ranging from enormous energy requirements to problems with penetrating the earth's atmosphere. Debate among scientists over the seriousness of these technological hurdles has been quite heated.[19] Nevertheless, there is a consensus of sorts that it would be possible to deploy a layered kinetic energy defense in the next fifteen years, and that a beam weapon defense would probably not be possible until after the year 2000. The real controversy is over the issue of whether or not such systems would prove effective when measured against potential enemy countermeasures.

For example, some scientists believe that the boost phase, which is the most attractive time to attack an ICBM, can be reduced from five minutes to less than a minute. ICBMs could also be made to spin so that beam weapons could not focus on one spot, or coated to make the skin of the missile less vulnerable to beam weapons. Also, many believe that the satellites necessary for detecting ICBMs and directing a BMD would be far easier to destroy than the ICBMs themselves. Antisatellite weapons could be used to attack space-based sensors and battle stations, and nuclear detonations in space prior to the ICBM attack could be used to confuse and disrupt sensors. Perhaps the most widely expected Soviet countermeasure would be a vast expansion of the Soviet offensive nuclear arsenal: more ICBMs to overwhelm the ballistic missile defenses; new low-trajectory, submarine-launched nuclear missiles; and thousands of low-flying nuclear cruise missiles to sneak in under U.S. coastal defenses.

In response, SDI supporters argue that there are countermeasures to countermeasures. Decoys that have little mass could be distinguished from warheads by neutral particle beam weapons. Particle beams cause gamma rays to be emitted when they hit a massive object like a warhead, but produce almost no emissions when they hit an object with little mass, like a decoy. Also, sensors might be able to detect decoys by the way they are released, expecting the lightweight decoys to move faster than the heavier warheads.

In addition, SDI supporters believe that some countermeasures are self-defeating. For example, a faster boost phase, which would require a lighter missile or more fuel, would require reducing the number of warheads the missile could carry. Similarly, coating the missile to make it less vulnerable would also add to its weight and reduce the payload it could carry. Finally, attempting to outrun a defense by increasing offensive arms production might be prohibitively costly.

The importance of the relative cost of offensive and defensive systems is a point on which most critics and supporters of SDI agree. In order for a BMD to be cost effective, it must be cheaper to intercept an added warhead than it would be to add the warhead to the offensive arsenal. If it cost $100 million to add a new space station that could destroy approximately ten missiles in their boost stage, but only $5 million to build another ten missiles, the builder of the missiles could bankrupt the builder of the defensive system in an arms race.

Another viewpoint holds that the above definition of cost effectiveness is too narrow. These observers claim the impact of defensive weapons on security and stable deterrence cannot be measured by a strict numerical trade-off. The mere existence of a defense, even if it cost more than its offensive counterpart, might be worthwhile if it added enough uncertainty about the possibility of a successful first strike to deter an adversary from taking such a gamble. In other words, a defensive system that could not destroy all incoming missiles on a cost-effective basis might still be profitable if it destroyed an aggressor nation's confidence that it could strike first with overwhelming success.

Strategic Implications

Debate over the strategic implications of ballistic missile defense can be divided into two separate issue areas: the long-term implications of a BMD system for defending the U.S. population, and the shorter-term contribution of a BMD system for the stability of nuclear deterrence. Despite the fact that it is not a short-term possibility, much of the early debate on SDI has focused on population defense. Population defense was the original justification for SDI research, and it will always be the most popular public justification for the huge sums being spent on strategic defense research.[20]

Population defense is popular among maximum flexible response theorists who believe damage limitation and war fighting capability are essential to a credible deterrence posture. It is also popular among many minimum assured destruction theorists and radical disarmers who have always argued for a transition away from aggressive offensive capabilities toward "defensive" military deployment postures. These groups often make their support for SDI contingent upon concomitant reductions in offensive weapons, though, since they fear an offensive-defensive weapons race.

There are those who question the value of a population defense against ICBMs. Some believe that if fear of nuclear war subsided, conventional war would become more likely.[21] Even some who previously argued that mankind's sole imperative in the nuclear age was to reduce the risk of nuclear war are against SDI research because they believe it is a technical impossibility. They fear that pursuing research on a BMD system will precipitate a dangerous arms race that will make nuclear war more likely.

There are other general arguments for and against a BMD system. Opponents argue that any BMD system could also be used against satellites, which the United States relies on more than the USSR. It would be better, they say, to leave outer space demilitarized altogether. Supporters of SDI respond that outer space is already militarized, and even if BMD systems were outlawed by treaty, antisatellite capabilities would remain.[22] Further, supporters argue that even a partially effective BMD system would be insurance against nuclear war starting from an accidental launch or smaller nuclear attacks from some lesser power controlled by a madman who obtained nuclear missiles.[23]

While much attention is given to the question of population defense, the more immediate issue is how a BMD system would affect mutual deterrence of nuclear war. Readers will recognize this part of the SDI debate as a direct continuation of the flexible response and assured destruction argument, with assured destruction theorists against and flexible response supporters for SDI research.

Flexible response advocates argue that a perfect population defense is not necessary. They are not concerned with a Soviet first strike against U.S. cities. Such a first strike is deterred by the threat of a similar attack in return by the United States. Instead, as mentioned in the first part of the chapter, flexible response theorists are concerned that the USSR might believe it could attack and destroy the vast majority of accurate U.S. ICBMs, leaving the U.S. without the means to respond in kind.

If the United States had a strategic defense against ICBMs, the USSR could not disarm the United States with a crippling first blow that could destroy U.S. ICBMs while leaving the vast majority of the U.S. population alive. As former Secretary of State Henry Kissinger argued in defense of SDI:

> If only an all-out attack can penetrate defenses and if a strategic defense makes it uncertain what weapons will get through, rational incentives for nuclear war will diminish.[24]

In other words, the defensive forces would make it impossible to determine if it was possible to destroy the overwhelming majority of U.S. ICBMs. Those not destroyed could be used in retaliation. After such an exchange and all the devastation it produced, neither side would be in a superior position from which it could dictate demands. Thus there would be no rationale for a surprise first strike in the first place.

The assured destruction theorists see the impact of strategic defense differently. It may be remembered that assured destruction theorists consider secure second-strike *counterforce* capabilities destabilizing because they also could be used for a first strike. Similarly, they believe a BMD system would be destabilizing because it would complement a first-strike capability. A state could launch a first strike that destroyed most of the enemy's ICBMs, and then defend itself against the enemy's surviving missiles with its ballistic missile defenses. Assured destruction theorists worry that during periods of high tension each side would be tempted to strike first and rely on its BMD forces to prevent retaliatory damage from whatever enemy missiles remained. The state that waited and absorbed a first strike would be at a disadvantage.

The fact that a defense against ICBMs would be very effective in defending against an enemy's weakened retaliatory capability following a first strike was pointed out in 1960, again by former Secretary of State Henry Kissinger:

> The problem of a technological breakthrough will always remain with us. Stability in numbers of offensive weapons . . . could be made irrelevant by a major advance in defensive weapons and systems. If one side developed a defense against ballistic missiles which it considered very highly effective, it could use even its controlled retaliatory force for blackmail since it might feel safe from a counterblow.[25]

All the assured destruction and flexible response arguments enumerated above apply to the debate over SDI.[26] Flexible response theorists, who have never recognized the separation of defense and deterrence, or the sharp delineation of the offensive and the defensive, see strategic defense as a way to make deterrence more credible and a first strike less likely. The assured destruction theorists continue to argue that nuclear weapons have forever separated defense and deterrence. That is, they do not believe defense is really possible, and attempts to defend against nuclear weapons are dangerous because they complement first-strike capabilities, and thus are destabilizing.

It was mentioned in the previous chapter that strategic defenses in the past, such as the Siegfried Line, were used to complement strategic offensives. This is the problem raised by a BMD system: it can both protect against an enemy first strike, and protect an attacking state after it launches a first strike. Thus if a transition from mutual assured destruction to mutual assured survival is desired, it would seem best if both the USSR and the United States had a ballistic missile defense good enough to prevent a first strike, but not good enough to completely negate an enemy's retaliatory strike.[27] Many believe that this kind of precise recipe for strategic stability would require negotiations.

Future Alternatives: Arms Limitation Negotiations and Strategic Defense

SDI supporters who claim that ballistic missile defenses eliminate any rational calculation that a counterforce first strike could be successful say that this fact would reduce the value of first-strike weapons. Thus it should be easier to negotiate their reduction. Negotiations would also be easier because a BMD system would provide a safety margin against cheating, thereby reducing the need for exceedingly stringent verification measures, a major stumbling block in past negotiations.

Some go further and argue that SDI makes offensive arms reduction agreements not just possible, but absolutely necessary in order to keep the number of offensive weapons from expanding to the point where they could overwhelm the BMD defense. Also, agreements might be necessary to prevent the testing of decoys and other BMD countermeasures. In summary, this is the vision of the SDI supporters: a BMD system accompanied by arms control agreements restricting offensive weapons, and thus a transition from a world of mutual assured destruction to a world of mutual assured survival.

Critics of SDI see a different future. They say a BMD would be destabilizing because it would be vulnerable to attack, vulnerable to countermeasures, and easily overwhelmed by thousands of new offensive missiles. They believe the USSR would feel compelled to counter a U.S. BMD system by proliferating Soviet offensive systems. Otherwise the USSR would be vulnerable to a U.S. first strike. Thus the net effect of a BMD would be a furious offensive-defensive arms race and a less secure world. For this reason critics argue the United States ought to take advantage of the negotiating leverage provided by SDI and try to get the USSR to agree to limits on its offensive nuclear arsenal in exchange for restrictions on SDI research and development.

Conclusions

The different perspectives of assured destruction and flexible response theorists on SDI were perfectly consistent and predictable from their past positions on nuclear deterrence strategy. This consistency has been obscured somewhat by the uproar over population defense, which is not a near-term possibility. Otherwise it is evident that for all its revolutionary technical goals, the controversy over the short-term merits and drawbacks to a BMD system is a continuation of the old and familiar assured destruction-flexible response debate.

As for current strategic arms policy, it remains to be seen whether or not the United States and the USSR can work out a cooperative path to mutual security through negotiations. It is clear, however, that the chances for success are greater when states are able to overcome their internal divisions and establish a unified negotiating position. A state with a unified and well-defined national security policy will enter negotiations with answers thought out in advance and its compromise positions carefully considered. Since obtaining goals in one area often means accepting concessions in other areas, it is important to have clear preferences as to the most acceptable combination of security objectives in addition to a list of absolute priorities. The next part of the book reviews nine of the most salient security questions that must be addressed when deciding on a negotiating strategy.

DISCUSSION QUESTIONS

1. What role, if any, should defense play in nuclear deterrence and arms limitation strategy?
2. Does credible nuclear deterrence require a secure second strike capability, and if so, should it be a secure counterforce or countervalue capability?
3. Nuclear weapons are often considered a radical innovation in weapon's technology which has transformed all previous calculations of deterrence. Is this true, and if so, would a successful BMD have an equally significant impact on deterrence doctrine?

4. Would an assessment of Soviet BMD research and development affect your position on SDI research in the United States, and if so, how?
5. Is population defense irrelevant, a long-range subsidiary benefit, or the only legitimate goal for the SDI program?

SUGGESTED READINGS FOR CHAPTER SIX:
THE CURRENT DEBATE ON ARMS CONTROL, NUCLEAR DETERRENCE, AND STRATEGIC DEFENSE

A. Nuclear Deterrence and Arms Control

GRAY, COLIN S. "Nuclear Strategy: The Case for a Theory of Victory." *International Security* 4 (Summer 1979): 54–87.
GRAY, COLIN S., and KEITH PAYNE. "Victory Is Possible." *Foreign Policy* 39 (Summer 1980): 14–27.
JERVIS, ROBERT L. *The Illogic of American Nuclear Strategy.* Ithaca: Cornell University Press, 1984.
KISTIAKOWSKY, GEORGE B. "Can a Limited Nuclear War Be Won?" *Defense Monitor* 10 (1981): 1–4.
KULL, STEVEN. "Nuclear Nonsense." *Foreign Policy* (1985): 28–52.
PAYNE, KEITH B. *Nuclear Deterrence in US-Soviet Relations.* Boulder, CO: Westview Press, 1982.

B. Strategic Defense and Arms Control

ARMSTRONG, SCOTT, and PETER GRIER. *Strategic Defense Initiative: Splendid Defense or Pipe Dream?* Headline Series, Foreign Policy Association, #275. September–October 1985. Reprinted from the series "Star Wars: Will it Work?" *Christian Science Monitor* 4–12 November 1985.
BETHE, HANS A., RICHARD L. GARWIN, KURT GOTTFREID, and HENRY W. KENDALL. "Space-Based Ballistic Missile Defense." *Scientific American* 251 (October 1984): 39–49.
BRZEZINSKI, ZBIGNIEW. "A Star Wars Solution: How to Break the Arms Control Impasse." *New Republic,* July 8, 1985, pp. 16–18.
CARTER, ASHTON, and DAVID SCHWARTZ. *Ballistic Missile Defense.* Washington, DC: Brookings, 1984.
CHALFONT, ALUN. *Star Wars: Suicide or Survival?* Boston: Little, Brown, 1986.
DRELL, SIDNEY, PHILIP J. FARLEY, and DAVID HOLLOWAY. *The Reagan Strategic Defense Initiative: A Technical, Political, and Arms Control Assessment.* Cambridge, MA: Ballinger Pub. Co., 1985.
FLETCHER, JAMES D. *Strategic Defense Initiative: Defensive Technology Study.* Washington, DC: U.S. Department of Defense, March 1984.
GLASER, CHARLES. "Why Even Good Defenses May Be Bad." *International Security* 9 (Fall 1984): 92–123.
JASTROW, ROBERT. *How to Make Nuclear Weapons Obsolete.* Boston: Little, Brown, 1985.
———. "Reagan Versus the Scientists: Why the President is Right About Missile Defense." *Commentary* January 1984, pp. 23–32.
———. "The War Against Star Wars." *Commentary,* December 1984.
MCNAMARA, ROBERT, GEORGE KENNAN, MCGEORGE BUNDY, and GERARD SMITH. "The President's Choice: Star Wars or Arms Control." *Foreign Affairs* (Winter 1984–85).
OFFICE OF TECHNOLOGY ASSESSMENT. *Ballistic Missile Defense Technologies.* Washington, DC: Government Printing Office, 1985.
PAYNE, KEITH. *Strategic Defense: "Star Wars" in Perspective.* Lanham, MD: Hamilton Press, 1986.

PAYNE, KEITH, and COLIN S. GRAY. "Nuclear Policy and the Defensive Transition." *Foreign Affairs* (Spring 1984).
RA'ANAN, URI, and ROBERT L. PFALTZGRAFF, eds. *International Security Dimensions of Space.* Hamden, CT: Archon Books, 1984.
SCHLESINGER, JAMES R. "Rhetoric and Realities in the Star Wars Debate." *International Security* (Summer 1985).
TSIPIS, KOSTA. "Laser Weapons." *Scientific American,* December 1981, pp. 51–57.
UNITED STATES CONGRESS. House. Committee on Foreign Affairs, Subcommittee on Arms Control, International Security, and Science. "Implications of the President's Strategic Defense Initiative and Anti-satellite Weapons Policy." Hearings before the Subcommittee on Arms Control, International Security, and Science. 99th Congress, 1st Session, April 24 and May 1, 1985. Washington, DC: Government Printing Office, 1985.
UNION OF CONCERNED SCIENTISTS. *The Fallacy of Star Wars: Why Space Weapons Can't Protect Us.* New York: Random House, 1984.
"Weapons in Space, Volume I: Concepts and Technologies." *Daedalus* (Spring 1985) and "Weapons in Space, Volume II: Implications for Security." *Daedalus* (Summer 1985).

NOTES

1. Lawrence Freedman, "NATO Myths," *Foreign Policy* (Winter 1981–1982): 59. Copyright 1981 by the Carnegie Endowment for International Peace.

2. Bernard Brodie, *Strategy in the Missile Age.* Copyright © 1959 by the Rand Corporation. Published by Princeton University Press, 1959, p. 173. Brodie also noted in 1946 that "the first and most vital step in any American security program for the age of atomic bombs is to take measures to guarantee to ourselves in case of attack the possibility of retaliation in kind." Bernard Brodie, ed., *The Absolute Weapon* (New York: Harcourt Brace, 1946), p. 76.

3. Glenn Snyder quoted in Harry Almond, "Deterrence Processes and Minimum Order," *New York Law School Journal of International and Comparative Law* 4, No. 2 (1983): 333, n. 156.

4. Brodie, *Strategy in the Missile Age,* pp. 173, 219–220.

5. Ibid., pp. 282, 394. Also, especially see Albert Wohlstetter, "The Delicate Balance of Terror," *Foreign Affairs* (January 1959): 211–234.

6. Ibid., p. 222.

7. Bruce Russett, *Prisoners of Insecurity* (San Francisco: W. H. Freeman & Co., 1983), p. 31.

8. Donald M. Snow, *Nuclear Strategy in a Dynamic World* (Alabama University: University of Alabama Press, 1981), p. 41.

9. As briefly mentioned in the previous chapter, the Japanese also launched a naval surprise first strike against Russia's Port Arthur to begin the Russo-Japanese War of 1904. As in 1941, they did so while Japanese diplomats were in the target country's capital, ostensibly negotiating a peace agreement. The 1904 surprise attack was much less successful than the 1941 strike, but ironically Japan won the 1904 war and lost World War II.

10. SDI, ABM, and BMD are nearly synonymous acronyms, but there are some nuances of difference. ABM usually refers specifically to the antiballistic missile systems developed in the 1960s that were missiles themselves and attacked nuclear warheads in their terminal phase (to be discussed below). BMD is the generic term for all kinds of ballistic missile defense, nuclear space mines, ABMs, lasers, and so forth. SDI is President Reagan's BMD program, which is understood to include a multilayered defense that would attack ICBMs at each of the various stages of their flight, and thus necessarily includes space-based components.

11. Laser is an acronym for Light Amplification by the Stimulated Emission of Radiation.

12. Whereas beam weapons travel at or near the speed of light, the fastest kinetic energy weapon envisioned by SDI officials would travel at twelve miles per second. In comparison, a bullet from an M-16 rifle travels at 3,000 feet per second. These figures, along with many of the

points expressed in this section, are taken from Scott Armstrong and Peter Grier, "Strategic Defense Initiative: Splendid Defense or Pipe Dream," (Headline Series #275, Foreign Policy Association, 1985). This handy pamphlet is a reprint of the series published by the authors in the *Christian Science Monitor* as "Star Wars: Will it Work?" The series of six articles ran in the *Monitor* from November 4–12, 1985. The entire series makes an excellent and very readable primer on SDI.

13. Robert McNamara, George Kennan, McGeorge Bundy, and Gerard Smith, "The President's Choice: Star Wars or Arms Control," *Foreign Affairs* (Winter 1984/85).

14. As late as June 1986 the President was still referring to SDI as "a shield that could protect us from nuclear missiles just as a roof protects a family from rain." "Overtures in Glassboro," *Time,* June 30, 1986, p. 38. Even his supporters seldom make this claim, and instead argue the merits of SDI on the grounds of improved deterrence and stability:

> Reagan, as is his wont, has oversold strategic defense, suggesting that it can provide an impermeable "shield" that could in no place be overwhelmed by the multiplication of Soviet offensive systems. A sufficient argument for strategic defense is that it would provide some real defense . . . to some of the U.S. retaliatory capability. Thus it would enhance deterrence by radically complicating the calculations and multiplying the uncertainties of any Soviet leader contemplating a first strike.

George Will, "The Barrenness of Arms Control," (c) *The Washington Post,* January 13, 1985, p. B7.

15. This criticism assumes an unlikely premise: that the first strike would be against cities rather than U.S. ICBMs. Most first-strike scenarios assume the opposite, that the purpose would be to eliminate the most potent part of an opponent's nuclear forces. First-strike scenarios do not generally assume attacks on population centers because such an all-out attack could only prompt a similar retaliatory response.

    The fact that the USSR might not use all of its warheads in a first strike, and that the targets might not be cities but ICBM silos, does not reassure critics of SDI. They believe any "leakage" in a defensive shield that allowed nuclear warheads to hit U.S. territory would be a disaster of the first magnitude.

16. Albert Wohlstetter notes that the advent of precision guided munitions is "in some ways more revolutionary than the transition from conventional to fission explosives or even fusion weapons." He points out that an improvement in accuracy by a factor of one hundred "improves blast effectiveness against a small, hard military target about as much as multiplying the energy released a million times." Wohlstetter goes on to argue that this kind of accuracy makes it quite feasible to limit collateral damage. See Albert Wohlstetter, "Bishops, Statesmen and Other Strategists on the Bombing of Innocents," *Commentary,* June 1983.

    It has also been estimated that advances in electronic technology could make nuclear ICBM attack impossible by the end of the century. See *Janes Military Communications, 1983* (London: James Publishing Co., 1982).

17. Armstrong and Grier, "Strategic Defense Initiative: Splendid Defense or Pipe Dream."

18. Ibid.

19. See, for example, the negative criticism of SDI by Hans A. Bethe, Richard L. Garwin, Kurt Gottfried and Henry W. Kendall, "Space-Based Ballistic Missile Defenses," *Scientific American,* October 1984, and the response to this article by SDI supporter Robert Jastrow, "The War Against Star Wars," *Commentary,* December 1984. Jastrow criticizes the authors of the *Scientific American* article, members of the Union of Concerned Scientists, for faulty analysis of scientific data.

20. The rhetorical turbulence surrounding SDI has revealed some glaring inconsistencies. For example, many flexible response advocates who support SDI have forgotten the flexible response tenet that clear delineations between offensive and defensive weapons are difficult and now defend SDI research because it is purely defensive.

    Similarly, assured destruction theorists who once argued that Soviet first-strike capability was not a destabilizing concern since some U.S. nuclear retaliatory capability would always remain, now argue against SDI research because a BMD system would give the United States a first-strike capability which would be destabilizing.

21. This argument can be developed more specifically. The United States depends on nuclear weapons to defend Europe, where the Soviet Union has an advantage in conventional forces. Some believe that a move by the United States and the USSR to strategic defense, which would remove the threat of nuclear holocaust, would also leave Western Europe vulnerable to conventional attack.

22. For further discussion, see *Arms Control in Space: Workshop Proceedings* (Washington, DC: U.S. Congress, Office of Technology Assessment, OTA-BP-ISC-28, May 1984).
    Satellites are important components of modern military capabilities. They are used for reconnaissance, guidance, weather monitoring, communications, and early warning. For this reason they are likely to become targets in a general war. In this connection SDI supporters note that a BMD could protect as well as destroy satellites.

23. Critics of SDI believe there are cheaper alternative safety features available, such as building detonation devices into ICBMs that could be used to destroy them if they were accidentally launched. They also argue that terrorists are more likely to deliver a bomb in a suitcase or a truck than on the end of an enormously expensive and sophisticated missile.

24. Henry Kissinger, "We Need Star Wars," (c) *The Washington Post,* September 8, 1985, p. C8.

25. Henry Kissinger, "Arms Control, Inspection and Surprise Attack," *Foreign Affairs* (July 1960): 571.

26. Review the chart in the last section of the previous chapter in light of the foregoing discussion on SDI.

27. In this respect the fact that the effectiveness of a BMD can never be known because it could never be tested in actual war conditions might be advantageous. An intending attacker would have to assume the defender's BMD system would be effective to some degree, but he could not count on his own BMD system to completely prevent nuclear warheads from getting through to destroy his cities.

Chapter Seven

Setting an Agenda for Negotiating Mutual Security with Other Nations

> It appears to your Majesty's slave that we are very deficient in means, and have
> not the shells and rockets used by the barbarians. We must, therefore, adopt
> other methods to stop them, which will be easy, as they have opened negotia-
> tions.
>
> —Kee-Shen: Ministerial Report to
> the Emperor of China during the
> Opium War with Great Britain;
> March, 1841[1]

There are two popular but conflicting views on the significance of all
international security negotiations, including arms limitation talks. One view,
reflected in the optimism of Kee-Shen quoted above, is that the outcome and
even the process of negotiations can substantially improve (or damage) state
security. The great French statesman, **Cardinal Richelieu,** was even more optimistic than Kee-Shen about the possibilities for negotiations. He considered
them "innocuous remedies which never do harm," and frequently bear fruit:

> States receive so much benefit from uninterrupted foreign negotiations, if they
> are conducted with prudence, that . . . it is absolutely critical to the well-being
> of the state to negotiate ceaselessly, either openly or secretly, and in all places,

even in those from which no present fruits are reaped and still more in those for which no future prospects as yet seem likely.

Richelieu reasoned that

> He who negotiates continuously will finally find the right instant to attain his ends, and even if this does not come about, at least it can be said he has lost nothing while keeping abreast of events in the world, which is not of little consequence in the lives of states.[2]

Richelieu qualified his assertion that negotiations never do harm with the assumption that they were "conducted with prudence," and not prematurely brought to an unfavorable conclusion. Yet not all leaders are endowed with Richelieu's renown patience and prudence, as an example from ancient history illustrates.

Before the art of siegecraft was well developed, city walls were virtually impregnable, and thus their condition was a critical security concern. The Samnites of ancient Italy once entered into a peace treaty "sanctioned by mutual oaths" that allowed their adversary to remove one row of stones from the wall of their capital city. The terms of the agreement did not seem unreasonable to the Samnite negotiators. They had to conclude otherwise, though, when their enemy, keeping to the terms of the agreement, collapsed the entire wall by removing its bottom row of stones.[3] The Samnite experience is not unique. On numerous occasions states have been dismayed by the discrepancy between the intended and actual results of negotiations. Napoleon even held it as a general axiom that "one can never foresee the consequences of political negotiations undertaken under the influence of military eventualities."

The Samnite example illustrates one viewpoint on negotiations: the belief that they can powerfully affect state security, either for better or worse. In contrast, some students of international relations believe that diplomacy in general and negotiations in particular predictably reflect existing power configurations. According to this point of view, negotiations offer no greater opportunities or dangers than already exist in the balance of power between negotiating parties. Proponents of this second viewpoint would dismiss the story of the Samnite wall as fictional. The only realistic option for the Samnites, once they saw how their adversaries were going to apply the terms of the treaty, would have been to abrogate the treaty, even at the risk of war. It would have been far better to contest the issue with arms than to meekly agree to the destruction of their principal source of security.

In short, regardless of what is written down on paper, national security is a function of a nation's ability to defend itself and project its power. Or, as U.S. General Walter Bedell Smith observed on his return from the Geneva Conference on Indochina in 1954, "Diplomacy has rarely been able to gain at the conference table what cannot be gained or held on the battlefield."[4]

Leaders can choose either of these two opposing views of negotiations, and the choice often reflects existing geopolitical realities. The rulers of the Byzantine Empire, besieged for centuries by numerically superior enemies, were renown for their masterful use of negotiations as a security supplement for military capabilities. Alternatively, some statesmen have considered security negotiations solely as a means of confirming power relationships. This attitude was well represented by this categorical statement from the U.S. delegation to the 1925 League of Nations Preparatory Commission for the World Disarmament Conference:

> The United States will not be a party to any sanctions of any kind for the enforcement of a treaty for the limitation of armament nor will it agree that such treaties to which it may be a party shall come under the supervision of any international body.

Observed some recent commentators: "This attitude was not entirely, or even largely, a product of willful isolationism, as is sometimes charged; rather, it was founded upon a confident sense of economic, moral, and military security, which this nation enjoyed during that decade."[5]

While some observers adhere exclusively to either of the foregoing points of view on the utility of diplomacy, it is possible to appreciate the element of truth in both. Some negotiations are merely symbolic exercises in public posturing or attempts at improving the atmosphere for future cooperative security efforts. Other negotiations are quite substantive, clarifying disputed power relationships and committing nations to procedures and obligations that involve security opportunities and liabilities. A treaty may increase the security of all the signatories beyond what it is possible to accomplish by means of sheer military power, or a treaty may harm a state's security. In principle a treaty can always be abrogated, but it is often not politically possible to do so; and if it is done, it may entail political and security costs. Thus in some circumstances negotiated agreements may involve opportunities and risks that exceed those already present in the balance of relative military capabilities.

SHOULD NONMILITARY FACTORS BE CONSIDERED IN NEGOTIATIONS?

> Exasperated that the mice had moved out of the stable to invade his kitchen, Farmer Brown announced his intention of acquiring a cat. Whereupon, the mice raised an uproar in the barnyard about the "militarization of the pantry," and proposed negotiations. At the first meeting, the mice offered Farmer Brown an "equitable, fair, and balanced arms control agreement."
> "If you don't get a cat, we won't get a cat."[6]

The specific provisions of any arms control or disarmament agreement must be considered in their larger strategic context. The demilitarization of the pantry proposed by the mice sounds agreeable, and indeed, it was perfect from the mice's point of view. It left them free to continue feeding in the pantry, and all they had to do was forego the right to acquire a cat, which of course they had no intention of doing in any case. But the agreement obviously did not satisfy Farmer Brown's primary security concern—the protection of his foodstuffs. Most likely his counterproposal would have been to agree not to eat in the mice's pantry if they would not eat in his.

To enhance security, negotiations must be consistent with a state's broadest security needs, which seldom can be calculated solely on the basis of comparative military forces. Other more fundamental security factors need to be considered, such as food self-sufficiency, geography, industrial might, population, and so forth.[7] Ancient Athens, for example, was critically dependent on food imports. Therefore it deemed naval superiority over its potential adversaries an essential prerequisite for national security. Japan and Great Britain, island states that are similarly dependent upon imports of raw materials, also have traditionally relied on superior naval forces for national security.

Geography is often the single most important factor influencing a state's security needs. Israel is a perfect example. Israel has been at war with neighboring countries on five occasions in its brief history. During these wars it acquired the West Bank, Golan Heights, and Sinai territories. Without the West Bank, Israel would be only 10 to 15 miles wide at its "waist," and could easily be cut in two by a sudden strike from Jordan. Occupation of the mountainous Golan Heights by Syria would give Syrian artillery a commanding position for bombarding the Huleh Valley at will, a position which would cost much Israeli blood to recover. In contrast, the Sinai, which is much larger than either the Golan Heights or the West Bank, is strategically much less significant. Israel was willing as part of a larger peace settlement to give Egypt back the Sinai, so long as it remained demilitarized. Israeli forces would have time to react in case of an Egyptian advance into the flat Sinai and thus the Sinai could serve effectively as a buffer zone. From the Israeli point of view, schemes for peace settlements that do not take these geographic realities into account are stillborn. Poland made a case similar to Israel's in 1931, demanding special consideration for its long border, the unfavorable shape of its frontiers, and its lack of natural defenses.[8]

The mutual and balanced force reduction (MBFR) negotiations provide another example of how geography can influence negotiations. The USSR has favored numerically equivalent reductions in troops in Central Europe by NATO and the WPO. NATO rejects numerically equivalent troop withdrawals for geographic reasons that have not changed over the course of more than fifteen years of deadlocked negotiations. As one Secretary of State explained in reference to the MBFR talks:

> The Warsaw Pact had far more troops than we had along the central front; its initial advantage would grow rapidly once mobilization began, particularly be-

cause of the proximity of Soviet divisions in European Russia. In such circumstances, agreed mutual reductions, if both sides reduced by an equal percentage, would compound NATO's problem; they would weaken the already thinly held NATO front without degrading the Soviet capacity to reinforce. . . . Inevitably this led to the view that the only safe agreement was "asymmetrical" reductions, in other words, that the Warsaw Pact would cut its forces by a larger amount than NATO.[9]

The United States would find it difficult to move troops back to Europe in the event of hostilities. The USSR, in contrast, enjoys a 2,400 mile advantage in proximity to Central Europe, and it could move its forces back into the area relatively quickly.

Actually the geographical configuration of the entire world can be considered a key factor conditioning superpower conventional arms negotiations. Assuming the goal of containing Soviet power to its present confines, the United States is at a geographic disadvantage. The Soviet Union is centrally located in the Eurasian land mass with secure lines of communication to potential war fronts on much of the world's land mass. The United States has blocked the expansion of Soviet power into adjacent territory on its periphery by the forward deployment of U.S. forces into the Indian Ocean, Europe, Korea, the Philippines, Japan, and parts of the Middle East. Demilitarization, neutralization, and weapon-free zones in these areas would all be to the advantage of the USSR since it could fill the void more quickly in time of tension or conflict. This partly explains the Soviet enthusiasm for demilitarizing the Indian Ocean and for nuclear-free zones in Northern Europe, Central Europe, the Indian Ocean, the Balkans, and the Mediterranean and the reluctance of the United States to give up its bases or its nuclear weapons in any of these regions.

From the Soviet Union's point of view, its central position on the Eurasian continent affords dangers as well as advantages. The USSR can claim that because it has more area to protect, force disparities with its neighbors are justified. They say their security requires larger numbers of troops and arms than would suffice for a smaller nation that can concentrate its forces. This issue arose in the early 1800s when Tsar Alexander III proposed a general reduction of arms in Europe to Lord Castlereagh, the British foreign minister. When Castlereagh replied that Russia had by far the largest army in Europe and that the Tsar could greatly forward the cause of disarmament by reducing his own troop levels, the Tsar balked, arguing that Russia needed such a large army to protect its Persian and Turkish borders.[10]

Nuclear weapons have not rendered geography insignificant. The more geographically dispersed a nation's urban and industrial centers are, the greater the number of nuclear warheads required to assure their destruction. Some analysts in the United States have used this argument in justifying the larger number of warheads in the U.S. nuclear arsenal. They note that the Soviet Union is a larger country than the United States with a more dispersed set of urban, industrial, and military targets. They further note that the Soviet Union enjoys an additional geographic advantage in that many more of these targets in the United States are located near the coast and thus are more vulnerable to Soviet nuclear cruise missiles launched from submarines.

The USSR also has its complaints about geography in nuclear arms control talks. It observes that the United States enjoys a great advantage in easy access to both the Atlantic and Pacific Oceans, and thus its nuclear armed submarines stand a much better chance of putting to sea in a crisis and avoiding detection and destruction. Moreover, U.S. submarines have the advantage of overseas bases and in a crisis could close within firing range of the USSR more rapidly than Soviet submarines could reach firing positions off the North American coast.[11]

Population is another nonmilitary factor influencing negotiations. Countries at a disadvantage in population will prefer agreements limiting the mobilization potential of their neighbors but safeguarding their own mobilization programs, especially reserve training. For example, the German kaiser resisted arbitration agreements at the First Hague Conference (1899) because he feared that in a crisis his adversaries would use arbitration procedures as a stalling tactic until they could bring their larger forces to full readiness, thereby negating Germany's faster mobilization potential.[12] Similarly, since surprise and preemptive attack are key weapons in the arsenal of a numerically inferior army, it might not be in the interests of a small country to agree to measures providing equally effective early warning capabilities unless the accord included compensating advantages such as buffer zones or international peacekeeping forces to serve as deterrents to attack by larger neighbors.

Economic power is also a powerful influence on a state's approach to negotiations. At the end of the first Punic War in 143 B.C. the Romans restricted Carthage's access to silver mines in Spain in order to weaken its military potential.[13] Germany and France have repeatedly ended wars with peace terms designed to cripple the economic power of the defeated party. However, treaties restricting access to raw materials and a state's economic potential are rarely voluntary. Since it is difficult to gauge the impact of a multilateral treaty on economic power, states are reluctant to enter into such agreements. For example, in 1955 the U.S. Senate passed a resolution charging the President of the United States to explore means of improving world living standards by restricting the use of raw materials for military preparations by governments. The idea was that

> An adequate number of key resources be selected and standards be drawn up for determining what ratio of each of these resources should be set as a maximum ceiling limiting the proportion of each of these resources which may be utilized for military purposes.[14]

However, after considering their own proposal, the cautious senators added so many qualifications that they doomed the initiative.

Two of the senators' provisions were particularly problematic. First, they demanded that "measures of inspection and control be enforced to prevent the diversion or conversion for military purposes of resources committed for peaceful uses, also that any diversion or conversion be considered automatic evidence of aggressive intent."[15] Effective inspection and control measures for the use of industrial resources require massive intrusions into the domestic life of a state, to which few governments would readily agree.

Second, the senators stated that "a **'freeze'** of existing resource allocations cannot be taken as a starting stage because it would freeze a pattern of continuing aggression for some nations, while keeping others relatively defenseless."[16] This clause revealed the senators' perception that it was not their country which was devoting excessive amounts of its resources to war preparation and their expectation that other states would be required to make larger cuts in resource allocations under the terms of any subsequent agreement. Whether or not this perception was justified, it was not likely to be shared by other states.

Because of the difficulties associated with negotiating agreements on nonmilitary sources of power, their inclusion in arms control and disarmament negotiations is controversial. Nonmilitary factors can be strategically critical determinants of a state's power, but reaching agreement on how to define their relative military significance is extremely difficult, if not impossible. In summary the dilemma is that nonmilitary factors may hopelessly complicate negotiations and doom them to failure, but ignoring them may relegate an agreement to marginal security significance.

SHOULD NEGOTIATORS TAKE INTO ACCOUNT MILITARY POTENTIAL OR EXISTING FORCES ONLY?

It has been observed quite correctly that "there are few characteristics of a society which do not affect, directly or indirectly, its ability to generate military power."[17] Yet some factors contributing to military power are more immediately significant than others, and distinctions must be made if arms control and disarmament agreements are to be negotiated. The dividing lines are admittedly debatable, but in general it can be said that economic might becomes military potential when it is organized for the production of materials immediately necessary for conducting war. When the military forces are actually produced and deployed, military potential becomes existing military force, or "force-in-being." The scope of arms control and disarmament negotiations can be limited to existing forces, or can include provisions for regulating military potential, or both.

It is not uncommon for victorious states to impose restrictions on both the military potential and the existing forces of their vanquished enemies. Again, the Treaty of Zama between Rome and Carthage and the Versailles Treaty ending World War I serve as examples. Rome prohibited the training of elephants in Carthage in addition to demanding the surrender of all trained elephants, and also limited the navy of Carthage to ten ships. After World War I the Allies imposed manifold limitations on the existing German armed forces, ranging from numbers of guns and ammunition of all types to the number of military medical units. They also made great efforts to limit German military potential.

"All measures of mobilization" were forbidden. The Allies reduced Germany's army to one hundred thousand men and required each soldier to serve a minimum of twelve years in order to prevent the army from being used as a training school for building up huge reserve forces. Also, "educational establishments, the universities, societies of discharged soldiers, shooting or touring clubs and, generally speaking, associations of every description, whatever be the age of the members, must not occupy themselves with any military matters." To prevent German citizens from acquiring military experience, Germany was prohibited from sending "German nationals . . . to become enrolled in the Army, Navy, or Air Services of any foreign Power," and all signatories agreed not to use any German nationals "for the purpose of assisting in the military training" of such forces.[18] In addition to the preceding measures calculated to limit military potential, both Carthage and Germany were forced to pay large war indemnities partly in order to prevent an economic recovery that could contribute to future military potential.[19]

A defeated state usually must accept whatever restrictions on military potential the victors can devise. Voluntary agreements on measures of military potential are much more difficult, but attempts have been made. For example, during the 1920s and 1930s debate on the relative importance of military potential and forces-in-being was prominent in European disarmament negotiations, especially between France and Germany. Germany, with its existing forces drastically reduced by the Versailles treaty, demanded that France reduce its forces to a similar level. France insisted that Germany's greater military potential made disarmament to low levels disadvantageous to France. In the event of war, if France and Germany had similar existing forces, mobilization potential would be critical, and in that respect Germany held the advantage. This debate between France and Germany was broadened at the 1932 World Disarmament Conference. When President Herbert Hoover proposed a reduction of all national forces by one third at the conference, many objected that because industrial states could mobilize faster, nonindustrial states should be allowed larger standing forces.[20]

Some observers believe that mobilization potential is no longer so significant. In a nuclear war there would be no time to bring additional forces into battle, so "forces-in-being are almost surely decisive—at least in an all-out war."[21] Some proponents of arms control make this point in arguing that stability for the balance of forces-in-being is a more important goal now than disarmament per se. The goal of disarmament always leads to a consideration of military potential as well as existing forces, thereby distracting statesmen from the critical goal of the nuclear age: reducing the incentives for first strikes with existing forces.

There are two possible objections, or rather exceptions, to this emphasis on forces-in-being. First, if one does not assume a war between the superpowers will automatically escalate to total war, then a state's potential for extended conflict is still significant. For this reason flexible response theorists are concerned about the reload capacity of ICBM **launchers** and wartime command and control facilities. Second, an exclusive emphasis on stability of forces-in-being ignores the means by which military potential is converted into existing forces, that is, the weapons design and development process. Even in the nuclear era technology and testing are necessary to ensure reliability and continued development and production of weapons.

For example, proponents of nuclear test ban treaties are trying to restrict military potential by inhibiting tests necessary for developing weapons. In fact, all treaties that try to limit technological progress in weapons development are efforts to limit military potential, as are many nonproliferation treaties. Thus it would be wrong to say that arms control and disarmament in the nuclear age are exclusively concerned with forces-in-being, although one may believe this is where the greatest emphasis ought to be placed.

The issue of military potential, like the nonmilitary factors discussed in connection with the previous question, invariably complicates negotiations and sometimes dooms them to failure. Even if questions arising from broader security considerations can be resolved technically,[22] the result of balancing the impact of unequal military potential is a treaty that requires unequal sacrifices from the various signatories. Such treaties are extremely difficult to negotiate. A strong tendency exists for each state to be more conscious of its own nonmilitary liabilities than those of others, and thus to believe other states should make the larger concessions.

As with nonmilitary factors, ignoring military potential may reduce any subsequent agreement to a position of marginal significance for international security, but including them may hopelessly complicate negotiations. This general trade-off may be considered a rule of thumb for arms control and disarmament negotiations: *a broader scope for negotiations increases their complexity and significance but also reduces the likelihood of reaching an agreement.* The number of participating states is yet another factor which broadly establishes the parameters of security negotiations and conforms to the general rule that there is a trade-off between scope and practicality in negotiations.

SHOULD NEGOTIATIONS BE BILATERAL OR MULTILATERAL?

No scheme for the reduction of armaments . . . can be fully successful unless it is general.

—The Temporary Mixed Commission for the Reduction of Armaments, 1921[23]

In bilateral negotiations, overcoming complexity requires finding a combination of trade-offs and compromises that will satisfy the security concerns of both sides. Multilateral negotiations compound the difficulty of arriving at unanimous agreement on a set of compromises because each state has its own particular security objectives. A good example is the 1932 World Disarmament Conference. A total of 232 delegates representing fifty-seven nations attended the conference in Geneva and introduced 337 separate proposals for disarmament. Under the circumstances, unanimous agreement on any proposal except adjournment was unlikely.

A large number of participants in negotiations does not necessarily mean failure. Yet the complexity that stems from large numbers of negotiating parties does often require an offsetting degree of simplicity made possible by narrowing the substantive scope of the negotiations. The large United Nations Special Session on Disarmament (May 23–June 30, 1978) and its progeny, the Committee on Disarmament (1979) are exemplary. They have produced nothing more than broad statements of general sentiments favoring nuclear-free zones, military budget reductions, and other arms control and disarmament plans. Their predecessor, the Conference of the Committee on Disarmament (CCD), which at its peak represented thirty-two nations, was more successful.

The CCD lasted from 1969 to 1978 and grew out of the Eighteen Nation Committee on Disarmament which was founded in 1961 by the USSR and United States. Under its auspices three major multilateral agreements were reached: the 1971 Treaty on the Prohibition of the Emplacement of Nuclear Weapons and Other Weapons of Mass Destruction on the Sea-Bed and the Ocean Floor and in the Subsoil Thereof; the 1972 Convention on the Prohibition of the Development, Production, and Stockpiling of Bacteriological and Toxin Weapons and Their Destruction; and the 1977 Convention on the Prohibition of Military or Any Other Hostile Use of Environmental Modification Techniques. These treaties were signed and ratified by numerous nations (as of 1982, respectively, by 87, 111, and 48 states) and they all entail formal obligations for their many signatories. However, none of the treaties has significant provisions for verifying compliance with their terms, and thus they are as much symbolic statements of intention as substantive guarantees of behavior.[24]

Some multilateral treaties include meaningful provisions for verification of compliance, for example, the 1968 Nonproliferation Treaty. Nuclear-weapons-free zones agreements, another popular form of multilateral nonproliferation treaty, also occasionally contain significant compliance and inspection clauses.

Alliances, as multilateral institutions, can complicate negotiations. During the SALT II negotiations the United States at times tailored its negotiating positions to allow for the concerns of its NATO allies, and at other times did not. One issue that was not resolved in the West Europeans' favor was the agreement to a moratorium on the testing and production of NATO **Ground**

Launched Cruise Missiles (GLCMs) and **Sea Launch Cruise Missiles (SLCMs)** with ranges greater than 600 miles in exchange for a Soviet pledge to limit intercontinental use of its new "backfire" bomber. Many West Europeans objected to the exchange because they viewed long-range nuclear armed cruise missiles as essential to the defense of Europe, whereas limitations on the "backfire" bomber were seen as primarily beneficial to the security of the United States.

Sometimes when allies do not consider a set of negotiations to be in their interests, they work to sabotage them. The efforts of Corinth to undermine the Peace of Nicias in 421 B.C. are an ancient example of how alliance partners may complicate agreements. After ten years of fighting, Sparta and Athens negotiated a peace agreement. Sparta put the treaty to a vote in a special assembly of all its allies. Except for Corinth and a few others, Sparta's allies voted in favor of the treaty. Thus the terms of the treaty went into effect and began to be fulfilled despite Corinth's opposition. "But," as the Greek historian **Thucydides** notes, "Corinth and various other cities in the Peloponnese were trying to upset the agreement." When it became apparent that some Spartan allies were not holding to the terms of the agreement, Athens suspected Sparta of bad faith and responded accordingly, which led to a renewal of the war.[25]

The scope and significance of treaties between rival alliances or leaders of alliances depend in varying degrees upon the support of all alliance members. Even where no alliances are involved, treaties that limit the number and type of weapons deployed by states may eventually require the cooperation of states that did not participate in the original negotiations. The Washington Naval Treaty of 1922 is a good example.

The treaty obligated five major naval powers, United States, Great Britain, Japan, France, and Italy, to limit their naval armaments. These five states realized that the continuing significance of the treaty presupposed that no other state would upset the balance of forces codified in the treaty by launching an aggressive naval armament program that threatened the security of any of the treaty signatories. Therefore Britain and the United States, which had the most incentive to support the treaty, lobbied other states to support the naval status quo as defined by the terms of the Washington treaty. In 1923, at the Santiago Inter-American Conference, the United States attempted to extend the "Washington naval principles" to Latin American nations, but with no success. Latin American countries refused to be bound by an agreement they had no part in making and no ready reason for observing. Britain received a similar reaction from other European states in 1924 when it tried to extend the terms of the Washington treaty at a naval conference held in Rome.

Eventually, though, the terms of the Washington Naval Treaty were enlarged upon by three of the original five signatories. In the London Treaty of 1930 the United States, Britain, and Japan agreed to maximum tonnage limitations on other categories of naval arms not covered in the Washington treaty. However, the absence of France and Italy substantially reduced the significance of this treaty because it required the insertion of a clause that "restored complete freedom of action to any signatory if in its opinion new construction by a nonsignatory adversely affected its national security."[26]

It is not possible to make any general observations about how many states must participate in an arms control or disarmament treaty before it can be considered militarily significant or impossible to negotiate. It depends on the subject matter and the purpose of the treaty as well as existing geopolitical conditions. For example, today many believe that the nuclear arsenals of the United States and USSR are so vastly superior to those of any other nation that bilateral nuclear arms reduction agreements between the superpowers need not be contingent upon the participation of any other states. On the other hand, non-proliferation treaties designed to restrict the spread of nuclear weapons obviously require the cooperation of all states with nuclear capabilities in order to be effective.

WHICH WEAPON SYSTEMS AND FORCES SHOULD BE INCLUDED IN NEGOTIATIONS?

The parable of the animals' disarmament conference is a popular and powerful illustration of the difficulties involved in determining what kinds of weapons should be controlled or limited by mutual agreement:

> The eagle, with an eye on the bull, suggested that all horns be razed off. The bull, with a squint at the tiger, thought that all claws should be cut short. The tiger, glaring at the elephant, was of the opinion that tusks should be pulled out or at any rate shortened. The elephant, staring at the eagle, thought it indispensable that all wings should be clipped. Whereupon the bear, with a circular glance at all his brethren, cried out: "Why all those half-way measures? Let all weapons be done away with, so that nothing remains in the way of a fraternal, all-embracing hug."[27]

A comparison of national military forces always reveals advantages and disadvantages peculiar to each nation. Like the individual members of the animal disarmament conference, states tend to focus on their neighbors' areas of advantage, which they find threatening, while deemphasizing their own particular strengths. Thus when it comes time to set an agenda for negotiating arms limitations, each side will try to exclude its own areas of advantage while making sure its adversary's advantages are included in the negotiations.

The previously mentioned controversy over the cruise missile and backfire bomber was a case when disagreement over which weapons would be included or excluded almost scuttled the entire negotiations. The USSR insisted its backfire bomber was a tactical weapon and should be excluded from strategic arms negotiations, but the United States believed that since the backfire

bomber could reach the United States, it should be included like other strategic bombers. As for cruise missiles, the United States contended that the SALT negotiations were to limit ballistic missiles, not air-breathing missiles like the cruise, but the USSR argued nuclear cruise missiles were just as threatening as intercontinental ballistic missiles. The impasse over whether or not to include these two weapon systems stymied SALT negotiations during the Ford administration.

The inclusion or exclusion of weapons that defy easy categorization— often referred to as gray area systems—requires negotiation. If trade-offs in various gray area advantages are possible, comparative but different weapon systems may be included in the negotiations. Otherwise they may have to be excluded as nonnegotiable. For example, submarine launched nuclear cruise missiles were a gray area weapon excluded from SALT I by mutual agreement. Both sides believed their inclusion would unduly complicate the negotiations, raising difficult considerations of verification and antisubmarine warfare.

There are several potential solutions to the general problem of determining which weapon systems will be included in negotiations. Sometimes it is easier to begin with limitations on weapons whose significance seems to be declining in the wake of advancing technological developments. For example it has been claimed that the 1922 Washington Naval Treaty agreements to scrap battleships reflected the growing consensus that the lessons of the first World War suggested the battleship was obsolete.[28] Another solution is to agree to a set number of weapon systems under general numerical ceilings.

The signatories then are free to deploy whatever combination of specific weapons they believe will best serve their security interests, as long as they do not exceed the general ceiling or any subceilings agreed upon. The SALT II accords, for example, would have allowed the United States and the Soviet Union to use any combination of bombers, ICBMs, and SLBMs under a general subceiling of 1,320 "**MIRV**ed launchers" for each side. There were additional subceilings under this general limit on strategic nuclear launchers, but each side was allowed a substantial degree of freedom to choose how it would configure its forces.

Broad categories do not eliminate the problem of definition, but they can allow flexibility in arranging compromises and trade-offs. Defense budgets would be the broadest category for use as a ceiling for weapons deployment, but the problem of definition and verification of a state's defense budget is generally considered an insurmountable problem. A defense budget could be construed to include or exclude veterans' benefits, the cost of internal security police, the storage costs of strategic raw materials, research and development projects, and so forth.

Occasionally negotiators can agree to a numerical disparity by trading off advantages in different categories of weapons. For example, in the MBFR negotiations mutual reductions in the NATO advantage in tactical nuclear weapons and the WTO advantage in tanks have been used as the basis for numerous proposed agreements, sometimes with mutual troop reductions included and sometimes not. The problem with this solution is that it is very difficult to agree upon a basis for comparison. For example, how many tanks does it take to equal one tactical nuclear warhead?

Along with deciding what types of weapons are to be limited, negotiators must determine the criteria for limitations. Some weapons—fighter aircraft for example—are more conducive to simple numerical limitation by individual weapon units. Other military units can be limited by a number of indices. For example, a line of forts could be limited by the height of their walls, the number of gun emplacements, total area covered, or all of these. Thus in many cases specific criteria for measuring numerical limitations are necessary.

WHAT UNITS OF MEASUREMENT WILL BE USED?

What types of forces are to be included in the negotiations and what units of measurement will be used to determine how the forces are restricted are closely related issues. The unit of measurement agreed upon to establish limits on a particular weapons system either assists or exclusively defines the type of forces being limited. For example, a naval agreement could limit all capital ships over 10,000 tons. Such an agreement in tonnage would limit aircraft carriers, whereas an agreement to limit capital ships by the number of 16-inch or larger guns they had would exclude aircraft carriers.

Since the unit of measurement adopted helps define what forces are included, it raises problems similar to those discussed above in reference to the types of forces to be limited. Negotiators naturally want a unit that does not limit areas in which they consider themselves to have an advantage. Thus for many years in strategic negotiations the United States avoided including nuclear capable bombers, an area in which it had an advantage, and the USSR has consistently avoided negotiating on the basis of ballistic missile throw weight,[29] an area in which it had a decisive advantage.

Frequently very general units of measurement are agreed to in order to provide each side with as much flexibility as possible for configuring its forces to its best advantage, as was mentioned above in reference to launch vehicles in the SALT accords. Broader units of measurement entail the same advantages and disadvantages as broad weapons categories; respectively, advantages in flexibility but disadvantages in comparability.

The decision to count strategic launchers in SALT I illustrates the advantages and disadvantages of general units of measurement. Launchers as units of measurement were easy to verify and avoided more difficult units of comparison, such as warhead accuracy and throw weight. However, many complained that these other potential units of measurement—such as the accuracy of missiles, the number of warheads each could carry, and their total megatonnage—were far more important indices of strategic nuclear power. One launcher could be much more destructive than another. Some argued the United States benefited the most from the focus on launchers because it had more warheads, while others claimed the USSR had the better deal because of its advantage in megatonnage.

Broader units of measurement than launchers have been recommended for reducing the nuclear inventories of the superpowers. One disarmer has proposed "nuclear device" as a unit of measure, so that each side would turn in an equal number of warheads, bombs, or artillery shells according to its own preference.[30] Again, this unit of measurement has the advantage of flexibility but the disadvantage of noncomparability. While each side could choose the units it wanted to dispose of, a nuclear artillery shell is not remotely comparable to an intercontinental warhead in terms of its security value. Each side would dispose of its least significant "nuclear devices" until one side concluded the remaining inventories left it with a decided security advantage. The side with the most nuclear devices could afford to trade off until it alone remained with a significant strategic inventory.

Defense budgets offer yet another example of how problematic general units of measurement can be. Budget limitations would give states maximum freedom in choosing how to build and deploy their forces, and in the words of one observer, they are "the most direct means for slowing the arms race without having to conduct endless technical bargaining over the equivalence of specific weapons systems."[31] Again, the advantage in flexibility is offset by the comparability problem. None of the available indices for limiting military expenditure, such as percentage of GNP or a ceiling in constant currency, would provide a realistic basis for comparison, and thus equal security. For example one nation might produce weapons much more efficiently than another, while others might pay their soldiers less money and thus be able to afford larger forces.[32]

Even units of military force that may seem to be extremely basic can raise noncomparability problems. Manpower is a good example. Britain's Lord Esher recommended in 1924 that each European nation organize its army into units of thirty thousand and reduce its troop levels to an agreed upon number of divisions, determined by reference to the size of the state's population, location, and so on. The plan was quicly rejected by virtually all military experts because the quality of divisions could differ so radically according to the training and outfitting of the troops.[33] More recently, the MBFR negotiations have been stymied in part by the Soviet conviction that a German soldier is a greater threat to Soviet security than any other NATO soldier. The USSR has always insisted on individual national ceilings in these negotiations in order to prevent the West German forces from increasing in proportion to other NATO countries.

In summary, the more general the categories and units of measurement, the more flexibility each side has in arranging their forces to conform to the agreement's general guidelines. Yet the more general the categories, the greater the problems of non-comparability. That is, the flexibility in arranging force composition makes comparison (and thus security equivalency) difficult to estimate. The converse of this flexibility-comparability trade-off also holds true. The more specific the weapon category and unit of measurement, the easier it is to compare them and arrive at an agreement on security equivalency. Such specificity reduces negotiating flexibility, though, forcing states to adopt force postures dictated by the precise terms of the arms limitation agreement, thereby placing ultimate importance on which forces will be included and excluded in the final agreement.

Another important influence on the choice of weapons categories and units of measurement is the ability to effectively monitor the terms of the agreement. In fact, the ability to verify compliance often *determines* the forces and units of measurement agreed upon, since many believe there is little sense in agreeing to limit forces or units that cannot be monitored. The next chapter explores the way negotiators handle the issues of compliance, verification, and violations of agreements.

DISCUSSION QUESTIONS

1. When, if ever, would it be wise to negotiate an arms limitation agreement with a state inferior in military forces?
2. When, if ever, might an arms limitation agreement be harmful to a state's security?

3. The United States has geographic advantages as a sea power, and the Soviet Union as a land power. Should each demand superiority according to its geographic advantages or disadvantages? What problems would have to be resolved for the USSR and United States to negotiate general limitations on all types of conventional forces?

4. In nuclear arms negotiations, is it military potential or only existing forces which need to be considered?

5. Should the superpowers conclude a strategic arms limitation agreement even if it raised strenuous objections from their allies?

SUGGESTED READINGS FOR CHAPTER SEVEN: SETTING AN AGENDA FOR NEGOTIATING MUTUAL SECURITY WITH OTHER NATIONS

DOUGHERTY, JAMES F. *How to Think About Arms Control and Disarmament.* New York: Crane, Russak and Co., 1973.

FORBES, HENRY W. *The Strategy of Disarmament.* Washington, DC: Public Affairs Press, 1962.

FREEDMAN, LAWRENCE. "The Dilemma of Theater Nuclear Arms Control." *Survival* 23 (January–February 1981).

GOLDBLAT, JOSEF. *Arms Control: A Survey and Appraisal of Multilateral Agreements.* London: Taylor and Francis, 1979.

LUCK, EDWARD C., ed. *Arms Control: The Multilateral Alternative.* New York: New York University Press, 1983.

KNORR, KLAUSS. *The Power of Nations.* New York: Basic Books, 1975.

———. *Military Power and Potential.* Lexington, MA: D. C. Heath and Co., 1970.

MORGENTHAU, HANS. *Politics Among Nations.* Fourth ed. New York: Alfred A. Knopf, 1967. pp. 107ff, 387.

NICOLSON, HAROLD. *Peacemaking, 1919.* Boston: Houghton Mifflin, 1933.

NOTES

1. From *Dictionary of Military and Naval Quotations,* compiled and edited by Colonel Robert Debs Heinl, Jr., USMC (Ret.). Copyright © 1966, U.S. Naval Institute, Annapolis, Maryland, p. 211.

2. *The Political Testament of Cardinal Richelieu,* trans. Henry Bertram Hill (Madison, WI: University of Wisconsin Press, 1961), pp. 94–95. Talleyrand had similar sentiments: "One must negotiate, negotiate, and always negotiate." Quoted in U.S. Congress, House, Committee on Foreign Affairs, *Soviet Diplomacy and Negotiating Behavior: Emerging New Context for U.S. Diplomacy,* Vol. 1, Committee Print, Prepared by the Congressional Research Service, Library of Congress, 1979, p. 534.

3. *Polyaenus's Stratagems of War,* trans. R. Shepherd (Chicago: Ares Publishers, 1914; reprint of original 1793 London edition), p. 245. See also footnote 24 in the following chapter.

4. Heinl, *Dictionary,* p. 88. This sentiment was expressed more succinctly by an earlier American: "You may cover whole skins of parchment with limitations, but power alone can limit power." John Randolph, quoted in Hans J. Morgenthau and Kenneth Thompson, *Politics Among Nations: The Struggle for Power and Peace,* 6th ed. (New York: Alfred A. Knopf, 1985), p. 189.

5. Walter R. Fisher and Richard Dean Burns, *Armament and Disarmament: The Continuing Dispute* (Belmont, CA: Wadsworth Pub. Co., 1974), pp. 216–217.

6. Patrick Buchanan, "Save the Poseidons!" *Washington Times,* January 9, 1985.

7. A good review of these factors can be found in Hans Morgenthau, *Politics Among Nations,* 4th ed. (New York: Alfred A. Knopf, 1967), pp. 107ff, 387.

8. Henry W. Forbes, *The Strategy of Disarmament* (Washington, DC: Public Affairs Press, 1962), p. 16.

9. Henry Kissinger, *White House Years* (Boston: Little, Brown, 1979), pp. 947–948.

   The MBFR talks are much more important than their low public profile would suggest. About one half of the approximately $500 billion spent annually on arms worldwide is spent on NATO and WPO forces in Central Europe.

10. H. A. Smith, "The Problem of Disarmament in the Light of History," *International Affairs* 10 (September 1930): 601.

11. Similarly, the USSR demands compensation for geographic asymmetries in the intermediate-range nuclear force (INF) talks with the United States. Naturally the Soviets view all nuclear weapons capable of striking the USSR as a threat and want the United States to take this into consideration by making allowances for British, French, and Chinese INFs, all of which have the range to strike the USSR, but not the United States.

12. James E. Dougherty, *How to Think about Arms Control and Disarmament* (New York: Crane, Russak and Co., 1973), p. 39.

13. On the terms of the Treaty of Zama, see Livy, *The War with Hannibal,* trans. Aubrey De Selincourt (New York: Penguin Books, 1965) and Brian Caven, *The Punic Wars* (New York: St. Martin's Press, 1980).

14. U.S., Congress, Senate, Subcommittee on Disarmament, *Disarmament and Security: A Collection of Documents, 1919–55* Committee Print, 84th Congress, 2d Session, p. 794.

15. Ibid.

16. Ibid.

17. Klauss Knorr, *Military Power and Potential* (Lexington, MA: D. C. Heath and Co., 1970), p. 24.

18. U.S. Congress, *Disarmament and Security,* pp. 1–6. Interestingly, the French secured for themselves an exception to the rule that German nationals could not be trained by any of the signatories to the treaty. The treaty did not "affect the right of France to recruit for the Foreign Legion in accordance with French military laws and regulations." Article 179.

19. Because of the economic chaos in Germany that apparently contributed to the rise of Hitler, the Allies were more careful in their demands for reparations after World War II. For example, although the Allies desired to provide for the "economic demobilization" of Japan after the war, they concluded that reparations should "not prejudice . . . the maintenance of a minimum civilian standard of living." See U.S. Congress, *Disarmament and Security,* pp. 585, 587.

20. See Frederick H. Hartman, *The Relations of Nations* (New York: Macmillan, 1983), pp. 276–277; and Dougherty, *How to Think,* pp. 43–46.

21. Henry Kissinger, "Arms Control, Inspection and Surprise Attack," 38 *Foreign Affairs* (July 1960): 557.

22. Henry Forbes relates two interesting attempts to define military potential:

    Two methods for determining the potential were contemplated. One was a mathematical scheme which tried to give numerical values to a country's manpower, its existing armament, its various industries, the raw materials available for wartime use, the geographic location, the communication system, and other related factors. Fantastic as it may seem, this method was debated extensively by the Temporary Mixed Commission in 1921–22. The other method was to let a body of military experts determine the greatest total force a nation could put into the field. The relative strengths thus determined were to have been put into the Disarmament Treaty.

    Forbes, *The Strategy of Disarmament,* p. 287.

23. Fisher and Burns, *Armament and Disarmament,* p. 215.

24. Primarily symbolic agreements are sometimes referred to as "cosmetic" treaties. This term

is used by Richard Dean Burns in the introduction to his *Arms Control and Disarmament: A Bibliography* (Santa Barbara, CA: ABC Clio, Co., 1977), p. 4.

25. Interestingly, Corinth was aided in its efforts to undermine the peace by a clause in the treaty that led Sparta's allies to "suspect that Sparta was planning to enslave them with the aid of Athens." Thucydides, *The Peloponnesian War,* trans. Rex Warner (Middlesex, England: Penguin Books, 1954, reprint 1980), p. 366.

    The United States and the Soviet Union are also occasionally accused of using negotiations to conspire against the interests of the rest of the world. See Alva Myrdal, *The Game of Disarmament: How the United States and Russia Run the Arms Race* (New York: Pantheon Books, 1976).

26. Morgenthau, *Politics Among Nations,* 4th ed., p. 390.

27. John Spanier and Joseph Nogee, *The Politics of Disarmament* (New York: Frederick A. Praeger, 1962), p. 201. This parable comes from Salvador de Madariaga, and also has been used by others, including Winston Churchill. It is no secret that the bear is symbolic of the USSR and its oft-repeated support for complete and total disarmament. See also note 17, p. 208, chapter 11.

28. Morgenthau, *Politics Among Nations,* 4th ed., p. 389.

29. Throw weight refers to the amount of weight that a missile can deliver from one point to another, and thus in practical terms, the number and size of the weapons (usually warheads) it can carry.

30. Noel Gaylor, "How to Break the Momentum of the Nuclear Arms Race," in Burns H. Weston, ed., *Toward Nuclear Disarmament and Global Security: A Search for Alternatives* (Boulder, CO: Westview Press, 1984), p. 398.

31. Harvey Brooks, "Potentials for Curbing the Qualitative Arms Race," in Weston, *Toward Nuclear Disarmament,* p. 422.

32. Most arms control and disarmament experts have given up on budget reduction agreements as impossible to negotiate, but the USSR and the United Nations still proclaim considerable interest in this approach. See *The United Nations Disarmament Yearbook, Vol. 5, 1980* (New York: United Nations, 1981), pp. 369ff.

33. Forbes, *The Strategy of Disarmament,* p. 19.

Chapter Eight

Considerations for Negotiating Mutual Security

The three issues reviewed in this chapter, verification, violations, and stability, are interrelated. This excerpt from a 1952 U.S. proposal to the United Nations Disarmament Commission illustrates how these negotiating concerns interact:

> The goal of disarmament is not to regulate but to prevent war by relaxing the tensions and fears created by armaments and by making war inherently, as it is constitutionally under the [UN] Charter, impossible as a means of settling disputes between nations.
>
> To achieve this goal, all states must cooperate to establish an open and substantially disarmed world, (a) in which armed forces and armaments will be reduced to such a point and in such a thorough fashion that no state will be in a condition of armed preparedness to start a war, and (b) in which no state will be in a position to undertake preparations for war without other states having knowledge of such preparation long before an offending state could start a war.[1]

As stated in this 1952 U.S. negotiating proposal, the purpose of disarmament is to enhance strategic stability by reducing the ability of states to wage offensive war, thereby reducing interstate tensions. At the same time, because states may cheat on a disarmament agreement, strategic stability also requires that compliance with the agreements be verified. These two objectives are not altogether compatible. Reductions in armaments may contribute to stability by making aggression more difficult, but arms reductions also may increase incentives to violate the arms limitation treaty since at lower levels of armaments smaller and fewer violations would be both strategically more significant and harder to detect. In other words, as levels of arms decrease, the ability of states to hide significant quantities of arms increases. For this reason it is generally agreed that verification capabilities must grow increasingly more rigorous as the number of arms decreases in order to offset the greater ability and incentive to cheat on the agreement.

In short, strategies for negotiating stabilizing arms limitation agreements must take into account the risk of violations, which is both a function and a determinant of a proposed agreement's security significance and verifiability. Thus negotiators cannot consider the issues of verification, violations, and stability in isolation. With this caveat in mind, it is possible for purposes of discussion to explore the three issues separately, beginning with what is perhaps the most immediate question for the negotiator: Can compliance with the agreement be verified?

CAN COMPLIANCE WITH THE AGREEMENT BE VERIFIED?

> Kings should be very careful with regard to the treaties they conclude, but having concluded them they should observe them religiously. I well know that many statesmen advise to the contrary, but without considering here what the Christian religion offers in answer to such advice, I maintain that the loss of honor is worse than the loss of life itself. A great prince should sooner put in jeopardy both his own interests and those of the state than break his word, which he can never violate without losing his reputation and by consequence the greatest instrument of sovereigns.
>
> —Cardinal Richelieu (1595–1642)

> Lysander used to say, "Boys were to be cheated with dice, but an enemy with oaths."
>
> —Polyaenus, *Stratagems of War*[2]
> (Lysander was a respected Spartan political leader in fifth century B.C. Greece.)

Arms control and disarmament negotiations would be much easier if Richelieu's advice were always preferred to Lysander's, but history informs us that this is not the case. It will be remembered from the previous chapter that after World War I Germany's military might was subjected to extremely rigorous controls. The victorious allies, especially France, tried to verify German compliance with the terms of the Versailles treaty, with more success during the immediate postwar years than later:

A German officer talking to a senior member of the British embassy in Berlin in 1933, made the odd remark that the British are gentlemen, but the French are not. Asked what he meant he explained: "One day in 1920, some of the Military Control Commission under a French and British officer, came to the barracks of which I had charge. They said they had reason to believe that I had a store of rifles concealed behind a brick wall, contrary to the terms of the peace treaty. I denied this. 'I give you my word of honor as a German officer,' I said 'that I have no rifles concealed in the barracks.'

"Well, your British officer was a gentleman. He accepted my word of honor and went away. But the French officer was not a gentleman. He would not accept my word of honor. He pulled down the brick wall. And he took away my rifles."[3]

Verifying compliance[4] is not so simple a choice between trust and tangible evidence as this anecdote suggests. Perfect verification is not possible, and thus an element of trust is always present in arms control and disarmament agreements. Nor is the question of how far another state can be trusted framed in terms of national or personal honor so much these days. Instead *trust is measured by the extent to which one is willing to assume another state(s) shares the conception of self-interest implied by the terms of the treaty.*

Those who demand the least rigorous verification procedures are those who are most convinced an agreement is in the interests of all the signatories and so all will naturally abide by it:

So it can be asserted with some confidence that states only enter into obligations of their own free will, and when they see some compelling reason to do so. Having made the positive and voluntary decision to conclude or join a treaty, they are likely to comply with its terms thereafter.

Neither the lack of centralized powers of enforcement, nor the possibility of non-compliance with a treaty obligation going unpunished, is then a crippling disability. . . . [5]

From this point of view, an obsessive concern with verification "may divert us from more serious problems with respect to future agreements, and it may lead to our not concluding agreements that would be advantageous."[6]

At the other end of the spectrum of opinion on verification are those who believe some states will abide by an agreement only so long as they cannot obtain an even better security arrangement by cheating while the other state(s) continue to observe the terms of the agreement.[7] From this point of view the more stringent the monitoring procedures, the more reassuring the agreement is for mutual security. However, if the verification procedures are too stringent they may preclude negotiated agreement.

For example in the 1920s world attention began to focus on the prospect of mass urban bombing made possible by advances in aviation, a concern that gained a particular sense of urgency as the Japanese began their terror bombing of mainland China in 1932. In 1932 a League of Nations committee convened in Geneva with a core of twenty attending delegations, but as many as sixty-one nations participated over the course of the deliberations. The negotiators agreed that the elimination of only military aircraft could not be verified, and therefore many delegates concluded all civilian aircraft would have to be replaced by international civil aviation services. However, these provisions proved impossible to negotiate. The same experience followed the atomic bombing of Japan. Despite world-wide concern with the prospect of nuclear war, the rigorous control and inspection procedures required to verify the complete elimination of nuclear weapons could not be agreed upon.

Between those who believe mutually advantageous agreements are self-enforcing and those who believe an agreement is only as good as its monitoring procedures, are those who advocate playing the percentages, so to speak. They point out that the likelihood of cheating is partly a function of the risk of getting caught at a violation, and of the incentive to cheat on the agreement. The risk of getting caught goes up with more rigorous monitoring procedures, and the incentive to cheat goes up with the military significance of the agreement. The purpose of monitoring, therefore, is to detect cheating and induce compliance, but also to allow time for an appropriate response in case violations that significantly affect a state's security are detected.

For an exaggerated example, an agreement to abolish all nuclear weapons would provide great incentives for cheating since the state that retained even a few nuclear weapons would gain an immense military advantage. An agreement with such security significance would have to include the most intensive monitoring procedures possible. This is why "complete and total disarmament," a goal very seriously pursued in the 1950s, depends upon cooperative monitoring procedures, which almost no state would willingly agree to, and thus is no longer seriously mentioned by arms control and disarmament experts except as a hope for a hypothetical future world.[8]

In contrast, an agreement to limit the growth of nuclear weapons when both sides have thousands of them would be less militarily significant, and thus would require less rigorous monitoring and inspection procedures. With the advantage to cheating reduced and the disadvantages to being caught at cheating well understood, monitoring procedures would not have to be as strict to produce a high degree of confidence that the agreement was being honored. From this point of view, then, the requirements for verification are relative to the military significance of the proposed agreement.

It follows that different assessments of an agreement's military significance can produce different assessments of an agreement's verification requirements. This is why disagreements between strategists over the sufficiency of monitoring procedures often reflect differences between their deterrence doctrines. For example, assured destruction theorists, who believe the U.S. nuclear arsenal already has an overkill capability, are less concerned than flexible response theorists with evidence that another state has acquired more nuclear weapons than allowed by treaty:

> Verification need not be perfect to be effective. Under an agreement that provides for adequate verification, cheating is deterred; any cheating that does occur

is likely to be revealed, and cheating that is not detected is likely to result in only marginal changes in military capabilities. In a world where the United States and the Soviet Union have about 20,000 strategic warheads between them, such changes will not have much military significance.[9]

In short, differing assessments of the strategic significance of incremental increases in weapons produces different assessments of verification requirements.

As negotiators decide how stringent monitoring procedures ought to be, they must also choose which monitoring procedures will be used. These may range from unilateral measures that require no cooperation, for example, satellites and electronic monitoring devices (often called **national technical means: NTMs**[10]), to so-called intrusive measures that require the consent and cooperation of governments, for example, examination of government spending records, on-site inspection of production facilities and storage areas, and public communication links with international officials so that citizens can report any suspicious behavior by their government. In discussion, intrusive verification measures are only limited by the human imagination. It has even been suggested that "truth serum" be administered to selected government officials to determine whether agreements are being kept.[11] In practice, governments have strongly resisted any intrusive inspection measures.

The 1899 Hague Conference almost immediately bogged down on the issue of inspection and control as practically all states complained that intrusive measures violated the fundamental principle of national sovereignty.[12] In 1926 a Belgian proposal for an international agency to publicize scientific advances in techniques of warfare "condemned by the opinion of the civilized world" was rejected because compulsory disclosure of such information was not deemed possible.[13] In fact, most of the League of Nations's disarmament efforts foundered on the reluctance of states to agree to intrusive inspection measures. The United States, Britain, Chile, Italy, Japan, and Sweden even joined together in a report to the preparatory commission for the Disarmament Conference to declare intrusive measures could create much ill feeling without any substantial benefits.[14]

The League of Nations did manage to set up some reporting commissions that it assigned responsibility for monitoring arms control and disarmament agreements; for example, the Dardanelles Straits Commission, which monitored the movements of warships between the Black Sea and the Aegean. The League also on occasion assigned a specific commission of inquiry to investigate possible violations of treaties, such as the Aland Island Commission, which investigated a Soviet-Finnish demilitarized island in the Gulf of Bothnia. These commissions were exceptions to the general experience of the League, which indicated intrusive measures were widely considered unacceptable and even counterproductive.

The problem of intrusive monitoring measures remains to this day a critical stumbling block to substantial disarmament agreements. Some believe it is the single most vexing problem in U.S.-Soviet arms control and disarmament negotiations. The Soviet reluctance to accept any form of on-site inspection led to years of debates that were, as one noted author points out, "monotonously similar":

> The Soviets accused the Western powers of desiring control and inspection without disarmament. The Western powers reciprocated by accusing the Soviets of seeking a purely "declaratory disarmament" without adequate verification of compliance.[15]

The USSR and the United States found a way around their differences on intrusive monitoring techniques in the late 1960s and 1970s when satellites and other NTMs convinced negotiators that more intrusive measures were not necessary to ensure verification. In this respect the SALT era and its focus on ICBMs parallels the naval treaties of the early 1920s and their focus on capital ships, which the negotiators of the 1922 Washington Naval Treaty felt were easily enough monitored (since they are so large and take so long to build) to list individually by name and tonnage.

Fig. 8.1   Cruise missiles: Can they be monitored without intrusive inspection techniques?
(Source: U.S. Air Force Photo)

Advancing technology can assist and complicate monitoring efforts. In some areas progress on NTMs technologies continues to produce new opportunities for arms control.[16] For example, the inability to effectively monitor underground nuclear testing was long considered a major stumbling block to a total test ban treaty. Recently, however, more and more scientists are concluding that with advances in seismic technologies it is possible to monitor compliance with a nuclear test ban treaty with extremely high confidence.[17] On the other hand there is also much agreement that advances in weapons technology have enormously complicated effective monitoring of arms limitation agreements. Sea-launched cruise missiles (SLCMs, or "slickems") are an example. After being fired from a ship or submarine, a SLCM skims over the ocean or land on the way to its target with either a nuclear or conventional warhead. SLCMs have been totally excluded from superpower arms control negotiations simply because no one knows how restrictions on them could be verified without intrusive inspection techniques.[18]

There are some signs that the superpowers may be able to reach agreement on on-site inspection in special circumstances. On-site inspection has been a serious topic in the MBFR negotiations for several years, and the USSR also has offered to discuss the issue in other forums with increasing regularity. In May 1986 the USSR agreed to allow U.S. scientists to establish three seismic monitoring stations on Soviet territory in exchange for similar stations in the United States. Then, in August 1986, Soviet spokesmen offered to open nuclear test sites to American inspectors and to allow aerial inspection of some military activities in Eastern Europe.[19] In March 1987, as U.S. and Soviet negotiators neared agreement on the elimination of **INFs,** serious on-site inspection clauses were included in the negotiating proposals. With the principle of on-site inspection apparently accepted by the USSR, the issue has become the number of inspections and where and how they are to take place.[20]

There are two additional problems for the negotiator to consider besides the monitoring procedures required to verify compliance. First, the negotiator must consider whether requirements for verification in a proposed arms limitation agreement are consistent with strategic stability. For example, some have argued that future strategic stability requires the deployment of mobile missiles (either SLBMs or ICBMs) which would not be vulnerable to and thus encourage a first strike during a crisis. However, missiles which cannot be located as targets (and thus are often considered stabilizing) cannot be monitored for arms control either. The reverse is true also. That is, exceedingly effective means of verification may be destabilizing because if it is possible to locate all enemy forces with great accuracy, it is much easier to plan a surprise first strike.

Second, negotiators must decide how much of their detection capability they should publicize in order to maximize deterrence of violations. The Arms Control and Disarmament Agency has observed that

> The deterrent value of verification depends to a considerable extent on a potential violator being ignorant of the exact capability of the intelligence techniques used to monitor his compliance with an agreement.[21]

Yet ignorance of an adversary's monitoring capabilities may result in a state deciding it can secretly violate a treaty when in fact it cannot. For example, before the USSR discovered that the U.S. KH-11 satellite was a photographic satellite it did not bother to conceal certain sensitive security activities. Since obtaining information on the KH-11's capabilities, the USSR has taken steps to conceal these activities.[22]

States must strike a balance between impressing other states with their detection capabilities in order to deter violations and not revealing so much about their capabilities that they demonstrate how detection can be avoided, thereby both compromising their detection capabilities and also giving a potential violator reason to believe it knows enough to plan successful violations. As with military deterrence, an element of uncertainty is helpful in deterring treaty violations, but too much uncertainty may encourage violations. Considering how to detect violations[23] leads to another question: What to do if violations are detected?

WHAT OUGHT TO BE DONE
ABOUT TREATY VIOLATIONS?

The Nature of and Motives for Violations

Evidence that another state is violating an agreement immediately raises three questions: Is the evidence compelling? If yes, why is the agreement being violated? Finally, how militarily significant are the violations? Answers to these questions will help to determine whether a response to the violation(s) is advisable, and if so, what the response should be.

Often the nature of violations can suggest motives. For example, interference with agreed upon means for monitoring compliance with an agreement might indicate a desire for violating the substance of the agreement, raising doubts about the violator's commitment to the arms control process in general. It is for this reason that the encryption of telemetry from ballistic missiles became a major issue in superpower strategic arms control. During missile tests, telemetry—the transmission of electronic signals—is monitored to ensure the missile being tested does not violate previous agreements. The SALT agreements prohibited interference with national technical means such as electronic surveillance of missile telemetry, but this prohibition was not always respected by the signatories.

The timing of violations also provides clues to the violator's motives. If a defense program that violates a treaty was in development well before the treaty was signed, perhaps the violation is a result of bureaucratic momentum, a proposition easily tested by complaining about the violations. If the offending program was planned during the negotiations it might indicate perfidy, since this would suggest top-level knowledge and approval at the very moment such programs were under review and ostensibly being abandoned in the interests of mutual security. If the program was begun well after the treaty then one might argue the violations reflect deteriorating relations that have encouraged a sense of insecurity and a move to secure unilateral defense guarantees.

An assessment of motives may help formulate options for responding, but it is the security significance of the violations that gives the response more or less urgency. An ancient chronicler tells how the Athenian soldier Agnon was assigned the task of establishing a new colony in hostile territory. He had almost arrived at his destination and was about to cross the Strymon, a strategically located river junction, when he found his way barred by local forces:

> Agnon, not in a condition to effect passage over it by force, concluded a truce with them for three days; who retired to their own residence, leaving him, for the time stipulated between them, quiet in his post. In the night he passed the Strymon with his army . . . and there he entrenched himself with palisades; resting in the day, and working at the fortifications every night. In three nights his works were completed. When the Barbarians returned, and, finding in what manner he had during their absence employed himself, they charged him with an infringement of the truce. "Of that," replied Agnon, "I am perfectly clear: the truce was for three days of inaction, which I religiously observed: the works you see, I erected in the intermediate nights." Such was the origin of the city, which Agnon built . . . and called Amphipolis.[24]

Whether Agnon violated the treaty depends on how *day* is defined (as daylight or as twenty-four hours), but no matter how slightly his violation stretched or deviated from the terms of the agreement, the military impact was critical, and this is the first criterion by which major violations of a treaty must be judged.

The anecdote about Agnon's interpretation of his agreement illustrates another important point about violations: They can be relative to the precision of the agreement's terms.[25] For example, in response to U.S. complaints that the USSR was violating SALT II by developing a new missile, the Soviets argued it was not a new missile at all, but rather a "modification" of their existing SS-13. Modifications were allowable under the terms of the treaty, so the question is when does a modification of a missile become a development of a new missile type? What one party to a treaty considers a violation another signatory might consider just a case of approaching the limits of the agreement.

Another problem that must always be considered is that the verification process may err. For example, in April 1986 the CIA announced that its previous calculations of Soviet violations of the Threshold Test Ban Treaty may have been overstated by as much as 50 percent. Also, the United States has been unnecessarily alarmed in the past when estimates of bomber and missile "gaps" between U.S. and Soviet forces turned out to be greatly exaggerated. Obviously the strength of the evidence of treaty violations is a first and constant concern, but for the purpose of discussion the rest of this chapter will discuss violations that are assumed to be real.

Major Violations

Somewhat curiously, but not inexplicably, leaders often seem less concerned about the possibility of major violations than minor ones. There are a couple of reasons why this is so. First, many people, such as U.S. Congressman Les Aspin, argue that major violations would certainly be detected, and any that are not detected could not be major violations:

> The multiple and duplicative methods of detection at the disposal of the United States are sufficient to reveal any cheating on a scale adequate to threaten this country militarily.[26]

Second, if a nation seriously believed the state's security was being undermined by adherence to the terms of a treaty, it could always promulgate an explanation (or excuse) for abrogating the treaty, do so, and then take whatever unilateral steps seemed necessary. Thus a response to major violations is presumably already anticipated in a state's contingency plans for treaty abrogation. Finally, major violations of an arms control agreement at least have the virtue of reducing doubt about an adversary's intentions. The very least one can conclude is that the violator does not value stability so much as military advantage, although the reasons for desiring military advantage may not be clear.

Minor Violations

Minor violations, which at least individually do not upset the military balance, are more difficult to explain. They might not even be intentional. Sometimes states claim to have inadvertently violated a treaty because low-level officials were unfamiliar with the precise terms of the treaty. If so the violation should be easy to have corrected. If a pattern of minor violations begins to emerge, protestations of inadvertent noncompliance will be less credible, and other explanations must be sought.

Minor violations of an agreement's terms may be the violator's way of testing the verification capabilities and political will of other parties to the agreement. By coming closer and closer and eventually crossing the line that separates violations of the spirit of a treaty from violations of its letter, a violator can observe the responses of the other signatories and draw conclusions about their detection techniques and willingness to risk confrontation over the violations.

It is also possible that such "creeping violations" may be designed to add up to a breakout capability; that is, a point at which the combined impact of the minor violations collectively constitutes a major violation that shifts the strategic balance, and which if further taken advantage of by abrogation of the treaty and unrestrained unilateral security actions, can radically alter the balance of power.

Responses

How a state responds to violations depends upon how it interprets their individual and collective significance, both in terms of the military balance and in terms of the adversary's intentions. If the violations are not critical militarily, a state may choose to ignore them for several reasons. First, a state may believe that despite the violations, the treaty is still advantageous. For example, according to the terms of the 1936 Montreaux Convention aircraft carriers larger than 15,000 tons cannot pass through the Turkish straits (the Bosporus, Sea of Marmara, and the Dardanelles). The Soviet Union has *Kiev*-class aircraft carriers on the Black Sea that exceed the 15,000 ton limit and which have transited the Turkish straits. In order to avoid abrogating the Montreaux treaty the USSR classifies its Kiev class aircraft carriers as "antisubmarine ships." The USSR is expected to refer to the larger 75,000 ton aircraft carriers it is building on the Black Sea as "air capable battleships" for the same reason. NATO and Turkey choose to accept these unique classifications because they still believe the Montreaux Convention, on the whole, is a worthwhile agreement.

Also, a state may decide that the violations are, if not justified, then at least understandable, and to complain about them and expose them would cause more political problems than it would solve. After World War I Germany managed to circumvent the Versailles treaty provisions by training men and building and testing weapons in other countries, notably the Soviet Union, Switzerland, and Spain. Germany also hid weapons caches from on-site inspectors, who were occasionally subjected to threats and personal attacks. Other states knew about Germany's cheating on the treaty (in one plant alone six hundred illegal 105-mm gun barrels were discovered),[27] but none were willing to fight or occupy Germany to stop the violations. Many people in Europe felt the Versailles treaty had been unreasonably harsh on Germany in the first place and there was inadequate public support for permanently occupying and policing Germany. Thus leaders concluded that all things considered, it was not worthwhile doing anything decisive about German treaty violations. Indeed, the problems presented by evidence of German violations were so politically unpalatable that the tendency was to discredit the evidence rather than confront its implications.[28]

Finally, a state may decide to do nothing about a treaty violation because it does not want to compromise a secret source of information. It may be decided that at least in the short term it is more important to retain the source of information than it is to reveal the violation. If so, it will be necessary to wait until complaining about the violation will not compromise the intelligence sources that detected the violations.

If it seems that the violations are not critical, but are still militarily significant, or that their cumulative impact will soon become militarily significant a state may decide to protest privately. If it protests, it will most likely receive one of the following reactions: (1) an explanation, apology, and correction of the violation; (2) an explanation that reveals the activity presumed to be a violation actually was not and the verification process erred; (3) an admission of the activity, but a denial that it constitutes a violation of the treaty; (4) outright denial that any such activity occurred or is occurring. In denying the activity, a violator may agree, or disagree, or ignore the question of whether or not such activity constitutes a violation.

Not all violations are symptomatic of larger trends, so either of the first two reactions (admissions) might not require any further response. In the case of either the third or fourth reaction (denials), a state must either accept the denial and reevaluate its assessment of the violation, or plan some further response. If a state believes its original assessment was correct and rejects the denial of the violation it may still decide to do nothing. Doing nothing, however, may encourage further and more significant violations. The state may decide to continue protesting privately, but if the protests are not accompanied by some sanctions the net result may be to create an even greater image of weakness.

Yet another response would be to publicly protest the violations in an attempt to use public opinion to pressure the violator into stopping its violations. This option is complicated by several factors. First, the violator will likely deny the allegations publicly as it did privately. It will be incumbent upon the accuser to prove the violations occurred. Unless evidence of the violations is unambiguous and easily presented, it may be difficult to convince public opinion that the violations took place.

In addition, the violator may try to distract the public and confuse the issue. For example, after Congress forced the Reagan administration to release a report on Soviet violations the USSR accused the United States of sabotaging the arms control process. Commenting on upcoming negotiations, a Soviet spokesman said:

> It is hard for us to trust in our partner's good will at the talks, if on the very eve of those talks an official paper is published in Washington, charging us with cheating and breaches of our previous treaty obligations, and a cynical campaign is organized to undermine confidence in all agreements, both existing ones and those which may be made in the future.[29]

Such complaints from an alleged violator can be very effective when public opinion wholeheartedly favors the arms control process. In this context one U.S. Congressman observed that "there is a widely held perception that arms control is more threatened by public discussion of violations than by the violations of the treaties themselves," and he noted the President of the United

States received more criticism for releasing the report than the Soviets did for breaking their commitments."[30]

In addition to public relations campaigns to counter the allegations of violations, a violator may also employ more elaborate disinformation measures. For example, when newsmen in 1935 reported that Italy was using poisonous gas against Ethiopians, the Italians successfully discredited the reports by secretly substituting the reporters' photographs with pictures of leprosy victims. These photos were published in the world press as evidence of gas warfare, but then discounted when prominent medical authorities revealed the victims were suffering from leprosy, not gas burns.[31] When the evidence is not wholly convincing the state which protested the violations may be accused of fabricating its charges in order to undermine the peace process.

If a state does not respond to violations it most likely will prefer to keep its concerns private in order not to give the impression that it is too weak to respond. For example, the Reagan administration, known for its distrust of the USSR, only released its report on Soviet violations at the behest of Congress in 1984 after several years of lobbying for the report by a group of conservative senators. Even then the report was released over State Department objections.[32]

If a government is determined to respond to treaty violations, it has essentially three options. First, it could continue to abide by the treaty while imposing sanctions commensurate with the detected violations. Such a tit-for-tat approach might not do much to deter future violations, but it would prevent the adversary from gaining a unilateral security advantage. Alternatively a state could respond to violations with stronger unilateral actions designed to convince the violator that violations are counterproductive to its security.

Third, if a state believed the violations were not likely to stop or had already severely undermined its security, it could simply abrogate the treaty and take whatever unilateral steps it considered necessary. Politically abrogation can be a difficult step to take. To publicly terminate a treaty, for whatever reason, is generally perceived as a step towards war. Consequently, states often prefer some alternative to abrogation such as unilateral steps to offset the violations while waiting for the treaty to expire. This is one reason some politicians and arms control experts advise negotiating treaties of short duration.

In summary, two alternative general preferences for dealing with violations may be identified. First, those who fear an arms race more than military inferiority usually rely on public opinion to deter violations. They believe responding to violations with sanctions will only end up fueling the arms race, and they tend to assume the motive for any violations, if they actually occurred, was a sense of insecurity on the part of the violator. This was the sentiment represented by twenty-three congressmen who wrote a letter to Soviet leaders in the spring of 1985 asking them to stop violating the SALT accords. They thought their appeal would be more fruitful than official U.S. complaints lodged in the Standing Consultative Committee (established by the

SALT I treaty to provide a forum for investigating complaints and resolving misunderstandings). They reasoned that the Soviets could not interpret their request as an attack on arms control per se since they all had long records of support for arms control agreements.

Alternatively many believe public opinion and protestations of goodwill have no efficacy whatsoever for preventing violations, and that only sanctions will succeed in convincing a violator that his security is better served by cooperation than by unilateral actions. The difficulty with this approach is determining what sanctions will convince another state to cooperate rather than retaliate. As with all alternative approaches to arms control and disarmament issues, these two differing sets of preferences for dealing with violations reflect different assessments of how best to achieve strategic stability.

WILL THE PROPOSED AGREEMENT ENHANCE STABILITY?

Strategic stability is often described as a condition reducible to a set of technical criteria, but it is really just a generic term for the desire to increase the chances of peace and reduce the potential for war. The technical criteria for stability can be discussed, but only after certain starting assumptions are accepted. Thus, this section will not review all the technical criteria for the stability of deterrence that were discussed in Part 2 of the book. Instead it will demonstrate how criteria for stabilizing agreements differ depending on whether one believes the greatest danger to stability in international political-military relations resides in arms per se, the arms race, or the way states configure and deploy their forces (national force postures).

Strengthening Stability by Improving Communication and Unilateral Safety Precautions

Most people agree there is a possibility that war can occur as a result of miscommunication between states which neither desire nor believe conflict is necessary. International agreements designed to illuminate the nonviolent intentions of states, such as the communication, administration, and confidence-building agreements mentioned in Chapter 2, are the standard remedies for reducing the risk of war through miscommunication. Few object to such measures, though some question their efficacy.[33]

Reducing the risks of accidental war resulting from a malfunction of some weapon's system or from some form of human technical error requires additional safeguards. There is a long and disturbing history of weapon malfunctions and accidents involving nuclear devices. In the past thirty years, a hydrogen bomb has been dropped by mistake, a missile site has caught fire, an ICBM warhead was blown out of its missile silo by accident, a ballistic missile submarine has been lost, and midair collisions have occurred with aircraft carrying nuclear weapons.

States can unilaterally implement any number of technical safety precautions to reduce the chances of nuclear accidents but some believe these measures are inadequate. In addition to the potential for technical and human errors, the threat of terrorist attacks on facilities that use or store nuclear materials is a constant concern. Some even worry that a meteor from outer space might collide with the earth, causing a nation to believe it had been attacked by a nuclear weapon and thus precipitating a nuclear war.

No amount of additional security precautions can guarantee that the worst will not happen, either through accident, miscalculation, natural disaster, or terrorism. Since this is true, many advocate complete nuclear disarmament as the only true prescription for stability. This preference for eliminating rather than controlling weapons points to a fundamental difference between disarmers and arms controllers on the meaning of stability.

Crisis and Strategic Stability

Disarmers consider the mere existence of weapons destabilizing, especially weapons of mass destruction, but they particularly fear the consequences of arms competition. They define stability as the *reduction* or *elimination* of weapons, not merely their "control":

> There is a need to create a downward momentum. Nations cannot confine their efforts to managing the existing high levels of armaments. Major reductions and constraints on qualitative "improvements" must be a dominant theme in future negotiations and agreements.[34]

Arms controllers show a greater concern with reducing incentives for surprise attack, and thus seek the elimination of conditions that might encourage a state to strike first in a crisis where the chances of war seemed high; conditions that might or might not require reducing the numbers of certain types of weapons. The veteran American arms control negotiator, Paul Nitze, has described crisis stability simply as

> a situation where, in a crisis threatening war, there would be no significant advantage to the side striking first, preempting, or launching from under indications of attack.[35]

Sometimes the differences between arms control and disarmament is equaled with the distinction between strategic stability and crisis stability.[36] Strategic stability requires stopping unrestrained armament competition between states (the arms race), whereas crisis stability is concerned with the more immediate goal of dissuading first strikes (primarily, but not exclusively stable deterrence). However, this distinction is not sufficiently subtle to explain the differences between arms control and disarmament. The associations between arms control and crisis stability, and disarmament and strategic stability exist but they are not exclusive.

It cannot automatically be assumed that disarmament is required for strategic stability, since it is at least theoretically possible to stabilize an arms race without major reductions in arms. Thus some arms controllers argue that the arms race is neither invariably a "race" nor a critical problem for strategic stability. Similarly it cannot be assumed that crisis stability is a simple matter of eliminating first-strike capabilities. Disarmers are also concerned with crisis stability, which they believe "major reductions in the more threatening or more vulnerable systems would enhance."[37] In short, arms controllers and disarmers may believe their policy preferences satisfy criteria for both *strategic* and *crisis* stability, and that an exclusive association between arms control and crisis stability, and disarmament and strategic stability, does not exist.

Disarming and Controlling

When considering the reduction or elimination of weapons, two questions must be addressed. First, it would make sense to begin reducing those weapons that are more offensive than defensive, and thus more threatening. This requires some rudimentary categorization of weapons as either offensive or defensive. Second, the disarmament negotiator must determine how far he wants to reduce the number of weapons. Depending on verification capabilities and other considerations, it may be that there is a point of diminishing returns on further reduction. For example, reducing the size of forces to relatively small numbers may require a higher state of force readiness, which would increase the risk of accidents.

Disarmers tend to assume, however, that existing stockpiles of weapons are so excessive that there is no need to worry about lower limits. For example George Kennan has received much attention for his proposal that the United States propose "an immediate across-the-board reduction by 50 percent of the nuclear arsenals now being maintained by the two superpowers." Other considerations would not be allowed to complicate this immediate objective:

> Whether the balance of reduction would be precisely even—whether it could be construed to favor statistically one side or the other—would not be the question. Once we start thinking that way, we would be back on the same old fateful track that has brought us where we are today. Whatever the precise results of such a reduction, there would still be plenty of overkill left—so much so that if this first operation were successful, I would then like to see a second one put in hand to rid us of at least two thirds of what would be left.[38]

Arms controllers view calls for indiscriminate reductions with alarm. Their concern is less with numbers per se than with controlling arms competition and preserving a combination of weapons that reduces the likelihood of preemptive or preventive war. The most immediate concern is with crisis stability, or reducing incentives to launch a first strike. However, they also see crisis stability as a means to strategic stability over time. Therefore arms controllers insist on a careful review of what comparative force postures would be left after reductions or the imposition of ceilings on armaments.

Transition Periods

The strong but not exclusive tendency of disarmers and arms controllers to focus, respectively, on the dangers of destabilizing arms competitions and destabilizing force postures is especially apparent in their differing concerns about periods of dramatic change in force postures. Whether the transition involves the development and deployment of a new military technology or the reduction of numbers of existing arms, the arms controller is concerned with ensuring that there are minimum incentives for surprise first strikes during and following the period of transition. Arms controllers are generally more open (or resigned) to new technologies. They usually want to manage or control the transition period rather than prevent it.

The disarmer, in contrast, almost automatically considers any transition designed to integrate a new military technology into a state's force posture as destabilizing because it is likely to elicit a response that will fuel the arms race. Similarly any transition to a lower number of weapons seems automatically stabilizing to the disarmer although, when and where possible, the disarmer would prefer to begin by reducing clearly offensive weapons.

The Offensive-Defensive Distinction

These differences between disarmers and arms controllers on how to strengthen crisis and strategic stability are often only a question of emphasis. Consider the following box chart:

COMPARATIVE FORCE POSTURES

STATE A'S FORCE POSTURE

		Offensive	Defensive
STATE B'S FORCE POSTURE	**Offensive**	#1 Highly Unstable	#2 Ambiguous Mix of Off. and Def. Capabilities
	Defensive	#3 Ambiguous Mix of Off. and Def. Capabilities	#4 Highly Stable

Both disarmers and arms controllers prefer box 4 over box 1, but as discussed in Part 2, there is a great deal of controversy over whether specific weapons and forces can be categorized as offensive or defensive (or first and second strike) or broadly configured for aggression or defense. The differing emphases of arms controllers and disarmers often reflect their varying degrees of optimism about the ability to distinguish offensive from defensive capabilities.

Disarmers are more confident that box 4 can be attained by the categorization of weapons than arms controllers. Disarmers seek to reduce the level of forces to a point where it is not possible to wage war against another state or to use the ubiquitous phrase of the 1920s and 1930s, "to the lowest point consistent with national safety." This goal presumes that offensive power can be limited without jeopardizing a "finite" defense and deterrence capability. Arms controllers, who tend to be less optimistic about the ability to distinguish categorically between offensive and defensive weapons, generally deny a lower level of arms necessarily reduces the likelihood of war. They believe it is only possible to maneuver in boxes 2 and 3, depending on a number of factors (for example, verification needs, the ability to control technology, and the nature of the weapons in question), some subject to manipulation and some not.

Summary

Both disarmers and arms controllers want national force postures that are nonthreatening yet capable of defending against or deterring attack. However, the disarmer is usually more concerned with numbers of weapons than their qualitative distinctions and combinations, whereas the arms controller is less concerned with numbers and more concerned with qualitative combinations as indicated in doctrine and deployment patterns. Thus the disarmer sets as his first priority halting and then reversing the arms race, both by stopping the development of all new weapons and by reducing the numbers of existing weapons or eliminating them entirely. His second priority is distinguishing between offensive and defensive weapons to the extent possible so that existing stocks of the former can be reduced first. The arms controller seeks not so much the reduction of old weapons or the prevention of new weapons and their development as the management of their deployment in a force posture that is nonthreatening to other states, but also quite capable of defending a state. Among themselves, arms controllers differ substantially as to how they believe this can best be accomplished, with some displaying much more sensitivity to the disarmer's fears of destabilizing arms races than others.

Negotiations presuppose a consensus on how stability is defined, yet for reasons explored above this consensus is not easily achieved. Whichever view of stability becomes state policy and the guiding purpose of negotiators is often determined in whole or in part by political factors that many people consider illegitimate, even if admittedly powerful, influences on the decision-making process.

DISCUSSION QUESTIONS

1. Is there a role for trust in the verification process?
2. In what circumstances should a state publically reveal evidence of treaty violations?
3. Would consistent public disclosure of suspected treaty violations strengthen or retard the arms limitation process?
4. Can overly stringent monitoring procedures be counterproductive? If so, how?
5. How might the distinction between offensive and defensive weapons affect the procedures necessary to monitor an agreement?
6. Considering current international political conditions and the state of world armaments, should crisis or strategic stability be a mere pressing concern?

SUGGESTED READINGS FOR CHAPTER EIGHT: CONSIDERATIONS FOR NEGOTIATING MUTUAL SECURITY

A. Verification, Compliance, and Cheating

BELLANY, IAN, and COIT D. BLACKER, eds. *The Verification of Arms Control Agreements.* London, Cass, 1984.
BILDER, RICHARD B. *Managing the Risks of International Agreements.* Madison: University of Wisconsin Press, 1981.
HAFEMEISTER, DAVID, JOSEPH J. ROMM, and KOSTA TSIPIS. "The Verification of Compliance with Arms Control Agreements." *Scientific American,* (March 1985), pp. 39–455.
HAFEMEISTER, DAVID W., PENNY JANEWAY, and KOSTA TSIPIS, eds. *Arms Control Verification: The Technologies That Make it Possible.* Washington: Pergamon-Brassey's 1986.
IKLE, FRED C. "After Detection—What?" *Foreign Affairs* (January 1961).
JASANI, BHUPENDRA, and FRANK BARNABY. *Verification Technologies: The Case for Verification by Consent.* Dover, NH: Berg Pub. for the Center for International Peacekeeping, 1984.
KATZ, AMRON H. *Verification and SALT: The State of the Art and the Art of the State.* Washington, DC: Heritage Foundation, 1979.
KRASS, ALLAN S. *Verification: How Much Is Enough?.* Stockholm International Peace Research Institute. London: Taylor and Francis, 1985.
LORD, CARNES. "Rethinking On-site Inspection in U.S. Arms Control Policy." *Strategic Review* 13 (Spring 1985).
MELMAN, SEYMOUR, ed. *Inspection for Disarmament.* New York: Columbia University Press, 1958.
MEYER, STEPHAN M. "Verification and Risk in Arms Control." *International Security* (Spring 1984).
POTTER, WILLIAM C., ed. *Verification and Arms Control.* Lexington, MA: Lexington Books, 1985.
The President's Unclassified Report to the Congress on Soviet Noncompliance with Arms Control Agreements. Washington, DC: Office of the Press Secretary, February 1, 1985.
ROWELL, WILLIAM F. *Arms Control Verification: A Guide to Policy Issues for the 1980s.* Cambridge: Ballinger, 1986.
TIMBERBAEV, R. M. *Problems of Verification.* Moscow: Nauka Pub., 1984.
U.S. CONGRESS, SENATE, COMMITTEE ON ARMED SERVICES. "Soviet Treaty Violations." Hearings, 98th Congress, 2nd Session, March 14, 1984. Washington, DC: Government Printing Office, 1984.
WRIGHT, SIR MICHAEL. *Disarm and Verify.* London: Chatto and Windus, 1964.

B. Stability

ALLISON, GRAHAM T., ALBERT CARNESALE, and JOSEPH S. NYE. *Hawks, Doves, and Owls: An Agenda for Avoiding Nuclear War.* New York: W. W. Norton, 1985.

BLAIR, BRUCE G. *Strategic Command and Control: Redefining the Nuclear Threat.* Washington, DC: Brookings, 1985.

BLECHMAN, BARRY M., ed. *Preventing Nuclear War: A Realistic Approach.* Bloomington: Indiana University Press, 1985.

BRACKEN, PAUL. *The Command and Control of Nuclear Forces.* New Haven: Yale University Press, 1983.

CALDER, NIGEL. *Nuclear Nightmares: An Investigation into Possible Wars.* New York: Viking Press, 1980.

JERVIS, ROBERT L. "Cooperation Under the Security Dilemma." *World Politics* 30 (1978): 167–215.

LEVY, JACK S. "The Offensive/Defensive Balance of Military Technology: A Theoretical and Historical Analysis." *International Studies Quarterly* 28 (June 1984).

NYE, JOSEPH S. "US-Soviet Relations and Nuclear Risk Reduction." *Political Science Quarterly* 99 (Fall 1984): 401–414.

SCHELLING, THOMAS C. "Confidence in Crisis." *International Security* 8 (Spring 1984): 55–66.

STEINBRUNER, JOHN D. "Nuclear Decapitation." *Foreign Policy* (Winter 1981–82): 16–28.

URY, WILLIAM L. *Beyond the Hotline: Crisis Control to Prevent Nuclear War.* Boston: Houghton Mifflin, 1985.

U.S. CONGRESS, SENATE, COMMITTEE ON FOREIGN AFFAIRS. "Nuclear Risk Reduction Centers." Report to Accompany Senate Resolution 329, 98th Congress, 2nd Session, Washington, DC: Government Printing Office, 1984.

NOTES

1. U.S. Congress, Senate, Subcommittee on Disarmament, *Disarmament and Security: A Collection of Documents, 1915-55,* Committee Print, 84th Congress, 2d Session, p. 188.

2. *The Political Testament of Cardinal Richelieu,* trans. Henry Bertram Hill (Madison, WI: University of Wisconsin Press, 1961), p. 101 and *Polyaenus's Stratagems of War,* trans. R. Shepherd (Chicago: Ares Publishers, 1914; reprint of the 1793 London edition), p. 45.

3. Salvador De Madariaga, *Disarmament* (New York: Coward McCann, Inc., 1929).

4. Sometimes there is confusion over the different meaning of the terms *monitoring, inspection, verification,* and *compliance.* Monitoring refers to the technical procedures implemented to determine if other states are abiding by an agreement, and usually implies means of detection removed from the territory of the state under surveillance. Monitoring can be conducted unilaterally or in cooperation with other states, including those being monitored. Inspection is a form of monitoring that usually connotes procedures based on access to the territory and military facilities of another state, which with the exception of spies, requires interstate cooperation. Verification is the process of producing a net assessment of whether another state is abiding by an agreement based on evidence collected from monitoring programs and political judgment. Compliance is the actual regulation of state behavior by state authorities to ensure that the state abides by the terms of an agreement.

5. Nicholas Sims, *Approaches to Disarmament* (London: Friends Peace and International Relations Committee, 1974), p. 26.

6. The Arms Control Agency Newsletter, quoted in Russell Warren Howe, *Weapons: The International Game of Arms* (Garden City, NY: Doubleday, 1980), p. 266.

7. The most frequently cited case for this point of view is Fred Charles Ikle's "After Detection—What?" *Foreign Affairs* (January 1961).

8. See Seymour Melman, ed., *Inspection for Disarmament* (New York: Columbia University Press, 1958).

Some believe, however, that progress in disarmament will make intrusive inspection techniques increasingly acceptable:

> The country that had successfully concealed a few nuclear weapons while the rest of the world had totally disarmed could blackmail all the rest. This discouraging thought can be countered, however, by the encouraging one that disarmament can progress only as fast as international confidence grows, and that with increasing confidence would come increasing acceptance of inspection and familiarity with its procedures; thus total disarmament and inspection would probably become possible simultaneously.

Jerome D. Frank, "Psychological Aspects of Disarmament and International Negotiations," in Burns H. Weston, ed., *Toward Nuclear Disarmament and Global Security: A Search for Alternatives* (Boulder, CO: Westview Press, 1984), p. 327.

9. "Arms Control Verification," Union of Concerned Scientists, Briefing Paper, 1985.

10. For a good brief review of various NTMs at the disposal of the United States, see "Monitoring the Soviet Military: Arms Control, Verification, and Treaty Compliance," *The Defense Monitor,* Vol. 14, No. 10 (Washington, DC: Center For Defense Information, 1985).

11. This unusual proposal was advanced during the 1960s, and is still considered realistic by some:

> The second approach to knowledge inspection is through direct interrogation of people who might know of violations. A scientist whose opinion must be respected believes that modern detection techniques using such physiological indices as changes in brain-wave patterns could be raised to a level of over 90 percent certainty; if so, this approach holds out substantial hope for checking the veracity of an official's public statements or statements to an adversary in negotiations. He would have to submit to the tests, of course, but since this would be part of the overall agreement, refusal to be tested would be a virtual admission of lying. Furthermore, a leader who suspected that his nation was about to be falsely accused could volunteer to undergo examinations.

Jerome D. Frank, "Psychological Aspects of Disarmament and International Negotiations," in Weston, *Toward Nuclear Disarmament,* p. 329.

12. James E. Dougherty, *How to Think About Arms Control and Disarmament* (New York: Crane, Russak and Co., 1973), p. 39.

13. Henry W. Forbes, *The Strategy of Disarmament* (Washington, DC: Public Affairs Press, 1962), p. 50.

14. Ibid., p. 67.

15. Dougherty, *How to Think,* p. 49. Soviet sensitivity to intrusive inspection techniques extends beyond its relations with the United States. Even though the USSR and United Nations are almost the only supporters of disarmament by budget limitations, when the United Nations came up with a standardized reporting system on military expenditures the Soviet Union objected, raising the old Western arguments about the incomparability of different states' defense expenditures. See Weston, *Toward Nuclear Disarmament,* p. 488.

16. For some optimistic accounts of new monitoring technologies, see Kosta Tsipis, ed., *Arms Control Verification: The Technology that Makes it Possible* (Washington: Pergamon-Brassey's, 1986) and David Hafemeister, Joseph J. Romm, and Kosta Tsipis, "The Verification of Compliance with Arms-Control Agreements," *Scientific American,* March 1985, pp. 39–45.

17. See "U.S. Detects Soviet's Smallest Nuclear Tests," *Washington Post,* August 10, 1985, p. A15, and "Test-Ban Cheaters Couldn't Prosper: Sophisticated Monitoring Raises the Need for a New Debate," *Los Angeles Times,* February 18, 1986.

18. See "Sea-based Missiles Defy Limiting," *Washington Post,* November 9, 1985, p. A8.

19. See "New Yorkers Sign Soviet Test Pact," *New York Times,* May 29, 1986, p. A3, and "U.S. Can See Test Sites, Soviets Offer," *Miami Herald,* August 30, 1986, p. 1.

20. For more on on-site inspection, see Carnes Lord, "Rethinking On-site Inspection in U.S. Arms Control Policy," *Strategic Review* 13 (Spring 1985): 45–51; and Richard Shearer, *On-site Inspection for Arms Control: Breaking the Verification Barrier* (Washington: National Defense University Press, National Security Monograph Series 84-7, 1984).

21. Howe, *Weapons,* p. 271.

22. The USSR obtained knowledge of the KH-11 (*KH* stands for "keyhole") from a CIA clerk. Soviet intelligence has compromised another type of U.S. spy satellite. Two years after its initial launch, Soviet spies obtained data on the Rhyolite satellite which was capable of listening to telemetry transmitted during Soviet missile tests. The Soviets subsequently began the encryption of their telemetry.

23. For additional sources on the general subject of verification, see: William F. Rowell, *Arms Control Verification: A Guide to Policy Issues for the 1980s* (Cambridge: Ballinger, 1986); Allan S. Krass, *Verification: How Much is Enough?* (London: Taylor and Francis, for the Stockholm International Peace Research Institute, 1985); William C. Potter, ed., *Verification and Arms Control* (Lexington, MA: Lexington Books, 1985); Bhupendra Jasani and Frank Barnaby, *Verification Technologies: The Case for Surveillance by Consent* (Dover, NH: Beng Publishers for the Center for International Peacebuilding, 1984); Ian Bellany and Coit D. Blacker, eds., *The Verification of Arms Control Agreements* (London: Cass, 1984); and for a Soviet view, R. M. Timerbaev, *Problems of Verification* (Moscow: General Editorial Board for Foreign Publications, Nauka Publishers, 1984).

24. *Polyaenus's Stratagems,* p. 258. For another similar example from this source, see p. 299, but for a more historically reliable case of a violation of the spirit, if not the letter, of an agreement, see Athens's treatment of its armistice with Sparta in 425 B.C. Thucydides, *The Peloponnesian War,* trans. Rex Warner (Middlesex, England: Penguin Books, 1954), pp. 277–278.

25. Some analysts trace allegations of superpower treaty violations to ambiguous wording in the treaties. See Strobe Talbott's analysis of Soviet violations in *Time,* June 23, 1986, p. 27, and "Monitoring the Soviet Military," *The Defense Monitor,* 1985 Vol. XIV, #10, p. 5, where Richard Perle is quoted as saying:

   If there were one single thing that one should do to improve verification, it would not be the addition of a new satellite or even the dispatch of inspectors to Soviet territory. It would be greater precision in the agreements themselves.

   Such precision can be elusive. As Richelieu long ago observed:

   The same words often have two meanings, depending on the one hand on the good faith and openness of men and on the other hand on their artfulness and subtlety. For those employing the latter it is very easy to twist the true meaning of a word into some preconceived interpretation. It is absolutely necessary, therefore, to utilize as negotiators those people who know the weight of words and how best to employ them in written documents.

   The Political Testament, pp. 98–99.

26. Congressman Les Aspin, quoted in Amron H. Katz, *Verification and SALT: The State of the Art and the Art of the State* (Washington, DC: Heritage Foundation, 1979), p. 21.

27. Forbes, *The Strategy of Disarmament,* p. 66.

28. See Katz, *Verification and SALT,* pp. 11–13. Some believe that there is a natural inclination to ignore evidence that other states are violating arms control agreements because violations threaten the validity of the entire arms control process, which is often considered a prerequisite for peace. Moreover, efforts to ensure the integrity of the arms control process may be politically and financially costly, and thus unpopular. For a specific example some arms control experts charge that U.S. intelligence estimates have been prejudiced by a desire not to sidetrack the SALT process. See Dr. William Van Cleave's testimony to the Senate Armed Services Committee, *Military Implications of the Proposed SALT II Treaty Relating to National Defense,* (Washington, DC: Government Printing Office, 1980), p. 1214; see also, p. 1251.

29. Dr. Georgi Arbatov, "On Soviet-American Relations," *International Studies Newsletter* 12, March 1985, from a speech delivered to the 26th Annual Convention of the International Studies Association. Many find the argument that violations and political atmosphere are interrelated convincing:

   Compliance questions are bound to arise even during periods of detente, because no arms control agreement can regulate every eventuality and because there will always be those who wish to pursue activities that are not expressly forbidden. In the current political environment the impulse to hedge bets at the expense of arms control agreements is far greater and the checks against doing so are weakened.

Michael Krepon, "Decontrolling the Arms Race: The U.S. and the Soviets Fumble the Compliance Issue," *Arms Control Today* 14 (March/April 1984): 1.

30. Jim Courter, Statement before the House Foreign Affairs Committee, July 25, 1984.

31. David Ziegler, *War, Peace and International Politics* (Boston: Little, Brown, 1981), p. 258. For a contemporary example with interesting parallels, see the case on Soviet use of chemical weapons in Robert L. Bartley and William Kucewicz, "Yellow Rain and the Future of Arms Agreements," *Foreign Affairs* (Spring 1983): 805ff.

32. As a general rule the Department of State is reluctant to see treaties abrogated because it believes abandoning a treaty removes the most significant means of available leverage. For an interesting account of historical continuity in the State Department's position, see the discussion on the State Department's reaction to a successful Jewish lobbying effort that obtained the abrogation of a seventy-nine-year-old Russian-American commercial treaty in 1911 in John Lewis Gaddis, *Russia, the Soviet Union and the United States: An Interpretive History* (New York: John Wiley and Sons, 1978), pp. 41–47. In contrast to the State Department, some argue that even if the abrogation of a treaty has no impact on another state's behavior, it is worthwhile for its sobering impact on public opinion and as a statement of political will. See George Will, "Yalta's False Promise," (c) *The Washington Post* January 6, 1985.

33. For a comprehensive review of various categories of unintentional conflict, see Daniel Frei, *The Risks of Unintentional Nuclear War* (Totowa, NJ: Rowan and Allanheld, 1983), p. 3. Frei's bibliography is a good source for studies on nuclear accidents and the risks and safeguards involved in modern weaponry.

34. Independent Commission on Disarmament and Security Issues," Elements of a Programme for Arms Control and Disarmament," In Weston, *Toward Nuclear Disarmament,* p. 405.

35. Quoted in Richard Nixon, *The Real War* (New York: Warner Books, 1980), p. 173.

36. For the distinction, see Frei, *The Risks of Unintentional Nuclear War,* p. x.

37. Noel Gayler, "How to Break the Momentum of the Nuclear Arms Race," Weston, *Toward Nuclear Disarmament,* p. 403.

38. George F. Kennan, "A Modest Proposal," in Weston, *Toward Nuclear Disarmament,* p. 394.

Chapter Nine

How Will Politics Affect Negotiations?

Once when a deputation visited Lincoln and urged emancipation before he was ready, he argued that he could not enforce it even if he proclaimed it.

"How many legs will a sheep have if you call the tail a leg?" asked Lincoln.

"Five," they answered.

"You are mistaken," said Lincoln, "for calling a tail a leg don't make it so."[1]

Calling international conferences arms control negotiations "don't make them so." There are numerous political factors that make negotiations something different than they appear to be at first glance.[2] The purpose of this chapter is to demonstrate how political forces that may seem extraneous to the publicly promulgated objectives of negotiators often influence the initiation, conduct, and outcome of meetings ostensibly convened to discuss specific areas of arms limitations. States take these political variables into account when they develop their negotiating strategies.

THE COMPARTMENTALIZATION
OF SECURITY CONCERNS

This section begins by discussing how a series of apparently independent arms control negotiations are linked by their broader political and security significance. In addition, the following set of examples will familiarize the student with the origins of some contemporary U.S. security concerns and provide background for further discussion.

Post–World War II United States-Soviet Negotiations

Concurrent with deteriorating U.S.-Soviet relations after World War II, the United States began plans for the defense of Western Europe against a Soviet attack. One of the first steps in this process was the formation of the North Atlantic Treaty Organization (**NATO**). Shortly after the ratification of the NATO Treaty in 1949, NATO analysts concluded that it would take roughly 96 NATO divisions (which were somewhat larger than those of the USSR) to counter the approximately 172 divisions of the Soviet Union. Meeting in Lisbon, in February of 1952, NATO ministers accepted the 96 division figure as a basis for military planning. It was not long, however, before it became apparent that the goal of 96 divisions could not be met.

Most NATO countries, still struggling to recover from World War II, were unable or unwilling to bear the fiscal and social burdens necessary for such a serious defense effort. As an alternative, it was decided that tactical nuclear weapons would have to be deployed as an additional deterrent to offset the imbalance in conventional forces. The rationale for the decision was summarized by then Secretary of State John Foster Dulles:

> The total costs of our security effort (and those of our allies) could not be continued long without grave budgetary, economic and social consequences. . . . The basic decision was to depend primarily upon a greater nuclear capacity to retaliate instantly by means and at places of our own choosing. As a result it is now possible to get and to share more basic security at less cost.[3]

By 1965, the United States had placed some seven thousand tactical nuclear weapons in Western Europe. From the European point of view, tactical nuclear weapons were a popular option at the time. With the United States possessing strategic nuclear superiority, it was inconceivable that the Warsaw Pact (the Soviet counterpart to NATO) would start a conventional war at the risk of nuclear war, and thus the deterrence value of tactical nuclear weapons seemed high and yet did not contribute unduly to fears that they would ever have to be used on European soil.

During the Kennedy administration, U.S. thinking on NATO doctrine began to change. The emphasis shifted from a strategy of massive nuclear retaliation to greater reliance on conventional defense capabilities. Western Europeans, however, still preferred reliance on nuclear weapons, which led to a heated intra-NATO debate. Finally a ''flexible response'' strategy was decided upon which provided for varying levels of both conventional and nuclear defense capabilities:

The West Europeans had feared that the risk of a conventional war confined solely to the European continent was increasing because of a U.S. desire to reduce the risk of a nuclear confrontation with the Soviet Union. Flexible response offered the notion of a seamless web of deterrence, emphasizing the likelihood that a conflict in Europe would turn into a superpower confrontation. NATO reached this compromise in 1967 after an acrimonious debate that had resulted in French withdrawal from NATO's integrated military command.[4]

Flexible response strategy was adopted but the building up of the conventional forces necessary to give the strategy meaning languished. Nothing had changed the dilemma confronted in Lisbon in 1952: How to deter the Soviets at a cost the West could afford without undue reliance on nuclear weapons. One possible solution to the dilemma was to see if the origins of the problem—the imbalance of forces in Europe—could be solved through negotiation.

At its ministerial meeting in Reykjavik in June 1968 NATO ministers decided to open up talks with the Soviet Union and Eastern Bloc countries in hopes that such negotiations would lead to a conventional force balance, thereby reducing reliance on tactical nuclear weapons without requiring an increase in defense spending for conventional weaponry.

The Soviet Union was slow to respond to NATO's initiative. It demanded a *quid pro quo* for negotiations on conventional forces in Europe, which it eventually received in the form of Western agreement to open negotiations that the USSR hoped would consolidate its territorial gains from World War II (these negotiations came to be called the Conference on Security and Cooperation in Europe, **CSCE**). The CSCE negotiations opened the way for the Mutual and Balanced Force Reduction (**MBFR**) talks on conventional forces in Europe, which began in Vienna in January, 1973.

The MBFR talks have not met with success. The two sides never have agreed on what forces should be counted or even on how many forces the USSR has deployed in Eastern Europe. Consequently, despite more than 15 years of negotiations on conventional armaments, NATO remains tied to its nuclear weapons for security. As hope for conventional arms reductions has faded, frustration and fear have grown, contributing to a rising tide of popular antinuclear sentiment in Europe.

Other factors also fueled antinuclear public protests. In 1979 the USSR invaded Afghanistan and the United States responded with a boycott of the Moscow Olympics and a grain embargo. As U.S.-Soviet relations hit a new all-time low, more and more Europeans began to fear that nuclear war between the two superpowers was possible, and considering the large number of tactical nuclear weapons stationed there, that such a war might begin in and even be limited to Europe.

At the same time public opinion was mobilizing against nuclear weapons on European soil, European leaders were becoming increasingly concerned about Soviet deployment of new theater nuclear weapons. Beginning in 1976–1977 the Soviet Union started deploying numerous SS-20 intermediate[5] range ballistic missiles which were capable of destroying European cities. Combined with the passing of U.S. nuclear superiority, this factor gave European leaders cause for alarm.

Prior to the 1970s, European leaders could count on the overwhelming nuclear advantage of the United States to protect them from a Soviet attack. But as the signing of SALT I in 1972 signaled, the Soviet Union had caught up with the United States in strategic nuclear forces. This "strategic parity" between the United States and the USSR meant their strategic weapons essentially offset one another, and the Europeans could no longer count on a U.S. strategic superiority to deter the USSR at lower levels of nuclear or nonnuclear competition. Hence, there had to be an offsetting parity at every level. When the Soviet Union began deploying intermediate range (INF) nuclear weapons (that is, SS-20 missiles capable of hitting Western Europe but not the United States) Western European leaders were concerned that an advantage in these INFs would allow the Soviets to threaten Europe while holding the United States at bay with its strategic arsenal.

As a result, West European leaders requested that the United States station new intermediate range forces in Europe to offset the new Soviet SS-20s and indicate to the USSR that the United States was still committed to the defense of Europe. NATO formally made the decision in December 1979 to accept 108 Pershing II and 460 ground launched cruise missiles (GLCM) which the United States had agreed to provide. Realizing the decision to deploy new INFs would meet resistance from elements of public opinion, NATO decided to present the decision as a "dual-track" approach to security; with Nato pursuing arms control and armament simultaneously.

NATO leaders suggested that if arms control negotiations were successful, the new intermediate-range missiles might not be necessary. To further soften the expected adverse public reaction to the news of the new INFs, NATO also announced the decision to unilaterally withdraw fifty-four nuclear-capable F4 aircraft, thirty-six older Pershing missiles, and one thousand nuclear warheads.

Despite NATO sensitivity to public opinion, the news of new missile deployments met significant public resistance. INF negotiations were not successful, and as the 1984 deployment date drew near, Europeans were taking to the streets in ever larger numbers to protest the new weapons. Antinuclear sentiment grew so strong that some governments of the nations that were to receive the weapons (Great Britain, Italy, Holland, Belgium, and Germany) were having second thoughts about proceeding with deployment.

Although the "peace movement" coalesced around opposition to the deployment of new INFs, there was widespread agreement from observers of many different political persuasions that the public protest was symptomatic of a more general fear of nuclear war. NATO politicians and officials recognized the surest way to reduce public fear was through progress in the second half of the 1979 dual track decision: arms control. Yet, as U.S. officials were fond of pointing out, progress in arms control was difficult when the Soviet Union had reason to believe West European public opinion might force NATO governments to unilaterally abandon their plans to match the Soviets' SS-20s with U.S. Pershings and GLCMs. This led to a dilemma.

While European leaders encouraged the United States to make progress in INF negotiations with the Soviet Union in order to shore up faltering public support, the United States encouraged West Europeans to stand firm on their decision to deploy the new INFs in order to elicit a reasonable negotiating attitude from the USSR. In short, a united NATO front was necessary for progress in the negotiations, but progress in the negotiations was politically necessary for maintaining a united front.

This dilemma led to a great deal of trans-Atlantic debate and acrimony. Out of all the controversy emerged two solutions to the dilemma that were especially popular.[6] The first solution was to reduce the deterrent value of nuclear weapons with a "no-first-use" policy (that is, declare that NATO would never use a nuclear weapon unless the Warsaw Pact did so first) or, more radically, unilaterally withdraw NATO's tactical nuclear weapons. Either of these options would require a substantial improvement in the conventional force balance to offset Warsaw Pact superiority and maintain stable deterrence. However, a conventional force balance would require very unpopular increases in defense spending, recognition of which led to the second solution, which was to conclude an MBFR agreement. Both proposed solutions made it clear that the basic security problem remained as defined in 1949—a Warsaw Pact conventional superiority which NATO prefers to offset with reliance on relatively inexpensive nuclear weapons rather than significant increases in defense spending.

Eventually, despite public opinion, the new NATO missiles were deployed in January 1984, and the Soviet Union walked out of both the INF and **Strategic Arms Reduction Talks (START)** in protest. Thus arms control negotiations at both the intermediate and strategic levels ground to a halt. Although the Soviet walkout only lasted until Ronald Reagan won reelection, the sequence of events ushered in the greatest amount of pessimism about the prospects for strategic arms control since the late 1950s.

The disappointing record of superpower arms control efforts did not go unnoticed by third world countries. As mentioned in Chapter 2, one of the key provisions of the NPT was the assurance to nonnuclear (mostly third world) countries that the United States and the Soviet Union intended "to achieve at the earliest possible date the cessation of the nuclear arms race and to undertake effective measures in the direction of nuclear disarmament." The continuing superpower nuclear arms competition has been used by some states to justify their refusal to sign the treaty. For example, India has expressed the sentiment that "the NPT seeks to disarm the unarmed while allowing the armed to keep arming."[7]

Nonnuclear countries that *have* signed the treaty have repeatedly reminded the superpowers of their commitment to disarmament. In May 1975 at a review of the NPT, twenty small nonnuclear NPT signatories requested that the United States, the USSR, and Britain suspend underground nuclear tests when NPT ratifications reached one hundred, and that the United States and the USSR decrease their nuclear arsenals by 10 percent for every ten new NPT signatories over a hundred. Neither the United States nor the USSR accepted this proposal for automatic linkage between horizontal and vertical arms limitation.[8]

The preceding topics, ranging from a regional security concern in Europe to the global security problem of nuclear proliferation, demonstrate how ostensibly separate arms control negotiations are linked by international and domestic political considerations and security needs. The conventional balance and MBFR negotiations are linked to public concern over nuclear arms and increases in defense spending, and also are considered possible antidotes to public protests over INF deployments and negotiations. In turn, INFs are linked to the advent of superpower strategic nuclear parity, codified in SALT I and at issue in the START negotiations, which are linked to the NPT and nonnuclear nations' concerns about vertical proliferation.

Thus while a nation's security may be compartmentalized for purposes of administration, discussion, or negotiating convenience, in reality it resists dissection. This is why arms control initiatives cannot fully be understood in isolation from one another or removed from their political context. It does not necessarily follow, however, that all arms control issues should be negotiated in one forum.

The Debate over the Preferred Scope for United States-Soviet Negotiations

When interest in arms control began to spread in the early 1960s, many of those theorizing on the subject concluded it was too much to expect the United States and the Soviet Union to settle all or even most of their differences in a single peace agreement. Conventional wisdom advised approaching security issues on a piecemeal basis, accepting limited improvements in the short term in order to build precedents for more significant agreements in the future. The idea was to build up a momentum toward mutual trust.

More than two decades later this consensus has been shattered. With thousands of negotiations in dozens of forums producing scant results, many arms control enthusiasts are now advocating a general approach:

> We should take all the pieces and put them back together in one package. . . . The piecemeal approach we've taken so far hasn't worked. We need to start with a broad framework that we discuss privately with the Russians and then approach individual negotiations within that framework.[9]

According to one advocate of the broad scope approach:

> It is impossible to see how anything can be accomplished without ultimately treating the issues of nuclear arms and arms control in their entirety. There is simply not enough room for bargaining and tradeoffs if things are to be fought out separately in different arenas.[10]

In contrast to those who support a broader scope for negotiations, others advise even "smaller scale, more manageable agreements" than have been attempted in the past. They argue that

> The more you go comprehensive, the more difficult it is to get any deal, because you link intractable issues with ones that may be tractable.[11]

These two sets of opinions are diametrically opposed; the first assumes more inclusive negotiations will loosen up the bargaining process by incorporating more areas for trade-offs, and the second argues a broader agenda will drag in areas of irreconcilable differences and stalemate the negotiations. Implicitly, the piecemeal approach assumes that negotiations can be conducted on primarily a technical basis and that each side has the same overall objectives. The broader approach is in keeping with the "moral disarmament" tradition which assumes states need to resolve broad outstanding political differences before progress can be made in areas requiring more technical security cooperation.

The broader approach to defining the scope of security negotiations raises the issue of **linkage**. The term "linkage" may have several different meanings in foreign policy literature, but here it refers particularly to whether or not willingness to negotiate on arms control should be linked to the behavior of an adversary in other areas of foreign policy.

Linkage

In the past the United States has demonstrated more sensitivity to linkage than the USSR. The United States postponed arms control negotiations after the Soviet invasion of Czechoslovakia in 1968, and scuttled the SALT II treaty after the Soviet invasion of Afghanistan in 1979. In contrast, the Soviet Union has apparently considered arms control negotiations an item separate from other areas of foreign policy. In 1972, shortly before a major summit between President Nixon and Soviet leader Brezhnev devoted primarily to arms control, the United States launched a massive B-52 attack on North Vietnam's Haiphong harbor, accidentally hitting four Soviet ships and killing some Soviet sailors. Domestic critics of the Nixon administration argued that this would force the USSR to cancel the summit meeting, but this did not happen.

Despite U.S. sensitivity about linkage, there is no consensus in U.S. foreign policy circles on the matter. To explain the linkage controversy, it will be useful to use two common designations for opposing foreign policy groups: "hawks" and "doves." In general, foreign policy doves are those who believe the greatest threat to national security is lack of cooperation between the two superpowers and the consequent danger of unrestrained arms competition. Hawks, in contrast, believe the greatest dangers to national security are the aggressive intentions of adversary states.

Neither hawks nor doves are of one mind on the issue of linkage. On the one hand, doves consider the spiraling arms race the greatest danger to peace, and consequently many believe little else should be allowed to stand in the way of attempts to negotiate its termination. The following comments by Senator Edward Kennedy are representative:

> And so we say that we dare not misuse what is wrong in the Soviet system as an excuse for denying what is right in Soviet-American relations—which is the overriding imperative of nuclear arms control. . . . An arms control treaty will not tame Soviet misconduct in other areas. And the refusal to negotiate such an agreement, even when it is in our national interest, will not free Afghanistan or break the repression in Poland. In short, we cannot punish the Russians by raising the risk of nuclear war. We hear about linkage—but we must not forget our fundamental common link as people on this planet—that we shall all live or die together.[12]

While doves would not hold arms control negotiations hostage to Soviet behavior in other areas, they would insist on the reverse; that is, they would contend that U.S. behavior should be recognized as having an impact on Soviet willingness to negotiate. In particular, they frequently argue that it is necessary to be flexible and conciliatory in order to encourage moderate elements in the adversary's government. Thus many doves chastized President Reagan for simultaneously professing eagerness for arms control and characterizing the Soviet Union as an "evil empire."[13]

Those doves who object to linkage either feel sure the USSR has no aggressive designs on the United States or feel that nuclear arms control overrides all other considerations. Other doves, less sure of Soviet intentions, may see arms control as a means of testing Soviet motivations. By being flexible in negotiations and allowing some ambiguous wording to conceal unresolved differences, an adversary can be tested for compliance with the spirit of the agreement. With this approach, moderate doves support linkage; that is, they consider Soviet behavior in other areas to be a critical index of the USSR's worthiness as a negotiating partner in arms control. Thus overtly hostile Soviet actions may lead these doves to feel as though their good intentions and willingness to give the USSR "the benefit of the doubt" have been betrayed.

The Soviet invasion of Afghanistan constituted such a betrayal in the minds of many dovish congressional representatives. Those in Congress who were previously willing to overlook some hawkish concerns about verification and accept SALT II as a reasonable approximation of a strategic balance, suddenly rejected the treaty *in toto* after the Soviet invasion.

Like doves, hawks were of two minds on the issue, with some supporting and others ignoring linkage. Moderate hawks, or those entertaining some doubts about whether cooperation with the USSR is at all possible, tend to support linkage. In reference to SALT II, they may have been willing to accept the treaty as a means of testing Soviet interest in strategic stability, moderating the ambitions of the Soviet regime, and stabilizing or even eliminating a dangerous nuclear arms competition. But those hawks who already had classified the USSR as hostile and aggressive could not feign surprise and anger over the invasion of Afghanistan. These hawks had never supported linkage as a means of testing Soviet intentions, which they professed to understand. Hence the SALT II negotiations made no sense except as a calculated move to enhance U.S. security, and they could hardly argue that it made sense to discard the treaty because the enemy chose to continue the struggle in other forums.[14] Thus hard-line hawks who were displeased with the agreement in the first place simply used the invasion as a convenient tool for dismantling remaining political support for the treaty.

Some hardline hawks do support linkage, but not as a means of testing Soviet intentions. Instead, they see linkage as useful for negotiating leverage. They argue that if the USSR wanted a treaty or negotiations more than the United States, then the United States could try to link the treaty to other foreign policy concerns and extract additional concessions or moderate Soviet behavior. Both Presidents Nixon and Reagan, generally acknowledged as quite hawkish, have proclaimed their support for linkage, apparently with this thought in mind, or with the thought that linking arms control with other political issues would emphasize the necessity of resolving outstanding political differences before arms control could be really meaningful.[15] Yet with respect to the value of the treaty per se, all staunch hawks either support an unambiguous treaty on its own merits as a contribution to U.S. security, regardless of Soviet behavior in other areas, or they do not support the treaty at all.

Much of the debate about linkage stems from uncertainty or differences of opinion about the negotiating intentions of other states. Hawks tend to assume the worst, doves the best, and moderates of both camps usually favor testing intentions. However one looks at the issue, there is little doubt that the compatability of negotiating goals is the most important factor influencing the likelihood of successful negotiations.

Alternative Goals for Negotiations

A state can negotiate on arms control and disarmament for basically three reasons. First, it may negotiate because it wants agreement and believes it is possible on a number of procedures and mutual commitments that will enhance the security of all states that are parties to the agreement. Second, a state may desire an agreement that will enhance its security by obtaining more favorable terms for itself than for the other signatories. Third, a state may seek not so much an improvement in its own security as a reduction in the security of other states so that they will be more vulnerable.[16]

These goals, respectively, may be referred to as stability, defense, and aggression. Only the first goal, stability, presumes negotiations can be a positive-sum endeavor, that is, one in which all the participants may emerge better off. The last two goals assume international arms limitations agreements are "zero-sum games" in which the needs of the participants are necessarily at odds and inversely proportionate. The third goal is obviously more ominous for prospects of peace than the second.

It is also apparent that the opportunity for productive negotiations is best when all participants desire stability. States must consider each of these three possibilities, and combinations thereof, since it is possible to have different goals for different sets of negotiations. For example, a state may seek a security advantage in one area, but stability in another, and this too must be considered by those looking for negotiating opportunities.

Unfortunately, the negotiating intentions of other states are often obscure. One important reason for this is that intentions are a composite of numerous domestic forces rather than one collective will.

DOMESTIC FORCES AND NATIONAL DECISION MAKING

A great deal has been written on the effects of domestic political forces on the course of negotiations.[17] Here it will be possible to describe the various types of domestic political forces that can influence the negotiating process only briefly in order to alert students to the danger of automatically assuming that states negotiate with one voice or with one concept of their national interest.

Political Systems and Cultures

Writing in the 1630s, the French statesman, Cardinal Richelieu, observed:

> Different nations have different characters, some quickly carry out what they have in mind, while others walk with feet of lead. Republics are in this latter category. They proceed slowly and one ordinarily does not get from them at first attempt what is sought. Rather it is necessary to be content with little in the hope of getting more later. For this reason it is wise to negotiate painstakingly with them in order to give them time, and to press them only when they are ready for it.[18]

Virtually all great statesmen, both before and since Richelieu, have noted that negotiating styles must be tailored to a negotiating partner's political system and culture.

Republics, or representative governments, for example, are encumbered by a more complex decision-making process, and as Richelieu observed, this can delay and hinder negotiations. The erratic history of U.S. arms control negotiations is illustrative. The United States has negotiated agreements which the Senate then refused to ratify or for which the Senate significantly delayed ratification, for example, the Covenant of the League of Nations, the Threshold Test Ban Treaty, and SALT II. As one observer has remarked:

> The key fact, as the *New Republic*'s Richard Strout has recently commented, is that "In a Congress of 535 members, 33 Senators plus one can block a treaty." This may be, as Strout remarks, "a queer system." But it is the system nonetheless.

President Carter echoed this sentiment, noting that the SALT II accords required as much negotiation within the United States as with the USSR.[19]

In other words, even if the negotiators reach agreement, the battle may be only half won. Following the conclusion of the 1930 naval talks in London, an American spokesman gushed:

> I can't too strongly impress upon you the fine spirit in which the Japanese and British have met us. There was no disposition to quibble on the part of any one of the three delegations. . . . I can't imagine a pleasanter negotiation than it has been. The result is not a victory for anyone, but an honorable and reasonable settlement between the three.[20]

Some very influential domestic politicians saw the results of the negotiations in an altogether different light, however:

> *Frederick Hale (before the U.S. Senate):* The British by the terms of this treaty have us hamstrung and hog-tied and there will keep us as long as limitations of armaments are the order of the day.

> *Winston Churchill (before the House of Commons):* I am astonished that any Admiralty board of naval officers could have been found to accept responsibility for such a hamstringing stipulation.

> *T. Inukai (before the Japanese Diet):* [the government has] betrayed the country by entering into an agreement at the London Conference inadequate for Japan's needs.[21]

In addition to resistance to (and pressure for) arms control treaties from domestic legislators, representative governments must also maneuver weapons programs through their legislative bodies, a requirement that often influences the negotiating process.

As Richelieu also noted, patience often pays off in negotiations with a representative government. There are several reasons why this is so. As a lengthy and comprehensive study by the Congressional Research Service on lessons from the history of U.S.-Soviet negotiations noted, the less centralized, more individualistic American negotiators usually display more initiative in negotiations. The willingness to cease the initiative can become a disadvantage, though, when confronted with the recalcitrance for which Soviet negotiators are justly famous. As American negotiators try new proposals out on their Soviet counterparts, they come closer and closer to the danger of self-negotiation, that is, churning out ever more conciliatory negotiating positions in hopes of finding one acceptable to the Soviets.[22]

Moreover, representative governments can experience frequent leadership changes which interrupt the negotiating process. In the four decades since World War II, the United States has had nine presidents, while the USSR, before a series of deaths in the 1980s racked the Politburo, had only three leaders, Stalin, Khrushchev and Brezhnev. Also, during the long tenure of the USSR's Foreign Minister, Andrei Gromyko, the United States had ten Secretaries of State. Even if a U.S. President manages to win reelection, two of his four years of office are not prime negotiating years. The first year is lost to the necessary starting-up costs involved in transferring the reins of power from one administration to the next, and the fourth year the President is absorbed in reelection politics.

In the past, election campaigns have hurt the possibility for negotiations. In 1956 Adlai Stevenson charged that President Eisenhower had allowed the Russians to forge ahead of the United States and open up a "bomber gap," and four years later during his run for the presidency, John F. Kennedy made the same claim in reference to a "missile gap." Neither claim was true (in fact the United States held a lead in both cases) but the controversy precluded any negotiations with the USSR. However, an upcoming election can hasten negotiations if a president prefers to make concessions in order to obtain an agreement that would be popular with the electorate.

Public Opinion

Public opinion is another factor that can influence negotiations. For example, if public opinion is hostile toward nondemocratic governments it may be difficult for elected representatives to start, much less conclude, negotiations. It is frequently noted that Eisenhower and Nixon, the two U.S. Presidents responsible for opening negotiations with the two largest communist powers, respectively the USSR and the People's Republic of China, were conservatives with long public records of anticommunist sentiments. Many believe that without their popularity with the conservative American public these negotiations would not have been impossible.

On the other hand, if the public is strongly disposed toward negotiations, other states can try to manipulate this sentiment to their advantage. As a nineteenth century Russian historian once remarked:

> From time immemorial, the idea of disarmament has been one of the most favored forms of diplomatic dissimulation of the true motives and plans of those governments which have been seized with a sudden "love of peace." This phenomenon is very understandable. Any proposal for the reduction of armaments could invariably count upon broad popularity and support from public opinion.[23]

The USSR has skillfully used Western public opinion in support of its negotiating positions. Sometimes the USSR is able to accomplish what it could not prevent through negotiations (for example, its successful campaign against the neutron bomb in the 1970s) but other times it only succeeds in complicating the Western decision-making process. The massive Soviet effort to influence Western public opinion against new INFs—including walkouts from both the INF and START negotiations—eventually came to naught, but only after causing serious intra-NATO turmoil and dissension.

In response to the Soviet efforts, the United States also turned to "public diplomacy." Popular but less than serious negotiating proposals were batted back and forth across the Atlantic by Soviet and American leaders as they wooed West European public opinion. Brezhnev promised a moratorium on new Soviet INFs already being deployed if NATO would abandon plans for its INFs, and Reagan countered with a proposal to eliminate all INFs (the "zero option"). Meanwhile, observers in Geneva reported that despite protestations to the contrary, serious negotiations were postponed while both the United States and the USSR courted public opinion and waited to see if public protest would succeed in sidetracking the deployment of the new INFs.

Perhaps learning from the INF experience, some Reagan administration officials apparently decided that the principal utility of agreeing to negotiate with the USSR is to maintain public support for defense programs. This is not a new conclusion. Previous administrations have seen that while representative governments may be subject to public pressure while negotiating, they also can use negotiations to thwart unwanted influence from public opinion. For example, many knowledgeable observers of the MBFR talks agree that NATO's principal motive for initiating the talks was the desire to stave off public demands in America for the reduction of U.S. troop levels in Europe and public demands in Europe for reductions in defense spending. NATO governments have repeatedly countered such pressure by arguing that the reductions would undercut NATO negotiators in the MBFR talks, since the USSR cannot be expected to agree to commensurate reductions if it seems that the West is willing to make unilateral concessions anyway.

Bureaucracies

Bureaucracies play an influential and well-documented role in negotiating arms control agreements. In the United States the **Arms Control and Disarmament Agency (ACDA)**, the Departments of State and Defense, the Joint

Chiefs of Staff, and the National Security Agency all have a chance to influence the negotiating process. As Steven Miller notes:

> The structure of the game is simple: each of the organizations involved will seek, within the limits of its influence and effectiveness in the bureaucratic politics of the situation, to preserve its own interests or, at the least, to avoid having them badly violated.
>
> Herein lies the crux of the problem. For while it is commonly said arms control and military policy are compatible and indeed ought to be integrated, the fact is that the *practice* of arms control, whether as a process or in the particulars of a given agreement, can and usually does affront the interests of some of the players in the game.[24]

The importance of a bureaucracy to lobby for or against agreements is well recognized in Washington. The ACDA was set up as a counter to the Department of Defense and for the express purpose of lobbying for arms control. Recent successful lobbying for the "U.S. National Peace Institute" was similarly designed to give proponents of arms limitation more weight in the bureaucratic battles constantly waged in the nation's capital.

It is commonly observed that top Soviet leadership must actively enter the negotiation process to overcome bureaucratic inertia, and while this is sometimes true for the United States as well, it is more often the case that a U.S. president must simply play bureaucratic forces off against one another and insulate the negotiating process from their influence as much as possible. If the president can do this successfully, the opinion of a few key individuals can become critically important.

INDIVIDUALS

> It is absolutely necessary to be discerning in the choice of ambassadors and other negotiators, and one cannot be too severe in punishing those who exceed their authority, since by such misdeeds they compromise the reputation of princes as well as the fortunes of states. The irresponsibility or corruptness of some minds is sometimes so great and the consuming ambition of others, who are neither weak nor bad, to accomplish something is often so keen that unless they are held within bounds prescribed for them in terms of fear and the threat of utter condemnation, there will always be some who allow themselves to be drawn into the making of a bad treaty rather than none at all.

Cardinal Richelieu went on to conclude that "I have had so many experiences with this truth that . . . I must say that anyone who lacks the necessary devotion to the welfare of the state will fail to be rigorous in such matters."[25] As Richelieu notes, individuals can play an important role in negotiations, and thus the beliefs and ambitions of key policy-makers merit close attention from students of arms control and disarmament. Both ancient and modern examples attest to the importance of individual decision makers. During a war between

Fig. 9.1 **Richelieu believed that individual negotiators could make a significant difference, a viewpoint that his own illustrious career helped substantiate.** (Source: The National Gallery, London)

the Spartans and the Athenians in the fifth century B.C. two Athenians played important roles in thwarting and facilitating negotiations with the Spartans. After six years of war and an Athenian victory at the island of Pylos the Spartans were ready to negotiate a peace treaty. However, an Athenian named Cleon, who opposed a negotiated settlement, demanded extraordinary concessions from the Spartans as a preliminary to negotiations. The Spartans naturally refused, thereby allowing Cleon to convince his fellow citizens that the Spartans were unwilling to negotiate with sincerity.

The war dragged on for four more years until Cleon was killed and another Athenian general and statesman, by the name of Nicias, decided that peace would be beneficial. The Greek historian Thucydides records that

> While still untouched by misfortune and still held in honor, Nicias wished to rest upon his laurels, to find an immediate release from toil and trouble both for himself and his fellow citizens, and to leave behind him the name of one whose service to the state had been successful from start to finish. He thought that these ends were to be achieved by avoiding all risks and by trusting oneself as little as possible to fortune, and that risks could be avoided only in peace.[26]

Nicias succeeded in negotiating an agreement that subsequently bore his name.

Interestingly, in the Reagan administration two prominent personalities were characterized as modern-day alter egos of Cleon and Nicias. Assistant

Secretary of Defense Richard Perle, was called the man "who did as much as any American to doom detente during the 1970s." He was characterized by arms control advocates as the single most significant roadblock to further progress on negotiating arms control agreements.[27] In contrast, Paul Nitze was cast in the role of Nicias. Nitze had a long and distinguished career during which he earned a reputation as an unyielding hawk. Yet some hard-liners in the Reagan administration suspected that he had moderated his views and was willing to compromise with the USSR in order to secure a treaty as a grande finale to his professional career.[28]

It is not so important whether these characterizations are accurate or not. Perle would no doubt deny the association with Cleon, whom Thucydides described as a deceptive manipulator of public opinion, and Nitze has scoffed at the allegation of personal motives for obtaining a treaty with the USSR. The reason the parallel is interesting is that it underscores the undeniable fact that individuals matter in politics, including the politics of negotiating arms control treaties. This is why appointments of senior officials are often subjected to intense scrutiny by ideological opponents in the Senate. For example, President Carter's nomination of Paul Warnke as head of the ACDA unleashed a storm of criticism from conservatives who argued that Warnke's understanding of the USSR was naive. Many Reagan appointees, including Perle, met with similar opposition from Senate liberals.

CONCLUDING REMARKS

Those with high hopes for arms control and disarmament negotiations may find political forces and their influence on negotiations disillusioning. It is true that political factors can complicate the negotiating process, but they do not necessarily represent insurmountable problems. In fact, at times extraneous political forces can facilitate arms control. The oldest known disarmament treaty was reportedly the result of personal ambition and domestic political forces that induced otherwise unwilling states to meet and talk.

According to Tso K'iu-ming, a pupil of Confucious, in 546 B.C. the principal powers in China held a disarmament conference:

> A statesman of Ho Nan, being on friendly terms with his colleagues of Shan Si and Hu Peh, conceived the idea of making a name for himself by proposing a cessation of armaments. He went first to Shan Si, and interviewed the Premier there; the Premier consulted his colleagues in the Shan Si ministry, and one of them said: "War is ruinous to the people, and a fearful waste of wealth; it is the curse of the smaller Powers. Although the idea will come to nothing, we must consent to a conference; otherwise Hu Peh will consent to it first, in order to gain favour with the Powers, and thus we shall lose the predominant position we now occupy." So Shan Si consented.
> Then Hu Peh was visited, and also consented. Then Shan Tung. Shan Tung did not like the idea; but one of the Shan Tung ministers said: "Shan Si and Hu

Peh have agreed, and we have no help for it. Besides, the world will say that there would be a cessation of armaments were it not for our refusal, and thus our own people will vote against us. What is the use of that?'' So Si also consented. Then the whole four great powers notified the minor states, and a great durbar was held at a minor court in Ho Nan.[29]

Even with these inauspicious beginnings, prompted by hopes of personal glory, fear of public opinion, and calculations of political advantage, the conference was a success insomuch as it brought an end to seventy-two years of war between Shan Si and Shen Si.

One may always hope for such serendipity, yet it is safe to say the chances for preventing war and securing peace are better when leaders specifically set out to accomplish these goals. The last three chapters discussed nine basic issues that must be addressed when negotiating arms limitation agreements. The next part of the book examines why there is so much disagreement on how—and whether—these issues can be resolved.

DISCUSSION QUESTIONS

1. If outstanding political differences could be resolved through negotiations, would there by any reason for arms limitation agreements?
2. If outstanding political differences cannot be resolved through negotiations, of what value are short-term limited arms limitation agreements?
3. Is public opinion a positive or negative influence on arms limitation negotiations?
4. Who should determine a state's negotiating strategy?
5. What are the advantages and disadvantages to short-term arms limitation agreements.
6. Do certain political systems or cultures have inherent negotiating advantages or disadvantages?

SUGGESTED READINGS FOR CHAPTER NINE: HOW WILL POLITICS AFFECT NEGOTIATIONS?

A. On U.S. Security and NATO

BUNDY, MCGEORGE, GEORGE F. KENNAN, ROBERT S. MCNAMARA, and GERARD SMITH. "Nuclear Weapons and the Atlantic Alliance." *Foreign Affairs* (Spring 1982): 753–768.
HOFFMAN, STANLEY. "New Variations on Old Themes." *International Security* 4 (Summer 1979): 88–107.
KAISER, KARL, GEORGE LEBER, ALOIS MERTES, and FRANZ-JOSEF SCHULZE. "Nuclear Weapons and the Preservation of Peace: A German Response to No First Use." *Foreign Affairs* (Summer 1982): 1157–1170.
PIERRE, ANDREW J., ed. *Nuclear Weapons in Europe.* New York: Council on Foreign Relations, 1984.
RUEHL, LOTHAR. "The Slippery Road of MBFR," *Strategic Review* (Winter 1980).

SABIN, PHILIP A. G. "Should INF and START be Merged? A Historical Perspective." *International Affairs* 60 (Summer 1984): 419–428.
SHARP, JANE M. "Arms Control and Alliance Commitments." *Political Science Quarterly* 100 (Winter 1985–86): 649–667.
STEINBRUNER, JOHN D., and LEON V. SIGNAL. *Alliance Security: NATO and the No-First Use Question.* Washington: Brookings, 1983.

B. On Domestic Decision Making and Arms Limitation

ALLISON, GRAHAM T. "What Fuels the Arms Race?" In Robert L. Pfaltzgraff, ed. *Contrasting Approaches to Strategic Arms Control.* Lexington, MA: Lexington Books, 1974.
BRAUCH, HANS GUENTER, and DUNCAN L. CLARKE, eds. *Decisionmaking for Arms Limitation.* Cambridge: Ballinger, 1983.
NEWHOUSE, JOHN. *Cold Dawn: The Story of SALT.* New York: Holt, Rinehart and Winston, 1973.
PAYNE, SAMUEL B. *The Soviet Union and SALT.* Cambridge: MIT Press, 1980.
SMITH, GERARD. *Doubletalk: The Story of SALT I.* New York: Doubleday, 1980.
TALBOTT, STROBE. *Deadly Gambits: The Reagan Administration and the Stalemate in Nuclear Arms Control.* New York: Alfred A. Knopf, 1984.
———. *Endgame: The Inside Story of SALT II.* New York: Harper and Row, 1980.
U.S. CONGRESS, HOUSE COMMITTEE ON FOREIGN AFFAIRS. *Fundamentals of Nuclear Arms Control, Part V.* "The Internal Dynamics of U.S. Nuclear Arms Control Policymaking." Report prepared for the Subcommittee on Arms Control, International Security and Science by the Congressional Research Service. Washington, DC: Government Printing Office, 1986.

C. On Domestic Forces and the Conduct of Diplomacy

CLARKE, DUNCAN L. *Politics of Arms Control: The Role and Effectiveness of the Arms Control and Disarmament Agency.* New York: Free Press, 1979.
DESTLER, I. M. "National Security Management: What Presidents Have Wrought." *Political Science Quarterly* (Winter 1980–1981).
HASS, RICHARD. "Congressional Power: Implications for American Security Policy." Adelphi Paper 153. London: International Institute for Strategic Studies, 1979.
MILLER, STEVEN E. "Politics Over Promise: Domestic Impediments to Arms Control." *International Security* 8 (Spring 1984): 67–90.
SLOSS, LEON, and M. SCOTT DAVIS. *A Game for High Stakes: Lessons Learned in Negotiating with the Soviet Union.* Cambridge: Ballinger, 1986.
U.S. CONGRESS, HOUSE COMMITTEE ON FOREIGN AFFAIRS. *Soviet Diplomacy and Negotiating Behavior: Emerging New Context for U.S. Diplomacy.* Vol. 1. Committee Print prepared by the Congressional Research Service, Library of Congress. Washington, DC: Government Printing Office, 1979.
U.S. CONGRESS, SENATE COMMITTEE ON LABOR AND HUMAN RESOURCES. "United States Academy of Peace Act." Hearings. 97th Congress, 2nd Session, April 21, 1982. Washington, DC: Government Printing Office, 1982.

NOTES

1. Taken from Edmund Fuller, *2500 Anecdotes for All Occasions* (New York: Dolphin Books, 1961), p. 97.
2. Since negotiating has value as a political statement, even the decision to open arms limitation talks and their general content are subject to preliminary negotiations. See Dusko Doder, "Chernenko Says U.S. Holds Key to Arms Talks," *Washington Post,* October 17, 1984, and "Spaced Out," *Time,* August 13, 1984, p. 27.

3. Robert McNamara, "The Military Role of Nuclear Weapons: Perceptions and Mispercepti-ons" *Foreign Affairs* (Fall 1983): 60–61.

4. Laurence Freedman, "NATO Myths," *Foreign Policy* (Winter 1981–1982): 51. Copyright 1981 by Carnegie Endowment for International Peace.

5. These missiles were designated *intermediate range* instead of *theater* in order not to exacer-bate suspicions about their intended use in the European theater.

6. Alternative, but less popular, nonnuclear solutions to NATO's conventional inferiority also have been advanced. See Gene Sharp, *Making Europe Unconquerable: The Potential of Civilian-Based Deterrence and Defense* (Cambridge: Ballinger, 1986). Sharp advocates train-ing for civilian nonviolent resistance of occupying forces.

7. Edward C. Luck, "Placing Conventional Arms on the Multilateral Agenda," in *Arms Con-trol: The Multilateral Alternative* (New York: New York University Press, 1983), p. 182.

8. Russell Warren Howe, *Weapons: The International Game of Arms, Money and Diplomacy* (Garden City, New York: Doubleday, 1980), p. 278.

9. Cited in "Arms Control at the Crossroads," *Newsweek,* October 1, 1984, p. 29.

10. See Henry Grunwald, "Foreign Policy under Reagan II," *Foreign Affairs* (Winter, 1984-85): 226. See also Alton Frye, "Strategic Synthesis," *Foreign Policy* (Spring 1985): 3–27.

11. "Arms Control at the Crossroads," p. 30. For similar sentiments, see John Steinbruner, "Arms Control: Crisis or Compromise" *Foreign Affairs* 63 (Summer 1985): 1036–1049.

12. Address by Edward Kennedy marking the twentieth anniversary of President J. F. Kennedy's disarmament speech at American University, April 8, 1983. Printed by the Foundation for a Democratic Majority, pp. 1, 3.

13. See *Time,* June 25, 1984, p. 12.

14. Secretary of State Shultz made this point after the USSR destroyed a civilian airliner:

    When the Soviets shot down the Korean airliner, in contrast, President Reagan was not derailed from his steady, firm, and realistic course. He never had any illusions about the Soviet Union. . . . He made sure the world knew the truth about the incident. But he also sent our arms control negotiators back to Geneva, because he believed that reducing nu-clear weapons was a critical priority.

    George Shultz, "Managing the U.S.-Soviet Relationship Over the Long Term," *Current Policy No. 624* U.S. Department of State, Bureau of Public Affairs, October 18, 1984, p. 2.

15. Richard M. Nixon, *The Real War* (New York: Warner Books, 1980), pp. 174–175; Reagan quoted in Charles W. Kegley and Eugene R. Wittkopf, *World Politics: Trend and Transfor-mation* (New York: St. Martin's Press, 1981), p. 414. Henry Kissinger believed the SALT negotiations were so important to the USSR that he could use them as leverage for enlisting Soviet cooperation in bringing the war in Vietnam to a halt:

    Gromyko's eagerness, within four days after a massive B-52 attack in the Haiphong area, dramatized to me that the summit could be used as a restraint on Soviet conduct while we pursued our strategy for ending the war.

    It is not evident that this effort at linkage was successful. Nor did President Carter's National Security Advisor, Zbigniew Brzezinski, succeed in his announced intention of link-ing SALT II and Soviet cooperation in Africa.
    Henry Kissinger, *White House Years* (Boston: Little, Brown, 1979), p. 1126. For Brzezin-ski's attempt at linkage, see Howe, *Weapons: The International Game of Arms, Money and Diplomacy* p. 272. Some hawks support linkage not because it is seen as an opportunity for leverage, but because without linkage they fear public opinion will force the pursuit of arms control as an end in itself. Secretary of State Alexander Haig voiced this concern:

    Pretending that there is no linkage promotes reverse linkage. It ends up by saying that in order to preserve arms control, we have to tolerate Soviet aggression. This administration will never accept such an appalling conclusion.

    Technically there is no reason why stabilizing arms control agreements could not be negoti-ated at the same time steps were being taken to counter Soviet aggression, but it would require the difficult task of simultaneously mobilizing the public for the goodwill necessary to pass treaties and the concern necessary to support active security measures. Haig quoted by William Van Cleave in Richard Staar, ed., *Arms Control: Myth Versus Reality* (Stanford, CA: Hoover Institution Press, 1984), p. 16.

16. For a good discussion of U.S. and Soviet security objectives, see U.S. Congress, House Committee on Foreign Affairs, *Soviet Diplomacy and Negotiating Behavior: Emerging New Context for U.S. Diplomacy* Vol. 1, Committee Print, Prepared by the Congressional Research Service, Library of Congress, 1979, p. 517ff.

17. Sources that investigate the impact of domestic politics on arms control negotiations are numerous, but two popular discussions of U.S. politics and arms control are John Newhouse, *Cold Dawn: The Story of SALT* (New York: Holt, Rinehart and Winston, 1973), and Strobe Talbott, *Deadly Gambits: The Reagan Administration and the Stalemate in Nuclear Arms Control* (New York: Alfred A. Knopf, 1984).

18. *The Political Testament of Cardinal Richelieu,* trans. Henry Bertram Hill, (Madison: University of Wisconsin Press, 1961), p. 97.

19. Steven E. Miller, "Politics over Promise: Domestic Impediments to Arms Control," *International Security* 8 (Spring 1984): 80, 83.

20. *London Naval Conference: Speeches and Press Statements by Members of the American Delegation* Conference Series #3 (Washington, DC, U.S. Government Printing Office, 1930), p. 36.

21. Richard Dean Burns, *Arms Control and Disarmament: A. Bibliography* (Santa Barbara, CA: ABC Clio, Co., 1977), p. 5.

22. U.S. Congress, *Soviet Diplomacy,* p. 117. For the U.S. tendency to seize the initiative, see p. 494. For centralized control of Soviet negotiators, see pp. 501–502.

Fred Charles Ikle, among many other experienced American negotiators, has commented on the problematic combination of American flexibility and Soviet recalcitrance at the negotiating table:

The marked preference for flexibility among many Western diplomats results, in part, from the fear that the opponent might choose no agreement if faced with a firm position. . . . But this tactic is self-defeating if the diplomats on the opponent's side want to prove their mettle by showing that they pushed you as far as possible. They cannot satisfy themselves (or their government) that they have reached the limit as long as you offer them a menu of choices, particularly if the menu keeps changing. This is the reason why Westerners have been warned against trying out many variant proposals in negotiating with the Russians.

This passage is cited in Alvin Cottrell and Walter Hahn, *Naval Race or Arms Control in the Indian Ocean?* Agenda Paper #8 (New York: National Strategy Information Center, 1978), p. 64.

23. E. V. Tarle quotation from *Dictionary of Military and Naval Quotations,* compiled and edited by Colonel Robert Debs Heinl, Jr., USMC (Ret.). Copyright © 1966, U.S. Naval Institute, Annapolis, Maryland, p. 90.

24. Miller, "Politics Over Promise," pp. 80–81.

25. *The Political Testament,* p. 102.

26. Thucydides, *The Peloponnesian War,* trans. Rex Warner (Middlesex, England: Penguin Books, 1954, reprint 1980), p. 357. For Cleon's activities, see p. 277.

27. Fred Hiatt, "Perle's Distrust Shapes U.S. Policy," *Washington Post,* January 2, 1985, p. 1.

28. See "The Nitze Approach: Hard Line, Deft Touch," *Time,* January 31, 1983, p. 22.

29. Edward Harper Parker, *Ancient China Simplified* (London: Chapman and Hall, 1908), cited in Trevor N. Dupuy and Gay M. Hammerman, *A Documentary History of Arms Control and Disarmament* (New York: R. R. Bowker, 1973), p. 3.

PART IV

THE PHILOSOPHY OF ARMS CONTROL—
Nine Critical Questions for Formulating an Opinion on
Arms Control and Disarmament

Chapter Ten

The Basic Question—
Why Do Wars Begin?

Abraham Lincoln had a profound understanding of mankind and history. He often took a long-term perspective on fundamental issues. His response to a friend's inquiry concerning what most impressed him about his first view of Niagara Falls is indicative. Most people seeing Niagara Falls for the first time are transfixed and awed by its enormous hectic power, but "The thing that struck me most forcibly when I saw the Falls", said Lincoln, "was where in the world did all that water come from?" The national security debate sometimes seems analogous to Niagara Falls. One can see the voluminous debate on arms limitation issues sweep by and fall away, apparently always progressing but never ending, with the same old topics and arguments eventually bubbling up to the surface. To understand how questions raised in previous chapters are resolved in the real hurly-burly world of arms control debate and policy formulation, we must explore even more fundamental questions. Like Lincoln, we must consider more than the ephemeral; we must examine the enduring issues which run well beneath the surface of the tumultuous contemporary national security debate. Of such questions, the most basic is why wars begin.

The human heart is the starting point in all matters pertaining to war.

—Maurice de Saxe, *Mes Reveries,*
1732

Esau was a cunning hunter, a man of the field; and Jacob was a plain man, dwelling in tents.

—Genesis, 25:27

Each government accuses the other of perfidy, intrigue and ambition, as a means of heating the imagination of their respective nations, and incensing them to hostilities. Man is not the enemy of man, but through the medium of a false system of government.

—Thomas Paine, *The Rights of Man,* 1791

Can cultural differences, forms of political organization or human nature explain the cause of war? There is hardly a more fundamental or controversial topic than the cause of war, nor a more important one for the study of arms limitation, since different arms limitation strategies result from different explanations for why wars begin.

It would be impossible to review here the vast amount of scholarly work on the origins of war. Theories have been advanced on a multitude of causes, including such general categories as balance of power politics, population growth and density, the dynamics of arms competition, economic and cultural imperialism, and the biological and psychological roots of human nature. However, it is possible to focus on one intermediary cause of war about which there is substantial agreement in the field of international politics: the anarchic international environment.

Nation-states have a hierarchy of authority, with formal and authoritative decision-making mechanisms and procedures for the resolution of conflicts and competing interests. No similar international structure with sufficient prestige and power exists, so states frequently find it expedient and necessary to define and protect their own interests and security concerns. The result is an international environment characterized more by anarchy than cooperation, where trust can be dangerous and all suffer the consequences of incessant mutual suspicion. Scholars of international relations generally refer to the anarchic structure of the international system and the insecurity it creates as the "security dilemma."

TWO VIEWS OF THE SECURITY DILEMMA

Historian of international relations Herbert Butterfield has called the security dilemma the "absolute predicament" which lies at the heart of all human conflict.[1] To better visualize the intractable nature of the security dilemma, imagine a situation where the local city government has been destroyed and police, courts, elected and appointed officials suddenly disappear. At first citizens might attempt to cooperate with one another and resurrect authority patterns and institutions. But if some citizens failed to meet their responsibilities and all suffered as a result of their neglect, cooperation would break down and each citizen would begin to look after his/her own interests. More ominously if some decided to use force to gain their ends, or exercised authority arbitrarily, the others would have to respond similarly or succumb to the will of the strongest citizens. To trust your fellow citizen in such a lawless and anarchic environment might be disasterous.

Hence the security dilemma: If individuals choose to trust others, they put themselves in vital danger; yet if all individuals arm themselves to provide for their own security, it seems inevitable that bloody disagreements will erupt. The same circumstances prevail in the international environment. States believe they cannot trust one another and they all arm themselves for self-defense. There is general agreement on the existence of the security dilemma as a function of the anarchic international system, but disagreement arises over alternative characterizations of the security dilemma.

The origins and nature of the security dilemma may be explained in two different ways. The two people most often invoked as representatives of these two alternative explanations are the seventeenth-century English philosopher Thomas Hobbes and the eighteenth-century French thinker Jean-Jacques Rousseau. There is an inevitable oversimplification in characterizing Hobbes and Rousseau as spokesmen for alternative viewpoints on the security dilemma. It is important to note that the two views of the security dilemma do not fairly represent their thought in all its subtlety and complexity. With the acknowledged risk of some oversimplification, we shall follow precedent and draft these two great thinkers as representatives of the two most popular explanations for war.

Hobbes believed that men were prone to aggression and that without a powerful social authority "the condition of man . . . is a condition of war of everyone against everyone." Thus he considered it reasonable for man

> by force or wiles to master the persons of all men he can so long till he sees no other power great enough to endanger him; and this is no more than his own conservation requireth and is generally allowed. Also, because there be some that, taking pleasure in contemplating their own power in the acts of conquest, which they pursue farther than their security requires, if others, that otherwise would be glad to be at ease within the modest bounds, should not by invasion increase their power, they would not be able long time, by standing only on their defence, to subsist.[2]

Notice that Hobbes does not say all men are naturally aggressive, but that because some are, all must respond accordingly. As a result, in an anarchic environment the intelligent man (or state) will accumulate as much power as possible until "there was no other power great enough to endanger him." Certainly it would be folly under such conditions to simply trust one's security to the goodwill of others.

Rousseau had a more benign interpretation of human nature, and he regretted Hobbes's pessimism:

> But above all things let us beware concluding with Hobbes, that man, as having no idea of goodness, must be naturally bad; that he is vicious because he does not know what virtue is; that he always refuses to do any service to those of his own species, because he believes that none is due them; that, in virtue of that right which he justly claims to everything he wants, he foolishly looks upon himself as proprietor of the whole universe.[3]

With a different conception of human nature Rousseau arrives at a different understanding of the security dilemma. Men in an anarchic environment do not fight because they are generally evil, or even because some are inherently hostile, but rather they all suffer because they do not learn to cooperate. Suppose, said Rousseau, that a group needs to eat and can eat well if all will cooperate, but will starve if they do not. The group goes hunting for deer:

> Was a deer to be taken? Everyone saw that to succeed he must faithfully stand to his post; but suppose a hare to have slipped by within reach of any one of them, it is not to be doubted but he pursued it without scruple, and when he had seized his prey never reproached himself with having made his companions miss theirs.[4]

Whereas Hobbes's view of an anarchic environment is one of man preying upon man, Rousseau only sees men failing to cooperate. Many theorists of international relations draw on Rousseau's characterization of anarchy to describe the international security dilemma. In fact, this view predominates in much contemporary international relations literature. It is the foundation (and inherent bias) of the popular ''prisoner's dilemma,'' a contribution to international relations from game theory that is often used to describe the security dilemma confronting states in the anarchic international system.

In the prisoner's dilemma two men are being held on murder charges. They are separated and interrogated. The police offer each man a deal. Each prisoner is told that if he turns state's evidence against his partner, he will escape life imprisonment and get a reduced sentence. If both men accept the deal, they will both be convicted and sentenced for life. If neither accepts the deal, the police will not have enough evidence to convict them and they will go free. If only one man accepts the deal he will get a reduced sentence and his partner will go to jail for life.

Only if each prisoner trusts the other will both achieve the most desirable end. If they are unable to trust one another, each will turn state's evidence and both will receive life terms. Calculating the rational choice for a prisoner to make in this situation can depend on several factors—for example, how many times the ''game'' is played—but as one student of the subject notes:

> The key to overcoming the prisoner's dilemma regardless of the context in which it is stated, is developing the ability to cooperate. As the situation is structured, this in turn requires the capacity of the players to trust one another so that they can engage in the cooperative behavior that is mutually beneficial."[5]

As in the Rousseauistic characterization of the security dilemma, all that is lacking is cooperation made possible by trust.

The Hobbesian conception of the security dilemma, which postulates an inherent desire for power on the part of some men, has no specific parallel in current game theory literature. Although some associate the Hobbesian security dilemma with the game of "chicken," wherein two cars drive toward each other at high speed, each trying to force the other to abandon the path of collision first, the association is misleading.[6]

"Chicken" is roughly analogous to some conceptions of the problem of **escalation** in **deterrence** strategy (especially nuclear deterrence), but does not provide a full appreciation of either deterrence or Hobbes's notion of inherently aggressive parties. The emphasis on escalation in the chicken analogy overemphasizes will at the expense of capabilities as well as the mutually self-destructive dynamics of the "game." Most aggressors prefer to enhance their power at minimum cost, and certainly not by threatening to destroy themselves in the process (even if they occasionally do), and they devise strategies accordingly. Hobbes's view of the security dilemma may not be well represented by game theory, but it was the foundation of the "realist" school of thought which dominated international studies in the 1940s and 1950s and which many would say has been the dominant view throughout history.

The state that accepts Hobbes's view is inclined to accumulate power whenever possible, reflecting the old adage that the best defense is a good offense. At the very least it will take all the precautions it can to protect itself from other states. A state accepting Rousseau's interpretation of the security dilemma would not necessarily object to defense precautions but would have hopes of educating people everywhere to cooperate. The two views are not absolutely contradictory, as it is possible to provide for defense and attempt to facilitate cooperation among people, but in practice they exist in uneasy tension with one another.

From these two alternative conceptions of human nature[7] and the security dilemma spring two alternative explanations for the origins of war: the aggressor theory and the spiral theory of war. Just as the assured destruction and flexible response schools of thought define the spectrum of opinion on stable nuclear deterrence, the spiral theory and aggressor theories of war define the origins of the most popular explanations for the cause of war.[8] This does not mean that one must be either a spiral or aggressor theorist. It is possible to accept both theories as generally valid explanations for war depending on historical circumstances. Nonetheless, in any given situation threatening international conflict interested parties will show a greater concern with either the spiral or aggressor theory of war.

1. The Spiral Theory of War

The blade itself incites to violence.

—Homer, *Odyssey,* xvi, 1000 B.C.

Wars spring from unseen and generally insignificant causes, the first outbreak being often but an explosion of anger.

—Thucydides, *History of the Peloponnesian Wars,* 404 B.C.

Nobody wanted war . . . the nations backed their machines over the precipice.

—Lloyd George, British prime minister, commenting on the origins of World War I[9]

The spiral theory explanation of the cause of war accepts a Rousseauistic understanding of human nature. People are not by nature aggressive, but in an anarchic environment, where the cooperation of others cannot be expected, each must look to his or her own interests. Spiral theorists very frequently draw parallels between Rousseau's hunting analogy and the international environment. If states could be sure all other states would cooperate, the best prize could be secured (a deer/peace). But since the defection of one for momentary gain (a hare/an increment in security or power from military advantage) can ruin the chances of others, none is willing to trust the others. Hence they arm themselves and hunt alone. They see each other arming and become alarmed and suspicious of each other's motives. Insecurity and fear intensify as an arms race develops until finally it spirals out of control and some incident touches off a war no one really wanted but that all felt powerless to prevent.

Proponents of this action-reaction model of mutual fear and misperceptions usually adopt World War I as their archetype. In 1913 Europe was armed to the teeth, with each nation certain that others were conspiring to subvert its security. Lord Grey, British foreign secretary during the war, admirably summarized the spiral theory of war in his explanation of the origins of World War I:

The moral is obvious; it is that great armaments lead inevitably to war. If there are armaments on one side, there must be armaments on the other sides. . . . While one nation arms, other nations cannot tempt it to aggression by remaining defenseless. . . . Each measure taken by one nation is noted, and leads to countermeasures by others.

The increase of armaments that is intended in each nation to produce consciousness of strength, and a sense of security, does not produce these effects. On the contrary, it produces a consciousness of the strength of other nations and a sense of fear. Fear begets suspicion and distrust and evil imaginings of all sorts, till each government feels it would be criminal and a betrayal of its own country not to take every precaution, while every government regards every precaution of every other government as evidence of hostile intent.[10]

All it took was a spark of passion to ignite the inferno. When a suicidal assassin succeeded in killing the Austro-Hungarian archduke, country after country declared war in a train of events analogous to a falling row of dominoes, and Europe was engulfed in an unimaginably ferocious and destructive war. No one conspired to start the war, but it seemed that no one could halt the events leading to it either.

According to spiral theorists if we can come to understand the dynamics of this action-reaction model, we can escape its conclusion. Just prior to the Cuban Missile Crisis in 1962, John F. Kennedy read Barbara Tuchman's *Guns of August,* a powerful "spiral theory" explanation for the causes of World War I. After the crisis passed, Kennedy cited the influence this book had had on his crisis strategy. He opened and maintained communications with the Soviet leadership and he left open options that would allow a mutual retreat from the brink of nuclear confrontation.

The Aggressor Theory of War

Men do not fight because they have arms. They have arms because they deem it necessary to fight.

—Hans Morgenthau

The greatest happiness is to vanquish your enemies, to chase them before you, to rob them of their wealth, to see those dear to them bathed in tears, to clasp to your bosom their wives and daughters.

—Jenghiz Khan

The pacifist humane ideal might be a very good one if first one man had made himself master of the world.

—Adolf Hitler[11]

Aggressor theorists see men, the security dilemma and the origins of conflict much differently from the spiral theorists. Along with Hobbes, they believe that some states are intrinsically aggressive. The prime minister of Great Britain, Margaret Thatcher, succinctly stated the aggressor theory of war at the United Nations's Special Disarmament Session in June 1982:

The fundamental risk to peace is not the existence of weapons of particular types. . . . The springs of war lie in the readiness to resort to force against other nations, and not in "arms races," whether real or imaginary. Aggressors do not start wars because an adversary has built up his own strength. They start wars because they believe they can gain more by going to war than by remaining at peace.[12]

The model for most aggressor theory analogies is World War II. Hitler was bent on aggression, and attempts to conciliate him only seemed to fuel his belligerent demands. First Britain and France acquiesced to Hitler's absorption of Austria, then of half of Czechoslovakia, and finally of all of Czechoslovakia. Neville Chamberlain, the British prime minister at the time, who perhaps felt he had no alternative, accepted Hitler's promise that Czechoslovakia was his "final territorial demand." In a speech in Birmingham on January 28, 1939, Chamberlain said, "It takes at least two to make a peace, but one can make a war," and he was right.[13] Nine months later Hitler sent the German army into Poland and the world plunged once again into war.

World War II began because no nation was willing or able to defy Hitler's Germany while it was still relatively weak. When finally France and Great Britain were ready to fight, Germany was strong enough to attempt world domination and very nearly succeeded. Hitler's behavior and the apparent consequences of trying to appease him popularized the aggressor theory. Since World War II, politicians have made countless references to Hitler and the necessity of diligently defying aggressors sooner rather than later. This was the rationale offered by two American Presidents for the U.S. participation in the Korean and Vietnam wars.

In his memoirs, President Truman relates how the North Korean invasion of South Korea in 1950 was reminiscent of Hitler's behavior, and how he then decided that a forceful response was required to prevent another world war, this time between communist and noncommunist states. President Johnson also recalled the legacy of appeasing Hitler when explaining the U.S. role in Vietnam:

> Everything I knew about history told me that if I got out of Vietnam and let Ho Chi Minh run through the streets of Saigon, then I'd be doing exactly what Chamberlain did in World War II. I'd be giving a big fat reward to aggression. . . . And so would begin World War III.[14]

The aggressor theorist believes war can best be prevented by standing prepared to punish those who threaten aggression. For example, in the critical days following the end of World War II Stalin began to pressure Iran and Turkey with territorial demands. Stalin withdrew Soviet troops from Iran and stopped threatening Turkey only when the United States dispatched its fleet to the Eastern Mediterranean and threatened to use force if Soviet pressure persisted. Such preventive deterrence is the aggressor theorist's remedy for war.

For both spiral and aggressor theorists, war results from miscommunication, but miscommunication of two very different messages. In the spiral theory of war no state really wants war, but it fails to communicate its peaceful intentions to other states in a sufficiently reassuring manner. In the aggressor theory of war at least one nation is willing to threaten war, and it is the failure of the other nations to communicate their resolve to defend themselves that encourages the aggressor to take steps that make war inevitable.

THEORIES OF WAR AND ARMS CONTROL

Do arms cause wars? If they do, then arms limitation can prevent war. The spiral theorist will say yes, arms cause war, inasmuch as their proliferation through arms competition and technological momentum contributes to international misperceptions of hostility and insecurity, which in turn lead to war. Spiral theorists draw on and stimulate research on arms races—how they start, how they can be controlled, and how they are likely to end. Spiral theorists generally support closer communication, negotiations, and international agreements:

> If the habit of cooperation can be established in the field of armament policy, it may well prove "catching" in other areas . . . [and] facilitate the achievement of some political solutions, which in turn would facilitate further measures of armament cooperation; and so on.[15]

On the other hand the aggressor theorist will say no, arms do not cause war. In fact, the absence of arms may contribute to war because they are needed to deter aggressors. Aggressor theorists draw on and stimulate studies on deterrence, how it can succeed and why it fails. Aggressor theorists worry that familiarity may breed contempt if the overtures communicate weak resolve, and thus they want to keep perceived enemies at arm's length, only communicating resolution to defend their state's interests. They will take a much more skeptical approach to negotiations, agreeing with Hobbes that "covenants without the sword are but words." Many aggressor theorists believe arms control to be dangerous because it can create a false sense of security,[16] and they are very selective in their support for arms limitation agreements.[17]

There are several other points worth noting about these two theories of war. First, a comparison of the spiral and aggressor theories of war helps to explain the unilateral-militarist spectrum of popular opinion on arms control and defense (see chart p. 62). An extreme spiral theorist who believes that armaments are all that stand in the way of peace will support unilateral disarmament. In the words of one spiral theorist:

> The most likely result of unilateral disarmament—whether it be undertaken by the United States or the Soviet Union—is that it would prevent war. The main reason which could impel either the Soviet Union or the United States to atomic war is the constant fear of being attacked and pulverized by the opponent.[18]

On the other end of the spectrum is the militarist, or the extreme aggressor theorist, who agrees with Hobbes that the only way to ensure security is to expand national power at the expense of adversaries who will surely be attempting to do the same.

A decision maker who is not sure which approach best anticipates the origin of the most probable future war will pursue both the arms control and defense options. The less extreme spiral theorist will grant that defense programs are necessary to deter the enemy until it is possible through arms control to convince the enemy he is not being threatened. The less extreme aggressor theorist will admit that arms control agreements between peaceful states and in some cases with aggressive states are helpful in the short term for providing some stability in an increasingly dangerous world.

A clear majority of policy advocates reside between the two extremes and believe in pursuing arms control and defense preparedness simultaneously. Yet decision makers require explanations for international events, and when they survey extant international conditions they usually conclude the evidence supports a greater concern with either the spiral or aggressor theory scenarios for war, which in turn predisposes them to defense or arms limitation when the two do not seem compatible.

Another point to keep in mind is that these two explanations of war have attendant policy prescriptions. Most importantly, wholeheartedly following the policy prescriptions of one approach will invariably alarm proponents of the other approach. A spiral theorist will consider an aggressor theorist's recommendations for a show of resolve as just another step in the escalation of misperceptions and hostility, while an aggressor theorist will consider a spiral theorist's recommendations for a unilateral demonstration of goodwill to break the spiral of fear as a signal of appeasement and an encouragement to aggression. In theory, this puts aggressor theorists and spiral theorists at loggerheads when it comes to policy, which explains the antagonism and the vehemency with which committed aggressor and spiral theorists argue their cases in public debate.

The last point is a general one. It is that the spiral theory of war and the aggressor theory of war are really the foundations of two very different approaches to peace, precisely because they are two very different explanations of the origins of war. The spiral theorist believes that peace is a construction project of sorts, to be built, slowly perhaps, but cumulatively, one block upon another. The aggressor theorist believes that peace is ever elusive because men are forever succumbing to aggressive tendencies. The decision maker must therefore always be on guard against undue optimism and false hopes, remembering that obligatory maxim so dear to the ancient Romans: "If you desire peace, prepare for war." In short, aggressor theorists, reflecting their acceptance of the Hobbesian interpretation of the international security dilemma, reject in principle the possibility of using arms control or disarmament to abolish military power. At best, military power can be stabilized. Spiral theorists believe it is possible to move beyond a precarious military stability to general cooperation and mutual trust.

A common denominator running throughout the preceding discussion is the issue of an adversary's intentions.[19] Important as they are, the intentions of states are far from evident. Doubt about the intentions of other states encourages a more moderate "carrot and stick" approach, which allows for deterrence but also for negotiating mutual security with those who prove responsive. Which side of this dual-track approach to security should be emphasized? Can enemy intentions be tested and modified? What are the preconditions to constructing a *modus vivendi,* the necessary first steps towards peace? Such questions are explored in the next several chapters.

DISCUSSION QUESTIONS

1. Is it possible for states to overcome the security dilemma?
2. Is the spiral theory or aggressor theory of war more convincing as a general explanation of armed conflict?
3. Based on your knowledge of history, do you consider the spiral theory or agressor theory of war a more convincing explanation for the following conflicts: The Korean War; the Vietnam War; 1968 Arab-Israeli War, 1973 Arab-Israeli War; the Falklands War; the Iran-Iraq War; the War in Afghanistan; the war in Nicaragua.
4. In what general respects do disarmament and arms control, respectively, accord or conflict with the spiral and aggressor theories of war?

SUGGESTED READINGS FOR CHAPTER TEN: THE BASIC QUESTION—WHY DO WARS BEGIN?

BLAINEY, GEOFFREY. *The Causes of War.* New York: Macmillan-Free Press, 1973.
BULL, HEDLEY. "Society and Anarchy in International Relations." In *Diplomatic Investigations.* Ed. Herbert Butterfield and Martin Wight. Cambridge, MA: Harvard University Press, 1966.
CARR, EDWARD H. *The Twenty Years' Crisis, 1919–1939.* New York: Harper and Row, 1964.
CLAUDE, INIS. *Power and International Relations.* New York: Random House, 1962.
DURANT, WILL and ARIEL. *The Lessons of History* Chapter XI. "History and War" New York: Simon and Schuster, 1968.
FALK, RICHARD A., and SAMUEL S. KIM, eds. *The War System: An Interdisciplinary Approach.* Boulder, CO: Westview Press, 1980.
GOLDMAN, RALPH M. "Political Distrust as Generator of the Arms Race: Prisoners' and Security Dilemmas." In Burns H. Weston, ed. *Toward Nuclear Disarmament and Global Security: A Search for Alternatives.* Boulder, CO: Westview Press, 1984.
HOBBES, THOMAS. *Leviathan.* Especially Part I, Chapter 13, "On the Natural Condition of Mankind, as Concerning Their Felicity, and Misery."
HOWARD, MICHAEL. *The Causes of War.* Cambridge, MA: Harvard University Press, 1983.
JERVIS, ROBERT. *Perception and Misperception in International Politics.* Princeton: Princeton University Press, 1976, especially pp. 58–111.
ROUSSEAU, JEAN-JACQUES. *A Lasting Peace Through the Federation of Europe and the State of War.* 1761.

STOESSINGER, JOHN C. *Why Nations Go to War.* New York: St. Martin's, 1974.
WALLACE, MICHAEL. "Armaments and Escalation: Two Conflicting Hypotheses." *International Studies Quarterly* 26 (1982): 37–56.
WALTZ, KENNETH N. *Man, State and War.* New York: Columbia University Press, 1959.
WRIGHT, QUINCY. *A Study of War.* Chicago: University of Chicago Press, 1942.

NOTES

1. Robert Jervis, *Perception and Misperception in International Politics* (Princeton, NJ: Princeton University Press, 1976), p. 66.

2. Thomas Hobbes, *Leviathan,* Vol. 23 of *Great Books of the Western World* (Chicago: Encyclopaedia Britannica, 1952), p. 85. Reprinted by permission from Encyclopaedia Britannica, Inc.

3. Jean-Jacques Rousseau, "On the Origin of Inequality," Vol. 38 of *Great Books,* p. 343. Reprinted by permission from Encyclopaedia Britannica, Inc. See also Jean-Jacques Rousseau, *A Lasting Peace through the Federation of Europe* (1761).

4. Ibid., p. 349.

5. Donald M. Snow, *Nuclear Strategy in a Dynamic World* (Alabama: University of Alabama Press, 1981), p. 165.

6. Herman Kahn described the basic game of "chicken" this way:

   Both cars straddle the white line and drive toward each other at top speed. The first driver to lose his nerve and swerve into his own lane is "chicken"—an object of contempt and scorn—and he loses the game.

   Cited in Louis René Beres, "Nuclear Strategy and World Order," in Burns H. Weston, *Toward Nuclear Disarmament and Global Security: A Search for Alternatives* (Boulder, CO: Westview Press, 1984), p. 224. Robert Jervis uses the chicken analogy as a representation of the essential elements of deterrence strategy. See Jervis, *Perception and Misperception,* pp. 63–67.

7. It bears repeating that while excerpts from Hobbes and Rousseau are used here to illustrate two alternative views of the security dilemma, these two views do not convey a full appreciation of the complexity of either Hobbes's or Rousseau's understanding of international relations.

8. For a thorough discussion of these two approaches to explaining the origin of conflict, see Jervis, *Perception and Misperception,* pp. 58–111.

9. From *Dictionary of Military and Naval Quotations,* compiled and edited by Colonel Robert Debs Heinl, Jr., USMC (Ret.). Copyright © 1966, U.S. Naval Institute, Annapolis, Maryland.

10. Philip Noel-Baker, *Disarmament* (New York: Garland Publishing, 1972), pp. 80–81.

11. Hans Morgenthau, *Politics Among Nations,* 4th ed. (New York: Alfred A. Knopf, 1967), p. 392; Jenghiz Khan quoted in Lynn Montross, *War Through the Ages* (New York: Harper and Row, 1960), p. 144; and Hitler quoted in Quincy Wright, *A Study of War* (Chicago: University of Chicago Press, 1940), p. 815.

12. Quoted in Joyce E. Larson and William C. Bodie, *The Intelligent Layperson's Guide to the Nuclear Freeze and Peace Debate* (New York: National Strategy Information Center, 1983), p. 22.

13. Heinl, *Dictionary.*

14. John Stoessinger, *Crusaders and Pragmatists: Movers of Modern American Foreign Policy* (New York: W. W. Norton, 1979), p. 180.

15. Donald Brennan, cited by William Van Cleave in Richard Staar, ed., *Arms Control: Myth Versus Reality* (Stanford, CA: Hoover Institution Press, 1984), p. 7.

16. Even so benign and superficial a treaty as the Kellogg-Briand Pact outlawing war was condemned by some U.S. senators who believed it would lull the United States into a state of

unpreparedness. More recently a top U.S. official complained, "This stuff [arms control] is soporific. It puts our society to sleep. It does violence to our ability to maintain adequate defenses." Alexander DeConde, *A History of American Foreign Policy,* Vol. 2, 3rd ed. (New York: Charles Scribner's Sons, 1978), p. 97, and for the comment by the US arms limitation official, see *Time,* April 18, 1983.

17. It is worth noting that both of the most elaborate efforts on behalf of peace by mankind in this century, the League of Nations and the United Nations, contain in their charters language that gives due consideration to both spiral and aggressor theorists' concerns. In the League of Nation's Charter, Article 1 represents the concerns of the aggressor theorist, and Article 8 represents those of the spiral theorist:

> To maintain international peace and security and to that end to take effective collective measures for the prevention and removal of threats to the peace, and for the suppression of acts of aggression and other breaches of the peace . . . (Article 1)

And:

> Maintenance of peace requires the reduction of national armaments to the lowest point consistent with national safety. (Article 8)

The corresponding passages in the United Nations's Charter are found in Articles 51 and 26:

> Nothing in the present charter shall impair the inherent right of individual or collective self-defence. (Article 51)

And Article 26 commits each member to promote peace with:

> the least diversion for armaments of the world's human and economic resources.

18. Erich Fromm, "Unilateral Disarmament," in Donald C. Brennan, ed., *Arms Control, Disarmament and National Security* (New York: George Braziller, 1961).

19. Or as Robert Jervis has asserted in the context of U.S.-Soviet relations:

> [The] explanation for differences of opinion between the spiral theorists and proponents of deterrence [aggressor theorists] lies not in differing general views of international relations, differing values and morality or differing methods of analysis, but in differing perceptions of Soviet intentions.

Robert Jervis, "Hypothesis on Misperception," *World Politics* (April 1968): 455.

A spiral theorist might object that the dynamics of an arms race can propel states toward war despite their leaders' intentions, and thus the issue is the arms race and not intentions. However, this position also requires an assessment of intentions—namely, that they are benign until influenced by fear generated by arms competition. See the discussion in chapter 13 on intentions and capabilities.

Chapter Eleven

Toward Peace—Which Comes First, Arms Control or Trust?

If trust is to be established in the area of relations between the Soviet Union and the non-Soviet world, it will be a consequence, and not a condition, of arms control.

—William T. Fox

The problem with disarmament was and is that the problem of war is tackled upside down and at the wrong end. . . . Nations don't distrust each other because they are armed; they are armed because they distrust each other. And therefore to want disarmament before a minimum of common agreement on fundamentals is as absurd as to want people to get undressed in the winter. Let the weather be warm and people will discard their clothes readily and without committees to tell them to do it.

—Salvador de Madariaga

Everyone will agree with what President Eisenhower has said so often: that it is desirable to work both for disarmament and for the settlement of political disputes; that work on both should go forward simultaneously; and that any progress on one will improve the hope of progress on the other.[1]

—Philip Noel-Baker

It is frequently observed that arms control presumes minimum levels of both trust and distrust between nations. Hedley Bull is often quoted on this point:

> Only the existence of international tension makes arms control relevant. It is relevant when tension is at a certain point, above which it is impossible and beneath which it is unnecessary. . . . where there exists political tension between nations above a certain degree some kinds of arms control appear out of the question. It should also be pointed out that where there exists political tension below a certain degree, when the relations between nations are marked by sympathy and amity, arms control appears to be irrelevant.[2]

In other words, arms limitation agreements are relevant when states are not sure of each other's intentions (hostile or peaceful). In such cases there is a possible but debatable role for trust and arms limitation agreements. The issue of trust and arms limitation may be specifically defined with two different questions, depending on how broadly or narrowly trust is construed. *Broadly understood, trust means a level of goodwill sufficient to resolve outstanding political differences.* Trust so construed is usually considered a long-term endeavor. *Defined more narrowly, trust connotes the amount of risk a nation is willing to tolerate in trusting that another nation will not suddenly seek to do it harm or gain unilateral advantages.* Trust in this context is a short-term issue involving the desire of an adversary for military stability, and it is always relevant to specific policy decisions on starting negotiations and accepting treaties.

Either of these two definitions of trust may be used when asking whether trust is a precondition or product of arms control. With trust broadly construed, the issue becomes: Must arms control and disarmament precede or follow the resolution of outstanding political differences? With trust narrowly construed, the question is: Do negotiated agreements require some trust and thus the acceptance of some risks, or can they only contribute to mutual trust if they entail virtually no risks?

TRUST BROADLY UNDERSTOOD

Following World War I, two major sets of treaties were signed, each of which assumed a different answer to the question of whether disarmament must precede or follow from the resolution of outstanding political differences. The Washington Naval Treaty of 1922 was the first most notable disarmament effort following the war. The treaty curtailed the number of capital ships to be produced by the signatories to the treaty, and it was widely viewed and explained as an attempt to improve the climate of trust by first halting the arms race. Years later, while attending another disarmament conference, Secretary of State Henry Stimson explained the United States's understanding of the Washington Naval Treaty's significance:

> Eight years ago . . . [the United States] . . . was engaged in building a fleet of battleships larger and more powerful than those of any other nation in the world. Fifteen of such capital ships were already in the course of construction and over $330,000,000 had been spent on their construction. In order to stop naval competition and to put an end to the consequent rivalry, suspicion, and fear between the nations which would grow out of such competition, America destroyed all of those new ships, together with thirteen older battleships in her possession. . . .
>
> More than this, and with the special purpose of reassuring Japan, America at the same time agreed to stop all work on her naval bases in the Orient and to leave them unfinished and unprotected. Nothing could have shown better her confidence in Japan. . . . The subsequent events have shown America was right. Japan has responded most cordially to this action, and the relations between Japan and America have become more friendly and mutually confident than ever before.[3]

At about the same time as the Washington Naval Treaty negotiations, a number of European states were tackling the security dilemma from the opposite direction; by first improving the atmosphere of trust in order to pave the way for substantive disarmament negotiations. The seven European nations who met in Locarno, Switzerland, in 1925 produced a series of treaties that resolved border disputes between Germany and her western neighbors, made provisions for arbitration of future disputes, renounced war as a means of resolving any disputes, and promised collective security action in case of aggression by any of the signatories—all in order to "hasten on effectively the disarmament provided for in . . . the Covenant of the League."

During the rest of the 1920s and early 1930s, professional opinion slowly came to the conclusion that trust (for which the term "moral disarmament" became a synonym) must *precede* actual reductions in weapons (generally referred to as "material" or "technical" disarmament). In part this shift in opinion was due to years of fruitless efforts to negotiate disarmament treaties in the aftermath of the remarkable Washington Naval Treaty. When the First General Disarmament Conference convened in Geneva in 1932, it

> proceeded on the conviction that "moral disarmament" is an essential preliminary condition of material disarmament, that this moral disarmament can only be achieved in an atmosphere of mutual confidence and security.[4]

The conference began with many expressions of goodwill and in an atmosphere of high hopes. But this "spirit of Geneva," as it was referred to then, and many times since,[5] failed to resolve political differences and did not lead to tangible results in material disarmament. Eventually failure and frustration led to two different responses, both of which retained the assumption that trust must precede disarmament.

Many of those believing trust was a necessary and possible precondition set about debating the means for building trust. Numerous peace leagues and pacts, both local and international, were established. Support for world government also reached the height of its popularity at this time. Many still believe that a large dose of trust must precede significant disarmament and that world government is the only way to produce such trust. The other response came from aggressor theorists who had no confidence in peace pacts or world government (which at that time meant the League of Nations). They agreed that trust was a prerequisite for disarmament, but argued that it was an impossible prerequisite given current political conditions, and thus disarmament was not practical. In other words, tension had risen so high between European states that arms limitation was no longer practical. As Winston Churchill said (speaking to the House of Commons on July 13, 1934), "It is the greatest possible mistake to mix up disarmament with peace. When you have peace you will have disarmament."

Churchill, an aggressor theorist, saw disarmament negotiations in the existing political climate as exercises in power politics rather than trust building.[6] Therefore he tried to shift the terms of the debate from disarmament to the outstanding political differences that stood in the way of peace. This basic difference of opinion over material and moral disarmament, and which should precede the other, has not changed. Most aggressor theorists still agree with Churchill that trust (or "peace") is a requisite for meaningful disarmament, and as such not a very likely precondition. As John Spanier and Joseph Nogee have put it:

> It is an illusion to expect nations to disarm in the absence of prior political agreement on the issues separating them. How can nations really be expected to agree to the elimination or reduction of the instruments with which they seek to protect themselves or gain their ends? If nations cannot settle their political differences, then they cannot end the arms race. If these differences could have been resolved, the arms race would never have started.[7]

Spiral theorists reject the assertion that prior resolution of political differences is a prerequisite for disarmament as unrealistic and impossibly pessimistic. First, since arms races breed so much distrust it is unrealistic to ever demand or expect the resolution of all political problems prior to arms control:

> The arms race, it has been suggested, is a symptom of political tension and the solution of political questions is therefore necessary to produce a favorable climate for negotiation on disarmament. This attitude has rightly been regarded as defeatist. . . . For it is impossible to conceive of settlements which remove all sources of dispute and thus the time for disarmament can never arrive.[8]

The spiral theorist believes the broad trust necessary to defuse political disagreements is possible, but especially so once arms control agreements have helped establish a basis for mutual trust by restraining arms competition. Thus, spiral theorists believe that arms control must precede trust, that is, the resolution of major political differences. As Philip Noel-Baker observed in 1958:

> The argument is sometimes stated [that]: "Disarmament can only be a conse-quence, and never a cause, of an improvement in international relations." Many historical examples could be given to prove the falsity of this assumption; two will suffice, one from the early nineteenth century, the other from the early twen-tieth. The Rush-Bagot Agreement of 1817, made against the wishes of the gen-erals in both Britain and the United States, totally disarmed the Canadian fron-tier. The Washington Naval Disarmament Convention of 1922 made very big reductions in the navies of Britain, the United States and Japan. Both produced the most remarkable "improvements in international relations." Since, as experi-ence shows and as present conditions only too clearly confirm, competition in armaments embitters international relations, producing mutual fear, suspicion and tension, it necessarily follows that the ending of an arms race by a disarma-ment treaty would improve international relations, reduce the tension, and facil-itate the settlement of outstanding political disputes.
>
> Indeed, there is much more substance in the counterargument used by those who favour disarmament, namely, that political disputes are much less likely to be settled while an arms race is going on, and that, if you want settlements, the arms race must first be stopped.[9]

Philip Noel-Baker's use of historical cases to support the spiral theorist posi-tion raises an interesting question. Does the bulk of historical evidence support the belief that arms limitation agreements must precede or follow significant improvements in interstate relations? The question is difficult to answer be-cause the historical evidence is often ambiguous. For example, the Rush-Bagot Agreement and Washington Naval Treaty cited by Noel-Baker for improving the general atmosphere of trust between nations are also cited by others to support the assertion that trust must precede disarmament.

Historical Ambiguity

Spiral theorists attribute the success of the Rush-Bagot Agreement to the fact that it suspended the arms race on the Great Lakes, and allowed a modi-cum of trust and eventually goodwill between the United States and Great Britain to develop. But aggressor theorists point out that the 1817 treaty was repeatedly violated, and reach the opposite conclusion:

> Contrary to what many schoolbooks say, the agreement was violated repeatedly. The worst violations occurred in the late 1830s, when the British sent armed ships into the Great Lakes to mount retaliatory raids against American sanctuaries for guerrilla parties who were raiding Canada. Land fortifications were maintained until 1871, when the United States signed a treaty with Britain settling claims arising from the Civil War. Only then was disarmament extended gradually and without formal agreement to the long land border. Not until the twentieth cen-

tury, when the possibility of war between Canada and the United States finally disappeared from the minds of policy-makers, did violations cease.

The Rush-Bagot Agreement is sometimes cited to prove that disarmament leads to peaceful relations between states. A close examination of the historical record seems to support the opposite view: Only when there are already peaceful relations between states is a disarmament agreement workable.[10]

Did the Rush-Bagot Agreement create the conditions necessary for a general reconciliation between the United States and Britain, or did a general reconciliation finally make the agreement effective, and eventually even unnecessary?

The Washington Naval Treaty of 1922 is also a historically controversial example of the interplay between trust and negotiations, primarily because it succeeded in obtaining dramatic reductions in some categories of naval armaments but seemed to spur on competition in other categories. To paraphrase Florence Nightingale's observation that whatever else hospitals did, they ought not to spread disease, one might say that whatever else disarmament negotiations do, they ought not to encourage the arms race. Yet many believe that all too often their net effect is to stimulate arms competition in new directions.

The Displacement Effect

The redirection of military efforts into channels purposefully excluded in negotiations is referred to in arms control literature as the "displacement effect." While the Washington Naval Treaty actually succeeded in reducing and limiting the capital ships of Great Britain, the United States, Japan, France, and Italy, it was followed by even more intense competition in cruisers, destroyers, and submarines. In fact, all the signatories began building new cruisers displacing almost 10,000 tons, which was the capital ship limit agreed upon in the treaty but still almost twice the size of previous cruisers. The "displacement effect" has also been noticeable in the aftermath of other treaties.[11] For example, while SALT I limited the number of missile launchers, the United States and USSR shifted their competition to warheads, putting more and more warheads on each missile.

Those who believe trust must precede disarmament are not surprised by the displacement effect. De Madariaga, a close participant in disarmament negotiations during the 1930s, described the internal dynamics of the negotiating process at the Washington Naval Treaty which produced the displacement effect described above:

> Every delegation goes to a disarmament conference determined to secure an increase in the *relative* armaments of its own nation, even though the conference may lead to an all-round reduction of *absolute* armaments. What matters for the expert is: (a) the national power standing in relation to that of the nation's potential adversary; (b) the national potential power (power for expanding armaments) in relation to that of the nation's adversary. It is clear that a cleverly conducted negotiation in conference may increase these two relative quantities even though the absolute values concerned be reduced.

This explains the atmosphere of profound distrust which prevails in disarmament conferences. Every delegate scrutinizes the most innocent-looking proposals with the utmost anxiety, *lest* his own relative position be sacrificed by his acceptance thereof.

Because of political differences which engender mutual distrust, de Madariaga concluded, "armaments are indispensable as instruments of power and therefore all disarmament discussions are bound to transform themselves into armament discussions."[12]

In other words, according to aggressor theorists, it makes little difference whether negotiators finally agree on higher or lower ceilings. Higher levels of arms allow the military competition to continue along well-worn paths, while lower ceilings force it to branch out in other directions. Like some amorphous blob in a science fiction horror film, arms competition can be channeled but not stopped. Aggressor theorists simply view this phenomenon, the displacement effect, as evidence of the distrust that precludes using negotiations to build trust and instead makes all negotiations exercises in redefining international power relationships.[13]

Spiral theorists acknowledge the displacement effect but they do not believe it is either inevitable or necessarily evidence that arms control cannot contribute to mutual trust. As one spiral theorist put it, "The closing of several holes in a porous dike may not necessarily be the reason for the leaks from the other holes."[14] In the first place, occasionally the displacement effect is a beneficial product of initial negotiations. For example, sometimes negotiators deliberately encourage the development of defensive or stabilizing weapons at the expense of offensive and destabilizing weapons in order to improve stability and security. Second, when the displacement effect *is* a product of distrust, it is often a function of domestic politics. That is, spiral theorists claim that often new spurts in weapons programs following arms control agreements are the result of having to appease domestic aggressor theorists who would not support the arms control treaty in question without being promised greater growth in programs not covered by the treaty.

Finally spiral theorists claim that the displacement effect just signals the need to follow up an initial treaty with additional treaties to further curtail the arms race and establish a momentum of mutual trust. They do not expect immediate success with the first treaty. Thus they maintain the Washington Naval Treaty did help ease political differences, and that it was the failure to follow up with additional treaties limiting other classes of naval armaments, especially submarines and aircraft carriers, that contributed to growing mistrust and eventually to war.

Sources of Distrust

One result of all the debate and disillusionment over disarmament in the 1930s was a better understanding of how difficult trust is to establish and nurture. Two sources of distrust often cited are national character and national form of government. Madariaga offers an example of the first:

> The history of the Franco-British dialogue on disarmament and security—for it was mostly a dialogue between two protagonists—is but the working out of this psychological contrast between the English and the French characters. The Frenchman said: "We are all agreed about principles; therefore, please sign this paper in which our agreed principles are set forth and developed to their logical conclusions." And the Englishman answered: "True, we are agreed about principles, there is no need to sign anything at all. When the time comes to apply them, we shall do so in the light of the circumstances, and since we are agreed on principles, there is no doubt but that we shall agree as to their application." Then the Frenchman was taken aback and went home full of misgivings: "He does not want to sign, therefore he does not really believe in the principles," he suspected. While the Englishman went home muttering: "He wanted to pin me down for ever. I wonder what he had up his sleeve." Thus does misunderstanding arise, and even mistrust is bred out of a mere difference in character.[15]

John Lewis Gaddis, citing George Kennan, offers an example of differences in forms of government making trust impossible:

> Further concessions to Moscow would be futile Kennan argued; the Stalinist regime would always remain hostile because it depended upon the existence of foreign threats to maintain its domestic authority. "Nothing short of complete disarmament, delivery of our air and naval forces to Russia and resigning of powers of government to American Communists" would come close to alleviating Russian distrust, and even then the Kremlin would probably "smell a trap and would continue to harbor the most baleful misgivings." Suspicion, Kennan noted in March, "is an integral part of [the] Soviet system, and will not yield entirely to any form of rational persuasion or assurance."[16]

Can arms control and disarmament negotiations, by emphasizing the shared concern of peace, slowly encourage mutual trust between nations with different national characters and political systems? The spiral theorist argues yes. For the spiral theorist these entrenched sources of mistrust are all the more reason to conduct negotiations on a regular basis, thereby demonstrating each side's commitment to peace. Aggressor theorists, on the other hand, believe trust must precede arms control, and they are most likely to believe such trust is not possible. In fact, some aggressor theorists go further and assert that negotiations are likely to generate suspicion and resentment and thus actually contribute to greater mistrust.[17]

These differing points of view on distrust explain the debate over detente in the 1970s. Spiral theorists were viewing detente as a long-term process of evolution toward mutual trust, and defended the SALT negotiations as "the centerpiece of detente." Aggressor theorists denied such goodwill was possible, and would only agree to SALT so long as it seemed to enhance the stability of deterrence. Thus, with respect to the details of the SALT negotiations, aggressor theorists strongly rejected the notion that any concessions were justified by the spirit of trust generated by the negotiations, while spiral theorists were willing to be more flexible. Other, more specific aspects of the U.S. domestic debate on the SALT I treaty amounted to a difference of opinion on whether trust—narrowly construed—was a precondition or a consequence of arms limitation agreements.

TRUST NARROWLY UNDERSTOOD

> There is an intimate, almost circular relationship between armaments competition and political conflict and thus the problem . . . is to determine the point at which we can intervene most effectively in the vicious circle.[18]

In the United States during the 1960s and 1970s less extreme spiral and aggressor theorists gained prominence and argued that modest arms control treaties could be negotiated between the United States and the Soviet Union despite deep distrust between the two countries. These proponents of arms control initiatives construed trust more narrowly, that is, as the amount of acceptable risk in negotiating a treaty rather than the level of goodwill necessary to establish world government or negotiate a major disarmament agreement (projects they considered unrealistic for the foreseeable future). These moderate spiral theorists and aggressor theorists agreed that arms control might be beneficial considering extant international conditions, but they often disagreed among themselves and with less moderate spiral and aggressor theorists about what risks were acceptable in 1) initiating the arms control process, and 2) concluding an arms limitation agreement.

Minimal Trust as a Prerequisite
for Negotiations

Negotiations do not just happen—they are planned. Aggressor theorists believe negotiations automatically entail risks, not least because the willingness to negotiate may suggest weakness as well as confidence. Always alert to the political significance of negotiating procedures, aggressor theorists approach negotiations with time-consuming caution. Negotiations have even been postponed due to disagreement over the shape of the negotiating table, which one side objected conferred political status to a party it considered illegitimate. Most spiral theorists have little patience for the aggressor theorist's perpetual pessimism and precautions on political symbolism which always seem to delay and complicate negotiations. As one experienced American diplomat noted:

> It's almost like an 18th-century minuet, where you have to go through all these formal steps. Some people think we ought to just go off and sit down with the Russians and say "This is what we're worried about, and what can we do to fix it?"[19]

Spiral theorists are especially sympathetic to this sentiment. If it seems necessary, they will even support unilateral gestures of restraint (for example, in weapons procurement) to get negotiations started and break the cycle of armaments and fear. The Greek historian Xenophon has recorded with great eloquence just such a unilateral gesture of trust designed to initiate negotiations between two potential belligerents. Twenty-four hundred years ago, as mutual suspicion arose between Greek mercenaries being escorted from Persia by a contingent from the Persian army, the leader of the Greeks approached his Persian counterpart and said:

> I observe that you are watching our moves as though we were enemies, and we, noticing this, are watching yours, too. On looking into things, I am unable to find evidence that you are trying to do us any harm, and I am perfectly sure that, as far as we are concerned, we do not even contemplate such a thing; and so I decided to discuss matters with you, to see if we could put an end to this mutual mistrust. I know, too, of cases that have occurred in the past when people, sometimes merely on the strength of suspicion, have become frightened of each other and then, in their anxiety to strike first before anything is done to them, have done irreparable harm to those who neither intended nor even wanted to do them any harm at all. I have come then in the conviction that misunderstandings of this sort can best be ended by personal contact, and I want to make it clear to you that you have no reason to distrust us.[20]

The Greek leader, aware of past spirals of insecurity that had led to preventive strikes and general war, decided to break the cycle of suspicion and through a unilateral gesture of goodwill convince the Persians to negotiate procedures for a reduction of tension.

Unfortunately, that decision turned out to be a mistake. The Persians

accepted the Greek overture and invited all the Greek leaders to a banquet. The Persians then slaughtered the Greek officers, evidently expecting the rest of the leaderless Greeks to quickly succumb. Instead, the Greeks elected new leaders and fought all the way across Persia and back to Greece.[21] Seldom do modern negotiators have to worry about their personal safety, but statesmen still worry about an adversary using negotiations as a distraction while it prepares a first strike or otherwise secures some unilateral advantage, for example, to manipulate public opinion while covertly building up a lead in armaments.

Aggressor theorists would cite the case of the Greeks and Persians as evidence that misplaced trust can encourage aggression, in the short term by enticing an aggressor to strike first, and over the long term by psychologically disarming a state overly anxious to reach accommodation.[22] Moderate aggressor theorists who support arms control negotiations are more flexible. However they justify negotiations as requiring no trust whatsoever, in part to assuage less compromising aggressor theorists and in part because of their own convictions. U.S. secretary of state George Schultz made this claim in 1984:

> Some say that if you cannot trust the Soviets, you should not negotiate with them. But the truth is, successful negotiations are not based on trust. We do not need to trust the Soviets; we need to make agreements that are trustworthy because both sides have incentives to keep them. Such incentives operate best when there are clear and working means to verify that obligations undertaken are, in fact, carried out.[23]

Secretary Schultz who supported negotiations was trying to postpone the issue of trust until after an agreement had been negotiated (when the question of trust would reopen in reference to verification procedures). He needed to argue that opening negotiations required no trust, and therefore no risks.

Referring to the case of the Greeks and Persians, the spiral theorist would say the incident only demonstrates why building trust must be an incremental process, and why in the short term both negotiations and defense are necessary. The Greeks should have arranged to meet on neutral ground with equal numbers of men. One cannot expect to dissipate a vast reserve of mistrust so soon. By offering too much trust too fast the Greeks encouraged the Persians to launch what the Persians thought would be a crippling first strike. The proper course would have been to investigate the possibilities for some sort of confidence-building measures.[24]

The spiral theorist would add, moreover, that there also are risks associated with refusing to take a unilateral step to check rising tensions. Edward Gibbon cites a case where "the flames of discord and mutual hatred burst forth into a dreadful conflagration," which he suggests could have been avoided if in a moment of crisis, Lupicinus, a Roman military governor in Thrace, had tried conciliation instead of revenge. When an "accidental quarrel" broke out between some Goths and Romans, Lupicinus "inflamed by wine and oppressed by sleep" issued a "rash command" for revenge. One act of violence led to another until finally the result was a long and destructive war which ended in a military disaster of the first magnitude for the Roman Empire and its citizens.[25]

Minimal Trust as a Precondition
for Treaty Ratification

After arms limitation negotiations are completed the debate shifts to whether or not accepting the provisions of the treaty requires any trust, and if so, how much trust is acceptable. The amount of trust required in accepting a negotiated agreement is equal to a state's inability to verify compliance (domestic political considerations aside). Hard-line aggressor theorists who do not want an arms control treaty insist on ironclad guarantees for compliance, and then argue that no control system can provide perfect verification of compliance, so there should not be a treaty.

The spiral theorist finds that even those moderate aggressor theorists who want an arms control treaty usually demand impossibly stringent standards for verification of compliance. There are always potential means of cheating on an agreement if a nation is determined to do so, but the small security advantage resulting from a successful violation of a minimum risk arms control treaty would not be worth the security costs of a renewed arms race and the public opinion costs should the violation be detected and made public. Therefore, asserts the spiral theorist, there is no net incentive to violate low risk agreements.[26] In addition, the spiral theorist concludes that whatever small risks are entailed in accepting imperfect verification procedures, they are outweighed by the greater risks of continued arms competition.[27]

In summary, whatever amount of trust is involved in a minimum risk agreement, the aggressor theorist sees it as the amount of risk his country must take, which he wants to minimize. The aggressor theorist also will insist on inspecting each new agreement with the same close scrutiny. The spiral theorist, in contrast, wants to maximize trust while remaining within the bounds of stability. He may want to begin slowly but also will want to enlarge upon the amount of trust involved in succeeding agreements in order to build what the aggressor theorist rejects in principle: a reassuring record of expanding mutual trust.

According to the spiral theorist, when enough low risk arms control agreements are in place and none are being violated, there will be a cumulative impact on the political environment which will contribute to mutual trust and the resolution of outstanding political problems. This process is facilitated by the fact that in negotiating an arms control agreement each side learns more about the other's capabilities, knowledge that contributes to deterrence and mutual respect. In contrast, the aggressor theorist believes that well-defined arms control agreements can only contribute to stability by reducing uncertainty about relative power configurations.

TRUST AND ALTERNATIVE WAYS OF NEGOTIATING

From the foregoing it should be clear that aggressor theorists see negotiations as a means of defining relative power configurations, while the spiral theorist sees negotiations as a means of improving mutual trust. This basic difference in perspective explains further disagreement on three important issues associated with negotiating arms limitation agreements: the "spirit and letter" of the agreement, weapons as "bargaining chips," and "informal" as opposed to formal arms control.

The Letter and Spirit of an Agreement

In negotiating an arms limitation agreement, states may make it clear that they will only recognize the precise obligations contained in the text of the agreement (the letter of the agreement). Alternatively, negotiators may encourage a broader interpretation of the treaty's significance by either using vague or ambiguous language where specific agreement is not possible, or by appending separate clauses of interpretation for points of unresolved contention (in effect, agreements to disagree). In seeking a more general significance for a treaty, the hope is that each side will refrain from taking steps that might not be prohibited by the letter of the agreements, but which the other signatory would surely consider a violation of the spirit of the agreements. In this way some calculated ambiguity can assist a move toward greater mutual trust.

An aggressor theorist objects to reliance on the spirit of an agreement for at least two reasons. First, it could actually increase mutual distrust. Edward Luttwak makes this point:

> Soviet leaders have been frank in stating that only the actual language of treaties is binding. . . . It has been *Western* statesmen who have insisted that this or that summit, or treaty, has generated a binding "spirit" of cooperation. . . . The Soviet refusal to accept voluntary inhibitions for the sake of the "spirit" of things merely requires that arms control agreements be drafted very carefully indeed. . . .
>
> While arms control can only be effectively pursued if negotiated limitations are defined with extreme precision, the United States has consistently tolerated ambiguities in its urgent pursuit of agreement for its own sake. As a result, a new and entirely artificial source of U.S.-Soviet tensions has been created. Changes in the Soviet strategic forces that would otherwise have passed almost unnoticed have excited suspicion and resentment when seen in high contrast against the poorly drafted texts of the 1972 Moscow accords. One side-benefit of each arms control agreement should be to build confidence for the next, but the tension creating ambiguities of SALT I have utterly defeated this purpose.[28]

Secondly, according to aggressor theorists reliance on ambiguity and the spirit of the agreement may also encourage bad behavior. Ambassador Averell Harriman observed in 1945 that Soviet moves to establish hegemony in Eastern Europe were in part a result of U.S. willingness at Yalta "to accept a general wording of the declaration on Poland and liberated Europe," and he said he had evidence that the USSR regarded the continued "generous and considerate" attitude adopted by the United States as a sign of weakness.[29]

There are historical cases that support the hopes of spiral theorists and some which substantiate the fears of aggressor theorists. Aggressor theorists often cite the Japanese and German use of naval treaties prior to World War II:

> While the Germans and Japanese made some attempt to conceal their naval building programs, most of their efforts were devoted to devising ingenious variations of those vessels prohibited under the treaty—variations that would fall outside the letter of the prohibition.[30]

It was impossible to match Japan's and Germany's violations of the spirit of the agreement when American and British public opinion saw the arms agreements as movement toward peace and were thus unwilling to fund new defense programs.

On the other hand, the Hittite-Egyptian treaty of 1296 B.C. mentioned in Chapter 2 is an example of a treaty designed with calculated ambiguity which appears to have been a success. The treaty was not only engraved on a silver plaque in two languages, but also in two versions. Like the modern U.S. and Soviet negotiators who wrote alternative interpretations of treaty provisions into the SALT I accords, the Egyptians and Hittites insisted on two versions "each being a revised translation of the paragraphs concerning the enemy's obligations, and in each case the phraseology [was] altered to suit the wishes of the revisers."[31] Despite much misgiving and distrust between the contracting parties, the ambiguous wording made the treaty possible, and the treaty helped end the recurring Egyptian-Hittite wars, bringing peace and stability to the region for quite some time.

Bargaining Chips

Differences of opinion on the relationship between trust and arms control are also manifest in disagreement over the use of weapons as "bargaining chips" for arms control negotiations. If a weapons system is not considered vital by spiral theorists, they are often willing to suspend its deployment as a unilateral gesture of restraint rather than use the threat of its deployment to extract concessions during negotiations. For example, President Carter believed the B-1 bomber was unnecessary in view of cruise missile development, so he canceled the program and rejected advice that it be used as a bargaining chip in the SALT II negotiations.

Aggressor theorists were alarmed by President Carter's decision. Since they see arms control negotiations as an exercise in defining power relationships, aggressor theorists are loath to forgo any weapons system without commensurate concessions from the other side. President Nixon criticized the Carter decision to cancel the B-1 as a unilateral concession:

> We cannot deploy, use, or employ for political effect or as bargaining chips missiles we were allowed to build but did not. If the United States unilaterally makes a concession in the hope of inducing concessions on their side, the Soviets take full advantage of this stupidity and push ahead with their programs.[32]

Moreover, argue aggressor theorists, without weapon programs under development for eventual deployment or use as bargaining chips, a state may feel compelled to accept a treaty even if it grants the adversary significant advantages. With defense preparations in limbo, the other side could "cash its chips" and lurch ahead in the arms race while the side that had already unilaterally forsaken developing "bargaining chips" would have to start new defense programs from scratch. Fearing this eventuality, a state might consent to a poor treaty, reasoning it would be better than none at all.

Sometimes arguments for bargaining chips are used as a ploy to secure domestic support for new armament programs. Several presidents have defended development of a weapons system as necessary for negotiating its termination, even when the President was personally convinced that deployment of the system was necessary for U.S. strategic stability. Nixon secured congressional acceptance of the Trident submarine by arguing it was necessary for successful completion of the SALT I negotiations, and President Reagan used the same argument in reference to the START negotiations in order to secure congressional support for the MX missile.

Informal Arms Control

"Informal arms control" is defined differently by aggressor and spiral theorists according to their differing approaches to the issue of trust in arms limitation agreements. For the spiral theorist, informal arms control means measures calculated to reduce mistrust and establish a cooperative relationship that will make formal negotiations possible. Declarations of goodwill, unilateral restraint, or concessions in military programs and informal public diplomacy are means to this end.

For example, since 1960 delegations of private (and prominent) U.S. and Soviet citizens have met in a series of conferences to improve mutual understanding and defuse dangerous tensions. These meetings are called the Dartmouth Conferences in reference to the first meeting held at Dartmouth College. The delegates discuss controversial bilateral issues off the record in an effort to diminish misunderstandings through informal dialogue. The Pugwash Conferences, initiated in 1957, and the World Disarmament Campaign launched by the United Nations in 1982 are similar examples of the spiral theorist approach to informal arms control. The Pugwash Conferences began at the behest of Bertrand Russell and Albert Einstein, who called on scientists of all nations to meet annually and discuss ways modern science could contribute to peace. The Campaign for World Disarmament was begun "in order that an international conscience may develop and . . . mobilize world public opinion on behalf of disarmament."

In contrast, the aggressor theorist, who does not strive for trust but rather for deterrence, defines informal arms control as unilateral steps designed to enhance strategic stability by improving strategic force postures. The purpose of these unilateral steps is to be informally communicated to adversaries in hopes that they will understand and reciprocate. As one example of the aggressor theorists' approach to informal arms control, Henry Kissinger has argued that the United States should forgo MIRVed ICBMs in favor of single warhead missiles in order to reduce the incentive to launch a first strike. While the Soviets should be encouraged to follow the U.S. lead, the United States should proceed unilaterally if necessary, and in either case, argues Kissinger, the move would improve conditions for strategic stability.[33]

CONCLUSIONS

Can apolitical agreements not requiring trust, that is, "technical" arms control and "material" disarmament agreements, precede and contribute to a level of trust sufficient to resolve outstanding political differences? Or can they only follow from the resolution of outstanding political differences? In summarizing the different ways spiral and aggressor theorists answer these questions, it is helpful to distinguish between negotiations aimed at short-term military stability and those aspiring to longer-term elimination of interstate hostilities.

Short-term formal treaties designed to enhance stability, or technical arms limitation agreements, assume two minimum elements of trust. First, it is assumed that each side desires stability, an assumption that many aggressor theorists doubt, and second, since there are no *perfect* verification procedures that are practical, it is assumed that each side has more reason to comply with the treaty than to circumvent its provisions. The spiral theorist accepts and assumes these minimum elements of trust. Aggressor theorists do not assume a minimum level of trust exists. If they support an agreement, so far as is possible they want strict verification procedures that require minimal trust and thus minimal risk. If such verification procedures are in place and the terms of the agreement are explicit and unambiguous, aggressor theorists may support a short-term arms limitation treaty as a contribution to stable deterrence.

Concerning long-term prospects for formal treaties, the spiral theorist and aggressor theorist find almost no room for agreement. The aggressor theorist concludes that trust, broadly construed, is a prerequisite for meaningful arms control and disarmament, but that such trust is impossible considering the nature of the international system and the adversary in question. The conclusion for many aggressor theorists, therefore, is that the long-term prospects for building goodwill through arms control are nonexistent.[34]

The spiral theorist has a more optimistic appraisal of the long-term prospects for building goodwill through negotiated agreements. Since the spiral theorist begins with the presumption that mistrust is a function of misperception, he sees arms control and trust as inextricably linked. The question is not an all or nothing proposition, but an inquiry about first steps toward mutual trust, the answer to which is that trust and arms control proceed virtually simultaneously. In the long term, the question of whether trust is a prerequisite for arms control is really misleading for spiral theorists since they believe trust and arms control proceed incrementally and are mutually reinforcing. A successful record of minimum risk agreements, they believe, can contribute to growing mutual trust and eventually the resolution of outstanding political differences. In this broad sense, the spiral theorist would assert that arms control can precede trust.

It bears repeating that the question of which precedes the other, arms control or trust, is not obscure and trivial. On the contrary, answering the question is critical for determining how and when arms control negotiations should begin, proceed and conclude.

The question of trust and arms control is also most relevant for an understanding of contemporary arms control negotiations between the United States and the Soviet Union. It is often argued that the United States attempts to negotiate "technical" agreements aimed at military stability (believing arms control can precede trust), while the USSR views arms control in a political context, believing trust must precede disarmament.[35]

President Reagan, an aggressor theorist, campaigned for office on the assertion that the dissimilar U.S. and Soviet approaches to arms control had been disastrous for the United States. He entered office believing too much had been left to trust in previous negotiations and that the Soviet Union had taken advantage of this trust to secure unilateral advantages:

> So far, the Soviet Union has used arms control negotiations primarily as an instrument to restrict U.S. defense programs and, in conjunction with their own arms buildup, as a means to enhance Soviet power and prestige.[36]

Not unexpectedly, President Reagan was in no hurry to negotiate an arms control agreement. Since he believed the USSR used arms control to redefine the strategic balance in its favor he did not believe it would see any reason to negotiate for stability or arms reductions until the United States reestablished strategic parity: "Unless we demonstrate the will to rebuild our strength and restore the military balance, the Soviets . . . have little incentive to negotiate."[37]

Opponents of the President either asserted there was still a basic parity in military power between the United States and the Soviet Union, or that even if one agreed that the balance of forces had been upset, the best way to establish parity was through negotiations rather than a renewed arms race. In essence the President and his detractors disagreed as to whether or not parity was a precondition or a consequence of arms control negotiations, a question examined in the following chapter.

DISCUSSION QUESTIONS

1. What is the safest and most effective way to determine how much trust is possible between two states?
2. Is it possible to determine from the historical record whether and to what extent a state may be trusted? Can the U.S. and the USSR be trusted, and if so, to what extent?
3. Can a series of arms limitation agreements based on minimal trust contribute to a broader trust between states which helps resolve their outstanding political differences? In what circumstances might limited agreements undermine broader trust between the signatories?
4. President Carter and the United States Senate disagreed on whether the minimal trust between the U.S. and USSR necessary for ratifying the SALT II treaty existed. Was the president or the Senate correct?
5. Is it possible for negotiators to avoid the 'displacement effect', and if so, how?

SUGGESTED READINGS FOR CHAPTER ELEVEN: TOWARD PEACE—WHICH COMES FIRST, ARMS CONTROL OR TRUST?

BLECHMAN, BARRY M. "Do Negotiated Arms Control Agreements Have a Future?" *Foreign Affairs* (Fall 1980).

BULL, HEDLEY. *The Control of the Arms Race: Disarmament and Arms Control in the Missile Age.* 2nd ed. New York: Praeger, 1965. Especially Chapter 4.

BURTON, JOHN W. *Peace Theory: Precondition of Disarmament.* New York: Alfred A. Knopf, 1962.

CARLTON, DAVID. "International Systemic Features Inhibiting Disarmament and Arms Control." In David Carlton and Carlo Schaerf, eds., *Reassessing Arms Control.* London: Macmillan, 1985.

CLARK, GRENVILLE, and LOUIS SOHN. *World Peace Through World Law.* Cambridge: Harvard University Press, 1966.

DE MADARIAGA, SALVADOR. *Disarmament.* New York: Coward McCann, 1929.

FRANK, JEROME D. "Psychological Aspects of Disarmament and International Negotiations." In Burns H. Weston, ed., *Toward Nuclear Disarmament: A Search for Alternatives.* Boulder, CO: Westview Press, 1984.

GRAY, COLIN S. *Strategic Studies and Public Policy: The American Experience.* Lexington, KY: University of Kentucky Press, 1982.

KENNAN, GEORGE F. *The Nuclear Delusion: Soviet-American Relations in the Atomic Age.* New York: Pantheon, 1982.

KINCADE, WILLIAM H. "Arms Control or Arms Coercion?" *Foreign Policy* (Spring 1986): 24–45.

LUTTWAK, EDWARD N. "Why Arms Control Has Failed." *Commentary,* January 1978, pp. 19–28.

MYRDAL, ALVA. *The Game of Disarmament: How the United States and Russia Run the Arms Race.* New York: Pantheon, 1977.

NOEL-BAKER, PHILIP. *Disarmament.* New York: Garland Publishing, 1972.

OSGOOD, CHARLES E. *An Alternative to War or Surrender.* Urbana: University of Illinois Press, 1963.

RANGER, ROBIN. *Arms and Politics, 1958-79: Arms Control in a Changing Political Context.* Toronto: Macmillan of Canada, 1978.

WEISS, SEYMOUR. "The Case Against Arms Control." *Commentary,* November 1984, pp. 19–23.

YORK, HERBERT T. "Bilateral Negotiations and the Arms Race." *Scientific American,* October 1983.

NOTES

1. Respectively, William T. Fox in *Daedalus,* Vol. 89, No. 4 (1960): 1005; Salvador De Madariaga, quoted by Barbara Tuchman, *New York Magazine,* April 18, 1982; and Philip Noel-Baker, *The Arms Race* (London: Atlantic Books, 1958), p. 86.

2. Hedley Bull, *The Control of the Arms Race* (New York: Frederick A. Praeger, 1961), p. 75.

3. Radio address by Secretary of State Henry L. Stimson from London, January 28, 1930, in *London Naval Conference: Speeches and Press Statements by Members of the American Delegation,* Conference Series #3 (Washington, DC: United States Government Printing Office, 1930), p. 6.

4. Denys P. Myers, *World Disarmament: Its Problems and Prospects* (Boston: World Peace Foundation, 1932), p. 3.

5. Salvador de Madariaga, *Disarmament* (New York: Coward McCann, 1929), pp. 245, 296.

6. Some aggressor theorists believe all disarmament negotiations invariably fail to produce trust, and instead become political exercises in defining power relationships with numbers:

   The nation that has aggressive tendencies against another or fears aggressive tendencies on the part of another—and all nations are in the latter category—is compelled by considerations of self-interest to keep the estimate of its own defensive needs as high as possible and to reduce those of its rivals to the lowest possible point. In other words . . . the retention and aggrandizement of their own power and the containment and reduction of that of their rivals is expressed [through negotiating positions] in numerical terms in the evaluation of their own and other's military needs. The standards they apply are determined by their political aims and not by anything remotely resembling objective criteria. Therefore, these standards can be determined through free agreement of the nations concerned only after they have agreed on a settlement of the political issues dividing them.

   Hans Morgenthau, *Politics Among Nations,* 4th ed. (New York: Alfred A. Knopf, 1967), p. 387.

7. John Spanier and Joseph L. Nogee, *The Politics of Disarmament* (New York: Frederick A. Praeger, 1962), p. 14.

8. Ernest Lefever, ed., *Arms and Arms Control* (New York: Frederick A. Praeger, 1962), p. 181.

9. Philip Noel-Baker, *The Arms Race* (London: Atlantic Books, 1958), p. 86.

10. David Ziegler, *War, Peace and International Politics* (Boston: Little, Brown, 1981), pp. 254–255.

11. After the signing of the Partial Test Ban Treaty, which prohibited atmospheric nuclear testing, the frequency of nuclear testing underground almost doubled. In the eighteen years before signing the treaty, the United States and the USSR tested 463 warheads. In the ten years following the treaty, they conducted 424 tests. After the signing of SALT I, the United

States deployed the Trident submarine, developed B-1 bombers and long-range cruise missiles, and the USSR added SS-16s, 17s, 18s, and 19s to its nuclear arsenal.

For a discussion of technology and the displacement effect, see G. W. Rathjens et al., *Nuclear Arms Control Agreements: Process and Impact* (Washington, DC: Carnegie Endowment for International Peace, 1974), pp. 21ff.

12. De Madariaga, *Disarmament,* pp. 61–62, 251.

13. Simply put: "Disarmament negotiations are, in brief, one form of the arms race itself, the aim of each nation being an increase in its relative power position." Spanier and Nogee, *The Politics of Disarmament,* p. 15.

Morgenthau makes this point at greater length:

> The conflict between the United States and the Soviet Union, like [that] between France and Germany of the early thirties, then, is being fought on two levels: on the superficial level of disarmament and on the fundamental level of the struggle for power. On the level of disarmament, the conflict resolves itself into a controversy between two theoretical conceptions: security first, disarmament later vs. disarmament first, security later. On the level of the struggle for power, the conflict is posed in terms of competition for military advantage, each side trying, at worst, to maintain the existing distribution of power and, at best, to change it in its favor. Of this competition, the controversy about nuclear disarmament is merely an outward expression, following the contours of the conflict as the cast of clay follows the shape of the form into which it is molded. As the cast can only be changed by changing the mold, so the problem of nuclear disarmament can only be solved through a settlement of the power conflict from which it has arisen.

Morgenthau, *Politics Among Nations,* p. 386. See also footnote 8 above. For examples of treaties that allow higher ceilings, see p. 390 of Morgenthau and any account of the 1974 Vladivostok accords.

14. Gert Krell, "The Problems and Achievements of Arms Control," *Arms Control* (December 1981).

15. de Madariaga, *Disarmament,* p. 25.

16. John Lewis Gaddis, *The United States and the Origins of the Cold War* (New York: Columbia University Press, 1972), p. 316. For an ancient example, see Demosthenes, "On the Liberty of Rhodes," in A. N. W. Saunders, *Greek Political Oratory* (Middlesex, England, Penguin Books, 1970), p. 183, or Plato's *Republic,* where he observes, "When the tyrant has disposed of foreign enemies by conquest or treaty, and there is nothing to fear from them, then he is always stirring up some war or other, in order that the people may require a leader." In other words, some believe that tyrannies require political tension for domestic stability.

17. This point of view has been expressed in a conclusion to the anecdote about the animals' disarmament conference mentioned in Chapter 7, p. 125. After much argument about whether to limit beaks, claws, horns, talons, or teeth,

> The discussion got so hot and angry, and all those animals began thinking so much about horns and teeth and hugging when they argued about the peaceful intentions that had brought them together that they began to look at one another in a very nasty way. Luckily the keepers were able to calm them down and persuade them to go back quietly to their cages, and they began to feel quite friendly with one another again.

Henry Forbes, *The Strategy of Disarmament* (Washington, DC: Public Affairs Press, 1962), 48.

18. James E. Dougherty, *How to Think About Arms Control and Disarmament* (New York: Crane, Russak and Co., 1973), p. 10.

19. William Hyland, quoted in John Powers, "Hiroshima Plus 37," *Boston Globe Magazine,* October 17, 1982.

20. Cited by Thomas Schelling, in "Confidence in Crisis," *International Security* (Spring 1984), p. 55.

21. Interestingly, this feat of Greek arms seemed to convince Macedonian and Greek leaders (for example, Philip of Macedon and Isocrates of Athens) that Persia could be had for the

taking, much the same way the USSR's inept invasion of Finland in 1939 convinced many Germans, including Hitler, that the USSR was vulnerable. The Macedonians and Greeks were right, Hitler was wrong.

22. This is a constant complaint of hard-line aggressor theorists. They see an aggressor strug-gling to gain enough of an advantage in armaments to succeed at coercion or aggression. They are therefore constantly concerned with falling behind in arms. For many aggressor theorists the archetypical example of a nation psychologically disarmed by disarmament negotiations is Britain in the 1930s. See Stefan T. Possony, "On Arms Control for 1984," *Defence and Foreign Affairs* (February 1984): 7.

For another example, see Walter Laqueur, "America and the World: The Next Four Years," *Commentary,* 1977. Laqueur also warns that the United States must not fall behind the USSR in arms, and parallels the evolution of U.S. policy with the British failure to keep step with Nazi Germany, which he divides into four stages: (1) the reports of German rearmament are claimed to be exaggerated; (2) the reports are true but Germany will never catch up; (3) Germany has attained parity but it is not threatening because Germany must also defend its Eastern borders; and (4) Germany has acquired superiority, so appeasement is the only sensible policy. To prevent such a process from evolving, aggressor theorists demand constant efforts to keep pace in armaments.

23. Secretary of State George Shultz, "Managing the U.S.-Soviet Relationship Over the Long Term," *Current Policy No. 624,* U.S. Department of State, Bureau of Public Affairs, Oc-tober 18, 1984.

24. See footnote 17, Chapter 3.

25. Edward Gibbon, *The Decline and Fall of the Roman Empire,* an abridged version by Dero A. Saunders (Middlesex, England: Penguin Books, 1952), pp. 520–523.

26. Alva Myrdal, *The Game of Disarmament: How the United States and Russia Run the Arms Race* (New York: Pantheon Books, 1976). Myrdal asserts that the benefits of agreeing to verification based on an element of trust reinforced with fear of violations being detected "would allow confidence tested by experience to grow gradually." p. 301.

27. See Stephan M. Meyer, "Verification and Risk in Arms Control," *International Security* (Spring 1984): 117–119, and 126, where Meyer concludes:

The issue of verification and the risks of arms control should be approached in terms of one fundamental question: Is the military and political threat posed by undetected cheating greater than the military and political threat posed by unconstrained military activity?

See also Michael Wright, *Disarm and Verify* (London: Chatto and Windus, 1964).

28. Edward Luttwak, *Strategy and Politics: Collected Essays* (New Brunswick, NJ: Transaction Books, 1980), pp. 133–134, 137.

29. Cited in Walter R. Fisher and Richard Dean Burns, *Armament and Disarmament: The Con-tinuing Dispute* (Belmont, CA: Wadsworth Publishing Co., 1974), p. 121.

30. Richard Barnet and Richard Falk, eds., *Security in Disarmament* (Princeton, NJ: Princeton University Press, 1965), pp. 20–21.

31. C. W. Ceram, *The Secret of the Hittites,* translated by Clara and Richard Winston (New York: Alfred A. Knopf, Inc., 1973), p. 190.

32. Nixon went so far as to conclude, "The Carter administration's cancellation of the B-1 in the summer of 1977 may have been one of the greatest strategic blunders this nation has ever made." Richard Nixon, *The Real War* (New York: Warner Books, 1980), p. 169.

For more on bargaining chips, see Robert J. Einhorn, *Negotiating From Strength: Lever-age in US-Soviet Arms Control Negotiations* (New York: Praeger, 1985).

33. See, for example, Henry Kissinger, "A New Approach to Arms Control," *Time,* March 21, 1983. Also, for arms control from the aggressor theorist's point of view, see Kenneth Adel-man, "Is Arms Control at a Dead End?" Address before the Commonwealth Club of San Francisco, U.S. Department of State, Bureau of Public Affairs, *Current Policy* #837, May 16, 1986.

34. For example, in advising the United States to adopt the "Soviet political approach" to arms control, Colin Gray concludes:

> This is sound advice in that the United States would, at long last, begin to understand much more fully why the Soviet Union advances particular arms control positions, and why particular weapon systems are deployed, contrary to the American logic. But accepting a political approach to arms control means, in effect, abandoning aspirations for arms control altogether. Through political arms control, all that can be accomplished is to register, in weapons referent guise, the political interests that divide states.

Colin S. Gray, *Strategic Studies and Public Policy: The American Experience* (Lexington, KY: University of Kentucky Press, 1982), p. 163.

35. Going further it is sometimes argued that since the USSR believes trust between the United States and the Soviet Union is impossible, it considers arms control and disarmament only as a means to enhance a state's political fortunes. This theme is a popular one, despite its profound implications. It is especially well developed by Robin Ranger in *Arms and Politics: Arms Control in a Changing Political Context* (Toronto: Macmillan, 1979), and by Gray, *Strategic Studies and Public Policy,* pp. 76ff, where Gray quotes the frustrated head of the U.S. delegation to negotiations in 1959, concluding

> We have sought to promote technical discussion and understanding. You [the Soviet Representative] have sought discussion of a selection of political proposals, for the most part not susceptible of technical assessment. . . . Our approach was designed to avoid, without prejudice to any national interests, a wide range of difficult political issues which do not admit of technical discussion and can only be handled in the give and take of diplomatic negotiations.

See also Barry Blechman, "Do Negotiated Arms Limitations Have a Future?" *Foreign Affairs* (Fall 1980): 107–108, and U.S. Congress, House, Committee on Foreign Affairs, *Soviet Diplomacy and Negotiating Behavior: Emerging New Context for U.S. Diplomacy,* Vol. 1, Committee Print (Prepared by the Congressional Research Service, 1979), p. 492, where John Newhouse is cited for his conclusion that SALT I was a political and not a technical achievement, and p. 498, where Ambassador Smith concludes:

> For the Soviets, arms control has seemed primarily to be "a matter of international policies having technical aspects," while for the Americans, though appreciating its high political significance, it was seen "more as a search for solutions to the complex technical problems of establishing force levels and weapons characteristics by international agreements."

36. Ronald Reagan, *Vital Speeches of the Day,* June 1, 1982.
37. Cited by William Van Cleave in Richard Staar, ed., *Arms Control: Myth Versus Reality* (Stanford, CA: Hoover Institution Press, 1984), p. 15.

Chapter Twelve

Which Comes First, Arms Control or Parity?

In our times security can be real and enduring only if it reposes on the prevailing rough military parity of the opposite forces and on subsequent reduction of their level. . . . [But] the U.S. administration does not want parity. It wants the world to identify parity with U.S. military superiority.

> —Leonid Brezhnev
> June 30, 1981

By the end of 1979, when Soviet leader Brezhnev declared, "a balance now exists," the Soviets had over 800 (SS-20) warheads. We still had none. . . . By last August, the 800 warheads had become more than 1,200. We still had none. . . . At this same time Soviet Defense Minister Ustinov announced "approximate parity of forces continues to exist." But the Soviets are still adding . . . and now have 1,300. . . . We still have none. So far, it seems that the Soviet definition of parity is a box score of 1,300 to nothing, in their favor.

> —Ronald Reagan
> April 15, 1983[1]

Public opinion tends to equate parity with fairness, and thus few nations publicly want to admit they are willing to accept disparity as a basis for negotiations. Consequently negotiations often proceed with parity as the declared goal regardless of what the negotiators are actually willing to accept in the best interest of their nation's security. If negotiations are unsuccessful, it is likely that each side will accuse the other of rejecting the principle of parity.

Before discussing parity, in more detail, and in particular whether parity is a cause or consequence of arms control two preliminary points must be made. First, as was true in the case of trust and arms control, equivocal usage of the term "parity" complicates discussion on whether it is a consequence or a precondition of arms limitation agreements. Sometimes parity is broadly construed as a general balance of power (strategic parity), at other times it is intended to mean an equality in overall forces (military parity), and then again parity is often used to suggest only a balance in a specific area of armaments currently under negotiation (negotiated parity). Second, despite its popularity, there are alternatives to parity.

ALTERNATIVES TO PARITY

Multilateral Ratios

Two years after the signing of the Washington Naval Treaty in 1922, several of its signatories tried to encourage other nations to follow their example and voluntarily limit their naval construction. A conference was convened in Rome in 1924, but scant progress was made in the discussions. Britain, historically very sensitive to the European balance of power in naval armaments, was particularly intent on seeing Spain, France, and Italy limit the size of their navies in accordance with the set of ratios used in the Washington Naval Treaty. These ratios, used to define the "status quo," were based on the relative European naval balance of power in 1921. Spain was particularly displeased with the "status quo" figure it had been allocated, arguing it unfairly reflected a time when the Spanish navy was unnaturally "depleted." One day, after the usual frustrating impasse in negotiations, the Spanish admiral cornered the British admiral and

> declared himself ready to accept the status quo. His British colleague was very much elated. Then the Spaniard added: "But we must discuss one point, the year to be chosen to define the status quo." "Why," said the Englishman, "1921." "Oh, no," said the Spaniard: "I suggest 1588."[2]

Of course, 1588 was the year the Spanish Armada sailed for England and the last year Spain ever held naval superiority over England.

Ratios are either determined by arbitrarily selecting a particular year as a basis for the "status quo," or by arguing the merits of alternative ratio systems in the context of extant security concerns. Either way the ratios are sure to be controversial.[3] In the 1924 negotiations mentioned above Spain would have considered naval parity with England a great victory, while England would have considered it a disaster (and vice versa in 1588). In the case of

England, parity with Spain was unacceptable because England felt its national security depended upon its navy more than did Spain's, and that it had to take into account other nations that it believed were a threat to its security, especially Germany. For the same reason, Britain accepted parity in capital ships with the United States in 1922 only when it felt it had no alternative, and rejected parity in cruisers until 1930 when again, it felt it could only restrain the U.S. shipbuilding program by accepting a negotiated parity. In these negotiations, the British argued that the defense of their worldwide sea lines of communication made parity unacceptable.

The problem of choosing between parity and a ratio system persists in contemporary arms control debate. Many in the United States today believe nuclear parity is incompatible with U.S. security interests in Europe. Parity might suffice to deter an attack on the United States, but they believe U.S. nuclear superiority is required to deter a Soviet attack on Western Europe, since only superiority would make the U.S. threat to escalate from nuclear war in Europe to a general nuclear war credible.

Trading Disparities or Seeking Strategic Parity with Military Disparities

How states define negotiated parity is partly a function of the scope of the negotiations and the similarity of their forces. Restricting the scope of the negotiations can reduce some dissimilarities in forces, thereby making comparison and a definition of parity easier. On the other hand, the broader the scope of the negotiations, the more room there is for trade-offs and compromises on relative advantages and disadvantages between dissimilar weapon systems. For example, a treaty may allow a disparity in one kind of weapon (for example, tanks) to be balanced by a reciprocal disparity in other kinds of military forces (for example, troop levels).

Or, if the scope of the treaty is broad enough, states may accept negotiated disparity in one area of military competition in order to achieve broader strategic parity or advantages. For example, the Japanese accepted numerical disparity and allowed the United States and Britain an advantage in capital ships in the Washington Naval Treaty. Yet, from the Japanese point of view this naval disparity in warships may have been acceptable in a larger strategic context since a nonfortification clause in the treaty prevented the improvement of existing British and U.S. military bases in the Pacific region.

Superiority

Besides political, geographic, and numerous other strategic considerations, parity can be rejected as the sole basis for negotiations because it is believed that mere parity will not deter states that are dissatisfied with the status quo. Senator Henry Jackson explained this point of view in straightforward fashion:

> International peace and stability depend not on a parity of power but on a preponderance of power in the peace-keepers over the peace upsetters.[4]

If two sides are only roughly equivalent in strength, an aggressor may presume that his nation's inherent military virtues will suffice to carry him to victory, especially if he takes full advantage of the element of surprise. Or, if the aggressor is more cautious, he still will have nothing to lose by constantly probing the target state's defenses, looking for an opportunity to seize momentary advantage until finally the balance of power has shifted to his advantage. For these reasons many aggressor theorists insist military superiority is necessary to deter an aggressor from both massive first strikes and more limited conflicts.

Occasionally a state which believes it is negotiating with an aggressive adversary will accept parity in an arms limitation agreement if a continuation of the arms race would be too dangerous, or if it appears the state would actually lose ground in military competition without the benefit of a negotiated parity. President Nixon's assessment of parity and his role in negotiating SALT I reflects the aggressor theorist's reluctant acceptance of parity.

Nixon argued that superiority was a legitimate goal for the United States. However, he defended the underlying strategic parity of the SALT I agreement, which he signed:

> In 1972 SALT I, with the Jackson Amendment, established parity . . . as U.S. policy. Parity is an uneasy condition . . . as long as we live in a situation of parity, we live with risk. But parity is better than inferiority, and parity is something about which negotiators can negotiate. Mutually beneficial arms restraints between the two major powers can only be agreed upon on a basis of parity. Strategic parity is a situation we can live safely with—but only if it is true parity and only if . . . we are strong enough in other areas—theater nuclear forces, conventional forces, the strength and cohesion of our alliances, the will and skill of our leaders—to check Soviet adventuring without holding a strategic advantage. If we fail in these other areas, then parity will no longer be sufficient; then we will have to resume an all-out arms race, and go all out to win. Otherwise, we will lose.

Nixon concluded, "Superiority would be preferable," but implied it was not possible, and argued that in special conditions, negotiated parity in strategic weapons was acceptable. Thus he defended the SALT I accords in part because they reflected parity and in part because he felt they were necessary to "buy time" for the United States.[5]

Spiral theorists are not concerned with deterring aggression but rather with halting the arms race. Naturally they reject superiority because it forces the other side to reciprocate, thus escalating the spiral of mutual fear and arms which leads to war. Negotiating limitations or reductions in armaments, or even accepting temporary inferiority through a negotiated freeze in weapons deployments, are sensible first steps to arresting the spiral of insecurity. Thus for the spiral theorist, parity rather than superiority is the legitimate basis for negotiating arms limitation agreements.

PARITY DILEMMAS

Parity is not the only possible objective of arms negotiations, but it often is considered the only realistic basis for arms limitations, especially in bilateral negotiations. Often it is even asserted that parity is a prerequisite for meaningful arms limitation negotiations because if too great a disparity in power exists between two parties, the superior party will prefer to dictate rather than negotiate the terms of agreement.[6] Just as wars often end when two sides agree neither is strong enough to force its will on the other, peace agreements often are signed when both sides agree their military forces are roughly equivalent and cannot be used to extort concessions.[7]

Yet if parity is a precondition for arms limitations, it cannot also be the goal of arms negotiations. This conundrum may be referred to as:

> *Parity Dilemma 1:* Meaningful negotiations are only possible when military parity exists. If there is disparity, the state that is ahead will feel no need to negotiate. Thus, the goal of arms control—parity—is a precondition for negotiations. Once the precondition of parity is met, the goal of arms control has been accomplished and there is no need for a negotiated agreement.

The rebuttal to parity dilemma number one usually takes one of two forms. First, formal negotiations and negotiated agreements which codify parity may be defended as confidence building measures which improve the political atmosphere. The second response to the dilemma is more involved and requires a distinction between rough and stable military parity.

It may be agreed that nations only have an incentive to negotiate when a *rough* military parity exists, but a more precise and stable parity is more easily achieved at the negotiating table than by means of a diverse, extended, and dangerous weapons competition. Without sitting down and actually hammering out a negotiated agreement as to what constitutes parity, each side, ever insecure about its military security, will tend to exaggerate the enemy's strength and underestimate its own, thereby providing the impetus for a dynamic arms race. Hence to suggest that arms control is unnecessary when two nations have military parity is to assume that parity is easily recognizable, relatively static, and informally agreed upon by both sides, none of which is true.

Aggressor theorists, who often find parity dilemma 1 compelling, may accept the spiral theorists' rebuttal which distinguishes between rough military parity (a precondition for negotiations) and a more specific stable parity (the goal of negotiations). If so, they are likely to demand a very precise negotiated parity. The slightest imbalance which favors an adversary will be rejected as acquiescing to enemy "superiority." Spiral theorists are not sympathetic to the aggressor theorists' demands for perfect parity. They believe it is virtually impossible, and in any case unnecessary, to have *perfect* parity between opposing forces. Breaking the cycle of mistrust is more important than quibbling over what constitutes perfect parity in military forces.

Moreover spiral theorists believe aggressor theorists make a logical contradiction when they fuss too much over whether the terms of an agreement amount to perfect parity. This apparent contradiction may be referred to as:

> *Parity Dilemma 2:* How can anyone worry about whether or not the terms of an agreement constitute perfect parity or whether there is the slightest imbalance in forces, when without an agreement the balance, or "parity," between opposing forces would be much more ambiguous.

The reasoning behind this rhetorical dilemma is particularly convincing to those who believe both sides have overkill capabilities. Senator Kennedy's plea for a "freeze" on the nuclear forces of the United States and the USSR is representative of this attitude:

> The United States and the Soviet Union now possess the equivalent of 3 million tons of T.N.T. for every man, woman and child presently living on this planet. Even in the unlikely event of a successful Soviet first strike against our land-based missiles, we would still have over 3500 warheads at sea and on bombers—enough to destroy every Soviet city and town seven times over. . . . Because this is so, a number of us in Congress . . . called for an immediate, mutual, and verifiable freeze. . . . for both great powers, arms control is a far saner way to preserve strategic parity than an endless arms race.[8]

Kennedy notes that parity is better preserved through negotiations, but his major point is that parity is not important because the United States has a secure second-strike capability, and even an overkill capability, in nuclear weapons. In other words, Kennedy believes there is no particular advantage in nuclear superiority, and thus it is not necessary to insist on strict parity.

There is a rejoinder to Parity Dilemma 2, and it came to the forefront of public debate after Secretary of State Henry Kissinger made a statement on the irrelevance of nuclear superiority during testimony before the U.S. Senate on the SALT I accord. While responding to criticism from senators who were dissatisfied with the SALT treaty because they believed it gave the USSR strategic superiority, Kissinger retorted:

> What in the name of God is superiority? What is the significance of it, politically, militarily, operationally? What do you do with it?[9]

Hard-line aggressor theorists immediately took Kissinger to task for his "what is superiority" comment. Harvard Sovietologist Richard Pipes made the following analysis of Kissinger's remark:

> It is often argued, sometimes with the invocation of heaven's name, that the concept of nuclear superiority is utterly meaningless because there is no way in which it can be exploited. National security, it is said, requires nothing more (nor less) than strategic parity or "essential equivalence." One does not have to be

an expert on formal logic to realize that the terms "parity" or "equivalence" postulate their contraries, which are "superiority" and "inferiority." He who says "parity" unavoidably, even if silently, admits to the possibility of "disparity"; that is, superior and inferior entities. Were this not the case, we would have no need for arms limitations. We could readily permit the Russians to squander their resources on accumulating, until the end of time, useless arsenals of still-bigger and more-accurate missiles while we enjoyed the good life behind our deterrent.[10]

In essence, Pipes responded to Parity Dilemma 2 with yet another parity dilemma. Dilemma 2 asks why the aggressor theorist nit-picks over a negotiated definition of parity when, however it is defined, it is more closely approximated in an agreement than in an arms race. The aggressor theorist's rejoinder is:

> *Parity Dilemma 3:* A precise definition of parity is critical because it is the sole reason for negotiating an arms control agreement. If superiority, or an imbalance in arms, is insignificant, then there is no need to bother negotiating parity. In other words, if a slight imbalance is not worth quibbling over, there is no need to try to move beyond rough parity, which is a precondition to negotiations and thus is obtained without the benefit of negotiations.

In the first parity dilemma, it is argued that if one is only concerned with an approximation of parity (rough parity)—such as those spiral theorists who use the overkill argument and claim there is no advantage in superiority—then there is no need for any negotiations because rough parity is a precondition for negotiations. If a more precise and stable definition of parity is the goal of arms limitation negotiations (as is argued in response to Parity Dilemma 1), then the aggressor theorist may agree that negotiations must precede parity, and thus have a legitimate function. However, the goal then becomes precise parity and the aggressor theorist feels justified in debating whether or not the agreement allows any imbalance in forces. If such an imbalance is not significant, then precise parity is not significant. If precise parity is not significant, there is no reason to negotiate since the commencement of negotiations implies *rough parity* already has been established.

The combination of the first and third parity dilemmas seem to put negotiators in the uncomfortable position of having to defend any arms limitation agreement as the codification of perfect parity, but this is not necessarily the case. One may argue that perfect parity is impossible, or at least endlessly debatable. What is needed is a negotiated parity that is more precise and much more stable than that which would be possible through an arms race, but does not claim to codify perfect parity, which is impossible to negotiate or ratify. In other words, spiral theorists desire a well regulated parity, or a "this is as close as can reasonably be expected" parity.[11]

Various U.S. administrations trying to justify strategic arms control agreements have tried to relieve pressure from aggressor theorists demanding perfect parity by dropping the term "parity" altogether when explaining their goal in strategic arms control negotiations. "Essential equivalence" or mere "sufficiency," for example, lack the implied precision of parity and thus psychologically dispose one to a more flexible definition of strategic parity.

Perhaps a more effective means of countering pressure for perfect parity is to put the aggressor theorist on the defensive with Parity Dilemma 2: how can one nit-pick over the fine details of parity when no agreement at all would leave the question of precise parity even more confused?

Aggressor theorists have an answer to this question. They argue that it would be dangerous to allow the other state to believe it had managed to gain even a minor military advantage. The willingness to accept any disadvantage, no matter how small, might communicate a lack of resolve and encourage aggression. A formal treaty is a powerful symbolic statement. An opponent may draw conclusions about resolve from a formal agreement which would not be justified in the turbulence and ambiguity of normal arms competition.

It even has been argued that accepting a numerical disparity in an arms limitation agreement can suggest weakness even where there is no actual military disparity:

> In 1972 . . . Edward Luttwak . . . recognized that "a near consensus of strategic experts would undoubtedly answer that the United States has conceded nothing" of military significance in the SALT I treaty. Yet such thinking, he argued, "totally discounted" the "prestige effects deriving from the possession of strategic weapons" that are "psychologically by far the most impressive of all instruments of power." He claimed that "with informed public opinion the world over" there is a "definite awareness that one side or the other has more. And 'more' is widely regarded as implying greater power."[12]

Aggressor theorists are so sensitive to the significance of perceived disparity that they are likely to reject disparity in any form, regardless of its military significance.

TWO QUALIFICATIONS TO THE PREMISE IN PARITY DILEMMA 1

The premise in Parity Dilemma 1 is that arms control agreements can ratify parities in force levels but cannot create them, since states will not negotiate when a significant disparity in military forces exists (the leading state having no reason to negotiate while it is ahead). There are at least two exceptions to the validity of this general rule. First, sometimes a state will willingly relinquish military superiority in favor of a more stable negotiated parity, either because it believes negotiated parity is better for its security than continuing arms competition or because it can no longer afford the financial and political costs of arms competition. For example the United States forsook strategic nuclear superiority during the 1960s and opted in favor of negotiated parity when it signed the SALT I agreement.[13]

The second exception to the assertion that rough parity must precede negotiations comes from those aggressor theorists who believe some states must be threatened with an effort to achieve superiority before they will agree to parity. They maintain that an aggressor, or a state used to superiority, will not agree to parity unless its opponent mounts an armament effort that suggests it is determined to acquire superiority if negotiations fail. This is bargaining chip strategy writ large, and it is designed to make negotiated parity an attractive option for states otherwise not inclined to accept parity.

For example in 1927 Allen Dulles explained the success of the Washington Naval Treaty in obtaining dramatic cuts in existing capital ships as a result of an American drive for naval superiority:

> The Washington Conference was a success because of the impelling influence exerted by the United States at a time when it was about to assume a controlling naval position. The results were purchased at a price which has often been criticized by our naval men, but which the country at large has approved. We gave up the opportunity to secure naval superiority in exchange for an agreement on the basis of equality with Great Britain.

With respect to the then current negotiations on cruisers and submarines, Dulles went on to argue:

> We must frankly recognize, however, that as a result we cannot now exercise the same effective influence for naval limitation as we did in 1921. No power has any reason to fear that we are now seeking naval supremacy and no power consequently would be particularly impelled to make concessions which they might be disposed to make in difficult circumstances.[14]

As a result Dulles believed the United States would have to "be content with relatively high maximum limitations in the various classes of vessels now unrestricted," which were better than "no limitations whatever." (These same arguments were offered as an explanation for the high ceilings agreed to in the Vladivostok accords which President Ford negotiated as a complement to SALT I.) In 1982 President Reagan justified his administration's arms negotiating strategy with the same explanation Dulles offered in 1927 for the success of the Washington Naval Treaty. Reagan claimed success in arms negotiations would require a determined arms program to induce the USSR to agree to substantial reductions in strategic arms.[15]

The parity dilemmas discussed above deal specifically with how balance in military capabilities affects negotiating positions. However, the different points of view on the validity of these arguments usually reflect different assessments of the intentions of other states. Similarly, the previous chapter concentrated on intentions as they are manifest in trust, yet also highlighted the effects of armaments (capabilities) on trust. This interrelationship between intentions and capabilities has been evident in subjects previously raised, such as the comparison between mankind and technology, will and capabilities (in deterrence), moral and material disarmament, and aggression versus the arms race as a cause of war. In the following chapter the relative importance of these two concepts is specifically addressed.

DISCUSSION QUESTIONS

1. Is arms superiority ever a legitimate national security goal, and if so, when?
2. Is the distinction between rough and precise military parity significant from the military strategist's point of view? From the negotiator's point of view?
3. Which of the following ought to be the goal of arms limitation negotiations: rough, well-defined, precise or perfect parity?

SUGGESTED READINGS FOR CHAPTER TWELVE: WHICH COMES FIRST, ARMS CONTROL OR PARITY?

BLECHMAN, BARRY and ROBERT POWELL. "What in the Name of God is Strategic Superiority?" *Political Science Quarterly* 97 (Winter 1982–83).

BURT, RICHARD R. "Implications of a Nuclear Freeze." *Department of State Bulletin* 83 (June 1983).

BUCKLEY, JAMES L. *Freezing Chances for Peace.* Washington, DC: U.S. Department of State, Bureau of Public Affairs, 1982.

DE MADARIAGA, SALVADOR. *Disarmament.* New York: Coward McCann, 1929.

FORSBERG, RANDALL. "A Bilateral Nuclear-Weapon Freeze." *Scientific American,* November 1982, pp. 52–61.

KENNAN, GEORGE. "A Modest Proposal." *New York Review of Books,* July 1981.

KENNEDY, EDWARD M., and MARK O. HATFIELD. *Freeze! How You Can Help Prevent Nuclear War.* New York: Bantam, 1982.

MOULTON, HARLAND B. *From Superiority to Parity: The United States and the Strategic Arms Race, 1961–71.* Westport CT: Greenwood Press, 1973.

WOHLSTETTER, ALBERT. "Is There a Strategic Arms Race?" *Foreign Policy* 15 (Summer 1974): 3–20; and "Is There a Strategic Arms Race?—Part II: Rivals but no 'Race.'" *Foreign Policy* 16 (Fall 1974): 48–81.

NOTES

1. Brezhnez quoted in Vassili Mamontov, *Disarmament: The Command of the Times* (Moscow: Progress Publishers, 1979), p. 7; Reagan in *Vital Speeches,* April 15, 1983.

2. Salvador de Madariaga, *Disarmament* (New York: Coward McCann, 1929), p. 106.

3. For examples from the 1920s and 1930s, see Henry Forbes, *The Strategy of Disarmament* (Washington, DC: Public Affairs Press, 1962), pp. 17–19.

4. Quoted in Patrick Morgan, *Deterrence: A Conceptual Analysis* (Beverly Hills: Sage Publications, 1977), p. 89.

5. Richard Nixon, *The Real War* (New York: Warner Books, 1980), p. 5 on the "drive for superiority"; pp. 153–55 for the comments on parity; and p. 167 for the need to "buy time."

At the same time Nixon, echoing Jackson, recognized an "aggressor's edge" which must be offset; see p. 153.

6. For example, two National Security Council reports in the 1950s (known as the Killian and Gaither reports), which concluded the United States was ahead of the USSR in the nuclear arms race, advised considering how to use this advantage to extract concessions from the USSR.

   The authors of the Killian report noted, "Our military superiority may never be so great again," and suggested that the possibilities for exploiting the situation for political benefit be explored. Similarly, the Gaither report observed that, "This could be the time to negotiate from strength, since the U.S. military position vis-a-vis Russia may never be so strong again." See Lawrence Freedman, *The Evolution of Nuclear Strategy* (New York: St. Martin's Press, 1981), pp. 158–163.

7. See Thucydides' discussion of the conditions that led to the Spartan-Athenian peace, Thucydides, *The Peloponnesian War,* trans. Rex Warner (Middlesex, England: Penguin Books, 1954), pp. 375–378. The Indian political theorist Kautilya also concluded parity was an advisable but not sufficient condition for peace, whether a state was growing, receding or stagnating:

   > If any two kings, hostile to each other, find the time of achieving the results of their respective works to be equal . . . [or] deteriorating, expect to acquire equal amounts of wealth in equal time . . . [or] in a stationary condition, expect to acquire equal amounts of wealth and power in equal time, they shall make peace with each other.

   But, since broad parity in capabilities does not ensure peace, Kautilya also advised that

   > When a king of equal power does not like peace, then the same amount of vexation as his opponent has received should be given to him in return; for it is power which brings peace between any two kings.

   R. Shamasastry, *Kautilya's Arthasastra,* 8th ed. (Mysore, India: Mysore Printing and Publishing House, 1967), pp. 295, 300. For a more modern argument based on more recent historical evidence that supports these ancient sources, see Geoffrey Blainey, *The Causes of War* (New York: Macmillan-Free Press, 1973).

8. Address by Senator Edward Kennedy marking the twentieth anniversary of President J. F. Kennedy's disarmament speech at American University, April 8, 1983. Printed by the Foundation for a Democratic Majority.

9. Quoted in Laurence Martin, "Is Military Force Losing its Utility," in John F. Reichart and Steven R. Sturm, *American Defense Policy,* 5th ed. (Baltimore: Johns Hopkins University Press, 1982), p. 35.

10. Quoted in Amrom H. Katz, *Verification and SALT: The State of the Art and the Art of the State* (Washington, DC: Heritage Foundation, 1979), p. 16.

11. This sentiment was expressed by Christoph Bertram, who thought the whole matter of parity and superiority a matter of educating the superpowers:

    > The Americans must learn that parity is a combination of asymmetries and that marginal advantages on one side or the other do not undermine stability.

    And the USSR must learn, said Bertram, that

    > Catching up with the leader is one thing, gaining superiority over him quite another.

    Christoph Bertram, "Arms Control and Technological Change: Elements of a New Approach," from Christoph Bertram, ed., *Arms Control and Military Force* (Montclair, NJ: Allanheld, Osmun and Co., 1980), pp. 160–61.

12. Steven Kull, "Nuclear Nonsense," *Foreign Policy* (Spring 1985): 31. Copyright 1985 by the Carnegie Endowment for International Peace. Kissinger, years after his SALT I testimony, agreed with Luttwak:

    > The arms race is driven by political as well as military factors. While a decisive advantage is hard to calculate, the *appearance* of inferiority—whatever its actual significance—can

have serious political consequences . . . Thus each side has a high incentive to achieve not only the reality but the appearance of equality.

It is not immediately clear whether Kissinger was referring to domestic or international political consequences or both. Kissinger quoted in Raymond L. Garthoff, *Perspectives on the Strategic Balance.* (Washington, DC: Brookings Institution, 1983), p. 4.

13. The French philosopher Fenelon even held it as a general rule that superiority ought to be relinquished in favor of parity. See his eloquent defense of parity in Hans Morgenthau and Kenneth W. Thompson, *Politics Among Nations: The Struggle for Power and Peace* 6th ed. (New York: Alfred A. Knopf, 1985), p. 390.

14. Allen W. Dulles, "Some Misperceptions about Disarmament," *Foreign Affairs* (April 1927): 413–414.

15. According to Reagan:

The United States wants deep cuts in the world's arsenal of weapons, but unless we demonstrate the will to rebuild our strength and restore the military balance, the Soviets, since they are so far ahead, have little incentive to negotiate with us. Let me repeat that point because it goes to the heart of our policies. Unless we demonstrate the will to rebuild our strength, the Soviets have little incentive to negotiate. If we had not begun to modernize, the Soviet negotiators would know that we were bluffing without a good hand because they know what cards we hold just as we know what is in their hand.

You may recall that in 1969 the Soviets did not want to negotiate a treaty banning antiballistic missiles. It was only after our Senate narrowly voted to fund an antiballistic missile program that the Soviets agreed to negotiate. We then reached an agreement.

Ronald Reagan, *Vital Speeches,* December 15, 1982.

Chapter Thirteen

Which Is More Important for Arms Control and Deterrence, Knowledge of an Opponent's Capabilities or Its Intentions?

How laudable it is for a prince to keep good faith and live with integrity, and not with astuteness, every one knows. Still the experience of our times shows those princes to have done great things who have had little regard for good faith, and have been able by astuteness to confuse men's brains, and who have ultimately overcome those who have made loyalty their foundation.

You must know, then, that there are two methods of fighting, the one by law, the other by force: the first method is that of men, the second of beasts; but as the first method is often insufficient, one must have recourse to the second. . . .

A prince being thus obliged to know well how to act as a beast must imitate the fox and the lion, for the lion cannot protect himself from traps, and the fox cannot defend himself from wolves. One must therefore be a fox to recognize traps and a lion to frighten wolves.

—Niccolo Machiavelli,
The Prince, Chapter 18

As Machiavelli suggests, prudence requires proper respect for both the physical capabilities of the lion and the ability of the fox to detect threats, that is, respect for what an adversary can do and what it plans to do. It is not easy to determine either the capabilities or intentions of another state, since both are always evolving. It is also difficult because assessments of capabilities and intentions are interrelated. State A's capabilities can influence the intentions of State B by being strong enough to deter B, or so strong that they alarm B, or so strong that they reduce B's willingness to defend itself, or so weak that they encourage B to act aggressively, and vice versa. State A's intentions can influence State B's capabilities by convincing State B that it needs a greater or lesser capability to defend itself, and vice versa.

Questions about capabilities and intentions become interesting only when both reach a significant level. Capabilities without any aggressive intention are not threatening, and neither are aggressive intentions without capabilities to fulfill those intentions. It is when an adversary has the capability to carry out aggressive intentions, but his intentions are not readily apparent, that debate over the relative importance of capabilities and intentions begins.

FACTORS INFLUENCING AN EMPHASIS ON EITHER CAPABILITIES OR INTENTIONS

Arnold Wolfers has summarized admirably some aspects of how intentions and capabilities interact:

> It takes more to deter an opponent whose assumed intention it is to extend his territorial control—if necessary by a resort to military force—than it does to check an opponent whose armaments are believed to be intended solely to preserve the status quo or to provide him with an adequate sense of security. The intentions of other governments and nations are at best, however, a matter of informed guesses, and it is a risky enterprise to reduce armaments in response to assumed changes in intentions. Also, the ticklish question may arise of whether a given "relaxation of tension," if it occurs, reflects the kind of change in adversary intentions that will diminish the threat to national interests. Some risk-taking in such instances may be justified if the refusal to take the risk would threaten even greater harm, as it might do if the existing level of armaments should prove too provocative.[1]

Aggressor theorists concentrate on Wolfers's first point, that it takes more military capabilities to deter an adversary with aggressive intentions than a nation that is satisfied with the status quo. Spiral theorists focus on Wolfers's second point, that some risk taking when an adversary's intentions are unclear may be necessary in order to break the dangerous cycle of spiraling competition in military capabilities.

Expanding on these observations, it is possible to identify among proponents of disarmament and defense preparedness tendencies to emphasize either capabilities or intentions. Disarmers and spiral theorists generally separate intentions and capabilities, focusing on the latter. They assume states would prefer peace, and that escalating military capabilities can propel states into conflict regardless of the good intentions of their leaders.

Proponents of defense preparedness and aggressor theorists concentrate on the importance of intentions. They do not think of intentions as a vague preference for either peace or war, but rather the price an adversary is willing to pay to obtain its objectives. Thus, prodefense preparedness policymakers emphasize intentions as they are manifest in an adversary's military and political strategies, which in turn define a state's needs in military capabilities. Arms control and disarmament agreements are frowned upon if they force a state to mold its capabilities to "what is negotiable" rather than what is needed for deterring the adversary's political and military strategy.

There are also short term technical and political reasons for emphasizing either capabilities or intentions. Occasionally a technical assessment of the current state of military technology may determine how a person views the relative importance of capabilities and intentions. For example, if one holds that existing technology favors defensive weapons intentions will be considered less significant since simply attending to defensive fortifications will ensure security. The superiority of defensive forces also would allow more flexibility for arms control negotiators by reducing the importance of verification and parity in offensive arms. If, on the other hand, one believes existing military technology could provide a decisive advantage to the offensive (especially in the case of a surprise attack), then the intentions of an adversary are crucial. There also will be a corresponding increase in the importance of verification procedures and strict parity.

Public debate on arms negotiations often reveals politically motivated emphasis on either intentions or capabilities. For example, if an adversary takes some action that seems belligerent, critics of negotiations will focus on intentions while those favoring the negotiations will try to shift the discussion to relative capabilities. If, on the other hand, an adversary appears to demonstrate restraint in weapons deployment, the pro–arms control forces will hail it as a sign of the adversary's intention to cooperate, while opponents of negotiations will want to discuss capabilities and show the gesture has no appreciable military impact on relative capabilities. Thus arms control debate often swings back and forth between discussion of an adversary's intentions, during which the question of trust predominates, and discussion of an adversary's capabilities, during which the issue of parity predominates.

A close examination of any major national security debate will illustrate the preceding points. However, to assist objectivity, it will be helpful to remove ourselves from our current historical circumstances and consider a case from ancient history. Thucydides, the Greek historian who recorded the events of the Peloponnesian War, provided an excellent example of a debate where assessments of capabilities and intentions were related but unevenly emphasized in national security deliberations.

A CLASSIC DEBATE ON INTENTIONS AND CAPABILITIES

In the winter of 415 B.C., an assembly of citizens sat down in their city's amphitheater to debate the security of their city-state. They were inhabitants of Syracuse, the wealthiest and most powerful city-state on the island of Sicily. Far to the east of Syracuse, in Greece, Sparta and Athens were locked in a titanic struggle which, after sixteen years of exhausting warfare, had settled down to an uneasy and deteriorating peace.

Syracuse had received intelligence reports indicating Athens suddenly had decided to launch an invasion of Sicily with the intention of conquering Syracuse and enlisting Sicilian resources in a renewed Athenian war effort against Sparta. The city fathers called an assembly to discuss the situation. After much debate it was evident that the Syracuseans were split over their assessment of Athenian intentions. Some speakers argued that the invasion was imminent, and that all haste and determination were necessary to provide an adequate defense. Other speakers claimed that the alleged invasion was just a rumor being circulated by warmongers. Still others thought that Syracuse should not be so concerned with Athenian intentions as with the relative capabilities of Athens and Syracuse.

According to Thucydides,[2] the most prominent aggressor theorist in the debate was Hermocrates. After assuring his listeners that the invasion was very real, he listed all the reasons he thought Syracuse could successfully defend itself if it acted quickly to enhance its military capabilities and solicit alliances with other Sicilian city-states. Then he went a step further, speaking as follows:

> What I think is the best thing of all for us to do at this moment is something which you, with your stay-at-home habits, are not in the least likely to see the point of; nevertheless I shall say what it is. If all the Sicilians together, or at least as many of us as possible, would be prepared to launch every available ship and, taking two months' supplies with us, would meet the Athenians at Tarentum and the promontory of Iapygia and make it clear to them that before there is any question of fighting for Sicily they will have to fight for their passage across the Ionian sea, this would have the most powerful effect on their minds.

Hermocrates went on to list all the military advantages of this bold naval maneuver, and concluded it would have a most disheartening effect on the Athenians. In fact, he said, it was entirely likely that the Athenians "would be so taken aback by this surprise move of ours that they would give up the expedition entirely." Hermocrates defended his preemptive strike strategy and assessment of Athenian intentions with hard-line aggressor theorist reasoning and convictions:

> The people who attack first, or at any rate make it clear to the aggressors that they are going to defend themselves, are the ones who are most feared, because it is then thought that they are ready to take up the challenge. This is just what would happen now to the Athenians. They are attacking us on the assumption that we are not going to defend ourselves, and they have a right to hold such a poor view of us, because we failed to help the Spartans to destroy them. But if they were to see us acting with a daring that they do not anticipate, they would be more frightened by the very unexpectedness of the thing than they would be by the power which we really have. It is this daring action, therefore, which I am most anxious that you should take; but if you will not, then I urge you to

make every other preparation for war as quickly as possible. . . . The Athenians are coming: the Athenians are, I am sure of it, already on their voyage: the Athenians are very nearly here.

According to Thucydides, Hermocrates's speech received mixed reviews, ranging from the few who believed him to those who "dismissed the idea [of an invasion] altogether and turned the whole thing into a joke." One of those who belittled Hermocrates was Athenagoras. He dismissed Hermocrates's concerns as mere rabble-rousing, and argued that the Athenians were not foolish enough to attack Syracuse:

> You, if you are sensible, will not take such reports [of an Athenian invasion] as a basis for calculating probabilities, but instead will consider what a clever and a widely experienced people, as, in my view, the Athenians are, would be likely to do. It is not likely that they would leave the Peloponnesians behind them and, with the war in Hellas [Greece] still not satisfactorily settled, would go out of their way to take on a new war on just as big a scale. In fact I personally am of the opinion that they are pleased enough to find that it is not a case of us going to attack them, considering the numbers and the strength of our cities.

However, continued Athenagoras, even if Athens were to launch an invasion, Syracuse was more than capable of defending itself. He considered Syracuse stronger "than their supposed army of invasion, even if it were twice as big as it is said to be." Moreover, pointed out Athenagoras, Athens would

face innumerable technical difficulties in mounting a successful invasion, such as transport of horses, a long sea voyage, arrangements for provisions and large quantities of equipment, lack of fortifications once in Sicily, and so forth. Athenagoras concluded that since this was the case, he doubted "whether they will be able to effect and consolidate a landing at all."

The danger to Syracuse, therefore, said Athenagoras, came not from Athens but from within Syracuse itself:

> But, as I tell you, the Athenians know all this, and I am quite sure they are occupied in safeguarding their own possessions. What is happening is that there are certain people here in Syracuse who are making up stories which are neither true nor likely to become true. . . . they resort to stories of this kind or even more villainous fabrications, and their aim is to make you, the mass of the people, frightened, and so gain control of the government themselves.

This twenty-four-hundred-year-old debate illustrates several general points about the relative significance of intentions and capabilities. First, the dialogue between Athenagoras and Hermocrates demonstrates how perceptions of enemy capabilities and intentions are linked— regardless of whether we prefer to emphasize one or the other. The two men differed over the sufficiency of Syracuse's defenses partly because they disagreed over Athenian intentions. Similarly, their assessments of Athenian capabilities reflected their assessments of Athenian intentions, with Hermocrates much more convinced than Athenagoras that Athens was capable of launching a potentially successful invasion.

Second, the debate shows how aggressor theorists tend to concentrate on intentions. They believe that enemy intentions define the defense capabilities necessary to deter or thwart aggression, which they usually find deficient. Also, for aggressor theorists, it is the enemy's intentions which must be targeted prior to hostilities. Thus, Hermocrates argued for preventive measures in order to give Athens cause to reconsider its expedition before it even reached Sicilian soil, and short of that, for enhancing preparedness with every other precaution possible.

In contrast, spiral theorists most often consider existing defense capabilities sufficient and thus dismiss assessments of enemy intentions as irrelevant. Athenagoras noted that Syracuse's capabilities should give Athens more cause for concern than vice versa. He also concentrated on the potential logistical problems of Athens and the easy sufficiency of Syracusean defenses which rendered Athenian intentions irrelevant as far as he was concerned. Athenagoras, like many spiral theorists, believed offensive forces in general must be superior to defensive forces to make aggression succeed. So, unlike Hermocrates, he saw no need for superiority. Simple parity was more than sufficient:

> Indeed, I am so sure of what I say that I think that, even if they brought with them here another city as big as Syracuse and planted it down on our borders and made war from it upon us—even then they would have very little chance of survival; and how much less of a chance will they have with the whole of Sicily united, as it will be, against them, with their own base a mere fortification thrown up by a naval expedition, living in tents, and only provided with the barest necessities, unable to move in any direction because of our cavalry? Taking everything into account, I doubt whether they will be able to effect and consolidate a landing at all; so very much superior, I think, are our forces to theirs.

Parity would be sufficient, but Athenagoras judged the difficulties of assuming the offensive so great that Athens was actually in a position of inferiority if it contemplated aggression.

The Syracuse debate also illustrates how political rhetoric and domestic politics creep into spiral-aggressor theorist differences over defense policy. With Hobbesian logic, aggressor theorists lament the parochial mentality of spiral theorists ("stay-at-home habits") and usually desire a more activist foreign policy to carry the struggle away from the home territory. They see spiral theorists as naive for giving an adversary the benefit of the doubt, and sometimes even accuse spiral theorists of lack of patriotism or, worse, implicit collaboration with the enemy.

Likewise, spiral theorists are often disposed to question the intentions of aggressor theorists more closely than those of foreign governments. Starting with the assumption that a foreign government does not want war, spiral theorists tend to "mirror-image" a potential adversary, meaning they assume it reasons as they do ("But, as I tell you, the Athenians know all this . . . "). They assume that the foreign government is of like mind and satisfied with peace, but they know that the aggressor theorists in their own country are preparing for war. Thus, spiral theorists frequently see the danger of war originating at home from aggressor theorists who, at best, genuinely but mistakenly fear enemy attack and, at worst, love conflict and want to use war to expand their domestic political power.

There is another point of view on the relative importance of capabilities and intentions which the debate in Syracuse demonstrates. After Athenagoras had spoken, a representative of Syracuse's military establishment stepped forward and gave a final opinion, after which the assembly was dissolved. He said:

> It is not a wise thing either for speakers to make these attacks on each other, or for the hearers to give countenance to them. Instead we should be giving our attention to the reports which have reached us and seeing how we can all of us— the State as a whole and each individual in it—best deal with the invaders. Even if there is no need, there is no harm in having the State furnished with horses and arms and everything that is glorious in war. We shall undertake the responsibility for this and see to the details. Nor is there any harm in sending to the [other] cities to find out what their feelings are and in doing anything else that

may be thought useful. We have seen to some of these matters already, and anything that we find out shall be brought to your notice.

The Syracusean general is relatively uninterested in enemy intentions, neither so sure of Athenian aggression that he would support Hermocrates's suggestion for preventive action, nor so sure Athens was not invading that he would support Athenagoras's sanguine assessment of existing defenses. He just argues for more resources for his special interest, the military establishment, without reference to a specific threat assessment, thus relying on vague notions of what general "preparedness" requires. The general's relative uninterest in enemy intentions and his concentration on Syracusean capabilities could reflect his belief that enemy intentions are unknowable, or his belief that one should always assume the worst about an adversary's intentions.

The Incalculable Nature of Intentions

As noted above, "the intentions of other governments and nations are at best a matter of informed guesses. There are numerous factors that complicate assessments of an adversary's intentions. For example, political posturing for the benefit of public opinion makes it difficult to distinguish aggressors from peacemakers. Peacemakers strike a rhetorical balance between appeals for diligent defense efforts and disarmament negotiations. John F. Kennedy's famous dictum: "Let us never negotiate out of fear, but let us never fear to negotiate," is exemplary. Aggressors also understand the usefulness of a rhetorical emphasis on peace negotiations, for the reason bluntly revealed in Fichte's maxim: "Promise peace that you may begin war with advantage."

A state's official ideology does not necessarily clarify its intentions. The ideology itself may be ambiguous. Marxism-Leninism, for example, postulates the inevitability of class conflict, which some take as evidence of aggressive intent. On the other hand there is the Marxist-Leninist faith in the historically inevitable victory of communism which some believe encourages patience and peaceful coexistence while waiting for the self-destruction of capitalism. And, of course, there is always the question of whether such ideologies are really the driving force behind national behavior.

Besides the problem of ambiguity there is the problem of *change* in motivations and intentions. For example, it is frequently observed that the United States has oscillated during its two-hundred-year history between periods of isolationism and internationalism, moving back and forth between the parochial sentiment of "no entangling alliances" and the interventionist promptings of "manifest destiny." Most nations go through periods of more or less interest in international involvement, including intermittent periods of conflict. Since it is frequently disputable who the aggressor is in any given conflict, the historical record is almost always confused enough to allow for different interpretations of a nation's proclivity for violence.

It also is extremely difficult to develop a static estimate of national aggressiveness because a state's intentions can change quickly. An originally modest national security objective, when successfully obtained, can encourage much bolder ambitions. Sometimes the flush of success is so intoxicating that a nation will believe it has a chance to achieve absolute security, to finish off its opponents for the foreseeable future. For example, Louis XIV of France began his conquests with a desire to secure defensible borders and ended up at war with practically all of Europe.

Occasionally it is asserted that national character and culture are critical indices of a state's trustworthiness and its penchant for limited security policies. A national commitment to honor may be a significant index of trustworthiness, but it is not a static one. For example, immediately following a Greek victory over the invading Persians, the Athenian leader Themistocles thought he saw a perfect opportunity to cripple Spartan naval power. The Spartan fleet had been beached near Gytheum during hostilities with the Persians, and Themistocles wanted to launch a surprise attack and burn the Spartan fleet, thereby giving Athens an insurmountable naval lead over its principal Greek rival. Since the success of the plan required absolute secrecy, Themistocles told Athens's assembly it should choose one man it trusted to hear the plan and pass judgment on its merits. The assembly chose Aristides, who after hearing Themistocles out, told the assembly Themistocles's stratagem was very expedient but not honorable. The assembly rejected the plan.[3] About sixty-five years later, however, an Athenian assembly voted in favor of the unprovoked war on Syracuse.

Testing Intentions

Those who believe intentions are important but obscure often propose exploring intentions in some methodical manner. For example, they may encourage unilateral peace initiatives of limited risk or unilateral restraint in defense programs in order to test the adversary's response. Alternatively, they may favor leaving some finer points of an arms control agreement unresolved in hopes that the enemy will respect the "spirit" of the agreement, thereby demonstrating its intention to cooperate on behalf of strategic stability. Many aggressor theorists believe that the opening of negotiations will soon reveal whether an adversary is serious about arms reductions or only interested in propaganda benefits. President Nixon said that he continued the SALT I negotiations begun by his predecessor partly in order to test Soviet intentions,[4] a policy his secretary of state, Henry Kissinger, had advocated a decade earlier in 1960:

> Soviet proposals so far have been consistent only with one of two interpretations: either the Soviet leaders have as much difficulty in understanding the problem as we do, or else they are using the negotiations in a deliberate effort to demoralize the free world and to induce it to disarm unilaterally. . . . Perhaps no serious negotiation is possible at all. . . . If the Soviet Union rejects proposals

which are designed to increase its security together with ours—and this is the essence of any responsible program—it will have given clear proof that there is no alternative to the arms race.[5]

In 1982, a decade after Kissinger negotiated the SALT I accord, he recommended again that the United States test Soviet intentions, only this time not with formal negotiations but by deploying mobile single warhead ICBMs to see if the USSR would follow suit. Kissinger believed the stabilizing advantages of this weapon were so obvious that their deployment "would be a serious test of Soviet intentions," and their refusal to respond with similar missile programs "would be a clear signal of a Soviet bid for superiority."[6]

Spiral theorists believe it takes something more than requests for reciprocal weapon deployment patterns or "serious" negotiating positions to test enemy intentions. Some distrust has to be swept away before these methods are likely to bear fruit. Charles Osgood's proposal for **"graduated and reciprocal initiatives in tension reduction" (GRIT)** is a popular spiral theorist proposal for testing enemy intentions. Osgood does not believe either the United States or the USSR wants war, so he suggested the United States should announce its peaceful intentions and how it intends to demonstrate its sincerity, and then follow up with unilateral measures of goodwill— usually suggested as reductions in armaments or withdrawal of some deployed forces.[7] To break deep-rooted mistrust, Osgood suggests it is necessary to continue the initiatives over a considerable period of time even if there is no reciprocity.

Both spiral and aggressor theorists have reservations about GRIT initiatives. The spiral theorist's concern is that if, for whatever reasons, the enemy is perceived as not having reciprocated, then the net result will be an increase in distrust as the lack of reciprocity is taken as evidence of ill will. For example, many U.S. senators were frustrated by the lack of a Soviet response to President Carter's unilateral decision to forgo development of the neutron bomb. From the aggressor theorist point of view, each concession made in order to test the intentions of an adversary tilts the balance of power in the adversary's favor and runs the risk of communicating lack of resolve.

A concern of both spiral and aggressor theorists is that GRIT initiatives will turn into opportunities for propaganda, with each side announcing concessions that are either not significant militarily or are never actually carried out. Both the United States and the Soviet Union have announced unilateral concessions in European-based forces and called for reciprocity, but these initiatives have not succeeded in gaining any momentum.[8]

Two Domestic Consequences of Obscure Intentions

National debate over the intentions of adversaries is often characterized by (1) the erosion of domestic consensus and (2) the shift to a discussion of capabilities. Taking place in an ever-evolving historical context, such debates often lead to conflicting opinions on the nature of an adversary's intentions which may increase as time passes.

For example, following World War I, initially both France and Britain attributed the origins of the war to German aggression. As time passed, the French continued to maintain Germany was inherently dangerous and that it was necessary for France to maintain military superiority in order to deter German aggression. In other words, France ascribed to the aggressor theorist point of view. But the English became increasingly persuaded by the spiral theorist point of view. English scholarship revised the popular explanation of the war from German hostility to mutual misperceptions and fear. The English began to consider the harsh peace terms imposed on Germany as unfair. Many considered Hitler's demands for military parity with France as only fair.[9] Aggressor theorists in England, such as Winston Churchill, resisted the increasing acceptance of the spiral theorists' point of view and a major public debate erupted over German intentions.

The same historical sequence was repeated in the United States after World War II. In the 1950s the USSR was commonly held responsible for the Cold War between the United States and the USSR. That being so, there was also a consensus in favor of U.S. military superiority. But during the 1960s the origins of the Cold War were reassessed and it became acceptable to apportion blame to both the United States and the USSR, both of which were deemed to have fallen victim to mutual fears, misperceptions, and overreactions. As the spiral theorists gained the upper hand in academic institutions and later in foreign policy circles, military parity with the Soviet Union replaced U.S. superiority as a legitimate goal for U.S. defense programs. As in England forty years earlier, die-hard aggressor theorists resisted the historical reassessment and are still warning the public about aggressive Soviet intentions.[10]

The point of the historical parallel is *not* to suggest the Soviet Union does or does not constitute a threat analogous to Nazi Germany, but rather to demonstrate the impact of evolving historical interpretations on national arms control and disarmament policies. With the passage of time and the lack of overwhelming evidence one way or the other, it is reasonable to expect a public consensus to erode and debate to heat up. During such debate many will voice the opinion that intentions are unknowable and thus cannot serve as the foundation for defense planning. When this happens, the emphasis in national security planning shifts to a discussion of relative capabilities, as happened in Syracuse when the General stepped forward to argue for military preparedness regardless of Athenian intentions.

The Syracuse General and many others since have portrayed defense and arms control as solely dependent upon relative military capabilities, but actually intentions and capabilities cannot be divorced so easily. Most capability analysts harbor their own estimates of enemy intentions which they either knowingly or unknowingly use to estimate their own national defense needs, and these assessments usually become evident when they are forced to pre-scribe specific defense plans. Justifying a weapons system often requires refer-ence to a broader concern—the enemy's strategy and military doctrine—which tends to bring intentions back into the discussion. The converse is also true. Those who emphasize intentions find it hard to ignore an assessment of rela-tive capabilities. Even if one is certain another state harbors hostile intentions, a strategy for dissuasion and defense still requires force planning and deploy-ment decisions based on an assessment of enemy capabilities.

CONCLUDING REMARKS

This chapter demonstrates when and why foreign policy analysts sometimes emphasize either intention or capabilities, and how in the final analysis it is not possible to separate the two when formulating arms limitation and defense strategy.[11] These points will be evident again in the following chapter where a specific aspect of military capabilities is discussed: advancing technology. In the abstract the advantages and disadvantages of changing technology may be considered independent of intentions, but when the impact of technology on current arms limitation policy is considered, an adversary's intentions usually figure prominently in the discussion.

DISCUSSION QUESTIONS

1. The role of will (the intention to defend oneself) and capabilities in credible nuclear deterrence are not equally emphasized by assured destruction and flexible response theorists. Why?
2. Should the United States base its defense planning, deterrence doctrine and nego-tiating policies on assessments of Soviet intentions or capabilities?
3. Would GRIT initiatives be beneficial for U.S. Soviet relations at the moment? If so, what type of initiatives would be most productive?
4. Do either the United States or the Soviet Union have hostile intentions toward the other? Which state has more powerful military capabilities?

SUGGESTED READINGS FOR CHAPTER THIRTEEN: WHICH IS MORE IMPORTANT FOR ARMS CONTROL AND DETERRENCE, KNOWLEDGE OF AN OPPONENT'S CAPABILITIES OR ITS INTENTIONS?

BLAKER, JAMES, and ANDREW HAMILTON. *Assessing the NATO/Warsaw Pact Military Balance.* Washington DC: Congressional Budget Office, 1977.
BROWN, THOMAS A. "Numbers Mysticism, Rationality, and the Strategic Balance." *Orbis* 21 (Fall 1977): 479–496.
GARTHOFF, RAYMOND L. "On Establishing and Imputing Intentions." *International Security* 2 (Winter 1978): 22–32.

GULICK, EDWARD V. *Europe's Classical Balance of Power.* Ithaca, NY: Cornell University Press, 1955.

MACHIAVELLI, NICCOLO. *The Discourses.* Especially Book II, Chapters 10, 13, 17, and 24; and Book III, Chapters 11 and 12.

MACGWIRE, MICHAEL. "Dilemmas and Delusions of Deterrence." *World Policy Journal* 1 (Summer 1984): 745–767.

OSGOOD, CHARLES E. *An Alternative to War or Surrender.* Urbana: University of Illinois Press, 1963.

PIPES, RICHARD. "Why the Soviet Union Thinks It Could Fight and Win a Nuclear War." *Commentary,* July 1977.

THUCYDIDES. *The Peloponnesian War.* Book IV, "The Debate at Syracuse."

NOTES

1. Arnold Wolfers in *The United States in a Disarmed World* (Baltimore: Johns Hopkins University Press, 1966), p. 6.

2. The entire dialogue may be found in Thucydides, *The Peloponnesian War,* trans. Rex Warner (Middlesex, England: Penguin Books, 1954), pp. 430–437.

3. Elizabeth Hazelton Haight, *The Roman Use of Anecdotes in Cicero, Livy and the Satirists* (New York: Longmans, Green and Co., 1940), p. 20. Haight also provides a few of the many examples of the role honor and good faith played in Roman diplomacy in the early days of the republic, as opposed to the later, more duplicitous, diplomacy of the Empire.

4. Richard M. Nixon, *The Real War* (New York: Warner Books, 1980), p. 167.

5. Henry Kissinger, "Arms Control, Inspection and Surpirse Attack," *Foreign Affairs* (July 1960).

6. Kissinger, "A New Approach to Arms Control," *Time* March 21, 1983. Both in this article and in his 1960 article (previous footnote) Kissinger argued that the willingness of the USSR to cooperate with technical solutions to stability would be a test of Soviet sincerity. Western analysts often suggest "technical" solutions to arms control problems in order to test the adversary's intentions. It is assumed that the purely technical solution has no underlying political implications, and thus it should be acceptable to any party negotiating in good faith for mutual security. In superpower negotiations the Americans proposing these technical solutions usually add that if the Soviet Union does not respond as they desire it will be a sign that it has no desire to negotiate seriously. For example, see Stanley Sloan, "East-West Troop Reductions in Europe: Is Agreement Possible?" Committee Print, Committee on Foreign Affairs, House of Representatives, 98th Congress, 1st Session (U.S. Government Printing Office, 1983), p. 2.

7. Charles E. Osgood, "GRIT: A Strategy for Survival in Mankind's Nuclear Age," in William Epstein and Bernard T. Feld, eds., *New Directions in Disarmament* (New York: Praeger, 1981). For Osgood's original work on GRIT see *An Alternative to War or Surrender* Urbana: University of Illinois Press, 1963. See also, Herbert Scoville, "Reciprocal National Restraints: An Alternative Path," *Arms Control Today* 15 (June 1985).

8. See William B. Prendergast, *Mutual and Balanced Force Reductions: Issues and Prospects* (Washington, DC: American Enterprise Institute for Public Policy Research, 1978), p. 13.

9. Hitler was willing to discuss arms control and disarmament. He rejected multilateral treaties as unrealistic, but signed numerous bilateral treaties. He declared he was

> perfectly ready to strengthen the Locarno Pact. She [Germany] was ready to agree to the abolition of heavy arms; to limit the use of other weapons—such as the bomber and poisonous gas— by international convention; indeed, to accept an overall limitation of armaments provided that it was to apply to all the Powers. Hitler laid particular stress on his willingness to limit German naval power to 35 per cent of the strength of the British navy.

As Alan Bullock notes, Hitler's "mastery of the language of Geneva was unequaled. He understood intuitively the longing for peace, the idealism of the pacifists, and uneasy conscience of the liberals, the reluctance of the great mass of their peoples to look beyond their own private affairs." Alan Bullock, *Hitler: A Study in Tyranny* (New York: Harper & Row, abridged ed., Perennial Library, 1964), pp. 186–187.

10. It is not difficult to find examples of aggressor and spiral theorist assessments of Soviet intentions. There is, for example, President Reagan's assessment that the USSR is an "evil empire," and, in contrast, former presidential candidate George McGovern's assertion that "the defense-minded, inward-looking Soviet Union—paranoid after three nearly fatal invasions from the West—is not analogous to Adolf Hitler, an expansionist psychopath." This McGovern quotation is from his book review, "Lessons of the Past," *Washington Post Book World,* March 30, 1986, p. 5.

11. Glen Snyder has noted the importance of the distinction between intentions and capabilities in the abstract:

> Much of the inconclusiveness of the recurring "great debates" about military policy might be avoided if the concept of "strategic value" could be clarified and clearly separated from the deterrent effects of military action. The strategic value of a particular piece of territory is the effect which its loss would have on increasing the enemy's *capability* to make various future moves, and on decreasing our own capacity to resist further attacks. The deterrent value of defending or attempting to defend that piece of territory is the effect of the defense on the enemy's *intention* to make further moves.

The problem is that the strategic and deterrent value of territory cannot be clearly separated, and even where they may be, "great debates" are not necessarily resolved. For example, as related in the Syracusean dialogue on the previous pages, Hermocrates wanted to defend the promontory of Iapygia because it would complicate the Athenians' ability to land in Sicily, but even more importantly because he thought it would dampen Athenian enthusiasm for such an undertaking. Athenagoras, on the other hand, would only consider the strategic value of Sicily proper, and paid no attention to the deterrent value of any territory because he believed in finite deterrence.

In other words, the Iapygian territory had both deterrent and strategic value; and these could not be "clearly separated." Thus, a distinction between intentions (deterrent value) and capabilities (strategic value) in the abstract could not solve the "great debate" between the two men. The quotation is from Glenn H. Snyder, *Deterrence and Defense: Toward a Theory of National Security.* Copyright © 1961 by Princeton University Press; reprinted as "The Theory of Deterrence," in Reichart and Sturm, *American Defense Policy,* p. 159.

Chapter Fourteen

Can and Should Technology Be Restricted?

The unresting progress of mankind causes continual change in the weapons; and with that must come a continual change in the manner of fighting.

—Mahan: *The Influence of Sea Power on History,* 1890

New weapons operating in an element hitherto unavailable to mankind will not necessarily change the ultimate character of war. The next war may well start in the air but in all probability it will wind up, as did the last war, in the mud.

—Report of the President's Board to Study Development of Aircraft for the National Defense, 1925[1]

The impact of advancing technology is a consideration that touches on most of the issues explored in this book. In this chapter the focus on technology is narrowed to two questions: How are arms control and disarmament affected by bias for or against technology? And how are they affected by opinions as to whether technology can or cannot be controlled?

TECHNOLOGY AND ARMS LIMITATION: THE OPTIONS
FOR CONTROL

Technological progress can both hinder and facilitate arms limitation negotiations. For example, the development of reconnaissance satellites and more accurate seismic recording devices have made monitoring arms control agreements easier,[2] and electronic locks (called permissive action links),[3] which make it impossible for one person alone to fire a nuclear weapon, have reduced the chances of accidental nuclear war. It is also true that various new technologies have hindered arms control. One example frequently cited is the development of smaller, highly mobile nuclear delivery systems such as cruise missiles. These missiles are critical strategic weapons, but they also are particularly difficult to monitor, and thus are difficult to include in arms limitation agreements.

Not everyone considers the development of highly accurate and mobile nuclear delivery systems counterproductive for arms control. How a new technology is evaluated often depends on one's understanding of what contributes to or undermines stability.[4] Some argue that "technology threatens the existing arms control forums because they are built around assumptions concerning the character of military technology that is on the verge of becoming obsolete."[5] However, arms control forums can adapt to new technologies if there is a consensus on which technologies are beneficial and ought to be developed, and which are counterproductive and ought to be controlled.

If it is decided that certain new technologies are counterproductive and ought to be limited, the new technologies can be restricted in one of three stages: during research and development, during testing of the weapon, or during the production and deployment of the weapon. Many believe the best place to start controlling a new weapon technology is at the beginning—in the research and development stage. As Marvin Goldberger points out, the initial impetus for the Manhattan Project, the U.S. atomic program in the 1940s, was the fear that Nazi Germany was well ahead in the race to produce an atomic bomb. Yet after Germany was defeated and it became evident that the Germans were not even close to this accomplishment, no one considered abandoning the U.S. effort. Instead the United States pursued the project to completion and used the result on Japan. Goldberger suggests the Manhattan Project's momentum was irresistible.[6]

The U.S. quest for a space-based ballistic missile defense is an even larger and more complicated research and development project, and there are many who want to stop this project in the research and development stage, so that unlike the Manhattan Project, it will not gather enough momentum to make its completion inevitable. Toward this end, and with encouragement from the Union of Concerned Scientists and the Federation of American Scientists, approximately 6,500 U.S. scientists and educators have pledged not to accept funds for research on SDI.[7] In response the U.S. government maintains it is not possible to verify restrictions on research and thus the United States must pursue SDI technologies just as the USSR is doing.

Verification of compliance with agreements to limit research and development of new weapons might be possible with instrusive monitoring techniques, but these are very difficult, if not impossible, to negotiate. To date no state has indicated a willingness to allow the massive international control system which would be necessary to monitor effectively national research programs. Thus there is almost unanimous agreement in the arms control field that controlling research and development of new technologies is the most difficult stage at which to control technology.

The second option is to control the testing of new weapons, which is easier to monitor than research. Most new weapons can be observed by satellites and other sensory devices in the testing stage. Also, as a general rule the more revolutionary the new technology, the more testing it will require when utilized in a weapon system, thereby allowing more opportunities for viewing by other states. Since history suggests that once a weapon has been tested and proven useful it is extremely difficult to restrict its deployment and use, there is a widespread belief that it is important to prevent the testing of a weapon in order to limit confidence in its ability to perform as planned.

A good example of the use of testing restrictions to control technology is the current debate over a total nuclear test ban treaty. Supporters of a total ban on nuclear testing argue that it is the most effective way to halt the nuclear arms race. Without testing new nuclear weapons could not be developed and confidence in the reliability of existing nuclear inventories would decline as time passed. For a long time opponents of a total test ban argued it would be impossible to verify compliance. More recently they have argued that even if verification is possible, a ban on testing is a bad idea. They want nuclear testing for the same reason test banners do not want it: to ensure the reliability of weapons already deployed and to bring new "stabilizing" systems such as SDI on line.

There are problems with trying to control new technologies by restricting weapons testing. Some weapons may need a minimum of testing before deployment. Even after testing there always remains an element of uncertainty about how a weapon will perform under battle conditions, but this does not prevent governments from constantly purchasing new weapons. There is also the possibility that some weapons may be tested clandestinely. Finally there is some question as to whether limits on testing would stabilize an arms race. As one study on the subject points out:

> In the absence of verifiable tests indicating the state of the weapons programme of the other side, military planners and technologists will tend to prepare for the worst case, namely that the opponent's procurement programme goes far beyond its tested elements.[8]

Nevertheless, if negotiators determine that a new weapon would be destabilizing and agree to prohibit it, and further decide that it could not be built and deployed safely without extensive testing, and finally that the testing process could be monitored, then restricting testing would seem to offer the best solution to preventing the introduction of new weapons technologies.[9]

If a new weapon has already been tested, negotiators can still agree to limit or prohibit its production. The major problems with limiting new weapons once they reach the production stage have already been mentioned: the tendency to deploy what has already proven effective, the inability to verify production and deployment limits, and the difficulty of devising a comprehensive negotiated definition of the new weapon technology which would prevent a state from changing a few relatively minor details of the weapon and then proceeding with its construction and deployment (thereby violating the spirit but not the letter of the agreement).

Limiting research, testing, and production and deployment are the options for controlling technology that statesmen and negotiators may consider. However, decisions on whether and how technology can be controlled are not simply the result of dispassionate technical analyses of available options. There is also the question of whether or not new technologies ought to be restricted.

BIASES ON TECHNOLOGY: FEAR AND FAITH

There have always been differences of opinion on whether the advance of technology better serve the cause of peace or war. Edward Gibbon, reflecting the optimism of the Enlightenment, supposed technology to be the salvation of civilization, which was forever plagued by barbarian threats:

> Cold, poverty, and a life of danger and fatigue fortify the strength and courage of barbarians. In every age they have oppressed the polite and peaceful nations . . . who neglected, and still neglect, to counterbalance these natural powers by the resources of military art. . . . The military art has been changed by the invention of gunpowder, which enables man to command the two most powerful agents of nature, air and fire. Mathematics, chemistry, mechanics, architecture, have been applied to the service of war, and the adverse parties oppose to each other the most elaborate modes of attack and defense. . . . Europe is secure from any future irruption of barbarians, since, before they can conquer, they must cease to be barbarous. Their gradual advances in the science of war would always be accompanied, as we may learn from the example of Russia, with a proportionate improvement in the arts of peace and civil policy.[10]

Today, many carry on with Gibbon's optimism, believing that science and technology favor "civilized" and peaceful people. For example, in discussions of nuclear terrorism one frequently finds the hopeful argument that anyone sophisticated enough to build and use a nuclear device would be civilized enough to object to its use for terrorism. Similarly, many have placed their faith in technology to eradicate the threat of nuclear war, most recently through the development of a space based defense against ICBMs.

Despite the hopes for strategic defense against ICBMs, many people today are inclined to be biased against, instead of for, technology, and it is readily apparent why. Mankind has finally reached the point of developing weapons capable of delivering instantaneous mass destruction, and this development appears ominous indeed when it is observed that "every technological advance in weaponry since the spear has been put to use on the battlefield."[11] The result is much visceral fear and ready support for any proposal that promises to rein in rampaging weapons technology.

CONTROLLING TECHNOLOGY: PREFERENCES AND POSSIBILITIES

Few people advise what they believe is impossible, but many people are prone to define the possible according to what they believe is preferable. Therefore many who argue technology can be controlled do so because they believe it should be, or even must be if mankind is to survive. Similarly, many who argue technology cannot be controlled do not believe it is critical, nor even always advantageous to limit advances in weaponry. Seldom does one find the opinion that the control of technology is imperative yet impossible, or that there is no special need to control technology but it could easily be accomplished. It is worthwhile, when reviewing three general sets of opinion on whether arms limitation agreements should seek to control technology, to note how they explain the origins of technological advances and the possibilities for their restriction.

"Technology Should Be Controlled"

Many believe that qualitative advances in weapons are the driving force in arms competition.[12] What states fear even more than falling behind numerically is that their adversaries will develop a decisive advantage in new weapons which they suddenly can utilize in war or for extracting political concessions.[13] Three possible conclusions can be drawn from this argument. Some consider all technological improvements in weapons pernicious since they fuel the arms race and arms races lead to war. For those holding this viewpoint, halting technology becomes an end in itself. They argue arms control policy should be designed to compartmentalize arms competition and that any negotiated agreement that prohibits the development or deployment of new weapons systems should be supported.

"Technology Should Not Be Controlled"

There are those who support unconstrained technology as a general security principle. They usually believe their state has an inherent or insurmountable advantage in qualitative arms development, and thus they feel their state can only be hurt by attempts to limit new weapons technologies. This point of view is found more frequently in advanced democracies or republics, where it is argued that technological advances are an inescapable function of free society. Where men are free to pursue their curiosity and rewarded for doing so, the inevitable result is innovation and new discoveries. Since an open society cannot long hide its technological secrets, it must aggressively pursue new technologies, always keeping several steps ahead in the game. In ancient Greece a leader of democratic Athens named Pericles distinguished between closed and open societies, observing that

> There is a great difference between us and our opponents: Our city is open to the world, and we have no periodical deportations in order to prevent people observing or finding out secrets which might be of military advantage to the enemy.

Pericles believed that Athens's security was critically dependent upon her naval superiority, which was a by-product of her system of free commerce. Because of their shipping industry, Athenians had been studying seamanship for decades, and Pericles argued that Athens could preserve its critical technological advantage with effort.[14]

Along with Pericles, many observers have concluded that free states must always rely on some qualitative advantages in military force, especially since closed authoritarian societies often enjoy other military advantages natural to their political circumstances, such as greater secrecy and no constraints from public opinion. In fact, some Americans today believe the United States is in a position where it cannot afford to relinquish technological superiority at any cost.[15] They believe the U.S. technological edge is the only real security advantage the United States has over the Soviet Union, and thus a critical factor in the overall ability of the United States to deter Soviet aggression.[16]

Others, however, argue that technological superiority is not the exclusive preserve of free societies, or any type of political system. Any state can devote the resources necessary for advances in weaponry. A qualitative arms race will just raise political tensions and may even tempt a preventive strike from a state that fears its adversary is about to deploy a new weapon that would significantly alter the existing balance of power. They believe technology can be controlled, and that "if the arms race had been halted two or three decades ago, civilization-threatening weapons would not have been attained."[17] In short, according to this viewpoint technology is not an inescapable function of human inventiveness. Instead, states explore new weapons because they are insecure. If alternative means of security can be found, such as arms control and disarmament agreements, the perceived need for new weapons will disappear.

"Only Some New Technologies Should Be Controlled"

Some observers believe the best approach is to craft arms control and disarmament policy to take advantage of positive developments in weapons and attempt to restrict destabilizing developments. These advocates argue against an endless quest for technological superiority, and they want to negotiate limits on some technologies. Yet they also argue that some advances in weapons can be positive insomuch as they reinforce deterrence and introduce uncertainties about force capabilities that discourage calculated aggression.[18] In certain circumstances, they believe mutual security may be enhanced by developing and sharing new technologies. For example, the United States gave the USSR information on how to protect its nuclear weapons from unauthorized use,[19] and President Reagan has suggested giving the Soviet Union new technologies for ballistic missile defense at some point in the future, if doing so would help secure both sides from the threat of nuclear war.[20]

This viewpoint agrees that free states may tend to excel in technological innovation, but also holds that any concentrated research and development program can be expected to produce advances in weapons. The point is that it may be in the interests of both open and closed societies to agree to limits on new weapons if they are destabilizing. The difficulty is determining which technologies undermine stabilizing arms agreements. One reason there is no consensus on which technological developments are stabilizing was illustrated by the discussion on SDI in Chapter 5. Different deterrence doctrines produce different assessments of which technological advances are stabilizing or destabilizing, and thus different opinions on which technologies should be banned and which should be developed.

CONCLUSION

It is a difficult task for states to determine whether and how to control technology. While the problem may be more acute today than ever before because of the accelerating pace of technological advances, difficult decisions on weapons developments have always confronted national security policymakers. Throughout history the great strategists have been those who could tailor military doctrine to take the best advantage of offensive and defensive forces as determined by the ever-evolving interaction between technology and terrain (on the tactical level) and more generally, geography (on the strategic level). The domestication of the horse, the command of the sea, the invention of

Fig. 14.1   If advances in weapon technology can not be halted, arms limitation negotiators must at least keep pace. (Source: U.S. Signal Corps)

steam locomotion, the advent of planes, tanks and submarines, and the rapid advances in communications and ballistic technology over the last few centuries have all changed human ability to attack or defend with the aid of terrain and geography.

Those who favor arms control limitation agreements argue that great arms control negotiators must parallel the efforts of great strategists. They must (1) determine whether current technology gives decisive advantages to either offensive of defensive forces; (2) based on these conclusions, negotiate stabilizing arms control agreements where desirable and possible; and (3) anticipate new technologies and, if possible, negotiate limits on those that would be destabilizing while preserving the freedom to acquire those that would be stabilizing. These tasks are easy to outline but very difficult to accomplish.

In the first place it is hard to correctly anticipate the rate and significance of technological change, even with the advantage of early demonstrations in combat. As one student of the subject notes:

> In 1939, the Russians and the French believed that modern antitank guns were as fatal to the tank as correctly emplaced machine guns were to the infantry. The Spanish Civil War was widely held to have proved that tank formations, as reasonably autonomous offensive instruments, had a very unpromising future. The notion that the defense had secured the upper hand was both a general truth concerning warfare and possibly even a truth concerning the state of the military art from 1939 to 1945.[21]

It is even more difficult to correctly estimate the impact of new technologies when they have never been tested or used in combat. For example, in 1945 the president of the prestigous Massachusetts Institute of Technology stated:

The whole idea that you could launch a missile from one continent and hit a target 4,500 miles away is too preposterous and absurd even to contemplate.[22]

Yet less than two decades later ICBMs were the preeminent weapon on the face of the earth.

Even when the feasibility of ICBMs was proven, it was not possible to develop a consensus on how they could be managed to the benefit of stability. In the 1960s many people strongly protested the deployment of ICBMs on submarines, yet today SLBMs are widely acknowledged to be a critical contribution to strategic stability.[23] Similarly, at the very time agreements on ICBM limits were being negotiated, the United States and USSR reserved the right to deploy MIRVs, which are now generally agreed to have made a major contribution to instability. Currently strategists and arms control experts are trying to determine the impact of new computer technologies on weapons and arms control, and in the area of strategic arms, whether new technologies have made ballistic missile defense more feasible.

Assessments of future technologies and man's ability to control them dispose a negotiator to certain approaches to arms control and disarmament. If one concludes technology cannot be controlled at all, the only option is for weapon designers and arms control negotiators to keep pace[24] with new weapon technologies by negotiating agreements on their deployment. If one believes that some new technologies can be indefinitely postponed or prohibited from use in new weapons, then ambitious qualitative and quantitative arms limitation plans are possible. If in addition a distinction can be made between dangerous offensive and safe defensive weapons, then disarmament (i.e. reductions in the destabilizing offensive weapons) is an attractive option.

If technology cannot be limited indefinitely, but only in some cases and for various durations, then negotiators may strengthen stability by temporarily delaying the arrival of new technologies in the form of new weapons systems. The eventual arrival of the new weapons will have a destabilizing impact on quantitative arms limitation agreements which are based on numerical ceilings and rely on static qualitative characteristics to keep the numerical ceilings equitable and secure. For this reason the alleged inevitability of technological advances is an effective argument arms controllers use against permanent disarmament schemes.

The argument for arms control as opposed to disarmament is strengthened further by the quickening pace of technological developments in the twentieth century. New weapons render older arms obsolete and thus cut short the time period for meaningful quantitative arms agreements. In other words the stability of quantitative agreements is a function of the pace of technology. Consequently, any disarmament agreement in a world of continually advancing technology must be subordinate to larger arms control regimes and their management of new technologies.[25]

Sometimes technology is perceived as evil because it always leads to greater and more efficient means of death and destruction, but it is also true that technology can produce defenses or weapons that will reduce the amount of damage and loss of life if war should occur. These assertions raise an important question. Does attenuating the horrors of war make war more likely? If it is the horror of war which makes men think twice about fighting, should not new and better means of mass destruction be welcomed, and new means of defense banned? These and other related questions are reviewed in the next chapter.

DISCUSSION QUESTIONS

1. Is it possible to delay or permanently restrict the application of new weapons technologies? If so, how?
2. Is it ever in the best interests of the United States to agree to limitations on new technologies?
3. If new technologies should be restricted, how should we determine which technologies to restrict?

SUGGESTED READINGS FOR CHAPTER FOURTEEN: CAN AND SHOULD TECHNOLOGY BE CONTROLLED?

BURT, RICHARD. "New Weapon Technologies: Debate and Directions." Adelphi Paper #126. London: International Institute of Strategic Studies, 1976.
GELBA, HARRY G. "Technological Innovation and Arms Control." *World Politics* 26 (July 1974): 509–541.
GUTTERIDGE, WILLIAM, and TREVOR TAYLOR, eds., *The Dangers of New Weapons Systems.* New York: St. Martin's Press, 1983.
HANRIEDER, WOLFRAM F., ed. *Technology, Strategy and Arms Control.* Boulder, CO: Westview Press, 1986.
HEAD, RICHARD G. "Technology and the Military Balance." *Foreign Affairs* (April 1978): 544–563.
KINTER, WILLIAM R. and HARVEY SICHERMAN. *Technology and International Politics: The Crisis of Wishing.* Lexington, MA: Lexington Books, 1975.
LONG, FRANKLIN A. "Advancing Military Technology: Recipe for an Arms Race." *Current History* 82 (May 1983): 215–219, 228.
PERRY, WILLIAM J. "Advanced Technology and Arms Control." *Orbis* 26 (Summer 1982): 351–359.
SCHROEER, DIETRICH. *Science, Technology and the Nuclear Arms Race.* New York: Halsted Press, 1984.

NOTES

1. Both quotations are taken from *Dictionary of Military and Naval Quotations,* compiled and edited by Colonel Robert Debs Heinl, Jr., USMC (Ret.). Copyright © 1966, U.S. Naval Institute, Annapolis, Maryland.
2. See Allan S. Krass, "Test-Ban Cheaters Couldn't Prosper: Sophisticated Monitoring Raises

the Need for a New Debate," *Los Angeles Times,* February 18, 1986. Reprinted in an April 1986 Union of Concerned Scientists *Pledge Bulletin.*

3. For additional citations of and sources on safety procedures and mechanisms made possible by advances in technology, see Daniel Frei, *Risks of Unintentional War* (Totowa, NJ: Rowan and Allanheld, 1983), pp. 161–162.

4. As Alvin Rubinstein has observed, many who originally criticized the advent of SLBMs as destabilizing later concluded they were a stabilizing technological development. See Alvin Z. Rubinstein, "Political Barriers to Disarmament," *Orbis* (Spring 1965): 145.

5. The quotation is from Col. Donald J. Stukel, USAF, "Technology and Arms Control," *National Security Affairs Monograph* (Washington, DC: National Defense University, 1978), p. 10. Stukel provides a fairly representative list of technological developments commonly considered stabilizing and destabilizing. Among stabilizing developments, he includes items that reduce vulnerability to surprise attack (for example, SLBMs, quickstart engines for bombers, harder ICBM silos), safeguards against accidental launch of ICBMs, increased reliability of early warning systems, improved means of verification, and weapons that reduce collateral damage (a more controversial assertion). Among destabilizing developments, he lists first-strike weapons (highly accurate ICBMs), weapons difficult to monitor, and capabilities to interfere with NTMs, like **ASATs.**

6. Marvin Goldberger, "Does the Technological Imperative Still Drive the Arms Race?" in Roman Kolkowicz and Neil Joeck, *Arms Control and International Security* (Boulder, CO: Westview Press, 1984), pp. 63–64.

    Senator Gore reportedly has made the same observation, suggesting that the scientists engaged in the MIRV development in the United States were probably inspired more by technical challenges than by the evidence of Soviet deployment of an ABM system. Senator Gore "mused that a scientist's response to a technical challenge could be likened to a mountain climber's response to an unscaled peak." Quoted in Frei, *Risks of Unintentional War,* pp. 26–27.

7. Malcolm W. Browne, "The Star Wars Spinoff," *New York Times Magazine,* August 24, 1986, p. 69. In a letter to the editor of *Time,* three physics professors claim that 57 percent of the faculty of the top twenty physics departments in the United States have refused to participate in SDI research, not because they "oppose all research on defense technology," but because SDI is "destabilizing. . . . a Star Wars shield would not be for defense but rather for offense and to assist in a first strike against the Soviet Union." John Kogut, Jon Thaler, and Mike Weissman, letter to *Time,* July 14, 1986, p. 6.

8. Chirstoph Bertram, "Arms Control and Technological Change: Elements of a New Approach," in Christoph Bertram, ed., *Arms Control and Military Force* (Montclair, NJ: Allanheld, Osmun and Co., for the International Institute for Strategic Studies' Adelphi Library #3, 1980), p. 164. The discussion here of problems involved in restricting weapons testing draws on points made by Bertram, pp. 162–164.

9. For an argument in favor of controlling technology in the testing process, see Herbert Scoville, "Problems of New Technologies and Weapons Systems," in William Epstein and Bernard T. Feld, *New Directions in Disarmament* (New York: Praeger, 1981).

10. Edward Gibbon, *The Decline and Fall of the Roman Empire,* an abridged version by Dero A. Saunders (Middlesex, England: Penguin Books, 1952), pp. 627–628. Gibbon found man's progress in technology much more impressive than his developments in other areas of civilized enterprise:

    If we contrast the rapid progress of this mischevious discovery [gunpowder] with the slow and laborious advances of reason, science, and the arts of peace, a philosopher, according to his temper, will laugh or weep at the folly of mankind.

    (Gibbon refers here to the Greek materialists, Democritus and Heraclitus, respectively known as the laughing and weeping philosophers.)

11. This comment was made by Senator Whitehurst at a meeting of the North Atlantic Assembly. He was explaining the understandable public fear of ever-expanding stockpiles of nuclear weapons. Chris Lamb, "Public Opinion and Nuclear Weapons in Europe," *NATO Review* (December 1981): 30.

12. See for example, "The New Arms Technology and What It Means," *Nation,* April 9, 1983; Franklin A. Long, "Advancing Military Technology: Recipe for an Arms Race," *Current History* 82 (May 1983); and John Tirman, *The Militarization of High Technology* (Cambridge, MA: Ballinger, 1984).

13. Fear of new invincible weapons is a very old concern. Plutarch, for example, related how Roman intelligence reports of new Parthian weapons "had a most depressing effect on the soldier's spirits:"

> They employ a new kind of missile which travels faster than sight and pierces through whatever is in the way before one can see who is discharging these weapons; and their armoured calvary has weapons of offense which will cut through everything and defensive equipment which will stand up to any blow.

Fall of the Roman Republic: Six Lives by Plutarch, trans. Rex Warner (Middlesex, England: Penguin Books, 1972, original printing 1958), p. 136.
Such fears persist. In 1984 Secretary of State Schultz noted:

> As long as international tension and conflict exist, there will be insecure or irresponsible leaders who seek to shift the balance of regional power dramatically by acquiring a "secret weapon."

Secretary George Schultz, "Preventing the Proliferation of Nuclear Weapons," Current Policy #631, U.S. Department of State, Bureau of Public Affairs, November 1, 1984, p. 1.

14. Thucydides, *The Peloponnesian War,* trans. Rex Warner, (Middlesex, England: Penguin Books, 1954), p. 146. For Pericles's observations on Athenian naval technological superiority, see pp. 121 and 166.

15. See, for example, Tom Bethell, "What's Wrong with Nuclear Superiority," *National Review* June 6, 1986; Francis X. Kane in Paul H. Nitze, James E. Dougherty, and Francis X. Kane *The Fateful Ends and Shades of SALT* (New York: Crane, Russak and Co., 1979); and especially Stefan Possony and J. E. Pournelle, *The Strategy of Technology: Winning the Decisive War* (Cambridge, MA: University Press of Cambridge, 1970).

16. The USSR may agree with this assessment. Barbara Tuchman cites an interesting USIA report on Russian fears:

> A study made in 1981 by the International Communications Agency . . . reports that while the Russians apparently do not fear direct attack, they suffer their own kind of apprehension about the United States as a power that can overwhelm them by superior military technology. In the popular view, the United States is seen as capable of changing the military balance of power in its favor overnight by some technological miracle that will leave the Soviet Union far behind in the arms race. Soviet governing groups, according to the study, harbor doubts "about the competence, reliability and effectiveness of their own forces."

Barbara Tuchman, "The Alternatives to Arms Control," in Kolkowicz and Joeck, *Arms Control and International Security,* p. 138.

17. Bruce Russett, *The Prisoners of Insecurity* (San Francisco: W. H. Freeman and Co., 1983), p. 59.

18. In addition, some believe that references to the qualitative arms race are misleading, and that technology has a certain momentum of its own:

> The action-reaction phenomenon is greatly overrated. I don't think you can say that *this* provokes *that*. The fact is, when we were developing MIRVs, so were they. I would say if you could get the secret plans for both sides, they'd look very much alike. . . . Technology has a life of its own. Something is funded. It's funded again. It moves even further.

William Hyland quoted in John Powers, "Hiroshima Plus 37," *Boston Globe Magazine,* October 17, 1982.

19. Charles A. Zacket, "Strategic Command, Control, Communication and Intelligence," *Science* (July 1984): 1311; and David Ziegler, *War, Peace and International Politics* (Boston: Little, Brown, 1981), p. 237.

20. The transcript of the presidential debate in which Reagan made this offer can be found in the *Washington Post,* October 22, 1984, A13.

21. Colin Gray, *Strategic Studies and Public Policy: The American Experience* (Lexington, KY: University Press of Kentucky, 1982).

22. Dr. Vannevar Bush, quoted by Caspar Weinberger in an address to the National Press Club on the subject of the U.S. Strategic Defense Initiative in early May 1984. See Ann Wood, ed., *Current News* # 1230, Special Edition, Strategic Defense Initiative, November 29, 1984, p. 6.

23. See footnote 4 above.

24. This was Hedley Bull's conclusion many years ago. Hedley Bull, *The Control of the Arms Race* (New York: Frederick A. Praeger, 1961), p. 199.

25. This fact was recognized by the signatories of the Washington Naval Treaty of 1922. The treaty provided that:

   In view of possible technical and scientific developments, the United States, after consultation with the other Contracting Powers, shall arrange for a conference of all the Contracting Powers which shall convene as soon as possible after the expiration of eight years from the coming into force of the present Treaty to consider what changes, if any, in the Treaty may be necessary to meet such developments.

   U.S. Congress, *Disarmament and Security: A Collection of Documents,* 1919–1955, Committee Print, 84th Congress, 2d Session, p. 25.

   For more on the impact of technological progress on arms control and disarmament agreements see Wolfram F. Hanrieder, ed., *Technology, Strategy, and Arms Control* (Boulder, CO: Westview Press, 1986).

Chapter Fifteen

Other Critical Questions for Peace Strategies

The issues reviewed in this chapter, uncertainty, escalation, attenuating the horrors of war, and weighing the respective risks of total and limited war, are all interrelated. Each of these topics offers a different perspective on essentially the same area of interest: peace strategies which make trade offs between the risks and intensity of war.

WOULD ATTENUATING THE HORRORS OF WAR
MAKE IT MORE THINKABLE, AND THUS MORE LIKELY?

> My factories may make an end of war sooner than your congresses. The day when two army corps can annihilate each other in one second, all civilized nations, it is to be hoped, will recoil from war and discharge their troops.
>
> —Alfred Nobel on the impact of his explosives.

> Nor is it possible to rely on fear of war, for fear never stopped man at the gates of folly.
>
> —Salvador de Madariaga[1]

Many modern arms control and disarmament proposals require taking a position on the ancient question of whether it is wise and moral to make efforts to limit the conduct of war. Speaking after the American Civil War, a scholar broadly summarized the two competing schools of thought on this issue:

> On this point two views, I am well aware, have been taken from the beginning, and still are advocated. On the one side, it is contended that warfare should be strictly confined to combatants, and its horrors and devastations brought within the narrowest limits. . . . But, on the other hand, it is insisted that such a method of procedure is mere cruelty in disguise; that war at best is Hell, and that true humanity lies in exaggerating that Hell to such an extent as to make it unendurable. By so doing, it is forced to a speedy end.[2]

Continuing, he argues that the cry of "War is Hell at best, [so] make it Hell indeed," has "echoed down the ages," but the result was not that war was made any shorter, "not by an hour," but only "needlessly bitter, brutal, and barbarous."

Arms control is basically sympathetic to this scholar's point of view. One of the three purposes generally attributed to arms control is the mitigation of death and destruction, should war occur.[3] The arguments against restraint in war are that: (1) restraining the conduct of war is not possible, (2) that efforts to do so end up dehumanizing people, (3) that restraint in war actually increases suffering and destruction, and (4) that reducing the horrors of war increases the frequency of war.

The first and most often voiced objection is that it is simply not possible to restrain behavior in war regardless of prior intentions. Many agree with the Roman philosopher Seneca that "Armed hands observe no limits. The drawn sword's fury none can soothe or check." Presuming otherwise, they argue, only makes men more likely to resort to war. This argument is made by assured destruction theorists who believe nuclear war could not be limited. Whether or not it is possible to limit the conduct of war was discussed in Chapters 1 and 2, and implicitly throughout much of this book. The issue cannot be resolved with any finality, but it is obvious that some constraints are more practical than others, and that a case-by-case analysis of the costs and benefits of making such efforts is required.

Besides the general criticism that it is impossible to restrain men in battle, there are several other objections to limiting the conduct of war. Surprisingly, some have argued that refining the rules of war could brutalize human sensitivities in the long run. The British historian T. B. Macaulay makes this argument:

> War ought never to be undertaken but under circumstances which render all intercourse of courtesy between the combatants impossible. It is a bad thing that men should hate each other; but it is far worse that they should contract the habit of cutting one another's throats without hatred.[4]

This same sort of complaint has been made by 20th century historians. Modern war, which is technically so sophisticated and fought so anonymously, becomes "a technologically dehumanized war [and] is bound to be morally dehumanized as well."[5]

Another argument in favor of unmitigated warfare is that efforts to limit war only have the opposite of their intended effect. If, as General von Moltke has proclaimed, "the greatest kindness in war is to bring it to a speedy conclusion,"[6] would not efforts to control or limit the war only succeed in prolonging it? Again Macaulay makes the case for maximum force and unrestrained efficiency in war:

> To carry the spirit of peace into war is a weak and cruel policy. When an extreme case calls for that remedy which is in its own nature most violent, and which in such cases, is a remedy only because it is violent, it is idle to think of mitigating and diluting. Languid war can do nothing which negotiation or submission will not do better: and to act on any other principle is not to save blood and money, but to squander them.

General William T. Sherman followed Macaulay's advice. His march through the South during the Civil War gave proof to his promise that "war is cruelty, and you cannot refine it." Sherman said that if Southerners "raise a howl against my barbarity and cruelty, I will answer that war is war. . . . If they want peace, they and their relatives must stop the war."[7]

Third, it has been argued that the more horrible the war, the longer will be the peace which follows. Sherman defended his unrestrained violence as an effort to make Southerners "so sick of war that generations would pass away before they would again appeal to it." The United States delegation to the First Hague Conference in 1899 (not a particularly cooperative participant[8]) made the same argument:

> It is doubtful if wars are to be diminished by rendering them less destructive, for it is the plain lesson of history that the periods of peace have been longer protracted as the cost and destructiveness of war have increased.[9]

The British said the same thing at the Second Hague Conference in 1907.[10]

It is not only memories of conduct in previous wars but also expectations of conduct in any future conflict that may condition the willingness to resort to violence. Deterrence of war by its anticipated horrors is a logic that has reached its zenith in the nuclear deterrence strategy of mutual assured destruction. Those who object to mutual assured destruction strategy point out that many new technological horrors have been thought to presage the end of war, but always man has adapted and continued to wage war.[11] Before the second World War it was thought that the effects of mass strategic bombing were so horrible to contemplate that they would preclude the outbreak of war. They were indeed horrible, but the war came and went nonetheless.

There are objections to each of the preceding points in favor of unrestrained war. To the concern that passionless war is dehumanizing, it may be argued that calm dispassionate violence is not so likely to corrupt men as giving their passions free reign. Indulging hatred and lust in time of battle has led to the most gruesome, heinous, and unnecessary acts of cruelty. Encouraging restraint and control may contribute to "cold-blooded" killing, but it instills the discipline necessary to secure military objectives with a minimum of collateral damage.

Secondly, it can be argued that unrestrained conduct of war is more likely to extend rather than shorten the conflict by stiffening the enemy's resolve. For example, at the siege of Malta in 1565, the Turkish Commander-in-Chief tried to demoralize the Christian defenders by displaying the crucified bodies of their lost comrades. The Christian commander promptly ordered the decapitation of all Turkish prisoners. Their heads were fired from cannons back into the Turkish lines. As one historian noted, from that point on no quarter or surrender on either side was possible.[12] Because such cruelty often produces the opposite of its intended effect, the following insight was long ago offered as a standing rule:

> Always give quarter to those who flee, lest otherwise the enemy should judge it better to hazard their lives in brave resistance, than be sure of losing them by running away.[13]

This advice was attributed to Lycurgus, a famous lawgiver of Sparta. A poet from Sparta's traditional rival, Athens, made another venerable argument in favor of restraint. The Athenian playwright, Aristophanes, who wrote during the Peloponnesian War and propagandized in favor of peace with Sparta, argued that personalized and passionate waging of war makes negotiated peace impossible. He took as a starting point the need to reduce popular hatred of the Spartans:

Mob Leader: Right? To come to terms with that lot? Don't you know that to a Spartan his pledged word, his oath, his most solemn sacrifice, counts for nothing?

Dikaiopolis: Oh, I know we always say hard things about the Spartans; but are they really responsible for everything?

Mob Leader: The Spartans not responsible?! You talk flat treason like that, and you expect to escape with your life?

Dikaiopolis: Yes, and I say it again, they're not responsible for everything. In fact I could prove to you quite clearly that they have a good many legitimate grievances against us.

Aristophanes' play, *The Archarnians,* won first prize and may have made some contribution to public acceptance of the Spartan-Athenian peace treaty which followed two years later. Aristophanes' concerns have been shared through the centuries by those who believe negotiated peace requires an ability to prevent the passions of war from foreclosing lines of communication between belligerents.[14]

It should be noted that the positions outlined above contradict one another in means, not ends. The overall goal is to reduce suffering and destruction. The debate is over whether or not this goal is best accomplished by increasing the severity of war in the short term. Since history and informed opinion support both general positions, political judgment that takes into account existing weaponry, social ethos, international conventions, and the nature of the antagonists is required. When and where to apply restraint in war is an abstract moral issue, but one which produces a number of concrete policy issues as the following two sections illustrate.

Unconditional Surrender

Many have felt that once war begins, a decisive result is necessary, and the more decisive the better; otherwise the issues that led to the war remain and are likely to lead to another round of war later. In his inaugural address of 1861, Abraham Lincoln noted

> Suppose you go to war, you cannot fight always; and when, after much loss on both sides, and no gain on either, you cease fighting, the identical old questions as to terms of intercourse are again upon you.

Lincoln's preference for decisive victory when war is unavoidable explains his policy of unconditional surrender during the Civil War which in retrospect seems to have been the correct choice. However, the lessons of history are not always so clear cut.

For example, World War I dragged on indecisively for years because neither side could publicly justify a negotiated peace based on military stalemate after so much sacrifice had been made in the defense of high ideals. Yet the conclusion of World War I was not decisive enough to prevent the second World War. Hitler explained the defeat in the first World War as a sellout by German negotiators, thereby building public support for policies that contributed to the second World War. Consequently, the Allies demanded unconditional surrender in the second World War. However, the policy of unconditional surrender was criticized for dragging out the war by hardening German resistance, making domestic opposition to Hitler less popular, and extending the time available for Nazi atrocities, not to mention making postwar reconciliation more difficult.

The advisability of unconditional surrender is a timeless issue, one debated centuries ago during the Punic Wars between Carthage and Rome and today in reference to the ongoing war between Iran and Iraq.[15] In the short term it seems obvious that a negotiated peace will reduce suffering and destruction, but whether this is true in the long term is questionable and requires a most difficult assessment of contemporary and future political trends. Discussing the relative merits of conditional and unconditional surrender in the abstract is further complicated because it requires an evaluation of higher social values that are both the justification for the awful price of war as well as the best reasons for prescribing rules of limitation.

Preventive War

Preventive war is a related issue since it can be argued that a decisive preemptive strike can shorten an unavoidable conflict and thus reduce the overall destructiveness of war. Montesquieu argued in favor of preventive war:

> Self-defense sometimes dictates aggression. If one people takes advantage of peace to put itself in a position to destroy another, immediate attack on the first is the only means of preventing such destruction.

Winston Churchill agreed, arguing, "There is no merit in putting off a war for a year if when it comes, it is a far worse war."

Yet how does one determine that a war cannot be indefinitely postponed, or that postponing it will necessarily make it worse when it comes? Otto von Bismarck once claimed that such certainty was impossible:

> I would never advise your Majesty to declare war forthwith, simply because it appeared that our opponent would begin hostilities in the near future. One can never anticipate the ways of divine providence securely enough for that.

Notice also that the argument in favor of preemption presumes the advantage of the offense and surprise, otherwise it would be better to await the attack from a defensive posture. But one principal goal of arms limitation has been to establish conditions that *reduce* the advantage of the offensive, for example, by providing both sides with early warning of attack and by negotiating limits on offensive but not defensive weapons.

The foregoing discussion on whether attenuating or intensifying war in the short term will reduce the net cost of war over the long term covers the full panoply of possible restraints, from the conduct of individual soldiers to noncombatants to national policies on unconventional and preventive war. A similar debate, of even broader scope, is the question of whether it is right to raise the risk of total war and the incalcuable destruction it would entail in order to reduce the risk of less destructive conflicts. Or would it be better to reduce the risk of total war at the cost of increasing the likelihood of lower-level conflicts?

IS THERE AN INVERSE RELATIONSHIP BETWEEN THE RISK OF TOTAL WAR AND THE RISK OF LIMITED WAR THAT CAN BE MANIPULATED BY ARMS CONTROL POLICY?

> To reap the harvest of perpetual peace. By this one bloody trial of sharp war.
>
> —Shakespeare,
> *King Richard III*, v, 1592

> For what can war but endless war still breed?
>
> —Milton, 1608–1674
> "Sonnet on the Lord General Fairfax"

There is a question to which many strategists have turned their attention, but which is eschewed by practicing politicians, who generally prefer to dwell on how to avoid war of any kind with minimum risk. The question is whether or not a state should be willing to threaten, or actually fight, limited wars as a means of perpetually forestalling a war of catastrophic proportions, or conversely, risk total war as a means of perpetually forestalling even limited war. This question may assume the entire gamut of nuclear and conventional conflict or it may distinguish between the two.

Nuclear Versus Conventional War

Winston Churchill is often quoted on his 1953 confession that he had had, on occasion,

> the odd thought that the annihilating character of [nuclear weapons] may bring an utterly unforeseeable security to mankind. . . . It may be that when the advance of destructive weapons enables everyone to kill anybody else no one will want to kill anyone at all.[16]

Those who carry Churchill's musing to its logical policy conclusion would advocate nuclear weapons proliferation, and indeed, some notable theorists do.[17] They point out that since the advent of nuclear weapons, there has been no general conflict between the major powers possessing nuclear arms. Therefore, they conclude the proliferation of nuclear weapons will most likely have the effect of depressing the tendency for war in other parts of the world also. Opponents of nuclear proliferation do not wish to accept the risk of total war, which they associate with nuclear proliferation, even if it would diminish the short-term risk of large-scale conventional war, and many do not believe it would.

Officially the United States government has always rejected the notion that the spread of nuclear weapons would strengthen general deterrence of war. Even so, the United States did purposefully exploit the risk of total war to prevent more limited conflict during the 1950s. This was the essence of John Foster Dulles's policy of "brinkmanship":

> The ability to get to the brink of war without getting into war is the necessary art. If you cannot master it, you inevitably get into wars. If you try to run away from it, if you are scared to go to the brink, you are lost. We've had to look it square in the face—on the question of enlarging the Korean war, on the question of getting into the Indo-China war, on the question of Formosa. We walked to the brink and we looked it in the face.[18]

Deterring limited war by threatening total war seemed less sensible, and less credible, when the enemy had a similar nuclear capability, and thus support for "brinkmanship" declined precipitously when the United States lost its recognizable margin of nuclear superiority.

Since the 1950s, confidence in the ability to fight a conventional war without triggering the use of nuclear weapons has increased in most parts of the world, particularly where one side does not possess nuclear forces. Nuclear powers began to refrain from threatening nuclear attack against nonnuclear powers during the 1950s, and such threats were virtually unheard of in the 1960s and 1970s. In 1982 Argentina became the first nonnuclear state to attack territory claimed and defended by an established nuclear power when it invaded the Falkland Islands. Argentina evidently considered the possibility of British nuclear retaliation unlikely, although it is not clear whether Argentina relied on British sensitivities or a vague notion of the disutility of nuclear weapons, or both.

The Argentine attack on the Falklands was evidence of what has been characterized as the stability-instability paradox. Many believe that nuclear weapons are so destructive that their only utility is in deterring other nuclear states from using or threatening to use nuclear weapons. Thus, according to some, the greater the confidence in the general stability of nuclear "self-deterrence," the greater the instability of conventional deterrence. That is, without the threat of escalation to nuclear war, the likelihood of conventional war rises.[19]

If it does not seem possible to prevent the outbreak of conventional war by threatening nuclear war, it still might be possible to terminate a conventional war by threatening to escalate to nuclear war:

> It is a tactic of letting the situation get somewhat out of hand, just because its being out of hand may be intolerable to the other party and force his accommodation. It would not only be necessary to be sufficiently rational to know the value of appearing irrational, but also to be sufficiently in control of matters to allow them to get out of control.
>
> Any escalatory move involved pushing matters more out of control. Thus a function of limited war was to "pose the deliberate risk of all-out war."[20]

Nuclear-armed states that suffer a conventional inferiority vis-a-vis their adversaries rely heavily on the threat of escalation to nuclear war to deter conventional attack. A good example is France, which uses the threat of nuclear retaliation to offset its conventional inferiority relative to Soviet forces stationed in Eastern Europe.

Total Versus Limited Nuclear War

The trade-off between risks in limited and unlimited war may be discussed in just a nuclear rather than a nuclear-conventional context. The assured destruction and flexible response nuclear deterrence strategies discussed in Chapter 4 assume fundamentally different assessments of whether trade-offs in risking total or limited nuclear war are possible and advisable. Assured destruction theorists advocate force postures that would make limited nuclear war technically more difficult in hopes of making any resort to nuclear weapons tantamount to initiating total nuclear war. They believe this increased risk of total nuclear destruction reduces the likelihood of any nuclear exchange occurring. The disadvantage of this strategy is that if nuclear weapons are ever used, there is a greater risk that the result will be catastrophic.

Noting the danger of uncontrolled escalation should nuclear weapons ever be used, flexible response theorists advocate a force posture that would make limited war more fightable and thus, in theory, more controllable. They do not believe it is possible to deter limited nuclear war by threatening total nuclear war because they do not believe an adversary will take such a threat seriously. Therefore flexible response strategy attempts to reduce the risk of total war by acquiring the means for damage limitation and escalation control of limited nuclear war. Many believe the negative side of this policy is the increased risk of limited nuclear war.

Total Versus Limited Conventional War

Finally, the question of trade-offs in risks between limited and unlimited wars may be considered in just the conventional context, and in particular through two competing approaches to conventional war and diplomacy. One view holds that international conflict is often a necessary condition for arms limitation and peace treaties. Fighting limited wars can convince an aggressor, or two equally hostile antagonists, that parity is established and that basic power alignments are consistent with existing political and military realities. This is essentially the balance of power approach to international relations. The English philosopher David Hume (1752) blamed his compatriots for straying from the prudent dictates of balance of power politics and waging war too passionately:

> In the first place, we seem to have been more possessed with the ancient Greek spirit of jealous emulation, than actuated by the prudent views of modern

politics. . . . In the second place, we are so declared in our opposition to French power, and so alert in defense of our allies, that they always reckon upon our force as upon their own; and expecting to carry on war at our expense, refuse all reasonable terms of accommodation. . . . In the third place, we are such true combatants, that, when once engaged, we lose all concern for ourselves and our posterity, and consider only how we may best annoy the enemy. . . . These excesses, to which we have been carried, are prejudicial; and may, perhaps, in time, become still more prejudicial another way, by begetting, as is usual, the opposite extreme, and rendering us totally careless and supine with regard to the fate of Europe.[21]

States that agree with Hume and act in accordance with the prescriptions implied in the classic balance of power approach to international relations will see arms control as a means for manipulating the balance of power in order to preserve their stability and limit the likelihood of revolutionary, unrestrained conflicts, that is, absolute war.

Another Englishman of Hume's era, Edmund Burke, made a much less favorable assessment of the balance of power approach:

The balance of power, the pride of modern policy . . . invented to preserve the general peace as well as the freedom of Europe, has only preserved its liberty. It has been the origin of innumerable and fruitless wars.[22]

These innumerable wars only perpetually postponed what many consider to be the real work of diplomacy: building enduring peace. Proponents of this point of view have a more ambitious plan for the prevention of war. They want all wars prevented, not just total war. They usually advocate disarmament and collective security as opposed to mere arms control and deterrence. Collective security pacts aim to prevent war by a mutual agreement requiring all the signatories to come to the aid of anyone attacked by an aggressor. The negative aspect of collective security is that it broadens what might otherwise be a local conflict by requiring all nations to respond by attacking the ''aggressor.''[23] Proponents of collective security accept the risks of large-scale war in order to reduce the chances of any war.

In summary, statesmen must consider whether it is preferable to adopt deterrence strategies, negotiating policies, and force-employment practices designed to increase the odds that any war will be a total war—which might help deter all wars—or those designed to increase the odds that any wars will be limited wars that can be kept limited, should they be deemed necessary. In resolving this issue many states prefer to distinguish between nuclear and conventional wars because they consider escalation in nuclear war inevitable whereas controlled conventional war seems more feasible. Whether a state distinguishes between conventional and nuclear wars or not, its estimate of the likelihood of controlling escalation is a critical consideration in how it decides to balance the risks of total and limited war.

IS ESCALATION INEVITABLE?

If we are to retain . . . a choice other than nuclear holocaust or retreat, we must be ready to fight a limited war for a protracted period of time anywhere in the world.

—John F. Kennedy

War will go on its own way withersoever chance may lead, and will not restrict itself to the limits which he who meddles with it would fain prescribe.

—Thucydides

Conflict escalation can be considered in several contexts: geographic escalation, escalation in conflict intensity (that is, proportion of social resources committed), and escalation in types of weapons used, from those of lesser to those of greater destructive capacity. In each of these areas arms control efforts usually assume escalation control is possible and beneficial. For example, arms control presumes that it is possible to control geographic escalation through neutrality pacts, arms embargoes, and nonproliferation treaties (either nuclear or nonnuclear) and that conflict intensity may be controlled with communication and administration agreements, mediation efforts, and established rules of war. Efforts to prohibit the use of certain types of weapons also presume the control of escalation since there would be little sense in negotiating restrictions if it was assumed that once a war began the intensity of the conflict would escalate beyond control.

There is a large body of literature on escalation in war. Political scientists have identified conflicts in which tacit agreements appeared to work to constrain the type and level of force employed, and eventually to terminate the conflict on mutually agreeable terms. Wars in which limits were established only to be broken, and wars that escalated without restrictions of any kind are also part of the historical record. Nuclear weapons confuse an already ambiguous empirical record. Because they have not been used since 1945, all discussion of nuclear weapons necessarily remains speculative. Some theorists believe that once the "nuclear firebreak" has been passed, conflict will inexorably escalate to all-out nuclear holocaust, while others believe the escalation process could be much more graduated. Herman Kahn, for example, identified forty-four rungs of the escalation ladder, with the employment of nuclear weapons commencing at rung number fifteen.

The likelihood of escalation is in part a function of national security strategy. Grand strategists draw a broad distinction between symmetrical and asymmetrical defense and deterrence strategies, the former advocating response to an attack in like manner and location and the latter based on retaliation in an alternative manner and location. One advantage of asymmetrical response is that it recovers the initiative for the defender. Following an attack the defender can choose where and how to respond in more favorable conditions. The disadvantage to asymmetrical response is that it escalates a conflict by drawing in new forces or by geographically broadening the conflict.

In the nuclear context the significance of differing opinions on escalation is most evident in domestic debate over nuclear deterrence strategy, and in the intra-NATO debate over extended deterrence.

NATO and Extended Deterrence

In theory the defense forces of the United States and NATO are "coupled" in order to prevent an attack on NATO anywhere along the conflict spectrum, from conventional to strategic nuclear attack. Thus NATO relies on the strategic nuclear weapons of the United States, which are "extended" in its defense. Disagreement between the United States and its European allies on extended deterrence revolves around the issue of escalation.

America's NATO allies do not want the balance of either conventional or nuclear weapons in Europe so stable that it appears a war could be initiated and terminated in Europe, that is, that escalation could be controlled. Therefore European NATO members want a deterrence policy that emphasizes escalation to total war in the hopes that this threat will prevent any war from occurring. Optimally this means weaker lower-level forces that would lead an aggressor to expect quick escalation by NATO, and U.S. strategic superiority that would leave no doubt in the aggressor's mind that total war could not be won.

In contrast, the United States does not want an imbalance in WPO and NATO conventional forces that would require an almost immediate resort to strategic nuclear weapons, that is, automatic escalation. The United States prefers not to use the threat of total war to reduce the risk of even limited war. It desires a more stable graduated deterrence that will make it easier to control escalation should war begin. At best this would mean escalation dominance, or superiority at every level of forces.

Escalation and Nuclear Deterrence Strategy

Domestic debate between assured destruction and flexible response theorists parallels the intra-NATO differences over the virtues of escalation and admirably demonstrates the importance of escalation in arms control and defense strategy. Assured destruction theorists want to convince potential adversaries that in the event of nuclear war escalation will be virtually automatic. In theory automatic escalation can be accomplished in one of two ways; either by convincing the other side that you have the will to escalate, which implies escalation can be controlled, or by convincing the other side that control is impossible and escalation is inevitable because any nuclear conflict will take on a dynamism of its own. Some assured destruction theorists emphasize the role of will, others emphasize the loss of control, and still others emphasize both simultaneously:

> No state can . . . take its population centers out of hostage; thus it is the willingness to run risks and the perceptions of this willingness that will determine whether a response is "realistic" and a threat is credible. . . . If one side denies that counterforce wars could be kept limited and convinces the other side that it believes this, the other side cannot safely act on its doctrine.[24]

In practice, convincing an enemy that escalation is to be expected involves some hard choices about force posture. Communicating a resolve to escalate often means taking steps to force escalation, as an example from the ancient historian Polyaenus illustrates:

> Memphis had been obliged to retreat before Ariboeus . . . but was determined not to be blocked up in his city. With this purpose he brought out whatever was valuable: his wives, his children, and his treasures he placed without the walls and destroyed the gates. Ariboeus saw in his conduct the marks of desperation and drew off his army—not judging it advisable to engage an enemy thus devoted to death or determined on victory.[25]

Memphis took active measures to foreclose his options. Assured destruction theorists also favor forgoing steps to assist damage limitation[26] and command and control capabilities.

There are numerous steps that could be taken to reinforce the perception and reality of uncontrollable escalation; for example, abandoning civil defense programs, targeting enemy decision-making centers for immediate retaliation, locating all missiles in urban population centers, and eliminating any force thresholds that could be seen as mutually agreed barriers for halting escalation.[27] The farthest one could go toward ensuring escalation would be to construct a "fail-safe" mechanism, which automates nuclear retaliation. Most assured destruction theorists stop far short of recommending the fail-safe option, and many avoid recommending other steps for increasing the likelihood of escalation as well. The reason they do not take all available steps to increase the likelihood of escalation is that doing so also means decreasing the chances of early war termination should, for whatever reason, nuclear weapons ever be used. Thus many assured destruction theorists prefer to rely on the uncertainty of escalation rather than take concrete steps to make escalation more certain.

In contrast to the assured destruction theorist, the flexible response theorist does not believe it is possible to convince an adversary that escalation will be automatic, not even with forces and doctrine designed to make escalation more likely. In the words of Albert Wohlstetter:

> We cannot assure that a nuclear war will never occur simply by repeating it would be an unlimited catastrophe. And we cannot eliminate the possibility of nuclear war simply by *assuring* that if it occurs it *will* be an unlimited catastrophe.[28]

From the flexible response theorist's point of view the ability to control escalation not only communicates determination instead of desperation, and thus constitutes a more credible deterrent; it also allows a greater possibility of war termination should a war start.[29] However, perfect escalation control is neither possible nor desirable for flexible response theorists either, since the threat of escalation beyond the wishes of the belligerents can be a key factor in mutual agreement to end hostilities. Thus, insomuch as the uncertainty of escalation can be used to help control escalation by making the results of crossing thresholds unpredictable, the flexible response theorist also requires an element of escalation uncertainty.

In summary, between a policy of automatic escalation and finely controlled escalation there is a middle ground of uncertainty about the likelihood of escalation that all strategists believe will enhance deterrence. On the other hand, most agree that at some ill-defined point, too much uncertainty, in both arms control and deterrence strategy, is counterproductive.

DISCUSSION QUESTIONS

1. Would attenuating or intensifying war in the short term be more likely to reduce the net cost of war over the long term?
2. Is it moral to use the threat of total war in hopes of reducing the chance of any war?
3. Is it possible to control escalation in conventional war? In nuclear conflict? Is it advisable to plan for escalation control?

SUGGESTED READINGS FOR CHAPTER FIFTEEN: OTHER CRITICAL QUESTIONS FOR PEACE STRATEGIES

A. Mitigating the Horrors of War

O'BRIEN, WILLIAM V. *The Conduct of Just and Limited War.* New York: Praeger, 1981.
"The Challenge of Peace: God's Promise and Our Response." Pastoral Letter on Nuclear War by the National Conference of Catholic Bishops. Washington, DC: U.S. Catholic Conference, May 19, 1983.
PFALTZGRAFF, ROBERT L. *National Security, Ethics, Strategy and Politics: A Layman's Primer.* New York: Pergamon-Brassey's, 1986.
RAMSEY, PAUL. *The Just War.* New York: Scribner's, 1968.
WALZER, MICHAEL. *Just and Unjust Wars: A Moral Argument with Historical Illustrations.* New York: Basic Books, 1977.
WOHLSTETTER, ALBERT. "Bishops, Statesmen, and Other Strategists on the Bombing of Innocents." *Commentary,* June 1983.

B. Limiting War and Controlling Escalation

BALL, DESMOND. "Can Nuclear War Be Controlled?" Adelphi Paper #169. London: International Institute of Strategic Studies, 1983.

BETTS, RICHARD K. *Surprise Attack.* Washington: Brookings, 1982.

BRODIE, BERNARD. *Escalation and the Nuclear Option.* Princeton: Princeton University Press, 1966.

FREEDMAN, LAWRENCE. *The Evolution of Nuclear Strategy.* New York: St. Martin's Press, 1981.

KAHN, HERMAN. *On Escalation: Metaphors and Scenarios.* New York: Praeger, 1965.

SCHEER, ROBERT. *With Enough Shovels: Reagan, Bush and Nuclear War.* New York: Random House, 1982.

SMOKE, RICHARD. *War: Controlling Escalation.* Cambridge, MA: Harvard University Press, 1978.

STEINBRUNER, JOHN. *"Nuclear Decapitation."* Foreign Policy (1981): 16–28.

NOTES

1. From *Dictionary of Military and Naval Quotations,* compiled and edited by Colonel Robert Debs Heinl, Jr., USMC (Ret.). Copyright © 1966, U.S. Naval Institute, Annapolis, Maryland; The Madariaga quote is from Salvador de Madariaga *Disarmament* (New York: Coward McCann, 1929), Preface.

2. General Adams, "War Is Hell," an address delivered in New York on January 26, 1903, at the Thirteenth Annual Dinner of the Confederate Veteran's Camp of New York, held in honor of Robert E. Lee. Quoted in Telford Taylor, foreword in Leon Friedman, ed., *The Law of War: A Documentary History,* Vol. 1 (New York: Random House, 1972), p. xx.

3. As mentioned in Chapter 2, the other two are to reduce the costs of defense and improve the state's security.

4. This and all the following quotations in this chapter which are otherwise not attributed are from *Dictionary of Military and Naval Quotations,* compiled and edited by Colonel Robert Debs Heinl, Jr., USMC (Ret.). Copyright © 1966, U.S. Naval Institute, Annapolis, Maryland.

5. Hans J. Morgenthau and Kenneth W. Thompson, *Politics Among Nations,* 6th ed., (New York: Alfred A. Knopf, 1985), p. 259.

6. Quoted in Michael Walzer, *Just and Unjust War,* (New York: Basic Books, 1977), p. 131.

7. Recently the "it's kind to be cruel" approach to war has been used in criticizing President Nixon's decision during the Vietnam war not to bomb North Vietnam into submission. The argument, made on purely utilitarian grounds, is that in the long run bombing restraint cost more lives than it saved, considering the mass killings which followed the Vietnam War:

    On assuming office, Nixon considers his options. Quit and go home. Use the "Knockout punch," not necessarily nuclear. Try to establish the "balance of power." Nixon went for the last. The "knockout punch" would have killed up to a million people. Bombing the dikes: 500,000. Dresdenizing Hanoi: 500,000. The price tag for the failed policy was much greater, perhaps by a factor of four to six. Nixon refused to adopt the humane solution.

    Jeffrey Hart, "Years of the Fish," *National Review,* May 3, 1985, p. 52.

8. The American delegation led the opposition to the only three concrete restrictions adopted by the conference. See William R. Hawkins, "Arms Control: Three Centuries of Failure," *National Review* August 9, 1985.

9. Walter F. Fisher and Richard Dean Burns, *Armament and Disarmament: The Continuing Debate* (Belmont, CA: Wadsworth Publishing Co., 1974), p. 215

10. James E. Dougherty, *How to Think About Arms Control and Disarmament* (New York: Crane, Russak and Co., 1973), p. 39.

11. Some who have no confidence that fear can deter governments from waging war still believe that in the nuclear age fear can succeed in ending war by galvanizing public opinion against war. See, for example, the argument Barbara Tuchman makes in "The Alternative to Arms Control," in Roman Kolkowicz and Neil Joeck, eds., *Arms Control and International Security* (Boulder, CO: Westview Press, 1984), pp. 136–141.

12. Ernle Bradford *The Great Siege: Malta 1565* (Middlesex, England: Penguin Books, 1964), pp. 139–140.

13. Evidently this advice became a staple of Spartan military doctrine. Hundreds of years after Lycurgus, Thucydides observed that:

    The Spartans will fight a long time, stubbornly holding their ground until the moment they have put their enemy to flight; but once this moment comes they do not follow him up a great way or for long.

    Thucydides, *The Peloponnesian War,* trans. Rex Warner (Middlesex, England: Penguin Books, 1954), p. 394.

14. Thomas Aquinas believed that cooling inflamed passions during war was a critical component of a "just" war. For Aquinas the initiation of a just war required competent authority, a just cause, and "right intentions." Right intentions were defined as limiting military objectives to the completion of the just cause, seeking a just and lasting peace, and finally, avoiding hatred of the enemy, which could lead to an unnecessary escalation of the war effort.

    See the discussion in Chapter 3 on just war, and in William O'Brien *The Conduct of Just and Limited War* (New York: Praeger, 1981).

15. Of course, the answer depends first of all on whether unconditional surrender is sought in order to exterminate the enemy, as the Romans did in the case of Carthage, or to seek such ends as were proclaimed by Polybius, the Greek historian who was present at the Roman siege of Carthage in 147 B.C.:

    It is not the object of war to annihilate those who have given provocation for it, but to cause them to mend their ways; not to ruin the innocent and guilty alike, but to save both.

16. Charles W. Kegley and Eugene R. Wittkopf, *The Nuclear Reader: Strategy, Weapons, War* (New York: St. Martin's Press, 1985), p. 7, fn. 1.

17. According to Kenneth Waltz:

    The world has enjoyed more years of peace since 1945 [the advent of nuclear weapons] than had been known in this century. . . . With more nuclear states the world will have a promising future. . . . Nuclear weapons make it possible to approach the deterrent ideal.

    Quoted in Leon Wieseltier, "When Deterrence Fails," *Foreign Affairs* (Spring 1985), p. 829.

18. Originally in *Life* January 11, 1956, quoted in Heinl, *Dictionary,* John Foster Dulles's strategy of massive retaliation was not limited to nuclear weapons, but was part of a broader asymmetrical deterrence strategy that took advantage of U.S. nuclear superiority. See the discussion of asymmetrical and symmetrical strategies below.

19. Thomas C. Schelling and Morton H. Halperin, *Strategy and Arms Control* (New York: Twentieth Century Fund, 1961), p. 31.

20. Lawrence Freedman, *The Evolution of Nuclear Strategy* (New York: St. Martin's Press, 1981), p. 220.

21. David Hume, from *Essays: Moral, Political, and Literary,* Part II, Essay 7, first published in 1752, in John A. Vasquez, ed., *Classics of International Relations* (Englewood Cliffs: Prentice-Hall, 1986), pp. 280–284.

22. Walzer, *Just and Unjust Wars,* p. 76.

23. Morgenthau observes that collective security as "a device intent upon making war impossible ends by making war universal." Hans Morgenthau, *Politics Among Nations,* 4th ed. (New York: Alfred A. Knopf, 1967), p. 402.

24. Robert Jervis, "Why Nuclear Superiority Doesn't Matter," *Political Science Quarterly* (Winter 1979/80), p. 620 and 631.

25. *Polyanenus's Stratagems of War,* R. Shepherd (Chicago: Ares Publications, 1914; unchanged reprint of 1793 ed.), p. 291. See also Niccolo Machiavelli *The Discourses* Bk III, Chp. 12, "A Skillful General Should Endeavor by all Means in his Power to Place His Soldiers in the Position of Being Obliged to Fight, and as Far as Possible Relieve the Enemy of Such Necessity."

26. Damage limitation efforts imply a belief in escalation control.

27. Ironically, the blurring of thresholds is aided by a flexible response force posture that includes a full range of nuclear capabilities from tactical nuclear weapons to "city busters."

28. Freedman, *The Evolution of Nuclear Strategy,* p. 373.

29. In this regard flexible response theorists may require some kinds of thresholds which could serve as a mutually agreed stopping point for escalation. In other words there must be some limits on the panoply of weapons if they desire to control escalation. As Colin Gray has noted, the "Davy Crockett" nuclear cannon and other very low-yield tactical nuclear weapons were withdrawn from service because of the belief

> that uncontrolled escalation was far less likely to occur if tactical nuclear weapons were fired late rather than early, and that the prospects for war termination and early termination short of cataclysm would be improved if an unambiguous threshold separated nonnuclear from nuclear weapons.

Colin S. Gray, *Strategic Studies and Public Policy: The American Experience* (Lexington, KY: University of Kentucky Press, 1982), p. 23.

Chapter Sixteen

Conclusion:

How to Think About Arms Control, Disarmament, and Defense

"Order and simplification are the first steps toward mastery of a subject."

—Thomas Mann, *The Magic Mountain*

This book has ordered and simplified subject matter which defies neat categorization. The purpose was to familiarize the reader with the perennial conceptual issues of arms limitation and national security, while also suggesting their interrelatedness, complexity, and subtlety; in short, to provide a framework for thinking about arms control, disarmament, and defense. Now it is appropriate to return to the question posed in Chapter 1 and see if thinking about the future really requires a knowledge of the past, which provides "a sense of the possible and the necessary, even if the necessary turns out to be the unprecedented."

HISTORICAL DISCONTINUITIES: AN ASSESSMENT OF ABSOLUTE AND LIMITED SECURITY STRATEGIES

My heart is in anguish within me, the terrors of death have fallen upon me. Fear and trembling come upon me, and horror overwhelms me. And I say, "Oh that I had wings like a dove! I would fly away and be at rest."

—Psalm 55:4–6

CHORUS:	Did you perhaps go farther than you have told us?
PROMETHEUS:	I caused mortals to cease foreseeing doom.
CHORUS:	What cure did you provide them with against that sickness?
PROMETHEUS:	I placed in them blind hopes.

—Aeschylus, *Prometheus Bound*

It was observed in Chapter 1 that, hoping for victory without end, some states have placed their faith wholly in power and sought the complete destruction of their enemies. Alternatively, some have hoped for peace through subservience or passive resistance, and placed their faith chiefly in the magnanimity, the reasonableness, or the humanity of their enemies. The historical record suggests these absolute security strategies have met with some success. Not all states choosing the glorification of power have been burdened with endless strife or ended in utter ruin. Neither have all states choosing to relinquish their freedoms been destroyed or subjected to ruthless tyranny. For example, the Roman, British, and Russian empires all obtained periods of extended peace for the bulk of their citizens by conquering neighbors and holding their enemies at bay. And many of their opponents paid for defeat with a loss of political sovereignty rather than wholesale loss of life.

Nevertheless, as discussed in Chapter 1, absolute security strategies more often than not require great sacrifices in human life and freedom. Moreover, many people believe that recent advances in technology have produced historical discontinuities which completely rule out absolute security strategies as reasonable hopes for securing peace in today's world. The advent of weapons of mass destruction which could eliminate whole nations if not the entire human race would seem to preclude total war as a reasonable security option. In a world armed with nuclear weapons any attempt at the total elimination of enemies runs the high risk of mutual self-destruction.

It is also argued that advances in technology have ruled out the absolute security strategies of pacifism and nonviolent resistance. As discussed in Chapter 1, the success rate of nonviolent resistance to aggression is not impressive, but much like the record on world empires, there are some notable exceptions.[1] However, the phenomenal technological advances in modern communications and modes of transportation may have rendered nonviolent resistance a hopeless gamble. Kenneth W. Thompson argued:

> The technological prerequisites for a stable world-wide empire are three in number: (1) enforced social integration through centralized control over the minds of the subjects of the empire, (2) superior organized force at any point of possible disintegration within the empire, and (3) permanency and ubiquity of these means of control and enforcement throughout the empire. None of these three military and political prerequisites has been achieved in the past, yet they are within the reach of our time.

Continuing, Thompson pointed out that most likely "a people once conquered will stay conquered," and "the chances are that the conqueror, through his monopolistic control of the means of communications, will have deprived it of the will to revolt as well."[2] In short, modern technology also poses a magnified threat to human freedom and dignity.

This, then, is the principal historical discontinuity between the modern and pre-modern world: now that mankind is armed with weapons of mass destruction and the globe has been shrunk by means of mass communication and transit, pacifism and militarism are security policies that risk the permanent loss of civilization as we know it. For those who care nothing for human life or who believe life itself rather than the quality of life is the highest value these risks may be deemed reasonable if there does not appear to be any practical alternative. However, an overview of history suggests there is a practical alternative to universal peace through conquest or submission.

HISTORICAL CONTINUITIES: AN ASSESSMENT OF MAN AND TECHNOLOGY

> If the debasement of arts and science to purposes of wickedness, luxury and the like, be made a ground of objection to the inventions of modern science, let no one be moved thereby. For the same may be said of all earthly goods: of wit, courage, strength, beauty, wealth, light itself, and the rest. Only let the human race recover that right over nature which belongs to it by divine bequest, and let power be given it; the exercise thereof will be governed by sound reason and true religion.
>
> —Sir Francis Bacon (1561–1626)[3]

Perhaps the most obvious point to be made about the historical record is that while people have eagerly professed peace they just as earnestly have prepared for war. This incongruity between profession and practice represents an old pattern in human affairs, as two excerpts from the Bible illustrate. The most renowned proclamation of peace is the prophet Isaiah's promise:

> they shall beat their swords into plowshares, and their spears into pruning hooks; nation shall not lift up sword against nation, neither shall they learn war any more. (Isaiah 2:4)

Isaiah's words are engraved on the outside walls of the United Nations' headquarters in New York City, and they are enjoined by an endless procession of diplomats inside the building. Yet the historical record, from prebiblical times to the present, demonstrates that nations eagerly harken to the advice of the biblical prophet Joel: "Beat your plowshares into swords, and your pruning hooks into spears." (Joel 3:10).

The words of Isaiah and Joel illustrate why arms limitation is necessarily a perennial item on the national and international political agenda. Whatever decisions men may make about whether to fashion the implements of war or the tools of peace, they nonetheless always retain the knowledge for both. Thus the choice between "swords into plowshares or plowshares into swords" can never be made with finality.[4] In principle, men and weapons must always coexist, though the level and sophistication of the weapons (and men too) may change. Mankind and weapons are the two major and inseparable factors in the age-old problem of war and peace. Throughout this book, subjects have been raised which represent a primary concern with either human relations or mankind's relationship to his material environment, and always it was apparent that each subject had its counterpart to which ultimately it was linked:

Human Relations and International Politics	Technological Capabilities
Human Hubris	Weapons Technology
Trust	Parity
Intentions	Capabilities
Aggressor Theory	Spiral Theory
Militarism/Pacifism	Offensive/Defensive Weapons
Moral Disarmament	Material Disarmament
Politics and Negotiations	Technical Parameters of Negotiations
Treaty Violations	Monitoring Capabilities

Thus, as argued in Chapter 1, it is at least as important to consider why people choose to apply technology on behalf of peace or violence as it is to think about the means with which they accomplish either of these ends. An exclusive focus on either human nature (people) or weapons (technology) as the source of conflict in international relations can lead to a tendentious—and either overly optimistic or overly pessimistic—historical assessment of human attempts to control weapons and violence.

For example, concentrating on weapons, the pessimist could argue that our situation is hopeless. The technology of war has accelerated through the centuries with every new weapon eventually being used for death and destruction. What reason is there to expect that we can escape nuclear, biological, and chemical holocaust? An optimist might respond by observing that throughout history many new armaments have shocked mankind so badly that there were initially labeled "doomsday weapons" capable of destroying civilization. There was a time when the rumble of thousands of war chariots portended quick and utter destruction. Many centuries later Alfred Nobel thought his new invention of dynamite was so horrible it would convince people to abandon hostilities rather than report to its awesome capabilities. And so it has been with respect to the machine gun, nerve gas, strategic bombers, and many others.

The reason war chariots, dynamite, and other major innovations in weaponry do not seem so threatening today is that offensive counters to deter the use of these weapons or defensive measures to render them less effective or obsolete have always been found. In fact, history records several cases of strategic defense in which technology played a critical role. The gateway to Europe, Constantinople, was protected from repeated Islamic onslaughts for centuries with the secret of "Greek fire"; and Great Britain survived a German submarine blockade and mass aerial bombings largely with the aid of sonar and radar. The technology of mass destruction has always been available, but the means to deliver or prevent destruction have constantly evolved with each new offensive capability producing a response in defensive capabilities. Thus it is reasonable to hope man will invent antidotes for poisonous gases and a defense against ICBMs, the two greatest technological threats of mass death facing mankind today. In short, technological innovations in offensive and defensive capabilities are not disputed, but pessimists stress the dangers of the latter and optimists hopes for the former.

If the focus is shifted from weapons to people, the pessimist may rejoin that all that the new weapons (offensive or defensive) do is to encourage the wish to test them in battle. The human record as a whole is one long series of bloody encounters. Despite periods of relative tranquility in some areas, it has been estimated that over fifty-five hundred years of history the world has averaged two and a half wars a year.[5] And, contrary to popular belief, war is not an outdated vice of previously unenlightened generations. Today numerous conflicts involving nations of diverse ideologies and differing levels of industrial development mar the face of the earth. In short, if one hopes to end war by fundamentally changing human behavior, it is a hope that ignores all of recorded history.

There is no easy rebuttal to this historical indictment, except the observation that despite all the violence, periods of extended peace have occurred also. However these periods of peace are explained, an understanding of the requisite conditions for peace could help minimize conflict in the future. If, as many believe, the same policies may at times and according to prevailing conditions encourage either peace or war, then a discerning political judgment becomes a principal requisite for peace. A judicious assessment of extant international conditions may enable a leader to prevent or minimize conflicts, but the historical record suggests there are limits to how long even the most talented of leaders can stave off conflict. The more specific concern of the pessimist remains: How can conflict-prone mankind prevent our extinction now that we possess weapons with the potential for instantaneous mass destruction? The optimist offers the following arguments.

First, the optimist points out that people always organize socially, and so organized, behave in socially purposeful ways. Even when the social goal is as violent as the extinction of a real or imagined enemy, societies have *always* exercised one minimal element of restraint in the use of force—self-preservation. We must be clear on this point. It is true that some groups have suffered catastrophic losses willingly, and fought fanatically even when all hope was abandoned, but never has a society moved purposefully towards self-annihilation. Moreover, socially purposeful groups not only seek to provide for their continued existence, they work to secure other group goals and thus may be expected not to act *consciously* against their own interests. Even the most militaristic and aggressive societies have restrained their behavior when it clearly seemed in their self-interest. If we can just continue this long record of minimal self-restraint then there is reason to hope that we may indefinitely postpone our extinction.

One could also add on behalf of mankind that most societies have exercised some degree of conscious restraint in the conduct of war above and beyond mere self-interest, as dictated by custom, belief, and faith. These additional margins of restraint cannot be depended upon, but they encourage the hope that we may not only avoid extinction but also may minimize conflict more generally through the development of appropriate social and religious mores (or, in Bacon's words sound reason and true religion).

Although they exist in tension, each of these four historical continuities contains truth. A judicious analysis of future prospects for survival would project each of these four truths into the future, giving each its due in order to produce a "net" assessment of man's historical record and anticipated future. Such an analysis would assume that brutal conflict, technological advances in weapons and defenses, and at least a bare minimum of restraint defined by self-interest will characterize the future as it has the past. Whether minimum restraint will suffice to prevent nuclear war, as it has for forty years, and the poisoning of large water supplies, as it has for centuries; or whether technological advances will render nuclear weapons obsolete; or whether the next decades will usher in a period of relative tranquility or burgeoning violence, cannot be determined from a study of the past.

REASONABLE HOPES

> Indeed, they fancied this was a perfectly safe thing to do, though, as was proved later on, the power of Athens was as great as had been their mistake in underestimating it. As it was, their judgment was based more on wishful thinking than on a sound calculation of probabilities; for the usual thing among men is that when they want something they will, without any reflection, leave that to hope, while they will employ the full force of reason in rejecting what they find unpalatable.[6]

> —Thucydides, *The Peloponnesian War*

The general historical observations from the previous two sections support two important conclusions. First, there is reason to hope. If the future is not likely to be free of conflict, it is at least possible to conceive of a future where the use of force is limited. Second, hopes for security must be reasonable. If history is a guide, it is not reasonable to expect plans for universal peace to succeed, or that some new technological development will forever end threats to security or that universal power (or government) could end human conflict. Absolute security strategies are not only historically unlikely candidates for success, they are prohibitively dangerous in light of twentieth-century technological advances.

If the risks associated with absolute security policies are unacceptable to the modern world, leaders must limit their hopes and accept the different risks and uncertainties involved in limited security policies. Limited security strategies require leaders to be able to recognize both threats to peace and opportunities for peace—a difficult task. In contrast to advocates of absolute security, who often imply history is irrelevant because the future requires an altogether new beginning (the argument of both pacifists and many ideological aggressors), partisans of limited security generally believe the historical record is a critical guide in defining the parameters of reasonable hope, including the role arms control and disarmament realistically can be expected to play in preventing war.

It was not the objective of this book to resolve the contemporary security issues facing advocates of limited security strategies. This would require arriving at firm conclusions to most of the issues raised in previous chapters. Rather, the goal was to help the reader learn to think about these kinds of arms control, disarmament and defense issues, primarily by posing appropriate questions, but also by encouraging the kind of historical perspective which is indispensable to prudent statecraft. Herbert Butterfield, the distinguished English historian of international relations, admirably made the case for cultivating a historical perspective:

> It is of considerable advantage to acquire one's basic knowledge of politics from distant examples, where the controversy is over, the story completed, the passion spent. By this method, one gains a notion of the structure of political conflict

which one can never gain in the fever of one's own contemporary world. Then, when one returns to the present, one is able to see it more analytically.[7]

Historical study is useful, therefore, not only for pointing to the general conclusions enumerated above, but also for assisting the student of international relations in developing a degree of analytical objectivity. Further, historical understanding helps us recognize patterns in social, political and technological developments which highlight current political opportunities and exigencies, and thus likely and unlikely solutions for the resolution of conflict in any given situation. In short, a historical perspective can improve tremendously our chances of successfully identifying correct limited security strategies.

The foregoing conclusions may be summarized by refering to the allegory of Prometheus introduced in Chapter One. Prometheus was trapped both by the knowledge he seized and by his unbending pride. Similarly, humanity is chained in its perilous condition by knowledge, through which it commands the means of human destruction, and by its nature, which is prone to hubris. Mankind cannot now abandon its knowledge or change its nature, which neither force nor education have ever fundamentally altered. Thus the solution to our dilemma cannot be the construction of a world devoid of weapons or inhabited by a new kind of human being.

Instead, we must face the world essentially as it is. In conversation with Hermes, Zeus' messenger, Prometheus commented that "Time in its aging course teaches all things," to which Hermes replied, "But you have not yet learned a wise discretion." Human knowledge has magnified itself many times in recent centuries, but it remains for us to learn a wise discretion. This is not too much to hope for. In our current circumstances, wise discretion simply means a prudence that acknowledges the great vulnerability of modern civilization, the limits of human control, and the importance of studying the historical record as the best possible preparation for managing our Promethean predicament.

NOTES

1. For additional examples of historical successes see Bruce Russett, *Prisoners of Insecurity* (San Francisco, W. H. Freeman & Co., 1983), pp. 60–65.
2. Hans Morganthau and Kenneth Thompson, *Politics Among Nations: The Struggle for Power and Peace,* 6th ed. (New York: Alfred A. Knopf, 1985), pp. 405, 407.
3. Sir Francis Bacon is quoted in Donald M. Kerr, "The Threat of the Neo-Luddites," in Roman Kolkowicz and Neil Joeck, eds., *Arms Control and International Security* (Boulder, CO: Westview Press, 1984), p. 71.
4. This is why the proliferation of nuclear energy programs is so controversial. As several authors noted in reference to Project Plowshare, a 1950s plan for peaceful use of nuclear explosions: "People think of swords that have been forged into plowshares as harmless because they cannot be used for war; but so-called "peaceful" nuclear explosions can destroy a city or other targets." At the time nuclear explosions were believed to have great potential for

construction purposes; for example, in the building of new ports and canals. Nuclear energy always was and still remains a double-edged sword with its constructive and destructive sides. See Albert Wohlstetter, Thomas A. Brown, Gregory Jones, David C. McGarvey, Henry Rowen, Vince Taylor, and Roberta Wohlstetter, *Swords from Plowshares* (Chicago and London: University of Chicago Press, 1977), p. viii.

5. Charles W. Kegley and Eugene R. Wittkopf, *World Politics: Trends and Transformation* (New York: St. Martin's Press, 1981), p. 352. Writing in 1968, Will and Ariel Durant concluded that in 3,421 years of recorded history, only 268 years had not seen war. Will and Ariel Durant, *The Lessons of History* (New York: Simon and Schuster, 1968), p. 81.

6. Thucydides, *The Peloponnesian War,* Book IV, 108.

7. The quotation is from Alberto Coll, *The Wisdom of Statecraft: Sir Herbert Butterfield and the Philosophy of International Politics* (Durham: Duke University Press, 1985), pp. 150. The historical examples used in this book to illustrate concepts and alternative points of view hopefully augmented the reader's historical sensitivity, but they are no substitute for serious historical study. Again, to quote Butterfield:

> A little history may make people mentally rigid. Only if we go on learning more and more of it—go on "unlearning" it—will it correct its own deficiencies gradually and help us to reach the required elasticity of mind.

p. 151.

Glossary

ABM: Antiballistic missile.

ABM Treaty: One of two agreements signed between the USSR and the United States in 1972 as part of the SALT I accords. This treaty of unlimited duration limits the number of antiballistic missiles the United States and the Soviet Union can deploy and also restricts development and deployment of ABMs.

ACDA: Arms Control and Disarmament Agency.

ADA: Atomic Development Authority.

Assured Destruction (AD): A nuclear deterrence strategy that requires the military capability necessary to inflict unacceptable damage on another state despite any preemptive or retaliatory measures it may take.

ALCM: Air launched cruise missile. (See cruise missile.)

Arms Control: Any measure intended to reduce the likelihood of war, or in the event that war does begin, to reduce the horrors of war and bring hostilities to an end quickly.

ASAT: Antisatellite weapon.

B-1 Bomber: A new nuclear capable supersonic transcontinental bomber to replace the B–52 bombers in the U.S. Strategic Air Command which was deferred by President Carter in 1977 and put into production under the Reagan administration.

Ballistic Missile. A missile that follows a trajectory without additional power after its initial thrust phase, relying on gravity and atmospheric drag to bring it back to earth. Ballistic missiles are usually armed with one or more nuclear warheads, operate beyond the earth's atmosphere for a portion of their flight, and in recent years have become exceedingly accurate.

BMD: Ballistic missile defense. Any system or combination of systems designed to track and destroy ballistic missiles before they reach their targets.

Bargaining Chip: An existing or planned weapons system that is limited, postponed, or forgone in exchange for some equal concession by another side in negotiations.

Catalytic War: A war between two major powers planned and provoked by a third country.

CBM: Confidence-building measure.

276

Collateral Damage: Damage sustained by surrounding population and nonmilitary resources as a result of an attack on a military target.

Counterforce Strikes: Attacks on military targets. A counterforce strategy requires more accurate weapons than a countervalue strategy.

Countervalue Strikes: Attacks on population centers. Since population centers are less well protected and larger targets, a countervalue strategy does not require weapons with the accuracy necessary for counterforce strikes.

Cruise Missile: A self-guided continuously self-propelled missile, either subsonic or supersonic, carrying nuclear or nonnuclear warheads, which usually stays close to the earth's surface in order to avoid detection by radar.

CSCE: Conference on Security and Cooperation in Europe.

Damage Limitation: Any measures taken to reduce direct and collateral damage resulting from a nuclear strike.

Deterrence: Preventing hostile action by an adversary by threatening retaliation.

Disarmament: The reduction or elimination of means for conducting war.

DoD: Department of Defense.

Escalation: An increase in the scope or intensity of actual or threatened violence during international hostilities. Escalation may be deliberate or unpremeditated.

First-Strike Capability: The military capability sufficient to destroy an adversary's will or capability to retaliate in kind before it can do so.

Flexible Response: A deterrence strategy that requires military capabilities sufficient to respond in kind to an attack of any intensity or duration.

Freeze: Any kind of negotiated agreement to limit armaments at the level of actual deployment at a particular point in time.

GCD: General and complete disarmament.

GLCM: Ground launched cruise missile. (See cruise missile.)

GRIT: Graduated and reciprocal initiatives in tension reduction.

Hague Conventions: Treaties creating a Permanent Court of Arbitration and a number of agreements on the conduct of land warfare. Twenty-six nations met in the First Hague Conference of 1899 and forty-four in the Second Hague Conference of 1907, both of which convened at the suggestion of Tsar Nicholas II of Russia.

Hard-Target Kill Capability: The combination of explosive power and accuracy necessary to destroy a protected strategic missile launcher.

IAEA: International Atomic Energy Agency.

ICBM: Intercontinental ballistic missile. (See ballistic missile.)

INF: Intermediate-range nuclear forces.

Launch on Warning: A policy of launching a retaliatory strike after determining that an attack by an adversary has been launched and is in progress but has not yet struck its targets.

Launcher: Any device from which a strategic weapon can be fired; for example, submarine missile tubes, aircraft, and missile silos.

Linkage: Tying progress in arms control negotiations to progress in the resolution of other bilateral foreign policy issues.

Locarno Treaties: A set of treaties signed in 1925 at the Swiss town of Locarno. The treaty signed by Germany, France, Belgium, Great Britain, and Italy guaranteed the Franco-German and Belgo-German borders. There also were various agreements on procedures for arbitrating conflicts and Franco-Polish and Franco-Czechoslovakian security pacts that provided for mutual assistance in the event of an attack on Germany. The sense of security created by these agreements led to a period of international goodwill widely referred to as the "spirit of Locarno."

Maginot Line: A series of French fortifications along the Franco-German border built in the 1920s. Named after French Minister of War Andre Maginot, the line of fortifications was considered impregnable. The Germans circumvented the Maginot line in 1940 and overwhelmed French forces.

MBFR: Mutual and balanced force reductions; ongoing negotiations since 1973 between NATO and the Warsaw Pact Organization over the reduction of conventional and tactical nuclear weapons in Central Europe.

MIRV: Multiple independently targeted reentry vehicle. The bus on a ballistic missile that carries multiple warheads, each of which may be detached from the bus and directed toward a separate target.

NATO: North Atlantic Treaty Organization. A mutual defense pact formed in 1949 between the United States, Canada, Belgium, Britain, Denmark, France, Iceland, Italy, Luxembourg, the Netherlands, Norway, and Portugal. West Germany, Turkey, and Spain joined later, and France withdrew its military forces from NATO in 1966.

NPT: Nonproliferation Treaty. An agreement signed in 1968 which included provisions for nuclear weapon states to cooperate in preventing the spread of nuclear weapon capabilities, and agreement by nonnuclear weapon states to abstain from producing nuclear weapon capabilities.

NTM: National technical means. Refers to techniques for monitoring compliance with arms limitation agreements which may be operated beyond the borders of the state being monitored, including such resources as reconnaissance satellites, land-and sea-based radar, and electronic eavesdropping devices.

NWS: Nuclear weapons states.

NNWS: Nonnuclear weapons states.

Nuclear Winter: An anticipated climatic consequence of general nuclear war which would produce drastic reductions in average temperatures, violent windstorms, and other devastating changes in the earth's ecosystem.

Preemptive Attack: An attack launched in the expectation that an enemy attack is imminent and that it would be advantageous to strike before the enemy does.

Preventive Attack: An attack launched when a state believes: (1) that an enemy will attack as soon as it is prepared to do so and (2) that striking first will allow it to fight under much more advantageous conditions, thereby preventing a more costly war later on.

PTBT: Partial Test Ban Treaty. Treaty signed in 1963 which prohibits testing nuclear devices in the atmosphere, outer space, and under the ocean, but not underground.

Punic Wars: A series of three wars between Rome and Carthage, a city which controlled Northwest Africa and part of Spain, and whose language was called "Punic." The first war lasted from 264–241 B.C., the second from 218–201 B.C., and The Third from 149–146 B.C. The total destruction of Carthage after the Third Punic War gave rise to the term, "Carthaginian Peace," meaning peace through annihilation of the enemy.

Richelieu, Cardinal Armand Jean du Plessis: Richelieu, a Cardinal of the Catholic Church and a consummate statesman, controlled the government of King Louis XIII of France between 1624 and 1642.

RV: Reentry vehicle.

Rush-Bagot Treaty: 1817 agreement between Britain and the United States demilitarizing the Great Lakes.

SALT: Strategic Arms Limitation Talks. Negotiations between the United States and the Soviet Union which began in 1969 and led to two agreements on limiting offensive and defensive strategic nuclear weapons. SALT I, signed in 1972, included the ABM Treaty (see ABM Treaty) and a set of numerical restrictions on U.S. and Soviet strategic offensive weapons. SALT II, signed in 1979, was never ratified by the U.S. Senate, but both states informally agreed to abide by its numerical limitations on offensive strategic weapons until 1986, when the United States announced it would no longer be bound by the agreement.

SDI: Strategic Defense Initiative. The U.S. research and development program aimed at producing a space-based ballistic missile defense. Often referred to as "Star Wars" by opponents of the program.

Second-Strike Capability: The military capability sufficient to sustain an enemy first strike and then respond in kind producing an unacceptably high level of damage to the attacker.

SIPRI: Stockholm International Peace Research Institute.

SLBM: Sea launched ballistic missile. (See ballistic missile.)

SLCM: Sea launched cruise missile. (See cruise missile.)

START: Strategic Arms Reduction Talks. Essentially a continuation of the SALT process, but the new designation by the Reagan administration was intended to put an emphasis on major reductions in strategic arms rather than relatively high but static ceilings.

Thucydides: An Athenian historian of fifth century B.C., Thucydides wrote a famous account of the Peloponnesian War (431–404 B.C.) which is still considered a classic work on international relations.

Triad: The U.S. strategic arsenal consisting of ICBMs, SLBMs, and manned bombers.

WPO: Warsaw Pact Organization. A military alliance formed in 1955 between the USSR, East Germany, Hungary, Poland, Czechoslovakia, Romania, and Bulgaria.

Selected Bibliography

ARMS CONTROL

ADELMAN, KENNETH. "Arms Control with or without Agreements." *Foreign Affairs* (Winter 1984–85).

ALFORD, JONATHAN. "Confidence-Building Measures in Europe: The Military Aspects." In Christoph Bertram, ed. *Arms Control and Military Force.* Montclair, NJ: Allanheld, Osmun and Co., for the International Institute for Strategic Studies, 1980.

BAILEY, SYDNEY D. *Prohibitions and Restraints in War.* New York: Oxford University Press, 1972.

BARUCH, HANS GUNTER. "Confidence Building Measures and Disarmament Supporting Measures." In William Epstein and Bernard T. Feld. *New Directions in Disarmament.* New York: Praeger Special Studies, 1981.

BLACKER, COIT D., AND GLORIA DUFFY, eds. *International Arms Control: Issues and Agreements.* Stanford, CA: Stanford University Press, 1984.

BLECHMAN, BARRY M. "Do Negotiated Arms Control Agreements Have a Future?" *Foreign Affairs* (Fall 1980).

BLECHMAN, BARRY, and ROBERT POWELL. "What in the Name of God is Strategic Superiority?" *Political Science Quarterly* 97 (Winter 1982–83).

BLOOMFIELD, LINCOLN P. "Arms Control Theory." In Walter Fischer and Richard Dean Burns, eds. *Armament and Disarmament: The Continuing Dispute.* Belmont, CA: Wadsworth Pub., 1974.

BRENNAN, DONALD G., ed. *Arms Control, Disarmament and National Security.* New York: Braziller, 1961. Based on the Fall 1960 issue of *Daedalus.*

BRODIE, BERNARD. "On the Objectives of Nuclear Arms Control." *International Security* 1 (Summer 1976): 17–36.

BULL, HEDLEY. *The Control of the Arms Race: Disarmament and Arms Control in the Missile Age.* New York: Praeger, 1961.

BUNDY, MCGEORGE, GEORGE F. KENNAN, ROBERT S. MCNAMARA, AND GERARD SMITH. "Nuclear Weapons and the Atlantic Alliance." *Foreign Affairs* (Spring 1982): 753–768.

BURT, RICHARD. "The Perils of Arms Control in the 1980s." *Daedalus* 110 (Winter 1981).

——, ed. *Arms Control and Defense Postures in the 1980s.* Boulder, CO: Westview Press, 1982.

CALDWELL, DAN. "Strategic and Conventional Arms Control: An Historical Perspective." *Stanford Journal of International Studies* 14 (Spring 1979): 7–27.

CARLTON, DAVID. "International Systemic Features Inhibiting Disarmament and Arms Control." In David Carlton and Carlo Schaerf, eds. *Reassessing Arms Control.* London: Macmillan, 1985.

COTTRELL, ALVIN, and WALTER HAHN, *Naval Race or Arms Control in the Indian Ocean?* New York: National Strategy Information Center Agenda Paper 8, 1978.

DOUGHERTY, JAMES E. *Arms Control and Disarmament: The Critical Issues.* Washington, DC: Center for Strategic Studies, 1966.

——. *How to Think About Arms Control and Disarmament.* New York: Crane, Russak and Co., 1973.

DUNN, LEWIS A. *Controlling the Bomb: Nuclear Proliferation in the 1980s.* New Haven: Yale University Press, 1982.

FAIRBANKS, CHARLES, JR. (Professor at Yale University and Research Director of Arms Races and Arms Control Project), "An Earlier Attempt to Limit Arms." *Wall Street Journal* (June 21, 1979): p. 26, col. 5.

GRAUBARD, STEPHEN R. Preface to "U.S. Defense Policy in the 1980s." *Daedalus* 109 (Fall 1980).

HARVARD NUCLEAR STUDY GROUP. *Living with Nuclear Weapons.* Cambridge: Harvard University Press, 1983.

HENKIN, LOUIS, ed. *Arms Control: Issues for the Public.* Englewood Cliffs, NJ: Prentice-Hall, 1961.

HOFFMAN, STANLEY. "New Variations on Old Themes." *International Security* 4 (Summer 1979): 88–107.

JASANI, BHUPENDRA. *Space Weapons: The Arms Control Dilemma.* Stockholm International Peace Research Institute. London: Taylor and Francis, 1984.

KAISER, KARL, GEORGE LEBER, ALOIS MERTES, AND FRANZ-JOSEF SCHULZE. "Nuclear Weapons and the Preservation of Peace: A German Response to No First Use." *Foreign Affairs* (Summer 1982): 1157–1170.

KINCADE, WILLIAM H. "Arms Control or Arms Coercion?" *Foreign Policy* (Spring 1986): 24–45.

KISSINGER, HENRY. "Arms Control, Inspection and Surprise Attack." *Foreign Affairs* (July 1960).

——. "A New Approach to Arms Control," *Time,* March 21, 1983.

KOLKOWICZ, ROMAN, and NEIL JOECK, eds. *Arms Control and International Security.* Boulder, CO: Westview Press, 1984.

KRELL, GERT. "The Problems and Achievements of Arms Control." *Arms Control* (December 1981).

LEFEVER, ERNEST, ed. *Arms and Arms Control.* New York: Frederick A. Praeger, 1962.

LUCK, EDWARD C., ed. *Arms Control: The Multilateral Alternative.* New York: New York University Press, 1983.

LUTTWAK, EDWARD N. "Why Arms Control Has Failed." *Commentary* (January 1978): 19–28.

NATIONAL ACADEMY OF SCIENCES. *Nuclear Arms Control: Background and Issues.* Washington, DC: National Academy Press, 1985.

OSGOOD, CHARLES E. *An Alternative to War or Surrender.* Urbana: University of Illinois Press, 1963.

PFALTZGRAFF, ROBERT L., ed. *Contrasting Approaches to Strategic Arms Control.* Lexington, MA: Lexington Books, 1974.

PIERRE, ANDREW J. *The Global Politics of Arms Sales.* Princeton: Princeton University Press, 1982.

——., ed. *Nuclear Weapons in Europe.* New York: Council on Foreign Relations, 1984.

RANGER, ROBIN. *Arms and Politics, 1958-79: Arms Control in a Changing Political Context.* Toronto: Macmillan of Canada, 1978.

RATHJENS, G. W., et al., *Nuclear Arms Control Agreements: Process and Impact.* Washington, DC: Carnegie Endowment for International Peace, 1974.

RUEHL, LOTHAR. "The Slippery Road of MBFR." *Strategic Review* (Winter 1980).

SABIN, PHILIP A. G. "Should INF and START be Merged? A Historical Perspective." *International Affairs* 60 (Summer 1984): 419-428.

SCHELLING, THOMAS, and MORTON H. HALPERIN. *Strategy and Arms Control.* New York: Twentieth Century Fund, 1961.

SHARP, JANE M. "Arms Control and Alliance Commitments." *Political Science Quarterly* 100 (Winter 1985-86): 649-667.

STAAR, RICHARD, ed. *Arms Control: Myth Versus Reality.* Stanford, CA: Hoover Institution Press, 1984.

STARES, PAUL B. *The Militarization of Space: U.S. Policy, 1945-84.* Ithaca, NY: Cornell University Press, 1985.

STEINBRUNER, JOHN D., and LEON V. SIGNAL. *Alliance Security: NATO and the No-First Use Question.* Washington: Brookings, 1983.

TUCHMAN, BARBARA. "The Alternative to Arms Control." *New York Times Magazine,* April 18, 1982. Reprinted in ROMAN KOLKOWICZ and NEIL JOECK, eds. *Arms Control and International Security.* Boulder, CO: Westview Press, 1984.

U. S. CONGRESS, House Committee on Foreign Affairs, Subcommittee on Arms Control, International Security and Science. *Fundamentals of Nuclear Arms Control: Part I.* "Nuclear Arms Control: A Brief Historical Survey." Report prepared for the Subcommittee on Arms Control, International Security and Science by the Congressional Research Service. Washington, DC: Government Printing Office, 1985.

WEISS, SEYMOUR. "The Case Against Arms Control." *Commentary,* (November 1984), pp. 19-23.

WISEMAN, HENRY, ed. *Peacekeeping.* New York: Pergamon Press, 1983.

DEFENSE AND NATIONAL SECURITY

A. Conventional and Uncoventional Security Strategies

FISCHER, DIETRICH. "Invulnerability without Threat: The Swiss Concept of General Defense." In Burns H. Weston. *Toward Nuclear Disarmament and Global Security: A Search for Alternatives.* Boulder, CO: Westview Press, 1984.

GADDIS, JOHN LEWIS. *Strategies of Containment: A Critical Appraisal of Postwar American National Security Policy.* New York: Oxford University Press, 1982.

GARTHOFF, RAYMOND L. "On Establishing and Imputing Intentions." *International Security* 2 (Winter 1978): 22-32.

GRAY, COLIN S. *Strategic Studies and Public Policy: The American Experience.* Lexington, KY: University of Kentucky Press, 1982.

GREGG, RICHARD B. *The Power of Nonviolence.* New York: Schocken, 1966.

KNORR, KLAUSS. *On the Uses of Military Power in the Nuclear Age.* Princeton: Princeton University Press, 1966.

———. *Military Power and Potential.* Lexington, MA: D. C. Heath and Co., 1970.

———. *The Power of Nations.* New York: Basic Books, 1975.

MERTON, THOMAS. *The Non-violent Alternative.* New York: Farrar, Strauss and Giroux, 1971.

MOULTON, HARLAND B. *From Superiority to Parity: The United States and the Strategic Arms Race, 1961-71.* Westport, CT: Greenwood Press, 1973.

REICHART, JOHN F., and STEVEN R. STURM. *American Defense Policy.* 5th ed. Baltimore: Johns Hopkins University Press, 1982.

SCHELLING, THOMAS C., and MORTON H. HALPERIN. *Strategy and Arms Control.* New York: Twentieth Century Fund, 1969.

SHARP, GENE. "The Political Equivalent of War: Civilian Defense." *International Conciliation* (November 1965).

——. *Exploring Non-violent Alternatives.* Boston: Porter Sargent, 1970.
SIBLEY, MULFORD Q. *The Quiet Battle.* Beacon Press, 1968.
VAGTS, ALFRED. *A History of Militarism.* New York: W. W. Norton, 1937.

B. Space-Based Strategic Defense

ARMSTRONG, SCOTT, and PETER GRIER. *Strategic Defense Initiative: Splendid Defense or Pipe Dream.* Headline Series, Foreign Policy Association, #275. September–October 1985. Reprinted from the series "Star Wars: Will it Work?." *Christian Science Monitor,* November 4–12, 1985.
BETHE, HANS A., RICHARD L. GARWIN, KURT GOTTFREID, and HENRY W. KENDALL. "Spaced-based Ballistic Missile Defense." *Scientific American,* October 1984, pp. 39–49.
BRZEZINSKI, ZBIGNIEW. "A Star Wars Solution: How to Break the Arms Control Impasse." *New Republic,* July 8, 1985, pp. 16–18.
CARTER, ASHTON, and DAVID SCHWARTZ. *Ballistic Missile Defense.* Washington, DC: Brookings, 1984.
CHALFONT, ALUN. *Star Wars: Suicide or Survival?* Boston: Little, Brown, 1986.
DRELL, SIDNEY, PHILIP J. FARLEY, and DAVID HOLLOWAY. *The Reagan Strategic Defense Initiative: A Technical, Political, and Arms Control Assessment.* Cambridge, MA: Ballinger Pub. Co., 1985.
FLETCHER, JAMES D. *Strategic Defense Initiative: Defensive Technology Study.* Washington, DC: U.S. Department of Defense, March 1984.
GLASER, CHARLES. "Why Even Good Defenses May be Bad." *International Security* 9 (Fall 1984): 92–123.
"Information Document on the Technology of Military Space Systems." (Brussels: North Atlantic Assembly, International Secretariat, Scientific and Technical Committee, 1982).
JASTROW, ROBERT. "Reagan Versus the Scientists: Why the President is Right About Missile Defense." *Commentary,* January 1984, pp. 23–32.
——. "The War Against Star Wars." *Commentary,* December 1984.
——. *How to Make Nuclear Weapons Obsolete.* Boston: Little, Brown, 1985.
MCNAMARA, ROBERT, GEORGE KENNAN, MCGEORGE BUNDY, and GERARD SMITH. "The President's Choice: Star Wars or Arms Control." *Foreign Affairs* (Winter 1984–85).
OFFICE OF TECHNOLOGY ASSESSMENT. *Ballistic Missile Defense Technologies.* Washington, DC: Government Printing Office, 1985.
PAYNE, KEITH. *Strategic Defense: "Star Wars" in Perspective.* Lanham, MD: Hamilton Press, 1986.
PAYNE, KEITH, and COLIN S. GRAY. "Nuclear Policy and the Defensive Transition." *Foreign Affairs* (Spring 1984).
RA'ANAN, URI, and ROBERT L. PFALTZGRAFF, eds. *International Security Dimensions of Space.* Hamden, CT: Archon Books, 1984.
SCHLESINGER, JAMES R. "Rhetoric and Realities in the Star Wars Debate." *International Security* (Summer 1985).
TSIPIS, KOSTA. "Laser Weapons." *Scientific American,* (December 1981, pp. 51–57.
UNION OF CONCERNED SCIENTISTS. *The Fallacy of Star Wars: Why Space Weapons Can't Protect Us.* New York: Random House, 1984.
UNITED STATES CONGRESS, House Committee on Foreign Affairs, Subcommittee on Arms Control, International Security, and Science. "Implications of the President's Strategic Defense Initiative and Anti-satellite Weapons Policy." Hearings before the Subcommittee on Arms Control, International Security, and Science. 99th Congress, 1st Session, April 24 and May 1, 1985. Washington, DC: Government Printing Office, 1985.
"Weapons in Space, Volume I: Concepts and Technologies." *Daedalus* (Spring 1985); and "Weapons in Space, Volume II: Implications for Security." *Daedalus* (Summer 1985).

DETERRENCE

ALMOND, HARRY. "Deterrence Processes and Minimum Order." *New York Law School Journal of International and Comparative Law* 4, No. 2, (1983).

BETHELL, TOM. "What's Wrong With Nuclear Superiority." *National Review,* June 6, 1986.

BRODIE, BERNARD, ed. *The Absolute Weapon.* New York: Harcourt Brace, 1946.

———. *Strategy in the Missile Age.* Princeton: Princeton University Press, 1959.

DYSON, FREEMAN. *Weapons and Hope.* New York: Harper/Bessie, 1984.

FREEDMAN, LAWRENCE. *The Evolution of Nuclear Strategy.* New York: St. Martin's Press, 1981.

GEORGE, ALEXANDER L., and RICHARD SMOKE. *Deterrence in American Foreign Policy: Theory and Practice.* New York: Columbia University Press, 1974.

GRAY, COLIN S. "Nuclear Strategy: The Case for a Theory of Victory." *International Security* 4 (Summer 1979): 54–87.

GRAY, COLIN S., and KEITH PAYNE. "Victory Is Possible." *Foreign Policy* 39 (Summer 1980): 14–27.

GREEN, PHILIP. *The Deadly Logic: The Theory of Nuclear Deterrence.* Columbus: Ohio State University Press, 1966.

GREENWOOD, TED. *Making the MIRV: A Study of Defense Decision Making.* Cambridge: Ballinger, 1975.

HERKEN, GREG. *Counsels of War.* New York: Alfred A. Knopf, 1985.

IKLE, FRED C. "Can Nuclear Deterrence Last Out the Century?" *Foreign Affairs* 51 (1973): 267–285.

JERVIS, ROBERT. "Deterrence Theory Revisited." *World Politics* 31 (January 1979): 289–324.

———. *The Illogic of American Nuclear Strategy.* Ithaca: Cornell University Press, 1984.

JERVIS, ROBERT, RICHARD NED LEBOW, and JANICE GROSS STEIN. *Psychology and Deterrence.* Baltimore: Johns Hopkins University Press, 1986.

KAHAN, JEROME H. *Security in the Nuclear Age: Developing U.S. Strategic Arms Policy.* Washington, DC: Brookings Institution, 1975.

KAHN, HERMAN. *On Thermonuclear War.* 2nd ed. New York: Macmillan, 1969.

KAPLAN, FRED. *The Wizards of Armageddon.* New York: Simon and Schuster, 1983.

KISTIAKOWSKY, GEORGE B. "Can a Limited Nuclear War Be Won?" *Defense Monitor* 10 (1981): 1–4.

KREPON, MICHAEL. *Strategic Stalemate: Nuclear Weapons and Arms Control in American Politics.* 1985.

KULL, STEVEN. "Nuclear Nonsense." *Foreign Policy* (1985): 28–52.

LEVINE, HERBERT. *The Arms Debate.* Cambridge, MA: Harvard University Press, 1963.

LUTTWAK, EDWARD N. *Strategic Power: Military Capabilities and Political Utility.* Beverly Hills, CA: Sage Publications, 1976.

MACGWIRE, MICHAEL. "Dilemmas and Delusions of Deterrence." *World Policy Journal* 1 (Summer 1984): 745–767.

MACLEAN, DOUGLAS, ed. *The Security Gamble: Deterrence Dilemmas in the Nuclear Age.* Maryland Studies in Public Philosophy. University of Maryland, 1984.

MORGAN, PATRICK M. *Deterrence: A Conceptual Analysis.* 2nd ed. Beverly Hills, CA: Sage Publications, 1983.

NAROLL, RAOUL, VERN BULLOUGH, and FRADA NAROLL. *Military Deterrence in History.* Albany: State University of New York Press, 1974.

NITZE, PAUL H. "Deterring Our Deterrent." *Foreign Policy* 25 (Winter 1976–77): 195–210.

PAYNE, KEITH B. *Nuclear Deterrence in U.S.-Soviet Relations.* Boulder, CO: Westview Press, 1982.

PIPES, RICHARD. "Why the Soviet Union Thinks it Could Fight and Win a Nuclear War." *Commentary,* July 1977.

PRANGER, ROBERT J., and ROBERT P. LABRIE, eds. *Nuclear Strategy and National Security: Points of View.* Washington, DC: American Enterprise Institute, 1977.

QUESTER, GEORGE H. *Deterrence Before Hiroshima.* New York: Wiley, 1966.

REICHART, JOHN F., and STEVEN R. STURM. *American Defense Policy.* 5th ed. Baltimore: Johns Hopkins University Press, 1982.

ROSENBERG, DAVID ALAN. "The Origins of Overkill: Nuclear Weapons and American Strategy, 1945-1960." *International Security* 7 (Spring 1983).

RUSSETT, BRUCE. *The Prisoners of Insecurity: Nuclear Deterrence, the Arms Race and Arms Control.* San Francisco: W. H. Freeman & Co., 1983.

SCHELLING, THOMAS C. *Arms and Influence.* New Haven: Yale University Press, 1966.

SNYDER, GLENN. *Deterrence and Defense: Toward a Theory of National Security.* Princeton: Princeton University Press, 1961.

STEGENGA, JAMES A. "Nuclear Deterrence: Bankrupt Ideology." *Policy Sciences* 16 (1983): 127–145.

STEINBRUNER, JOHN D. "Beyond Rational Deterrence." *World Politics* 28 (January 1976): 223–245.

U.S. CONGRESS, Senate Foreign Relations Committee, Hearing on "The Arms Control and Foreign Policy Implications of the Scowcroft Commission Report." Washington, DC: Government Printing Office, 1983.

WESTON, BURNS H., ed. *Toward Nuclear Disarmament and Global Security: A Search for Alternatives.* Boulder, CO: Westview Press, 1984. Chapter 5: "Rethinking Deterrence."

WIESELTIER, LEON. "When Deterrence Fails." *Foreign Affairs* (Spring 1985).

WOHLSTETTER, ALBERT. "The Delicate Balance of Terror." *Foreign Affairs* (January, 1959).

DISARMAMENT

BARNET, RICHARD, and RICHARD FALK, eds. *Security in Disarmament.* Princeton, NJ: Princeton University Press, 1965.

BECHOEFER, BERNHARD. *Postwar Negotiations for Arms Control.* Washington, DC: Brookings Institution, 1961.

BUCKLEY, JAMES L. *Freezing Chances for Peace.* Washington, DC: U.S. Department of State, Bureau of Public Affairs, 1982.

BULL, HEDLEY. *The Control of the Arms Race: Disarmament and Arms Control in the Missile Age.* 2nd ed. New York: Praeger, 1965. Especially Chapter 4.

BURT, RICHARD R. "Implications of a Nuclear Freeze." *Department of State Bulletin* 83 (June 1983).

BURTON, JOHN W. *Peace Theory: Precondition of Disarmament.* New York: Alfred A. Knopf, 1962.

DE MADARIAGA, SALVADOR. *Disarmament* New York: Coward McCann, 1929.

DOUGHERTY, JAMES E. *Arms Control and Disarmament: The Critical Issues.* Washington, DC: Center for Strategic Studies, 1966.

———. *How to Think About Arms Control and Disarmament.* New York: Crane, Russak and Co., 1973.

DULLES, ALLEN W. "Some Misperceptions about Disarmament." *Foreign Affairs* (April 1927).

EPSTEIN, WILLIAM. *Disarmament: 25 Years of Effort.* Toronto: Canadien Institute of International Affairs, 1971.

FISHER, WALTER R., and RICHARD DEAN BURNS. *Armament and Disarmament: The Continuing Debate.* Belmont, CA: Wadsworth Publishing Co., 1974.

FORBES, HENRY W. *The Strategy of Disarmament* Washington, DC: Public Affairs Press, 1962.

FORSBERG, RANDALL. "A Bilateral Nuclear-Weapon Freeze." *Scientific American,* November 1982, 52–61.

———. "Confining the Military to Defense as a Route to Disarmament." *World Policy Journal* (Winter 1984).

Independent Commission on Disarmament and Security Issues. *Common Security: A Blueprint for Survival.* New York: Simon and Schuster, 1982.

KALDER, MARY. "Disarmament: The Armament Process in Reverse." In Burns H. Weston, ed. *Toward Nuclear Disarmament and Global Security: A Search for Alternatives.* Boulder, CO: Westview Press, 1984.

KENNAN, GEORGE. "A Modest Proposal." *New York Review of Books,* July 16, 1981.

KENNEDY, EDWARD M. Address marking the 20th Anniversary of President J. F. Kennedy's disarmament speech at American University, April 8, 1983. Printed by the Foundation for a Democratic Majority.

KENNEDY, EDWARD M., and MARK O. HATFIELD. *Freeze! How You Can Help Prevent Nuclear War.* New York: Bantam, 1982.

LIEBERMAN, JOSEPH L. *The Scorpion and the Tarantula: The Struggle to Control Atomic Weapons, 1945–1949.* Boston, 1970.

MAMONTOV, VASSILI. *Disarmament: The Command of the Times.* Moscow: Progress Publishers, 1979.

MILLIS, WALTER. "Essential Conditions of Disarmament." *Social Sciences* (October, 1958).
MYERS, DENYS P. *World Disarmament: Its Problems and Prospects.* Boston: World Peace Foundation, 1932.
NOEL-BAKER, PHILIP. *The Arms Race.* London: Atlantic Books, 1958.
———. *Disarmament.* New York: Garland Publishing, 1972.
NOGEE, JOSEPH. *Soviet Policy Towards International Control of Atomic Energy.* Notre Dame, IN: University of Notre Dame Press, 1961.
RUBINSTEIN, ALVIN Z. "Political Barriers to Disarmament." *Orbis* (Spring 1965).
SCHELL, JONATHAN. *The Abolition.* New York: Alfred Knopf, 1984.
SIMS, NICHOLAS. *Approaches to Disarmament.* London: Friends Peace and International Relations Committee, 1974.
SMITH, H. A. "The Problem of Disarmament in the Light of History." *International Affairs* 10 (September 1930).
SPANIER, JOHN, and JOSEPH L. NOGEE. *The Politics of Disarmament.* New York: Frederick A. Praeger, 1962.
TUCHMAN, BARBARA W. *The Proud Tower.* New York: Macmillan, 1966.
WESTON, BURNS H., ed. *Toward Nuclear Disarmament and Global Security: A Search for Alternatives.* Boulder, CO: Westview Press, 1984.
WHEELER-BENNET, J. W. *Disarmament and Security Since Locarno, 1925–31.* New York: Macmillan, 1932.
WOLFERS, ARNOLD, et al. *The United States in a Disarmed World.* Baltimore: Johns Hopkins University Press, 1966.
YEFREMOV, A. Y. *Nuclear Disarmament.* Moscow: Progress Pub., 1980.
YOUNG, WAYLAND. "Disarmament: 30 Years of Failure." *International Security* 1 (Fall 1976): 98–116.

DOMESTIC POLITICS, DIPLOMACY AND NEGOTIATIONS

ALLISON, GRAHAM T. "What Fuels the Arms Race?" In Robert L Pfaltzgraff, ed. *Contrasting Approaches to Strategic Arms Control.* Lexington, MA: Lexington Books, 1974.
BARUCH, HANS GUENTER, and DUNCAN L. CLARKE, eds. *Decisionmaking for Arms Limitation.* Cambridge: Ballinger, 1983.
CLARKE, DUNCAN L. *Politics of Arms Control: The Role and Effectiveness of the Arms Control and Disarmament Agency.* New York: Free Press, 1979.
COLL, ALBERTO R. *The Wisdom of Statecraft.* Durham, NC: Duke University Press, 1985.
HASS, RICHARD. "Congressional Power: Implications for American Security Policy." Adelphi Paper 153. London: International Institute for Strategic Studies, 1979.
MILLER, STEVEN E. "Politics Over Promise: Domestic Impediments to Arms Control." *International Security* 8 (Spring 1984): 67–90.
MORGENTHAU, HANS. *Politics Among Nations.* 4th ed. New York: Alfred A. Knopf, 1967.
NEWHOUSE, JOHN. *Cold Dawn: The Story of SALT.* New York: Holt, Rinehart and Winston, 1973.
NICOLSON, HAROLD. *Peacemaking, 1919.* Boston: Houghton Mifflin, 1933.
PAYNE, SAMUEL B. *The Soviet Union and SALT.* Cambridge: MIT Press, 1980.
The Political Testament of Cardinal Richelieu. Trans. Henry Bertram Hill. Madison, WI: University of Wisconsin Press, 1961.
SLOSS, LEON, and M. SCOTT DAVIS. *A Game For High Stakes: Lessons Learned in Negotiating with the Soviet Union.* Cambridge: Ballinger, 1986.
SMITH, GERARD. *Doubletalk: The Story of SALT I.* New York: Doubleday, 1980.
TALBOTT, STROBE. *Endgame: The Inside Story of SALT II.* New York: Harper and Row, 1980.
———. *Deadly Gambits: The Reagan Administration and the Stalemate in Nuclear Arms Control.* New York: Alfred A. Knopf, 1984.
U.S. Congress, House Committee on Foreign Affairs. *Soviet Diplomacy and Negotiating Behavior: Emerging New Context for U.S. Diplomacy.* Vol. 1. Committee Print prepared by the Congressional Research Service, Library of Congress. Washington, DC: Government Printing Office, 1979.

U.S. Congress, Senate Committee on Labor and Human Resources. "United States Academy of Peace Act." Hearings. 97th Congress, 2nd Session, April 21, 1982. Washington, DC: Government Printing Office, 1982.

U. S. Congress, House Committee on Foreign Affairs. *Fundamentals of Nuclear Arms Control, Part V.* "The Internal Dynamics of U.S. Nuclear Arms Control Policymaking." Report prepared for the Subcommittee on Arms Control, International Security and Science by the Congressional Research Service. Washington, DC: Government Printing Office, 1986.

YORK, HERBERT T. "Bilateral Negotiations and the Arms Race." *Scientific American,* October 1983.

RESOURCE BOOKS AND CLASSICS

BURNS, RICHARD DEAN. *Arms Control and Disarmament: A Bibliography.* Santa Barbara, CA: ABC Clio, CO., 1977.

DOUGHERTY, JAMES E., and ROBERT PFALTZGRAFF. *Contending Theories of International Relations.* 2nd ed. New York: Harper and Row, 1981.

DUPUY, TREVOR N., and GAY M. HAMMERMAN. *A Documentary History of Arms Control and Disarmament.* New York: R. R. Bowker, 1973.

FERENEZ, BENJAMIN B. *Defining International Aggression in the Search for World Peace: A Documentary History and Analysis.* Dobbs Ferry, NY: Oceana Publishing, 1975.

FINE, MELINDA, and PETER M. STEVEN. *American Peace Directory.* Institute for Defense and Disarmament Studies, 1984.

FRIEDMAN, LEON. *The Law of War: A Documentary History.* New York: Random House, 1972.

GOLDBLAT, JOSEF. *Arms Control: A Survey and Appraisal of Multilateral Agreements.* London: Taylor and Francis, 1979.

———. *Agreements for Arms Control: A Critical Survey.* London: Taylor and Francis, 1982.

———. *Arms Control Agreements: A Handbook.* London: Taylor and Francis, 1983.

KEESINGS SPECIAL REPORTS. *Disarmament: Negotiations and Treaties.* New York: Charles Scribner's Sons, 1972.

London Naval Conference: Speeches and Press Statements by Members of the American Delegation Conference Series #3 Washington, DC: United States Government Printing Office, 1930.

MORGENTHAU, HANS. *Politics Among Nations: The Struggle for Power and Peace.* 4th ed. New York: Alfred A. Knopf, 1967.

MORGENTHAU, HANS J., and KENNETH W. THOMPSON. *Politics Among Nations.* 6th ed. New York: Alfred A. Knopf, 1985.

SHAMASASTRY, R. *Kautilya's Arthasastra.* Mysore, India: Mysore Printing and Publishing House. 8th ed. 1967.

Stockholm International Peace Research Institute. *World Armaments and Disarmament: SIPRI Yearbook 1985.* London: Taylor and Francis, 1985.

United States Arms Control and Disarmament Agency. *Arms Control and Disarmament Agreements.* New Brunswick, NJ: Transaction Books, 1982.

U.S. Congress, Senate Subcommittee on Disarmament, *Disarmament and Security: A Collection of Documents, 1915–55,* Committee Print, 84th Congress, 2d Session. Washington, DC: Government Printing Office.

VASQUEZ, JOHN A., ed. *Classics of International Relations.* Englewood Cliffs: Prentice-Hall, 1986.

TECHNOLOGY

BERTRAM, CHRISTOPH. "Arms Control and Technological Change: Elements of a New Approach." In Christoph Bertram., ed. *Arms Control and Military Force.* Montclair, NJ:

Allanheld, Osmun and Co., for the International Institute for Strategic Studies' Adelphi Library #3, 1980.

BURT, RICHARD. "New Weapons Technologies: Debate and Directions." Adelphi Paper #126 London: International Institute of Strategic Studies, 1976.

GELBA, HARRY G. "Technological Innovation and Arms Control." *World Politics* 26 (July 1974): 509–541.

GOLDBERGER, MARVIN. "Does the Technological Imperative Still Drive the Arms Race?" In Roman Kolkowicz and Neil Joeck. *Arms Control and International Security.* Boulder, CO: Westview Press, 1984.

GUTTERIDGE, WILLIAM, and TREVOR TAYLOR, eds. *The Dangers of New Weapons Systems.* New York: St. Martin's Press, 1983.

HANRIEDER, WOLFRAM F., ed. *Technology, Strategy and Arms Control.* Boulder, CO: Westview Press, 1986.

HEAD, RICHARD G. "Technology and the Military Balance." *Foreign Affairs* (April 1978): 544–563.

KINTER, WILLIAM R., and HARVEY SICHERMAN. *Technology and International Politics: The Crisis of Wishing.* Lexington, MA: Lexington Books, 1975.

KUZMACK, ARNOLD. "Technological Change and Stable Deterrence," *Journal of Conflict Resolution* 9 (September 1965).

LONG, FRANKLIN A. "Advancing Military Technology: Recipe for An Arms Race." *Current History* 82 (May 1983): 215–219, 228.

PERRY, WILLIAM J. "Advanced Technology and Arms Control." *Orbis* 26 (Summer 1982): 351–359.

POSSONY, STEFAN, and J. E. POURNELLE. *The Strategy of Technology: Winning the Decisive War.* Cambridge, MA: University Press of Cambridge, 1970.

SCHROEER, DIETRICH. *Science, Technology and the Nuclear Arms Race.* New York: Halsted Press, 1984.

SCOVILLE, HERBERT. "Problems of New Technologies and Weapons Systems." In William Epstein and Bernard T. Feld. *New Directions in Disarmament.* New York: Praeger, 1981.

STUKEL, COL. DONALD J., USAF. "Technology and Arms Control." *National Security Affairs Monograph.* Washington, DC: National Defense University, 1978.

VERIFICATION AND COMPLIANCE

BELLANY, IAN, and COIT D. BLACKER, eds. *The Verification of Arms Control Agreements.* London, Cass, 1984.

BILDER, RICHARD B. *Managing the Risks of International Agreements.* Madison: University of Wisconsin Press, 1981.

GARN, JAKE. "The Suppression of Information Concerning Soviet SALT Violations by the U.S. Government." *Policy Review* (Summer 1979).

GRAY, COLIN S. "Moscow is Cheating." *Foreign Policy* 56 (Fall 1984).

HAFEMEISTER, DAVID, JOSEPH J. ROMM, and KOSTA TSIPIS. "The Verification of Compliance with Arms Control Agreements." *Scientific American,* March 1985, pp. 439–455.

HAFEMEISTER, DAVID W., PENNY JANEWAY, and KOSTA TSIPIS, eds. *Arms Control Verification: The Technologies That Make It Possible.* Washington, DC: Pergamon-Brassey's, 1986.

IKLE, FRED C. "After Detection—What?" *Foreign Affairs* (January 1961).

JASANI, BHUPENDRA, and FRANK BARNABY. *Verification Technologies: The Case for Verification by Consent.* Dover, NH: Berg Pub. for the Center for International Peacekeeping, 1984.

KATZ, AMRON H. *Verification and SALT: The State of the Art and the Art of the State.* Washington, DC: Heritage Foundation, 1979.

KRASS, ALLAN S. *Verification: How Much Is Enough?* Stockholm International Peace Research Institute. London: Taylor and Francis, 1985.

———. "Test-Ban Cheaters Couldn't Prosper: Sophisticated Monitoring Raises the Need for a New Debate." *Los Angeles Times,* February 18, 1986. Reprinted in an April 1986 Union of Concerned Scientists' *Pledge Bulletin.*

KREPON, MICHAEL. "Decontrolling the Arms Race: The U.S. and the Soviets Fumble the Compliance Issue." *Arms Control Today* 14 (March/April 1984).
———. "Both Sides Are Hedging," *Foreign Policy* 56 (Fall 1984).
LORD, CARNES. "Rethinking On-site Inspection in U.S. Arms Control Policy." *Strategic Review* 13 (Spring 1985).
MELMAN, SEYMOUR, ed. *Inspection for Disarmament.* New York: Columbia University Press, 1958.
MEYER, STEPHAN M. "Verification and Risk in Arms Control." *International Security.* (Spring 1984).
POTTER, WILLIAM C., ed. *Verification and Arms Control.* Lexington, MA: Lexington Books, 1985.
The President's Unclassified Report to the Congress On Soviet Noncompliance with Arms Control Agreements. Washington, DC: Office of the Press Secretary, February 1, 1985.
ROWELL, WILLIAM F. *Arms Control Verification: A Guide to Policy Issues for the 1980s.* Cambridge: Ballinger, 1986.
TIMERBAEV, R. M. *Problems of Verification.* Moscow: Nauka Pub., 1984.
U.S. Congress, Senate Committee on Armed Services. "Soviet Treaty Violations." Hearings, 98th Congress, 2nd Session, March 14, 1984. Washington, DC: Government Printing Office, 1984.
WALLOP, MALCOLM. "Soviet Violations of Arms Control Agreements: So What?" *Strategic Review* (Summer 1983).
WRIGHT, SIR MICHAEL. *Disarm and Verify.* London: Chatto and Windus, 1964.

WAR: ITS PREVENTION, INITIATION, LIMITATION, ESCALATION AND TERMINATION

ALLISON, GRAHAM T., ALBERT CARNESALE, and JOSEPH S. NYE. *Hawks, Doves, and Owls: An Agenda for Avoiding Nuclear War.* New York: Norton, 1985.
BALL, DESMOND. "Can Nuclear War Be Controlled?" Adelphi Paper #169. London: International Institute of Strategic Studies, 1983.
BETTS, RICHARD K. *Surprise Attack.* Washington, DC: Brookings, 1982.
BLAINEY, GEOFFREY. *The Causes of War.* New York: Macmillan-Free Press, 1973.
BLAIR, BRUCE G. *Strategic Command and Control: Redefining the Nuclear Threat.* Washington, DC: Brookings, 1985.
BLECHMAN, BARRY M., ed. *Preventing Nuclear War: A Realistic Approach.* Bloomington: Indiana University Press, 1985.
BRACKEN, PAUL. *The Command and Control of Nuclear Forces.* New Haven: Yale University Press, 1983.
BRODIE, BERNARD. *Escalation and the Nuclear Option.* Princeton: Princeton University Press, 1966.
BULL, HEDLEY. "Society and Anarchy in International Relations." In *Diplomatic Investigations.* Ed. Herbert Butterfield and Martin Wight. Cambridge, MA: Harvard University Press, 1966.
CALDER, NIGEL. *Nuclear Nightmares: An Investigation into Possible Wars.* New York: Viking Press, 1980.
CARR, EDWARD H. *The Twenty Years' Crisis, 1919–1939.* New York: Harper and Row, 1964.
"The Challenge of Peace: God's Promise and Our Response." Pastoral Letter on Nuclear War by the National Conference of Catholic Bishops. Washington, DC: U.S. Catholic Conference, May 19, 1983.
CLARK, GRENVILLE, and LOUIS SOHN. *World Peace Through World Law.* Cambridge: Harvard University Press, 1966.
CLAUDE, INIS. *Power and International Relations.* New York: Random House, 1962.
The Effects of Nuclear War. Office of Technology Assessment. Washington, DC: Government Printing Office, 1979.
FALK, RICHARD A., and SAMUEL S. KIM., eds. *The War System: An Interdisciplinary Approach.* Boulder, CO: Westview Press, 1980.

FREI, DANIEL. *Risks of Unintentional War.* Totowa, NJ: Rowan and Allanheld, 1983.

GOLDMAN, RALPH M. "Political Distrust as Generator of the Arms Race: Prisoners' and Security Dilemmas." In Burns H. Weston, ed. *Toward Nuclear Disarmament and Global Security: A Search for Alternatives.* Boulder, CO: Westview Press, 1984.

HOBBES, THOMAS. *Leviathan.* Especially Part I, Chapter 13, "On the Natural Condition of Mankind, as Concerning Their Felicity, and Misery."

HOWARD, MICHAEL. *The Causes of War.* Cambridge, MA: Harvard University Press, 1983.

JERVIS, ROBERT. *Perception and Misperception in International Politics.* Princeton: Princeton University Press, 1976.

———. "Cooperation Under the Security Dilemma." *World Politics* 30 (1978): 167–215.

KENNAN, GEORGE F. *The Nuclear Delusion: Soviet-American Relations in the Atomic Age.* New York: Pantheon, 1982.

KAHN, HERMAN. *On Escalation: Metaphors and Scenarios.* New York: Praeger, 1965.

LEVY, JACK S. "The Offensive/Defensive Balance of Military Technology: A Theoretical and Historical Analysis." *International Studies Quarterly* 28 (June 1984).

LEWIS, K. N. "The Prompt and Delayed Effects of Nuclear War." *Scientific American,* 1979.

NOEL-BAKER, PHILIP. *The Arms Race.* Oceana, 1958.

NYE, JOSEPH S. "U.S.-Soviet Relations and Nuclear Risk Reduction." *Political Science Quarterly* 99 (Fall 1984): 401–414.

O'BRIEN, WILLIAM V. *The Conduct of Just and Limited War.* New York: Praeger, 1981.

OSGOOD, CHARLES E. "GRIT: A Strategy for Survival in Mankind's Nuclear Age." In William Epstein and Bernard T. Feld, eds. *New Directions in Disarmament.* New York: Praeger, 1981.

PFALTZGRAFF, ROBERT L. *National Security, Ethics, Strategy and Politics: A Layman's Primer.* New York: Pergamon-Brassey's, 1986.

RAMSEY, PAUL. *The Just War.* New York: Scribner, 1968.

ROUSSEAU, JEAN-JACQUES. *A Lasting Peace Through the Federation on Europe and the State of War.* 1761.

SAGAN, CARL. "Nuclear Winter and Climatic Catastrophe." *Foreign Affairs* (Winter, 1983–1984).

SCHEER, ROBERT. *With Enough Shovels: Reagan, Bush and Nuclear War.* New York: Random House, 1982.

SCHELL, JONATHAN. *The Fate of the Earth.* New York: Alfred A. Knopf, 1982.

SCHELLING, THOMAS C. "Confidence in Crisis." *International Security* 8 (Spring 1984): 55–66.

SCHROEDER, PAUL. "Does Murphy's Law Apply to History?" *Wilson Quarterly* 9 (1985): 84–93.

SMOKE, RICHARD. *War: Controlling Escalation.* Cambridge, MA: Harvard University Press, 1978.

STEINBRUNER, JOHN D. "Nuclear Decapitation." *Foreign Policy* (Winter 1981–82): 16–28.

STOESSINGER, JOHN C. *Why Nations Go to War.* New York: St. Martin's, 1974.

URY, WILLIAM L. *Beyond the Hotline: Crisis Control to Prevent Nuclear War.* Boston: Houghton Mifflin, 1985.

U.S. Congress, Senate Committee on Foreign Affairs. "Nuclear Risk Reduction Centers." Report to Accompany Senate Resolution 329, 98th Congress, 2nd Session, Washington, DC: Government Printing Office, 1984.

WALLACE, MICHAEL. "Armaments and Escalation: Two Conflicting Hypotheses." *International Studies Quarterly* 26 (1982): 37–56.

WALTZ, KENNETH N. *Man, State and War.* New York: Columbia University Press, 1959.

WALZER, MICHAEL. *Just and Unjust Wars: A Moral Argument with Historical Illustrations.* New York: Basic Books, 1977.

WEINBERGER, CASPAR W. "The Potential Effects of Nuclear War on the Climate: A Report to the U.S. Congress." *Congressional Record,* 99th Congress, 1st Session, (March 6, 1985).

WOHLSTETTER, ALBERT. "Is There a Strategic Arms Race?" *Foreign Policy* 15 (Summer 1974): 3–20; and "Is There a Strategic Arms Race?—Part II: Rivals but no 'Race.'" *Foreign Policy* 16 (Fall 1974): 48–81.

———. "Bishops, Statesmen, and Other Strategists On the Bombing of Innocents." *Commentary,* June 1983.

WRIGHT, QUINCY. *A Study of War.* Chicago: University of Chicago Press, 1942.

Index